The Woman Painter in Victorian Literature

The Woman Painter in Victorian Literature

ANTONIA LOSANO

The Ohio State University Press
Columbus

Cover: Dante Gabriel Rossetti, *A Parable of Love (Love's Mirror)*. Reproduced by permission of the Birmingham Museums & Art Gallery.

Copyright © 2008 by The Ohio State University.
All rights reserved.

Library of Congress Cataloging-in-Publication Data
Losano, Antonia Jacqueline.
   The woman painter in Victorian literature / Antonia Losano.
     p. cm.
   Includes bibliographical references and index.
   ISBN-13: 978-0-8142-1081-9 (cloth : alk. paper)
   ISBN-10: 0-8142-1081-3 (cloth : alk. paper)
   1. English fiction—19th century—History and criticism. 2. English fiction—Women authors—History and criticism. 3. Art and literature—Great Britain—History—19th century. 4. Women artists in literature. 5. Aesthetics in literature. 6. Feminism in literature. 7. Art in literature. I. Title.
   PR878.W6L67 2008
   823.009'9287—dc22
                                         2007028410

This book is available in the following editions:
Cloth (ISBN 978-0-8142-1081-9)
CD-ROM (ISBN 978-0-8142-9160-3)
Paper (ISBN: 978-0-8142-5736-4)
Cover design by Melissa Ryan
Type set in Adobe Garamond Pro
Type design by Juliet Williams

In Memoriam
Sarah Louise DeRolph Wampler
1908–2000

Contents

List of Illustrations		ix
Acknowledgments		xiii
Introduction		1
Chapter One	Prevailing Winds and Cross-Currents: Public Discourse and the History of Victorian Women Painters	23
Chapter Two	Desire and Feminist Aesthetics in Anne Brontë's *The Tenant of Wildfell Hall*	63
Chapter Three	Ekphrasis and the Art of Courtship in *Jane Eyre*	96
Chapter Four	Making A Living: Howitt, Eliot, Oliphant	119
Chapter Five	The Afterlife of Angelica Kauffman	149
Chapter Six	Disfigurement and Beauty in Dinah Craik and Charlotte Yonge	180
Chapter Seven	Painting the New Woman: Mary Ward and the Woman Artist	209
Coda	Contemporary Representations of the Woman Painter	232
Notes		239
Works Cited		267
Index		283

 List of Illustrations

Chapter One

Figure 1.1	"Found Out." Anonymous. *Punch* 89 (February 14, 1885).	28
Figure 1.2	"Female School of Art." Anonymous. *Punch* 66 (May 30, 1874).	29
Figure 1.3	George DuMaurier, "Varnishing Day at the Royal Academy." *Punch* 73 (June 19, 1877).	35
Figure 1.4	Emily Mary Osborn, *Nameless and Friendless*, 1857, private collection. Source: The Bridgeman Art Library. Reproduced with permission.	37
Figure 1.5	Emily Mary Osborn, *Sketch after a Portrait of Barbara Bodichon* (of original oil painting from 1884, whereabouts unknown). Source: Helen Blackburn, *Women's Suffrage* (London: Williams and Norgate, 1902).	40
Figure 1.6	Laura Alma-Tadema, *The Sisters*, 1883. Engraving. Whereabouts of original unknown. Source: Pamela Gerrish Nunn, *Problem Pictures*, illustration 5.7.	41
Figure 1.7	Kate Greenaway, *Little Loves. The Illustrated London News*, Christmas number, 1877.	42

Figure 1.8	Detail from "Let us join the Ladies" article, *Punch* 29 (July 18, 1857).	48
Figure 1.9	Florence Claxton, detail from *The Adventures of a Woman in Search of her Rights* (London: The Graphotyping Co., 1872), 17.	50
Figure 1.10	Dante Gabriel Rossetti, *A Parable of Love (Love's Mirror)*, 1850? Birmingham City Art Gallery. Reprinted with permission.	51
Figure 1.11	John Singer Sargent, *The Fountain, Villa Torlonia, Frascati, Italy*, 1907. Art Institute of Chicago. Reproduced with permission.	53
Figure 1.12	George Du Maurier, "Removal of Ancient Landmarks." *Punch* 82 (June 25, 1881).	55

Chapter Two

Figure 2.1	Anne Brontë, *Sunrise at Sea, or Woman gazing at a sunrise over a seascape*, 1839. Brontë Parsonage Museum. Reproduced with permission.	66
Figure 2.2	Mary Ellen Best, *An Artist in her Painting Room*, 1837–39. York City Art Gallery. Reproduced with permission.	80
Figure 2.3	Jessica Hayllar, *Finishing Touches*. Originally displayed at the Institute of Oil Painters, London, 1887. Present whereabouts unknown. Source: Deborah Cherry, *Painting Women*, plate 7.	81

Chapter Five

Figure 5.1	Angelica Kauffman, *Self-Portrait in the Character of Painting Embraced by Poetry*. The Iveagh Bequest, Kenwood. Source: *Angelica Kauffman: A Continental Artist in Georgian England*, ed. Wendy Wassyng Roworth. Published by Reaktion Books in association with the Royal Pavilion, Art Gallery and Museums Brighton, 1992.	153
Figure 5.2	Angelica Kauffman, *Self Portrait: Hesitating between the arts of painting and poetry*. Nostell Priory, W. Yorks. Source: *Angelica Kauffman: A Continental Artist in Georgian England*, ed. Wendy Wassyng Roworth. Published by Reaktion Books in association with the Royal Pavilion, Art Gallery and Museums, Brighton, 1992.	154

Figure 5.3	"Damerian Apollo." "Studies from Nature: A Model to Make a Boy." Anonymous engraving, 1789. British Museum. Reproduced with permission.	166
Figure 5.4	Margaret Dicksee, *'Miss Angel'—Angelika Kauffmann, introduced by Lady Wentworth, visits Mr Reynolds' studio*. Royal Academy, 1892. Current whereabouts unknown. Source: Fine Art Photographic Library. Reproduced with permission.	177
Figure 5.5	Helen Paterson Allingham, *Angelika Kauffmann in the Studio of Joshua Reynolds*, 1875. Wood engraving; whereabouts unknown. Source: Pamela Gerrish Nunn, *Victorian Women Artists*, 111.	179

Chapter Six

Figure 6.1	"Lady Students at the National Gallery." *Illustrated London News* 87 (November 21, 1885).	184

Chapter Seven

Figure 7.1	Frances Macdonald, *A Pond*, 1894. Glasgow School of Art Collection. Source: National Museums Liverpool. Reproduced with permission.	214
Figure 7.2	Frances Macdonald, *'Tis a Long Path That Wanders to Desire*, 1912–15. Hunterian Art Gallery, University of Glasgow. Source: National Museums Liverpool. Reproduced with permission.	215
Figure 7.3	Illustration from *The Mating of Lydia*, facing page 68. Photo by author.	224
Figure 7.4	Illustration from *The Mating of Lydia*, facing page 490. Photo by author.	225

Acknowledgments

This book could not have been written without enormous help from numerous people. Dorothy Mermin, Laura Brown, and Mary Jacobus at Cornell University encouraged me in the early stages and offered kind and wise advice throughout the process. Many friends at Cornell read drafts of varying coherence and made invaluable comments: Bonnie Blackwell, Jen Hill, Jodie Medd, Vera Palmer, Anne Mallory, Michelle Elleray, Anne Lyden, and Scott MacKenzie were particularly astute and patient readers. I thank Middlebury College for a generous leave year and my colleagues there for their encouragement and assistance throughout this project and my teaching career. Alison Byerly, Timothy Billings, Marion Wells, John Elder, Cates Baldridge, David Price, and many others at Middlebury have read drafts, made suggestions, and provided much-needed support and friendship. Robyn Warhol at the University of Vermont deserves special thanks for her meticulous reading of numerous drafts, and for the extraordinary quality of her commentary. Many thanks are due to Sandy Crooms and her colleagues at The Ohio State University Press for their gracious support of this project. My parents, stepparents, and in-laws have shouldered countless burdens (often in the shape of two young children) to make this book possible, and I thank them with all my heart. Finally, I thank Dan Brayton for being both my safe harbor and my far horizon for nearly two decades. There are no words to acknowledge the depth, patience, and intelligence of his contributions to this and other endeavors.

Introduction

> "What power! This is the way women should assert their rights!"
> George Eliot, on seeing a painting by Rosa Bonheur.
> (Letter to Sara Hennell, August 19, 1857. *George Eliot Letters,* 2: 377)

I.

WHY SHOULD George Eliot, who used words to assert her rights, declare that *painting* was the medium in which women could best demonstrate social power? Painting had enormous resonance and significance for Eliot, so it is understandable that she might have seen in a female painter the promise of women's political and artistic success.[1] But a remarkable number of other nineteenth-century women novelists shared Eliot's belief that the woman painter was the century's strongest source of female social and creative potential, and they translated that belief into the creation of fictional women painters. Virginia Woolf's Lily Briscoe did not emerge from a vacuum; Woolf would have seen the figure of the woman painter surprisingly often in the works of her Victorian foremothers. Charles Tansley's stuttered pronouncement—"women can't paint, women can't write"—that haunts Lily throughout *To the Lighthouse* and stifles her creativity makes it clear that Woolf, like the Victorian writers I discuss in this study, recognized the intense interplay between her own medium and Lily's. Woolf echoes numerous Victorian women writers in her belief that these two media of female aesthetic production are intimately connected in myriad ways, their fortunes rising and falling in tandem.

That Victorian women novelists embraced the figure of the woman painter as emblematic of the "Woman Question" more generally is perhaps unsurprising given the public prominence of women painters at the time: the nineteenth century saw a marked rise both in the sheer numbers of women active in art professions and in the discursive concern for the woman artist in the periodical press, art history, and political debate. Census figures show that the number of women who chose to officially call themselves professional female artists doubled between 1851 and 1871; the number steadily increased as the century wore on.[2] As the numbers increased, so did the public debate over the role of women in the visual arts; one art historian has aptly termed the increasing public discourse concerning women in art an "unprecedented fuss" (Gillett 1990, 3). The Victorian woman painter was a "contested image," to use Mary Poovey's term;[3] she was a figure whose ideological constitution and function (how she was perceived and constructed by the culture) varied tremendously. As Poovey argues, "Any image that is important to a culture constitutes an arena of ideological construction rather than simple consolidation" (1988, 9). The woman painter, like Poovey's well-known example of the governess, posed a considerable ideological problem: on the one hand, women were considered "naturally" artistic—sensitive and devoted to beauty—yet were simultaneously thought to be incapable of true artistic creativity or judgment. In a similar paradox, women were seen as necessary to art as models and muses, yet at the same time discouraged from participating in the artistic arena for modesty's sake (one might think here of M. Paul's reaction to Lucy Snowe's viewing of the Cleopatra painting in Charlotte Brontë's *Villette*). But in spite of these ideological tensions, women were demonstrably entering the art world in droves and increasingly succeeding, causing enormous upheaval in the aesthetic as well as social beliefs of the time. And precisely because of these tensions, the woman painter was an "ideological formulation," in Poovey's words again (1988, 3), which was put to use by different institutions, individuals, or groups for different purposes.

The Victorian women writers I consider here used the figure of the woman painter as a kind of Foucauldian "dense transfer point" of power relations to engage with and intervene in the symbolic economies of gender (in particular those that underpinned the discourses of aesthetics, sexual desire, and professional identity) that were at work during the nineteenth century (Foucault 1990, 103). At the outset, I attempt to give some sense of the broader cultural discourse surrounding the woman painter—a discourse to which the women novelists considered next both contributed and reacted. While feminist literary scholarship of the past thirty years has extensively and perceptively studied the nineteenth-century woman writer, no sustained examination of the historical and discursive connections *between* women painters and women writers in the nineteenth century has yet been undertaken; nor has the immense influence of the history, aesthetics, and economics of women's painting on women's fiction been explored. I set out here to examine how the complex involvement of women in the nineteenth-century art world impacted the work of women writers of the same period, roughly 1848–1900. At base is the assumption that women's achievements in the visual arts and the public fervor surrounding their struggles to achieve artistic success were neither unknown nor unimportant to women working in other disciplines.[4]

In examining fictional representations of women painters, I focus in particular on what I term the *scene of painting*, which includes not just descriptions of fictional artwork but representations of the act and process of painting and, equally often, of the reception and judgment of women's artworks. I argue that these scenes of painting offer fully formed and often radical aesthetic, literary, and social critiques. These scenes function as sites from which women writers articulate a wide variety of concerns: the fraught material and ideological conditions of women's artistic production, the changing social role of the woman artist, the gender bias of philosophical aesthetics, and the persistent eroticization of women in art. Simply put, these scenes of painting offer us contained aesthetic and sociopolitical treatises in narrative form.

In these fraught fictional moments, Victorian women writers pose a series of fundamental social, ideological, and aesthetic problems. They ask the traditional aesthetic questions—what is art? what is beauty? what are the criteria for judging the two? what qualities are required in a great artist?—but add to each of these the explicit rider, *when the artist or viewer is a woman,* a woman moreover impacted by specific historic, cultural, and ideological forces? If aesthetics itself, as Terry Eagleton writes, "began as a discourse of the body" (1990, 13), surely, then (although Eagleton rarely considers it), the *gender* of that body is profoundly important. The novelists discussed in this study ask how women artists fit into the grand traditions of Art, and they expose what might be incoherent, illogical, or just plain wrong with those traditions. What happens, these texts ask, to the history of aesthetic perception when the art object under consideration has been created by a woman? Can a woman's art ever be judged without reference to her gender? Can the art world be made accessible to women, and at what cost? What kind of social, economic, and ideological barriers limit a woman artist's development, and how can these be broken down? How can women artists unravel the seemingly inextricable link between art and erotic desire? How can women mine the liberatory potential of art as a source of emotional, spiritual, or financial satisfaction and tap the potentially radical transformative power of the woman artist to make significant changes in social, cultural, and political arenas?

Finally, these women writers question the ways in which women's painting might mirror women's writing. I suggest throughout this book that women novelists use the figure of the woman painter not only to engage with social and aesthetic debates about art in general, but also to consider the cultural position of their own medium. Indeed, both artistic media (painting and literature) were undergoing similar transformations during the period. For example, the Victorians inherited the eighteenth-century hierarchy that ordained History painting as the highest of High Art, with landscape art, portraiture, and still life taking their places farther down the totem pole. But by the mid-nineteenth century, the popularity of genre art began to scramble the old hierarchies; the art public flocked to see William Powell Frith's *Derby Day* and hailed it as High Art as well as a representation of everyday life. With the rise of the aesthetic movement, the influence of the egalitarian art theories of Ruskin and Morris, and the increasing public interest in interior design, the old notions of High Art—as confined to a few genres and available only to the elite—crumbled still further. Women entered this changing art world as engravers, illustrators, designers of textiles or china—or as painters in the traditional genres of High Art. The novel participated in a similar opening up of hierarchical conceptions of art. At the start of the nineteenth century, the novel stood in the shade of Poetry, which was considered the highest of literary arts. As the century progressed, this devaluation of the novel gave way—in dramatic fashion—to the enormous prestige of the Victorian realist novel.[5] But many women novel writers still struggled, as did women painters, against an ingrained ideology which insisted that cultural productions by women, no matter the media, were inherently barred from the realm of High Art. Only two of the writers I examine here—George Eliot and Charlotte Brontë—were in their lifetime or after considered solidly High Art; the others were considered popular writers and have subsequently been relegated to "noncanonical" status (Anne Brontë is the exception here, resting as she does uneasily on the border between the two). My focus on noncanonical women writers—specifically Margaret Oliphant, Anna Mary Howitt, Anne Thackeray Ritchie, Charlotte Yonge, Dinah Craik, and Mary Ward—means that questions of the gendering of aesthetic value are never far from the center of my analysis. By dramatizing the experiences and productions of women painters, these women writers were able to offer—however obliquely—their views on the shaky position of the woman's novel in Victorian culture. By reexamining these largely forgotten novels, contemporary scholars can similarly theorize the place of women writers in the Victorian canon.

II.

In investigating the interplay between literature and painting, my project is part of a large body of recent criticism called "interart criticism," alternately called "word and image studies"—both being a branch of the much larger and vibrant field of "interdisciplinary studies." Interart criticism is an enormous and varied field, including studies of the influence of painting on particular authors,[6] broader studies that argue for similarities across art media in the same historical period,[7] studies in the way narrative relies on or makes use of the more formal elements of painting (description, perspective, fore- and background, etc.),[8] and theoretical or historical studies of "the visual" as such.[9] Most frequently, of course, interart literary criticism is a mixed bag, relying on historical, stylistic, biographical, and theoretical investigations. Recent interart scholarship on the Victorian novel—and on Victorian culture more generally—has highlighted the extremely visual nature of the genre and the social order in which it flourished. As Kate Flint argues, "The Victorians were fascinated with the act of seeing, and with the question of the reliability—or otherwise—of the human eye, and with the problems of interpreting what they saw" (2000, 1). In *The Victorians and the Visual Imagination*, Flint explores the proliferation of visual images, techniques, practices, and theories that exploded in the nineteenth century. Historians (literary and otherwise) of the nineteenth century have written extensively on this explosion in a number of registers; the century saw, among other visual events, the advent of photography (plus a host of other technological marvels); the popularity of illustration in fiction; a rise in scopic controls within psychology, law, and empire; scientific treatises on vision and the structure of the eye; and not least an overwhelming literary obsession with visual description.[10] Literary critics have explored the different ways that literature can borrow from, depend on, and interact with painting; many critics have suggested further that nineteenth-century writers in particular were indebted to, and even obsessed with, the visual arts. Victorian writers themselves regularly celebrated the connection between writing and painting: "The analogy between the art of the painter and the art of the novelist is, so far as I am able to see, complete," writes Henry James in *The Art of Fiction* (1984, 187). More subtly, and slightly later, Virginia Woolf muses in her essay on Walter Sickert on the similarities: "Let us hold painting by the hand a moment longer, for though they must part in the end, painting and writing have much to tell each other; they have much in common. The novelist after all wants to make us see" (1950, 181).

Sophia Andres argues that this obsession with the visual realm, particularly with painting, put heavy pressure on Victorian writers. The perceived intimacy between the two arts generated "a set of pictorial demands placed on novelists, [who were] expected not only to be masters of the art of narrative but also to be familiar with the visual arts. . . . They were expected to understand painterly techniques to such an extent as to be able to employ them in their narratives or, even further, to transform pictorial into narrative techniques" (2005, xix). In this same vein, numerous critics draw the connection between the centrality of the visible and the rise to prominence of realism as an artistic ideal; the lexicon of painting was thought to provide writers with the techniques they needed to generate satisfactory realist texts. Mack Smith, for example, argues that "the language of the realism movement has such a strong bias for visual metaphors because the movement itself is grounded in painting" (1995, 243). Similarly, Peter Brooks writes that realism "makes the visual the master relation to the world . . . ; knowing those things is a matter of viewing them, detailing them, and describing the concrete milieu in which men and women enact their destinies. To know, in realism, is to see, and to represent is to describe" (1993, 88). Nancy Armstrong, too, argues that practices of visual representation and strategies of literary representation evolved together; fiction came to "equate seeing with knowing and made visual information the basis for the intelligibility of verbal narrative" (1999, 7–8).

The obsession with the visual arts meant that Victorian writers not only used painterly techniques in their works but also regularly included in their novels paintings themselves—real or imagined. Smith offers, in an appendix to *Literary Realism and the Ekphrastic Tradition,* a remarkably concise rundown on the possible meanings of painting in realist nineteenth-century fiction. Most frequently, he argues, novelists use painting as a "reflexive tool" (1995, 244), a way to express and define their aesthetic principles (Zola is the writer Smith most associates with this tradition). In specific instances, novelists use painting to depict failed representation, or a flawed form of representation that is set against the more successful form of the novel itself. Dickens, for example, in *Little Dorrit* contrasts the dishonest (misrepresentational) portraits painted by Henry Gowan with the more honest representations of the novel itself. Paintings may also be used to express character, as when Jane Eyre's three watercolors are seen to "reflect her view of herself and the world,"[11] or when a painting is seen as a harbinger of death or a similar narrative signal.

Other critics argue for specific narrative uses of specific kinds of visual arts. Françoise Meltzer, for example, in *Salome and the Dance of Writing* focuses on verbal representations of portraits in literary texts from a wide range of time periods. She writes, "The presentation of a portrait in a text particularizes the hierarchical stance writing wishes to assume in the face not only of the eidetic image (which . . . writing always strains to reduce to its own medium), but of representation itself as well" (1987, 215). Meltzer also argues that "the portrait is so convenient a measure for the power given to representation in a text" (2), but for Meltzer the portrait, because it "retains an element of alterity" (11), is often an unwanted presence within a literary work. In Meltzer's terms, the image often "play[s] Arachne to literature's Minerva" (215) and is finally punished for its difference. Concentrating more specifically on nineteenth-century literature, Alison Byerly's investigation of references to visual art, music, and theater in realist fiction leads her to a similar argument: she suggests that such references are "insistent reminders of the disjunction between art and life" which "threaten to sabotage the realist claim to unmediated representation. Such persistent allusions to art must, it would seem, have a purpose beyond mere decoration in order to be worth the risk" (1997, 2). In both these analyses, reactions to art within the novel model modes of aesthetic judgment and artistic consumption; paying particular attention to scenes of aesthetic judgment in fiction allows us to decode writers' theories of representation.

In addition to such studies of the inclusion (or intrusion) of visual arts in literature, we must add investigations of painter-figures as characters within narrative. As Bo Jeffares and Mack Smith argue, the nineteenth century saw a proliferation of the painter-hero in English and Continental fiction. Jeffares and Smith consider almost exclusively male painter-figures;[12] although a varied bunch, male painters in literature can be characterized broadly as partaking powerfully of the Romantic ideal even once the value of that ideal had markedly depreciated. Male painters were depicted as outsiders; Casteras notes that male artists in novels "establish recognizable traits of an idealized romantic artist who was bohemian, flamboyant, tormented or struggling, moody or soulful, and often imbued with a Promethean spirit that allied him with the alleged divinity of genius" (1992, 209). The female artists depicted by Victorian women novelists regularly partake of this mythos—they too are represented as being in diverse ways outside the scope of traditional bourgeois culture. Their artistic impulses are both the psychological cause and the narrative effect of their otherness; in other words, these novelists represent a woman's artistic nature as both responsible for her desire to escape gender norms and the symbol of that desire. But as we shall see, these women painters' outsider status is materially and socially instantiated, rather than emotionally depicted as it is with the male artist-heroes of the period. Artist-heroines are generally too busy trying to make a living to indulge in expressions of artistic angst.

In this study, I ask what narrative work is done by references to painting and painters in fiction by women, arguing that such narrative references are self-reflexive moments, articulating not simply writers' large-scale aesthetic and social opinions but their literary theories as well. However, I make several departures from current interart scholarship. Critics have tended to read the painter figure as a simple extension of the writer; Deborah Ellen Barker, for example, argues persuasively (apropos of painter-heroines in American fiction) that "the woman painter-as-heroine . . . provided women writers with an artistic alter-ego, and allowed them to explore issues of creativity and sexuality which conflicted with the limitations of feminine decorum that readers and critics often expected of the woman writer" (2000, 2). Although it is certainly accurate to suggest, as Barker does, that women painters in both Britain and America were often more radical (sexually and politically) than their sister artists (women writers), it is an oversimplification to see the painter-heroine as a mere fictional double for the woman writer. I therefore rarely draw a one-to-one correspondence between the woman writer and the woman painter, for while this is certainly a significant part of the story, I hope to suggest here that the painter figure in these novels goes well beyond an alter ego; these are *Künstlerromane*, certainly, but not primarily personal ones.[13] If these fictional women painters do not easily lend themselves to biographical readings, they likewise cannot be read as simple historical reflections; that is, few of the artist-heroines in these novels are directly modeled on historical characters. Rather, the fictional women artists appear to be composite creatures, cobbled together out of known public figures, the author's acquaintances, and her fantasy ideal of a woman painter. Similarly, there are few one-to-one correspondences between fictional scenes and real historical paintings to be found in these texts. What Andres calls "isomorphic equivalents" (2002, 374) or "narrative reconfigurations" (2005, xvi)—that is, fictional scenes that call to mind specific Victorian paintings[14]—are rare.[15]

In another departure from recent interart scholarship on Victorian fiction, I regularly consider fictional representations of the *act* of painting rather than simply ekphrastic representations of the artifact of painting,[16] thus emphasizing art as a *social* process involving multiple ideological pressures. In such scenes of painting, the woman painter was a nodal point for discussions of numerous problems relating to women and the social realm: access to education and training, professionalization, economic freedom, property rights, and other similar issues. Representing the difficult *process* of women's artistic production and its aftermath (public scenes of judgment, common to all the novels I consider) enables women writers to engage not just with aesthetic concerns but with the social issues that inevitably arise out of these public scenarios. When I do turn my attention to ekphrastic descriptions of paintings themselves, I focus the discussion on the gender implications of these references. By considering representations of women's paintings in texts by women writers, I introduce the issue of gender into the critical discourse surrounding textual ekphrasis. Ekphrasis has been most simply defined as "the verbal representation of visual representation" (Heffernan 1993, 3); unlike pictorialism, which represents natural objects and scenes, ekphrasis deals with visual works of representational art per se. W. J. T. Mitchell, in *Iconology*, explains that the relationship between the word and the image has always been essentially paragonal; that is, it turns on the *antagonism* between the two.[17] At different moments in history and in the works of different artists, one or the other medium has emerged as dominant—dominance here meaning that one medium is considered more successful in reproducing or expressing reality. As Starzyk explains, discussions of the antagonism between word and image are based on the "continued dominance of mimesis" (Starzyk 2002, 1). Although some critics, such as Jean Hagstrum (1958), have suggested that (at least until the late eighteenth century) the relationship between word and image is amicable (since both media are involved in the attempt at representing an immutable truth), most critics contend that by the Romantic period ekphrasis marks some form of rivalry between the two media. Starzyk, for example, contends that in the Romantic and Victorian periods, the verbal and the visual exist in a dialectical relationship, serving as *both* "duplicates *and* rivals" (2002, 5; emphasis in original). Nineteenth-century ekphrastic writers are therefore "simultaneously enamoured of and terrified by the image they gaze upon" (7).

Throughout the critical history, ekphrasis has been theorized as an implicitly gendered phenomenon. Critics have uniformly coded the word as male in ekphrastic encounters, while the silent and beautiful image that cannot speak for itself is, unsurprisingly, feminized. Keats's "Ode on a Grecian Urn" is the quintessential example here: the artwork, described as a "still unravish'd bride of quietness," is immobile ("still"), potentially sexualized ("unravish'd"), feminized ("bride"), and mute ("quietness"), and is then subjected to the verbal attentions of a masculine poetic speaker eager to pin "her" down with concrete description.[18] James Heffernan has taken up this binary formulation and interpreted various moments of ekphrasis as the

> struggle for dominance between the image and the word. . . . First, because it evokes the power of the silent image even as it subjects that power to the rival authority of language, it is intensely paragonal. Second, the contest it stages is often powerfully gendered: the expression of a duel between male and female gazes, the voice of male speech striving to control a female image that is both alluring and threatening, of male narrative striving to overcome the fixating impact of beauty poised in space. (1993, 1)

He writes later in a similar metaphoric register, "Ekphrasis stages a contest between rival modes of representation: between the driving force of the narrating word and the stubborn resistance of the fixed image" (6).

Historians of ekphrasis find that this gendering extends far back into literary history; scholars of the Early Modern period, for example, contend that the development of ekphrastic texts mirrors the courtly love poem.[19] The poet in both genres worships an unwilling, mute, or immobile feminized object and describes it in an attempt to possess it. The "blazon" or detailed description of the beloved is therefore structurally similar to an ekphrastic description of an artwork, as Nancy Vickers's foundational article on the blazon suggests.[20] Both use detailed description to control a female object. Similarly, Marion Wells writes (also apropos of Shakespeare's Lucrece) of "the destructive power of emotionally charged visual description" (2002, 98) known as *enargeia*, a related rhetorical device. Although enargeia tries to make an object "live" for the reader through unusually potent sensory description, it more frequently has the opposite effect, Wells argues, by entombing the object and simultaneously causing a lost of selfhood in the viewing subject, so absorbed does he (in most cases) become in the object.[21] This destructive power is arguably a major component of ekphrastic literature beyond the Early Modern period as well; ekphrasis seems always to slide inexorably into violent appropriation, and even eulogistic ekphrasis like Keats's still serves to metaphorically entomb a feminized art object.

How might it be possible to rethink the traditional gendering of ekphrasis? To begin with, we must first uncover a canon, so to speak, of women's ekphrasis, in which women occupy any or all of the possible subject positions involved in ekphrasis: viewer, describer, author, or producer of the art object itself.[22] Thus far, every major critic of the sister arts fails to consider any texts describing images made by women. This may be understandable for the Classical and Early Modern periods, but it is less so for subsequent literary eras. W. J. T. Mitchell, who includes no women artists in his analyses, does at least make a quick gesture in their direction when he concedes at the end of his chapter on ekphrasis in *Picture Theory* that "All this would look quite different, of course, if my emphasis had been on ekphrastic poetry by women" (1994, 181). How different would it look, for example, if the ekphrastic scenario involves a woman viewing an artwork? or a woman describing another woman's artwork? or a woman describing her own artwork, as happens in artists' memoirs? Or when an artwork being described has—at least within the fictional world of the text—been created by the *same* woman artist who creates the ekphrasis?

Once a suitable object of study has been found, we can begin to reconceive the model of ekphrasis with which critics have been working for decades.

Heffernan gives a useful place to begin when he argues that some ekphrastic moments offer hints—but only hints, and generally ineffectual ones—of gender resistance. He writes:

> Ekphrasis entails prosopopeia, or the rhetorical technique of envoicing a silent object. Ekphrasis speaks not only about works of art but also to and for them. In so doing, it stages—within the theater of language itself—a revolution of the image against the word, and particularly the word of Lessing, who decreed that the duty of pictures was to be silent and beautiful (like a woman), leaving expression to poetry. In talking back to and looking back at the male viewer, the images envoiced by ekphrasis challenge at once the controlling authority of the male gaze and the power of the male word. (1993, 7)

Heffernan purports to consider "an alternative genealogy" (46) of feminine ekphrasis where we might see this revolution, but the only art form he considers is women's weaving (in the cases of Philomela and Arachne) as described by exclusively male authors. Furthermore, his "alternate genealogy" focuses *solely* on images of *rape* (the chapter is titled "Weaving Rape"), arguing that "violated women speak in and through pictures of violation" (89). While these images of rape may provide a "radical alternative to the pictures of still unravished beauty" typical of the male ekphrastic tradition, they forcibly suggest just how little power women are permitted within this tradition: the only thing women's visual representations have to say here is "Help, rape!" In Heffernan's argument, woven depictions of rape ekphrastically described by male writers bear the burden of enacting "a revolution of the image against the word" (90); yet Heffernan nowhere considers the possibility of *women* writers offering ekphrases of women's visual representations, nor of male writers representing women's artistic productions that represent something slightly more revolutionary than rape.

Writing about rape and ekphrasis together is also not an isolated incident. Heffernan's focus on narratives of rape comes, obliquely at least, from Suzanne Langer's well-known comment about relations between the various arts. Unlike more contemporary interart theorists like Mitchell, Langer argues that true interart blending is impossible. Opera, for example, might have elements of drama but is, in Langer's mind, fundamentally music; one art form always subsumes another. In this context she writes, rather alarmingly, "There are no happy marriages in art—only successful rape" (1957, 86). Such a statement most clearly articulates the paragonal quality Heffernan and others see in interart relationships and has proved a useful paradigm for thinking through the gender politics of many of the classic ekphrastic texts by men in the Western canon, "Ode on a Grecian Urn" and Robert Browning's "My Last Duchess" among them.

In this study, I look exclusively at fictional ekphrastic scenes created by women writers to describe artworks produced by women. I should note that I am dealing here solely with what John Hollander calls "notional ekphrasis," descriptions of *imaginary* works of art. Ekphrases of real, existing works of art he terms "actual ekphrasis"; this group includes such examples as Auden's "Musée des Beaux Arts" or Williams's poems on Brueghel. Actual ekphrastic poetry or fiction about women's paintings by women writers of any era is extremely rare;[23] I have found no nineteenth-century works by women which ekphrastically describe real artworks by other women (other than descriptions in nonfiction works such as memoirs or art criticism), although the occasional woman poet writes of artworks produced by men.[24] Notional ekphrases such as the ones I examine are more common, but still significantly less common than similar descriptions by male writers; why this might be so is one of my underlying questions in this study. Are women writers less likely to use ekphrasis? and if so, why?

In the cases of notional ekphrasis that I examine, I ask if the interart relationship between word and image is necessarily still violent or antagonistic when a woman writer describes a work produced by a woman painter, and if the traditional gender associations (male word and female image) need apply. The overwhelming answer is no. Several of the novelists I consider here offer a complete reversal: scenes in which the image (even though produced by a woman) is implicitly male and the describing voice female. Others envision a mutually interdependent and potentially supportive interaction between word and image rather than the "revolution of the image against the word" noted by Heffernan in his alternate genealogy or the disciplining of the image by the word as in traditional ekphrases.[25] Ekphrasis is still about power in these texts, certainly, but not necessarily the power of one medium (the word) over another (the image). Descriptions of women's paintings by women writers are rather an attempt to consolidate female power; by controlling ekphrastic description, these writers attempt to control interpretation as well. My aim is to explore the nature and narrative ramifications of the nonparagonal theory of ekphrasis which arises when we look specifically at how women writers represent the productions of their sister artists.

In the texts I consider here, ekphrasis is further transformed by being repositioned with regard to the narrative that encloses it. Traditional ekphrasis is considered paragonal not just because it controls a female object with language but because that art object is explicitly set apart from the narrative that describes it; the object becomes confined in a textual frame. Ekphrastic moments are typically understood as therefore halting narrative progression. (Classical examples of this occur when Homer pauses his narrative of events to describe the construction of Achilles' shield or in Virgil's similar description of the images on Aeneas' shield.) This obstruction of narrative serves (seemingly) to highlight the absolute difference between the art object and the temporal movement of narrative. Ekphrasis can be read, then, as a way for writers to tout the strength of their own medium (temporal, fluid) over the image (static); it can also be read as narrative's way of borrowing the positive qualities of visual art. As Alison Byerly argues, references to the visual arts in fiction can on the one hand serve to validate the power of realist narrative by contrasting it with art objects put forward as "obviously" unreal within the context of the narrative. On the other hand, however, moments of ekphrastic description can signal independence: "Artistic allusion in the novel attempts to confer upon particular passages the autonomy and uniqueness of the artifact" (1997, 4).

In ekphrastic scenes by women describing women's artworks, we see most often the latter investment. The visual realm is conceived less as a failure or a threat to fiction than as a threat to *women,* and hence something which must be negotiated and assimilated if women are to become successful artists. As critics since Laura Mulvey's influential work have argued, the problem of being looked at is of central concern to women; as the texts I consider here demonstrate, it is even *more* of a problem if you are a woman producing art that you wish to be looked at. Ekphrasis becomes a way for women to reclaim power over the visual realm by refocusing narrative attention on women's artistic *productions* rather than upon their bodies.

III.

In blending traditional aesthetic questions with social and material debates, the women writers I discuss in this book anticipate much of the recent debate over aesthetics. After enjoying centuries of high status, the field of philosophical aesthetics came under serious attack by numerous late-twentieth-century critics who argued that the conditions and categories of aesthetic debate were, in fact, heavily weighted with considerable ideological baggage. Terry Eagleton's massive study *The Ideology of the Aesthetic* ripped open the major aesthetic writers from the mid-seventeenth century onward to reveal their historical and political underpinnings, suggesting finally that, because of such ideological motivations, aesthetics is and has always been largely incapable of doing what it purports to do: offer an objective definition and evaluation of art. If Eagleton's tome attempts an exhaustive reinterpretation of aesthetic history, his project—and that of others engaged in salvaging the aesthetic from its purely formalist bent—can be found in embryo, short and sweet, in one paragraph in Raymond Williams's discussion of aesthetics in *Keywords*. Williams writes:

> It is clear from this history that aesthetics, with its specialized reference to art, to visual appearance, and to a category of what is "fine" or "beautiful," is a key formation in a group of meanings which at once emphasized and isolated subjective sense-activity as the basis of art and beauty as distinct, for example, from *social* or *cultural* interpretations. It is an element in the divided modern consciousness of *art* and *society*: a reference beyond social use and social valuation which . . . is intended to express a human dimension which the dominant version of *society* appears to exclude. The emphasis is understandable but the isolation can be damaging, for there is something irresistibly displaced and marginal about the now common and limiting phrase "aesthetic considerations," especially when contrasted with *practical* or utilitarian considerations. (1985, 32; emphasis in original)

Much of Williams's critical work and the tradition of Materialist critical thinking that he inspired attempts to overcome this "damaging" definition of aesthetics as divorced from social, political, or historical forces. In this vein, for example, Martha Woodmansee dismisses traditional aesthetics as "great minds speaking with one another over and above the historical process" (1994, 7) and advocates shifting critical attention away from formal aesthetic evaluations and toward the material and social conditions of artistic production. In Tony Bennett's succinct terms, aesthetics is simply "really useless knowledge." (Bennett 1987).

More recently, however, the term has enjoyed something of a revival, as critics attempt to find ways to balance the traditional concerns of aesthetics—artistic quality, emotive response, beauty, and more—with a politically informed methodology. A volume of critical essays on aesthetics contains in its title the two critical terms that have come together in recent approaches to aesthetics: *The Politics of Pleasure* (Regan 1992). Michele Barrett's essay in this volume coins the phrase "materialist aesthetics" to describe attempts to locate the universal and metaphysical discourse of aesthetics in its historical framework; such scholarship treats aesthetics as a subject in the history of knowledge, as historically contingent and ideologically inflected.[26] Other critics provide similar ways to approach aesthetics with an eye to ideology.

George Levine, for example, sees aesthetics as a potentially disruptive force within dominant ideologies (1994), while Susan Wolfson argues for a "productive, generative meeting" between aesthetics and ideology (1998, 3). Isobel Armstrong also argues against the recent dismissal of the category of the aesthetic; in her view, "The politics of the anti-aesthetic [exemplified for Armstrong by Eagleton] rely on deconstructive gestures of exposure that fail to address the democratic and radical potential of aesthetic discourse" (2000, 2).[27] Armstrong's democratic aesthetic is a balancing act: she is struggling to find a way to blend Marxist or materialist thinking (which is sensitive to issues of class, race, and gender) with an evaluative discourse on beauty and affect (which has historically not been sensitive to these issues, as the materialist critics have pointed out) to create a new, radical aesthetic. Adorno, whose *Aesthetic Theory* (1984) Armstrong admires, also argues for a balance between Marxist methodology of aesthetic investigation (what are the conditions of production for art objects?) and a formalist view of the necessary autonomy of art. Art, for Adorno, is not a separate realm, yet it retains a certain autonomy even as it interacts with social reality.

The women writers I discuss in this book make it clear that this attempt at formulating a materialist aesthetic—while being absolutely crucial—is not a new project. Victorian women writers shared Armstrong's desire to achieve the fine balance between formalism and materialism, and they expressed their theories in narrative form. Because nineteenth-century women rarely wrote formal aesthetic treatises, they are often left out of aesthetic history. Elizabeth Bohls has argued that women writers of the Romantic period inserted themselves into the aesthetic tradition—a powerfully masculine and confined tradition—by encoding aesthetic treatises within travel narratives, memoirs, journals, and other types of nonfiction writing. These late-eighteenth-century women writers thereby opened out the tradition of aesthetics, radicalizing the discourse to make space for female subjectivity. Bohls writes:

> Instead of restricting aesthetics to a narrow, prestigious genre of academic or theoretical writing, I define it more broadly as a discourse, or a closely related set of discourses, encompassing a set of characteristic topics or preoccupations as well as a vocabulary for talking about these. Aesthetic discourse deals with the categories and concepts of art, beauty, sublimity, taste and judgment, and more broadly with the pleasure experienced from sensuous surfaces or spectacles. (1995, 5)

Similarly, I argue here that Victorian women writers use the figure of the woman painter to offer sophisticated, detailed, and often radical aesthetic theories within their novels—indirectly, perhaps, but still emphatically. Through their aesthetic debates, these women writers attempt to theorize female subjectivity through art; in doing so they also critique the philosophical discourse of aesthetics itself, that privileged field which, as Luc Ferry writes, "holds the sediments of the history of democratic individualism or modern subjectivity" (1993, viii). Women novelists use the woman painter as a figure for radical female subjectivity, at once engaged in the production, reception, and judgment of art. I see, I paint, I judge; therefore I am.[28]

The Victorian women novelists who are the focus of this study try to answer the "classic" questions of traditional (derived from late-seventeenth- and eighteenth-century models) aesthetics but are never unaware of the political nature of aesthetics. That is, these nineteenth-century women writers are *already* practicing a materialist aesthetics in their fiction. When they make their heroines artists, women writers recognize the social and political conditions of that status, and any discussion of the value or beauty of art is tinged inescapably with a self-conscious awareness of the political ramifications of aesthetics. In their representations of painter-heroines, these novelists show us ways in which aesthetics is conditioned by social ideology—how, for instance, women's art cannot be evaluated without the lens of gender ideology and beliefs about femininity, and how femininity is constructed in part by beliefs about art and aesthetic response. These writers consistently question the possibility of an aesthetic even temporarily abstracted from ideologies of civil society.[29] Thus, rather than assume that the materialist or historicist insight into aesthetics (that aesthetics is historically contingent) is a twentieth-century "discovery," we must acknowledge that nineteenth-century women writers were themselves aware of the ideologically constructed nature of a supposedly universalist discourse of beauty and were exploiting and exploring this connection in fiction.

As well as critiquing the aesthetic tradition, women writers were also participating in it. Numerous recent critics have argued persuasively that the nineteenth century saw a radical shift in the experience of the aesthetic, a shift that forcibly impacted women artists of all kinds. Eighteenth-century aesthetics theorized art from the point of view of the spectator and the art object; as Nietzsche writes of Kant, "all I wish to underline is that Kant, like all philosophers, instead of envisaging the aesthetic problem from the point of view of the artist (the creator), considered art and the beautiful purely from that of the 'spectator,' and unconsciously introduced the 'spectator' into the concept 'beautiful'" (*Genealogy of Morals* 1887; quoted in Agamben 1999, 1). The spectator, in Kantian aesthetics, approached the art object with disinterest; the aesthetic experience was an ideal meeting between an unconscious art object and an unselfconscious viewer. Nineteenth-century aesthetics, on the other hand, introduced the artist into this scenario; as Agamben writes, "The focal point of the reflection on art moves from the disinterested spectator to the interested artist" (1999, 2).[30] Following Nietzsche, Agamben takes the mythical sculptor Pygmalion as the model for this transformation in aesthetics. In classical and eighteenth-century aesthetics, art was considered dangerous because it could (for Plato) destroy the moral foundation of a city or (for the eighteenth-century writers) inspire the spectator with a kind of divine terror; both functions of art profoundly affected the *spectator*. In the nineteenth century, aesthetics shifts its focus from spectator to *artist*. Writes Agamben, "To the increasing innocence of the spectator's experience in front of the beautiful object corresponds the increasing danger inherent in the artist's experience" (3). This "danger" is not always danger in any negative sense. As the Pygmalion example dramatizes, the experience of the artist can be awful in the older sense of the word: awe-inspiring. The artist becomes a creature for whom art is a passion, a life-and-death erotic experience.[31]

In Adorno's historical account of the aesthetic, the period from the late eighteenth through the late nineteenth century is similarly pivotal and conflicted. For Adorno, this is the era in which "genius" comes into being as a concept that isolates individuals from society, a turn which Adorno deplores: the idea of genius "tends to diminish the status of the work, glorifying instead its author out of a false sense of enthusiasm" (1984, 243–44). Similarly, "[The obsession with the artist/genius] glorifies pure creation by the human being without regard to purpose . . . and it relieves the viewer of the task of understanding the artistic object before him, giving him instead a surrogate—the personality of the artist or, worse, trashy biographies of him" (245). Thus it would seem that art pulls farther away from society, becomes less concerned with quotidian realities, by virtue of the fact that art's creator is set above the common run of humanity.[32]

We can look to numerous nineteenth-century writers for support of these claims that the aesthetic experience became artist-centered during the nineteenth century. Carlyle, in an article on the importance of Biography published in *Fraser's Magazine* in 1832, argues that

> In the Art, we can nowise forget the Artist: while looking on the *Transfiguration*, while studying the *Iliad*, we ever strive to figure to ourselves what spirit dwelt in Raphael; what a head was that of Homer. . . . The Painter and the Singer are present to us; we partially and for the time become the very Painter and the very Singer, while we enjoy the Picture and the Song . . . this is the highest enjoyment, the clearest recognition, we can have of these. (1832, 254)

What Carlyle goes on to call the "Biographic appetite" (255) is, he argues, at work in our appreciation of narrative fiction as well as poetry, history, and painting: we read or view art simply to find out what artists think. Two years later, Anna Jameson similarly claimed that it was "atheistical" to ignore the artist. She writes (with rather surprising foreshadowing of Oscar Wilde):

> What Goethe says of poets must needs be applicable to painters. He says, "If we look only at the principal productions of a poet, and neglect to study himself, his character, and the circumstances with which he had to contend, we fall into a sort of atheism, which forgets the Creator in his creation." I think most people admire pictures in this sort of atheistical fashion; yet, next to loving pictures, and all the pleasure they give . . . equal with it, is the inexhaustible interest of studying the painter in his works. . . . Almost every picture has an individual character, reflecting the predominant temperament—nay, sometimes the occasional mood of the artist, its creator. Even portrait painters, renowned for their exact adherence to nature, will be found to have stamped upon their portraits a general and distinguishing character. (1834, 169–70)

Such an obsession with artists led, according to Julie Codell, to a proliferation of artists' biographies during the Victorian era; in turn these biographies marked a dramatic change in the public perception of artists (particularly in the latter half of the Victorian period), who were constructed no longer as "agonized geniuses" but instead as "gentlemen and ladies . . . thoroughly socialized, not alienated and suffering in garrets. . . . Victorian artists were models of success, decorum, proper manliness and femininity and, ultimately, of Britishness, all intended for public consumption" (2003, 2–3); such art writing served to "domesticate the artist" (23). Codell writes, "Victorian artists' lifewritings were predicated on the presentation of a mutually reflecting mirror between public and artist, not on distinguishing the artist radically from the public" as in the Modern period (6). Furthermore, the artist came to be identified as a figure "contributing to the public good" (15) rather than a figure opposed to public morality; artists were written about as insiders rather than Romantic outsiders. Arguably, artist-biographies were part of what Linda Dowling termed the "aesthetic democracy" of the period: a prevalent Victorian discourse that advocated opening up art for a wider public.[33] That emergent art-loving public read artists' biographies in droves and found the life of the artist to be part of the consumable aesthetic package. In part because of this public interest, the artist became a social figure to be reckoned with; from being artisans of the working class, artists became their own class, outside traditional hierarchies.³⁴ On the one hand, Victorian artists' "increasing agency" (9) was embraced by women artists, who "exploited male professional culture and identified themselves with it as a strategy for success" (11). On the other hand, because this newfound agency made artists more independent and liberated than ever before, women were more stridently debarred from entering the ranks of a profession that might allow them similar freedoms.

John Ruskin was perhaps the best-known contributor to this repositioning of the artist as central within the aesthetic system during the nineteenth century. If, as Ruskin believed, the art of a society could be used as a gauge of the quality of that society in other registers, then the artist had a considerable responsibility. "You can have noble art only from noble persons," wrote Ruskin in *Lectures on Art* (1903–12, 20: 139). Or again, in *Queen of the Air,* he writes: "Great art is the expression of the mind of a great man" (ibid. 19: 212). In Ruskin's writing, this concern for the ethical qualities of the artist devolves perpetually on a concern for the *physical* being of the artist, whose very *body* becomes an object for intense scrutiny. Thus, when in *Lectures on Art* he attempts to delineate the spiritual power of a great artist, he fixates on the artist's body before moving out again from that body to ethical realms:

> Try, first, to realize to yourself the muscular precision of that action [drawing a line], and the intellectual strain of it . . . imagine that muscular firmness and subtlety, and the instantaneously selective and ordinant energy of the brain, sustained all day long . . . and all this life long. And then consider, so far as you know anything of physiology, what sort of ethical state of body and mind that means! . . . what fineness of race there must be to get it, what exquisite balance and symmetry of the vital powers! (ibid. 20: 149)

Similarly, in volume 2 of *Modern Painters,* Ruskin asserts that "a great painter must necessarily be a man of strong and perfect physical constitution" (1866–84, 2: 78).

The refocusing of the aesthetic gaze on the figure of the artist, rather than the spectator or the art object, occasioned a considerable crisis for Victorian women artists, their critics, and their supporters. Should the woman artist, too, be "sensitive, active and vigorous" like Ruskin's male artist? Need she be able to hold her pencil all day and all life long with "muscular firmness"? Intellectual and spiritual genius aside, is it possible for a woman to have the physical qualities Ruskin imagines are necessary to produce great art? Few scholars of Victorian aesthetics consider the impact of gender on the changing aesthetic theories of the period (most, like Jonah Siegel, continue to use the pseudo-universal "he" to refer to "the artist"),³⁵ but it seems clear that women had an enormous role to play in the theoretical as well as the social aspects of art in the era. If there was what Paula Gillett describes as a "continuing lack of consensus concerning the role of the artist in society, and the legitimate functions served by the painter's work" (1990, 14) during the Victorian era, women painters were not able to merely insert themselves into an already codified ideology of The Artist. As Clarissa Campbell Orr writes in her introduction to *Women in the Victorian Art World*, the struggle for women painters to gain acceptance was "not just a question of being admitted to art schools or the Royal Academy, but of *challenging the whole notion of what an artist was*" (1995, 7; emphasis added). Women painters could and did actively contribute to the nineteenth-century conception of the character and role of the artist; and women writers who represented women painters in their fiction were therefore inserting themselves into an extremely volatile moment in aesthetic history.

It was certainly in women painters' best interest to help reconfigure the public conception of the notion of artistic genius, to make "the artist" a public, domestic, social individual. As Christine Battersby writes in *Gender and Genius*, "The Romantic conception of genius is peculiarly harmful to women. Our present criteria for artistic excellence have their origins in theories that specifically and explicitly denied women genius" (1989, 23). Women, she argues, were denied genius "even though qualities previously downgraded as 'feminine' had become valuable as a consequence of radical changes in aesthetic taste and aesthetic theory . . . cultural misogyny remained (and even intensified) despite a reversal in attitude towards emotionality, sensitivity and imaginative self-expression [qualities which continued to be defined as feminine]" (ibid.). The cult of genius (a more focused and gender-biased version of the cult of the artist) posed particular problems for women; the very definition of "genius" articulated by Romantic theorists precluded women from inclusion in the ranks. As the century progressed, however, young artists and the viewing (and purchasing) public began increasingly to hold the Romantic concept of artist as "misunderstood genius" in disfavor—a notion many women painters of the time shared. Bracketed by early-nineteenth-century Romanticism on the one hand and late-century Aestheticism on the other, the art of the middle decades of the nineteenth century (when women artists were entering the scene in greatest numbers) might be best summarized as "art for the public's sake." Here women could excel. Women painters, by virtue of their gender, were already in a position to present themselves as moral guardians; it was regularly argued that women painters' work could have a beneficial influence on society. This influence wasn't always conceived as elevating or ennobling (such would be the effects of masculine High

Art), but women's art was thought to educate, soothe, or amuse—as the *Punch* review discussed in chapter 1 will show. In tension with this moral conception of art, the tradition of the Byronic hero certainly lived on in the radical bohemians of the Pre-Raphaelite set—the debauched artist (often perceived as a dangerous French import) lived alongside the Victorian ideal of the socially responsible artist whose art was intended to stimulate public morality. As we shall see, however, women painters of fact and fiction most often attempted to align themselves (at least publicly) with the image of the artist as a moral and domestic creature.

IV.

Relying on interart theory, materialist aesthetics, and a range of art historical documents, this book examines the scene of aesthetic production as depicted in Victorian novels by women in which the focus is as much on the figure of the woman artist—her body and her place in the social body—as it is on the art object being produced. In chapter 1, I look more closely at ideological discourse surrounding the woman painter during the second half of the nineteenth century, examining periodical articles and nonfiction writings that introduce key problems in the historical conditions of women painters. The remainder of the study looks at fictional works, beginning in chapter 2 with Anne Brontë's undervalued *The Tenant of Wildfell Hall*. The heroine of *Tenant*, Helen Graham, offers a seminal example of the fictional woman painter, whose development as an artist allows Anne Brontë to articulate her critique of social and aesthetic systems which confine women (literally and figuratively in this case). In chapter 3 I turn to Anne's sister Charlotte's descriptions of a woman's paintings in *Jane Eyre,* a novel well known for its obsession with the visual realm. Jane's artwork—wild and strange—has frequently been read as a sign of her similarly untraditional interiority; I shift the focus of the discussion to consider Jane's art as part of Charlotte Brontë's dismissal of key social conventions on the one hand and her reconceptualizing of classic ekphrasis on the other. Both Brontë sisters use the figure of the woman painter to intervene in an aesthetic history conceived as erotically charged and in a social history seen as obstructing women's professional or emotional development.

Chapter 4 discusses works that specifically diffuse the erotic component of women's experience in the aesthetic realm. Margaret Oliphant's *Miss Marjoribanks,* Anna Mary Howitt's novella "Sisters in Art," and George Eliot's *Daniel Deronda* look more specifically at the social and economic concerns surrounding that experience. Chapter 5 introduces a little-known fictionalized account by Anne Thackeray Ritchie of the eighteenth-century painter Angelica Kauffman, titled *Miss Angel and Fulham Lawn*. Ritchie's heroine—the only fictional woman artist explicitly based on a real painter—offers a stunning example of women painters' inability to shed their skin and to be viewed as artists rather than as women. Chapter 6 offers two examples of fictional women painters who do manage to escape the problematic female body, but only because they are physically deformed or disabled. The physical disabilities of the painter-heroines of Dinah Craik's *Olive* and Charlotte Yonge's *Pillars of the House* allow them to escape traditional gender expectations. My final chapter looks at fictional women painters in the work of Mary Ward, whose wavering and conflicted commitment to feminist goals translates into similarly conflicted representations of women artists. Finally, in my coda I take a brief look at late-twentieth- and early-twenty-first-century representations of women painters in the public press to suggest, rather dolefully, that the ideological pressures facing women painters in the Victorian era have yet to leave us.

CHAPTER ONE

Prevailing Winds and Cross-Currents

Public Discourse and the History of Victorian Women Painters

I.

AT THE END of the eighteenth century and into the early decades of the nineteenth, painting and drawing were required accomplishments for women in England. Even before large numbers of women began to work as professional painters in the Victorian era, drawing and watercolor painting formed part of the standard education for middle- and upper-class ladies. In 1810, a popular art critic saw the rise of women's amateur art as a "revolution":

> It is impossible to congratulate our fair countrywomen too warmly on the revolution which has of late years taken place, when drawing and fancy-work of endless variety have been raised on the ruins of that heavy, unhealthy and stupefying occupation, needlework. Drawing, the groundwork of refined taste in the arts, is now considered, and very justly, as an indispensable requirement in the education of both sexes. In that of females in particular, it has opened a prodigious field of the excursions of imagination, invention, and ingenuity. ("Observations on Fancy Work" 1810, 397)

Similarly, Ellen Clayton, a Victorian historian of women in art, noted that "Drawing and painting became, in the days of King George the Third as fashionable accomplishments with young ladies as Greek and Latin had been with their Tudor predecessors, or pianoforte playing and amateur acting with their Victorian successors. . . . Art had become a craze . . . it was a necessary addendum to a superior education" (Clayton 1876, 1: 336).

Women's amateur artistic endeavors became highly commercialized and institutionalized at the start of the nineteenth century; a flood of art shops, art books (there were more, and more varied, art manuals in the 1800–50 period than ever before, many directed at women), sketching clubs, and new exhibit sites appeared (see Bermingham 2000, 132–33). Art was becoming part of women's social life. For example, Ackermann, an entrepreneur as well as a writer, kept a shop that was something between an art gallery, an art supply store, and—gradually—a feminized tea shop. Such a blend was part of a gradual change in retail shops to "adjust . . . shops to the needs and tastes of their female customers" (ibid. 175). Alongside this commercialization of women's art came a gradual but inevitable division between men's production of original works of (possible) genius and women's production of derivative works meant for amusement or home decor. Women were thought incapable of originality and relegated to the role of copyists; the female amateur was thus debarred from the masculine world of anticommercial, anticonsumer High Art. Writes Bermingham of the early nineteenth century, "The professional artist expressed his genius and imagination; the lady amateur practiced art for amusement and to display her taste and skill, to strengthen the domestic bonds of love and duty, to serve the community, and to improve her taste and that of the nation" (180).

As the century progressed, however, many women began to take their artistic skill more seriously. Elizabeth Ellet, writing a history of women painters in 1859, insists that "The progress of female talent and skill . . . has become more remarkable than ever within the last fifty years. The number of women engaged in the pursuits of art during that time far exceeds that of the whole preceding century" (234). We can see this transformation from amateurism to professionalism recorded almost unwillingly in the works of Sarah Stickney Ellis, the Victorian antifeminist moralist. While Ellis insists that women should not intrude on the professional male province of High Art, she nevertheless advocates a surprisingly rigorous brand of art-as-accomplishment. Ellis's collection of short conduct manuals, written beginning in 1838 for the "Women, Daughters and Wives of England" and collected into a volume titled *The Family Monitor,* encouraged women to buttress masculine superiority by obliterating their own selves. Directed particularly to middle-class *women* (rather than upper-class *ladies*), Ellis's trilogy schools female readers in "the minor morals of domestic life" (1848b, 3). One such "particular minutia of practical duty," as Ellis terms them, is the proper application of women to the fine arts. But not of course so that they might become professional artists (Heaven forbid!). Drawing and painting serve for Ellis as ways to discipline the feminine mind and to keep it out of trouble. She extols the virtues of drawing as follows:

> Among [drawing's] advantages, I will begin with the least. It is quiet. It disturbs no one; for however defective the performance may be, it does not necessarily, like music, jar upon the sense. It is true, it may when seen offend the practiced eye; but we can always keep our productions to ourselves. In addition to this, it is an employment which beguiles the mind of many cares . . . drawing is of all other occupations the one most calculated to keep the mind from brooding upon self, and to maintain that general cheerfulness which is a part of social and domestic duty. (1848a, 38)

Ellis is insistent that women should not study the art of painting to the extent that, or with the intent that, the productions might enter the public sphere. Women must remain, instead, domestic artists, since there is danger in achieving too great a skill in (and sensibility for) art: "In every object . . . the painter perceives at once what is striking, characteristic, harmonious, or graceful . . . he feels himself the inhabitant of a world of beauty, from which others are shut out" (ibid. 39). Women, in Ellis's system of belief, are not supposed to "shut out" others; women are connective tissue, uniting families, communities, and the nation. For a woman to become an Artist, then, would violate the principles of femininity Ellis is attempting to prescribe.

Yet when Ellis offers her plan for a proper education in art, one begins to wonder how any woman who completes such rigorous training could remain an amateur. For a woman to learn to draw properly, Ellis argues, she must first study perspective, the preliminary step in "the *philosophy* of picture-making, or, in other words, the relation of cause and effect in the grouping and general management of objects, so as to unite a number of parts into a perfect and pleasing whole" (ibid.; emphasis added). As a "philosophy," perspective becomes imbued with considerable depth and intellectualism—gone is any sense that drawing provides quiet entertainment in the hours of women's ennui. After conquering perspective, the eager amateur must then gain a solid knowledge, writes Ellis, of botany and entomology, a field of study that sends Ellis into a positively bloodthirsty fervor of excitement. Although she bemoans the "sacrifice of life most revolting to the female mind," she admits that any detailed study of insect life requires "those regular rows of moths and beetles pricked on paper." From entomology, women must move on to study in the "*whole range* of natural history" (ibid. 41; emphasis added). By this point, one wonders what dutiful female student would have time for marriage or childbirth—especially since drawing is but *one* of the accomplishments a young woman is expected to have under Ellis's plan. Regardless of this formidable array of knowledge Ellis encourages women to amass in search of artistic production, Ellis still desires women to remain amateurs in art, putting any artistic talent they may gain in the service of husbands, children, or the moral regeneration of the community. But Ellis is writing these conduct manuals at precisely the moment when women's relation to the art world was changing dramatically, a change reflected in the strange excess of Ellis's plan of study for young women.

Artistic accomplishment—that quiet, private act done solely for the moral improvement of the amateur artist or the genteel amusement of a suitor—begins to give way to serious art training for women. By the 1840s, demand for more formal art training for women including just such subjects as Ellis suggests rose dramatically. If a young nineteenth-century woman discovered in herself a taste and talent for art, how could she get the education she required? Women born into artistic families had a much easier time securing a satisfactory art education, since many were given instruction by fathers and brothers—sometimes with the view to training women as studio helpers (painting in backgrounds, etc.), but often with the result that these women became artists in their own right (see Cherry 1993, chap. 1). If her family was not artistic, a budding young artist's first recourse, if she was reasonably well-off and her parents approved, might be to hire a drawing master to teach her in her home. The Brontë sisters received such training sporadically (aided by the fact that Branwell Brontë intended to become a painter—the sisters piggybacked, in a sense, on their brother's training).[1] If a young woman's family was unwilling or unable to hire an in-home art teacher, what other options were there? Again with parental approval, a young woman might attend one of the local Schools of Design, the London Female School of Art, or one of the few private art schools in England that accepted women students. The number of art schools or private salons that accepted women students increased from mid-century onward, although few offered women the same course of study as male students until the turn of the century. Women students were accepted at Slade's, Cary's, Shaw's, and Cass's, which were all privately run; public schools that accepted women students by mid-century included the South Kensington School of Art, the Royal Academy female schools, and the Crystal Palace School (mainly offering classes in the decorative arts). Larger towns had their public School of Art or School of Design to which women were often admitted (the young artist in Oliphant's *Miss Marjoribanks,* discussed in chapter 4, attends and then teaches in just such a school). Private schools specialized in training wealthier young women: Mrs. Henrietta Ward, wife of Edward Ward, R.A., and herself a well-known painter, records in her memoirs that several of Queen Victoria's daughters studied at her school, as well as many duchesses and countesses. Mrs. Ward's school also boasted such notable visiting professors as Alma-Tadema, John Horsley, Marcus Stone, Luke Fides, and William Powell Frith—all prominent Royal Academy members of the time, and friends of Mrs. Ward and her husband.[2]

Training abroad was another option for artistically minded young women. Many women artists report in their memoirs that art schools in France, Germany, or Italy were more likely to accept or encourage women students, and that opportunities for artistic freedom were greater once one got free of Mother England. America, too, offered freedoms not to be found in England.[3] The painter Louise Jopling, for example, began her career as an artist in France, where she entered a state technical school in Paris. Jopling writes, "In France one is expected to cultivate what little talent one possesses. How my relations in England would have stared, and thought me little less than mad, to entertain the idea of becoming a 'professional'—I, a married woman!" (1925, 5). Anna Mary Howitt records a similar liberating experience studying art in Germany in her memoir *An Art Student in Munich* (1854). And May Alcott's book *Studying Art Abroad* (1879) includes chapters on London, Paris, and Rome (Alcott was American); she makes it quite clear that London, although still an important center for art, has less to offer the female student than does the Continent.

One area of artistic education proved particularly troublesome for English women: painting the unclothed human figure. Considered by many the pinnacle of the painter's art and often the most lucrative, painting the nude human body requires a solid grounding in anatomy and access to nude models. But even after the national network of Female Schools of Design was instituted, women still were forbidden by public art institutions to study "from the life" (that is, from nude models) until the end of the century. Many public and private art schools permitted women, in carefully segregated classes, to draw from the *draped* figure, and occasionally a private school would allow advanced female students segregated access to nude models, but until the end of the century women had no *public* access to nude models.[4] Women artists often grouped together, pooled their money, and hired models for private sessions (Clayton 1876, 2: 83). Part of the problem was, of course, that delicately nurtured females were considered too modest to be confronted by nudity. Both because they had little access to models and because of the intense public disapproval, extremely few women artists dared publicly exhibit nudes. Anna Lea Merritt and Henrietta Rae were two of the

Figure 1.1. "Found Out." Anonymous. *Punch* 89 (February 14, 1885).

few painters brave enough to send nudes to the Royal Academy shows, and this only in the last two decades of the century—and they caught hell for it. Another part of the problem was that the artist/model relationship, hitherto defined exclusively as male/female, had long been considered a site and source of erotic desire, as the cartoon in figure 1.1 dramatizes.

For a woman to paint from the life, then, embroiled her in a potentially erotic scenario, but one with radical permutations of the key players. The cartoon in figure 1.2 satirizes this potential problem: a roomful of female art students gaze longingly on a male model, whose pose suggests both seduction and affection. The scene calls into question the motivations of female art students, who appear here to simply be embracing the opportunity to look at an attractive man; the dandified, languid appearance of the male model further implies a demasculinization of men who might become the subjects

FEMALE SCHOOL OF ART—(*Useful Occupation for Idle and Ornamental Young Men*).

Figure 1.2. "Female School of Art." Anonymous. *Punch* 66 (May 30, 1874).

of women's artwork. It's not hard to imagine what the public would have thought of women art students gazing on a *nude* male model. Painting nude female models was equally problematic, raising as it did the specter of lesbian desire.[5]

Even finding clothed models was difficult for many women painters. Some relied on friends, family members, or female patrons for models. The well-known Impressionist Berthe Morisot, for example, painted family members and friends to save money on hiring models. Similarly, the English painter and portraitist Louise Jopling recalls in her memoirs how she circumvented the high cost of models when she was just entering the painting profession: "I started painting a three-quarter length of myself from my reflection in the mirror in my little bedroom; and this because my model cost me nothing, and never looked bored." On another occasion she resorts to "borrowing" a model; she writes, "The Romer family were away for a summer holiday, so I utilized their pretty cook as a model" (1925, 10–11). Countless other women artists were forced to discover similar stratagems to learn and exercise their trade. In the absence of live models, women's only available subjects were local landscapes, flowers, or domestic subjects. Access to the sort of subject matter that formed the basis for elevated genres of art in the period (the nude, exotic landscapes, etc.) was often impossible for Victorian women painters, who regularly echo a remark made by Helen Graham in Anne Brontë's *Tenant of Wildfell Hall*: "You see there is a sad dearth of subjects. I took the old hall once on a moonlight night, and I suppose I must take it again on a snowy winter's day, and then again on a dark cloudy evening; for I really have nothing else to paint" (A. Brontë 1979, 69). For all the hardships, there were still considerable motivations for women to become professional painters. Art was one of the few professional fields open to women in the period, which made it desirable if not easy. As Dinah Mulock Craik (whose novel *Olive*, discussed in chapter 6, features an artist heroine) writes in her treatise on women's work, *A Woman's Thoughts about Woman*, "Female professions, as distinct from what may be termed female handicrafts, which merit separate classification and discussion, may, I think, be thus divided: the instruction of youth; painting or art; literature; and the vocation of public entertainment—including actresses, singers, musicians and the like" (1860, 66). Though many women were employed in design, as engravers, or in other branches of what Craik calls "handicrafts," the middle of the century saw increasing agitation for women to be allowed access to the professional aspects of artistic endeavor. Women painters struggled to achieve the kind of education that could enable them to stop painting flowers and fruit and paint instead in the most respected genres—history paintings, landscape, portraiture, and figure painting—which were also the most lucrative.

II.

The debate over art education was logically tied up with the problem of employment for women. After receiving proper training, how could a woman make a living as an artist? Finding a place to send your artwork so that people could see it and buy it was the first step. The process of exhibition was made more difficult for Victorian women for a number of reasons: because they had little access to the better-known schools, they also had less pull with the various exhibition galleries or art shops, which were often tied to specific schools. An unknown artist (of either gender) who had not passed through one of the respected art schools would have had a difficult time placing a picture in an important gallery or shop. Women painters had a harder time than their male colleagues, however, because of the taboo against women actively participating in any professional market; relying (as does Helen Graham in *The Tenant of Wildfell Hall*) on a male relative was often essential. The founding of the Society of Female Artists in 1856 (as well as several other women-only galleries) smoothed the path for numerous women painters. The SFA was founded by Harriet Grote, Barbara Bodichon, and other women artists and boasted such supporters and members as Eliza Fox, Henrietta Ward, and Anna Jameson. The society offered struggling women artists a London venue to introduce their work to the public; it also offered established women artists a place to send small sketches or studies to gather meager but much-needed profits. The SFA provided many women a stepping stone to more prestigious galleries.

To make a living as a painter in England, no matter one's gender, it was helpful (if not entirely necessary) to get a picture accepted to the Royal Academy. Although this old and august institution was regularly attacked and rival progressive galleries (like the Grosvenor) were regularly set up to challenge its staid aesthetics, the R.A. remained the best place for an artist to sell his or her works. The R.A. shows were large, frequently exceeding a thousand pictures. The 1862 exhibit, to take a random example, had 1,142 works by 1,142 different artists, 146 of which were Academicians (whose works were guaranteed to be shown at R.A. exhibitions) and 996 outsiders (who had to submit paintings for consideration) (Nunn 1987, 91). Of this number, 55 were women (and of course none of those women were Academicians, women being formally debarred from membership from the late eighteenth century until the early twentieth century); the number of women exhibitors in the R.A. ranged from fifty to one hundred during the nineteenth century. By contrast, the smaller SFA shows included from three hundred to four hundred works of art by approximately a hundred fifty artists. At the SFA, however, prices were considerably lower. One of the SFA's goals was to provide lesser-known women artists a venue for selling their works, and it followed that the prices were low. The *Englishwoman's Review* writes:

> Some people like to read penny newspapers and sixpenny monthlies, and some people like to buy cheap pictures. For our own part we could spend a good deal of money with great pleasure in purchasing pictures in the Female Artists's Exhibition. If we had a limited amount of money and wanted to buy pictures to decorate our drawing room we should go there to buy them. If our supply of money were unlimited we confess we should go elsewhere. If we wanted a newspaper and could afford it we should take *The Times*, but if we were poor we should take a penny print, and be glad there were such things as cheap newspapers. ("Gallery of Lady Artists" 467)

The review continues by arguing that this cheapness is a public service: it provides the public with decent decoration and tantalizes them with the possibility of getting for a low price something that will increase in value if the artist gains a name for herself. Standard prices at the SFA were between two guineas at the lowest to 50 pounds at the absolute highest.[6] Lower prices notwithstanding, however, painting was still one of the rare ways by which a woman of the middle or upper classes in Victorian England could support herself and often a family, and the number of women embracing art as a profession rose steadily throughout the century.

If achieved, status as a professional artist could provide a secure social position for a woman, since the social status of the artist rose gradually over the course of the eighteenth and nineteenth centuries. After the founding and gradual rise to prestige of the Royal Academy during the eighteenth century,[7] art production became increasingly professionalized during the early nineteenth century; by the mid-nineteenth century the R.A. and other institutions of art had developed schools, procedures, laws, and bylaws; art was now publicly visible as a *career*, not just an accomplishment or a quasi-spiritual vocation but a respectable and financially rewarding profession. The 1850s and 1860s saw the dramatic rise of an art public with unprecedented purchasing power; in turn, these decades brought considerable wealth and social stature to those professional artists willing and able to provide the sort of artworks favored by the rising middle classes: genre works on contemporary subjects, sentimental realism, portraiture, and landscape art. For those supplying this market, the mid- and late nineteenth century saw an enormous increase in the average price paid for paintings. The years from 1860 to 1914 have been called the golden age of the living painter, with artists collecting as much as 7,000 guineas for a single painting. A relatively well-known (male) artist might regularly earn £1,000 to £4,000 for a large canvas.[8] Compare this to the £150–200 per year which comprised the average merchant or lawyer's income, and it becomes evident that artists could easily become quite rich, and hence quite respectable. Joshua Reynolds (one of the first to raise the painter to the status of the gentleman), Edward Burne-Jones, William Powell Firth, and George Frederic Watts were among those artists of middle- and lower-class backgrounds for whom art became a source of wealth and status (Burne-Jones was knighted; Watts was twice offered the hereditary title of baronet but declined).[9] In addition to economic prosperity, another contributing factor in the rise of respectability of art as a profession was the influx of "gentlemen" into the professional art world. Many male artists began their careers already independently wealthy, or at least from titled or wealthy families. Sir Francis Grant (R.A. president, 1866), Lord Leighton (R.A. president, 1878), William Morris, and Philip Gilbert Hamerton were well-born gentlemen when they began their careers. (Morris, however, took great pains not to appear the well-born gentleman he actually was.)[10]

Artwork by women unsurprisingly failed to earn the same prices as did works by male artists, nor did women painters achieve the same level of fame as their male colleagues, although a few became well known. In an article in the *Englishwoman's Review,* Jessie Boucherett writes of an exhibit in the Gallery of Lady Artists, "We believe the pictures in this gallery to be at present depreciated below their real worth, partly by the bad times, partly perhaps by the fact that they are generally painted by young women artists who have yet their fame to win. We should not be surprised if some years hence the purchasers of today were to find that their pictures had largely increased in value" (1881). Women's work in various galleries (Royal Academy, Society of Female Artists, Society of British Watercolours, Old Watercolour Society, etc.) ranged in price from £10 to, at the very top end, £100, with the average between £15 and £30 (Nunn 1987, 114–18). The few women on the high end of the scale, painters like Emily Mary Osborn or Elizabeth Thompson Butler, occasionally sold large canvases at the Royal Academy shows for over £1000. But Butler was an astute businesswoman, and she knew how to capitalize on enormous public success, a rare thing for a woman painter in the nineteenth century. As a contrast, when Frederic Leighton made his debut in 1855 as an entirely unknown but male artist at the R.A., he sold his *Cimabue's Procession* to the Queen for 600 guineas (Gillett 1990, 209).

III.

Even women like Butler who became successful professional artists still had battles to fight. In particular, women painters (like many other professional women) faced intense ideological disapproval because of their participation in the public realm. As Harman argues, "From the mid-nineteenth century onward . . . as women increasingly sought access to the public sphere—to political discussions, to education, to the professions, and to the vote—the debate about female publicity took a more prominent place in the collective cultural discussion" (Harman 1998, 1–2).[11] The public sphere was unusually problematic for women painters. Whereas women writers could and often did remain anonymous, carrying out their trade at discreet distance in modest solitude,[12] a painter couldn't very well hide her endeavors. Paint and paintings have a visible (and olfactory) physical presence; brushes and paint pots can't be whisked out of the way at a moment's notice; canvases and easels take up space. Art education, too, was a particularly thorny problem, since it was generally done in public and the specter of drawing from life always lurked in the background. The rare woman painter who successfully carved out a space in which to paint, secured an artistic education, and painted a good picture had yet more work to do in the public arena. Whereas the Brontë sisters could interact with editors by *mail* and remain physically in Yorkshire (for the most part), a large painting on canvas was not something one sent by post. Instead, paintings were carried or carted to art dealers or exhibit halls; generally the artist needed to be present to supervise the transportation and to negotiate with dealers or purchasers.

And there was yet more public work to be done, even once the painting arrived at its destination. It might seem obvious that artworks are made to be seen, but in the nineteenth century this meant *public* viewing, in newly created galleries, museums, or academies. In the eighteenth century, an artist could be successful and yet have his or her works seen by only a few patrons or people at court, but this changed early in the Victorian era. As Jan Marsh writes, "display is integral to artistic practice . . . being seen is what works of art are for, and certainly in the nineteenth century public exhibition was the first goal of the aspiring artist" (1995, 36). But not only the artworks were on display. To begin with, the Victorian art world was a highly gregarious arena; for example, Varnishing Day, the day before the opening of the Royal Academy exhibit each year, was a huge event, a time for painters to interact with one another. Painters (male or female) worked side by side putting the finishing touches on their work directly in the gallery (see figure 1.3). The Royal Academy Exhibit itself, in addition, was a see-and-be-seen event, a time for artists to mingle with the art public who were, as we have seen, increasingly fascinated with the artists themselves rather than simply the artworks.[13]

The R.A. Summer Exhibit averaged 355,000 paying visitors during the 1880s and 1890s—earlier figures were likely similar, with perhaps a rise in attendance during the "boom" years of the 1860s. As this suggests, art viewing in the nineteenth century was a profoundly public event; visits to the Royal Academy were part of the social rounds, and exhibits at galleries like the Grosvenor or the Female School of Art were also important public events, attended by the rich and famous as well as by the middle classes and always covered by the press. As Kate Flint writes, "by stressing . . . social gathering rather than the paintings themselves, depictions of art shows, whether in paintings or in periodical publications, ultimately serve to reinforce the point that spectators are participating in social rituals, however much any individual act or spectatorship may involve individualized, subjective apprehension and judgment" (2000, 176).

Prevailing Winds and Cross-Currents: Public Discourse 35

Figure 1.3. George DuMaurier, "Varnishing Day at the Royal Academy." *Punch* 73 (June 19, 1877).

If the Royal Academy and other galleries weren't public enough, as the century progressed artists' own studios increasingly became spaces for socializing and, crucially, marketing.[14] The Sunday before a show's official opening, wealthy clients would "go the rounds" of studios to decide on possible purchases or to give orders for portraits or other pictures. This Picture Sunday—or Show Sunday as it was often called—allowed for early sales; it also allowed artists to hobnob with the fashionable art-loving public and with one another. Additionally, it permitted an increasingly curious public a sight into the artist's private and working life. Mrs. E. M. Ward wrote in her memoirs that "Artists appear to possess a peculiar attraction.... A deep curiosity exists to see the inner workings of studio life" (1925, 113). By the 1880s, Show Sundays were so popular that "there was a spillover from one designated day to almost any Sunday, or sometimes both Saturday and Sunday" (Gillett 1990, 194). It was also quite common for Victorian artists to paint with a crowd of spectators present; the solitary genius image of the Romantic period gave way in the Victorian era to a socially visible and active artist.

Because of the public visibility inherent in her line of work, the woman artist had to be seen—and, problematically, the public often found it difficult to decide which of the dyad (artist/work) was the more interesting and attractive spectacle. Emily Mary Osborn's painting *Nameless and Friendless* (1857) dramatizes this scenario in exemplary visual form (figure 1.4).[15] The painting depicts the trials a young woman painter might have faced when attempting to sell her productions. The young painter stands, gazing forlornly down, before the counter in an art dealer's shop, where the dealer scrutinizes her small oil painting. By her clothing we can see that she is poor; the painting's title reinforces this reading. That she is "nameless" suggests that her painting has brought her neither fortune nor fame; that she is "friendless" further marks her situation, as she has no one to intercede for her in the art world. The young woman's face registers sorrow and, perhaps, shame—the shame of being in a public place with the intent of selling her productions for profit. She modestly does not look at the dealer; the small boy (perhaps a brother, or a boy hired to help carry her art supplies—but obviously poor himself, wearing trousers which are much too big for him and a coarse coat), however, looks straight at the dealer as he critically examines the painting, as if the boy (because of his gender) is ready to take charge of any economic exchange which might ensue. The young woman registers her nervousness by twisting a piece of string between two very dainty and delicate hands—hands, the viewer may be meant to imagine, which were once the hands of a woman of leisure but are now the hands of a working woman, who has become a "victim of the art market" (Casteras 1992, 221).

While the young woman artist and the boy form the central triangle of the painting, there are two other scenes in the background that contrast with the scene in the foreground. In the rear center we see the back of a wealthy woman in a fancy hat, an ornate hairdo, and a bustled dress; just behind her is another small boy carrying something rolled up under his arm. The boy, too, is well dressed and groomed, and is likely the wealthy woman's son. Is this a

Figure 1.4. Emily Mary Osborn, *Nameless and Friendless*, 1857, private collection. Source: The Bridgeman Art Library. Reproduced with permission.

wealthy patroness of the arts, departing with her latest purchase? Certainly her upright bearing and her clothing make her a strong contrast to the poor, huddled young woman exhibiting her paintings before the critical dealer. The other background scene depicts two men who hold between them a drawing of a ballet dancer in a very exuberant and exposed posture—arms above her head, one leg pointed outward and up. The men however, instead of looking at the aesthetic object before them (an image of a beautiful public woman), look askew (one sidelong, one just under his hat) at the young woman painter by the counter. The intensity of their gazes registers the public scrutiny a woman painter received: just as her artwork is thoroughly examined, so too is her person monitored.

The painting presents the viewer with three warring representations of female identity. There is the wealthy, well-dressed woman customer leaving the shop, spending money rather than earning it. Second, there is the ballet dancer whose image we see held by the two men on the left. The dancer represents the spectacle of the female body, a professional body open to the most intense public scrutiny; she is an object of desire and aesthetic appreciation, and Osborn hints that she may be as much for sale as is the drawing of her. The woman painter in the center, as Deborah Cherry writes, "introduces a third figuration of femininity, the middle-class working woman who could not easily be categorized . . . and whose respectability, the basis of her class identity and her sexuality, is at risk" (1993, 79). The risk involved in the painter's profession is precisely her public visibility, which radically repositions her socially and erotically. On the one hand, the act of painting causes her intrusion as an economic producer (rather than consumer) into a male business enclave; on the other hand, becoming a painter threatens to reposition women within the traditional erotic structure of art. The woman is traditionally looked at (as is the dancer); painting is an attempt to escape this aesthetic position by producing an object which receives visual attention. But Osborn suggests that this attempted escape is a failure: the woman artist remains subject to public scrutiny.

IV.

Osborn's painting functions explicitly as a feminist critique of the art world, and numerous other women painters also used their art—and their lives—to make similar social arguments, often embracing the publicity that inevitably accrued to them as a political tool. As Deborah Cherry has argued, the history of the woman painter in Victorian Britain is inextricable from the history of British feminism in the period; the art scene was frequently a locus for political rebellion by nineteenth-century feminists (see Cherry 2000). An enormous number of women artists or art critics played an integral part in the emergent nineteenth-century feminist movement. Barbara Bodichon, Anna Jameson, Lady Eastlake, Eliza Fox, Mary and Anna Mary Howitt, Henrietta Ward, Louise Jopling,[16] and numerous other women who made their names in the art scene were also actively involved in the women's rights movement. When the suffrage movement began, for example, a huge portion of the signatories of the 1889 *Declaration in Favour of Women's Suffrage* were women artists (nearly sixty of the over two hundred signatories stated their profession as "artist" on the document).[17] By contrast, the *Appeal against Female Suffrage* featured only one woman artist: Laura Alma-Tadema.

The driving force behind much of the Victorian feminist agitation—both in politics and in the arts—was Barbara Leigh Smith Bodichon, who combined in one woman the intertwined goals of art and feminism.[18] Bodichon worked primarily as a watercolorist and regularly exhibited paintings at the Royal Academy and other galleries; she was one of the few women artists in the century to have her own gallery shows as well. Because of her wealth, however, Bodichon didn't need the income she gained from her artworks; she used the money to finance her numerous feminist ventures: *The Englishwoman's Journal,* the founding of Girton College, political activism around women's rights bills, and other activities of the Langham Place Group, of which she was the leading force. She founded the *Englishwoman's Journal* in 1857; it was devoted to widening professional opportunities for women and published a great deal of art criticism and exhibition news. In 1859 Bodichon helped draft a petition to the Royal Academy demanding women's admission to the R.A. schools. The petition was signed by most of the prominent women painters of the time: Laura Hereford, Eliza Fox, Anna Blunden, Florence Claxton, the Mutrie sisters, Emily Mary Osborn, Rebecca Solomon, Margaret Gillies, and Mary Thorneycroft. The writer Harriet Martineau also supported the petition, giving it publicity in an article in the *Edinburgh Review* of April 1859.

One of the most visible political places of connection between Bodichon's feminism and her experiences in the art world was the agitation surrounding the Married Woman's Property Act (MWPA). Of the twenty-four signers of the Petition for Reform of the Married Woman's Property Act presented to Parliament in 1856, six were closely associated with the nineteenth-century art world as painters or art critics.[19] The petition for the MWPA was developed both to preserve married women's inherited economic assets and to protect those married women who were beginning, in greater numbers, to earn money independently as artists and writers. The petition states explicitly, in its first paragraph, that income from the arts is at stake:

> The Petition of the undersigned Women of Great Britain . . . Humbly Sheweth—That the manifold evils occasioned by the present law, by which the property and earnings of the wife are thrown into the absolute power of the husband, become daily more apparent. That it might once have been deemed for the middle and upper ranks, a comparatively theoretical question, but it is so no longer, *since married women of education are entering on every side the fields of literature and art, in order to increase the family income by such exertions.* (Holcombe 1983, 237; emphasis added)

Some of the immediate inspiration for the MWPA came from the notorious case of Caroline Norton, whom I discuss in chapter 2. Norton, separated from her husband, had great difficulties maintaining control over her income earned as a well-known writer. But countless other nineteenth-century women, as they entered the arts in greater numbers, demanded ownership of the fruits of their labors. The MWPA—defeated in Parliament successively

Figure 1.5. Emily Mary Osborn, *Sketch after a Portrait of Barbara Bodichon* (of original oil painting from 1884, whereabouts unknown). Source: Helen Blackburn, *Women's Suffrage* (London: Williams and Norgate, 1902).

in 1857 and 1868 and finally passed in 1870—was designed to protect the economic rights of just such working women.

Although Bodichon is better known today for her extensive contributions to the women's right's movement, in her own time she was equally well known as an artist. Indeed, as her biographer Pam Hirsch notes, Bodichon thought of herself first and foremost as an artist—for example, she entered "Artist" under the column for profession on her marriage certificate (1998, 129).[20] The portrait of Bodichon (see figure 1.5) by her friend and fellow artist Emily Mary Osborn also supports this emphasis on Bodichon's artistic career: though designed to celebrate Bodichon's involvement with Girton College, the portrait nevertheless portrays Bodichon before her easel even as it strives to represent Bodichon as a traditional scholar.

As Deborah Cherry writes, "It is significant that the founder of this first university college for women was portrayed as an artist" (1995, 65). Cherry further notes that Osborn elected to portray Bodichon as an oil painter rather than as the watercolorist she was—a decision motivated perhaps by the greater prestige of oil painting at the time.

Figure 1.6. Laura Alma-Tadema, *The Sisters*, 1883. Engraving. Whereabouts of original unknown. Source: Pamela Gerrish Nunn, *Problem Pictures*, illustration 5.7.

The work of Bodichon and other feminist artists had wide-ranging effects. By 1870, the Royal Academy schools had begun to admit women students intermittently. Other schools were numerous and largely available to women. By the turn of the century, women could enter most art schools and could study from the nude model in several. Women artists had numerous options for exhibition and were accepted, more or less, in the public realm of art. However, the nineteenth century does not offer a completely rosy picture of a gradual increase in the prestige and public acceptance of women painters. The story is certainly one of increased access to training facilities, Royal Academy

Figure 1.7. Kate Greenaway, *Little Loves. The Illustrated London News,* Christmas number, 1877.

schools, and exhibition galleries. But in the later decades of the nineteenth century, a backlash in public opinion concerning women artists brought ideological setbacks,[21] which might best be exemplified by the career of Laura Alma-Tadema, who came to prominence in the 1880s—her detailed, small, domestic subjects were considered appropriately feminine (see figure 1.6), and contrasted sharply with her husband's enormous neoclassical history subjects.

Similar, too, was the art of the enormously popular Kate Greenaway (see figure 1.7), whose images of adorable children and flowers were thought highly suitable for a woman artist. The public outcry against New Women artists, which I discuss in chapter 7, sets out the terms of the backlash. Well into the Modernist period and beyond, the woman painter has continued to struggle against social restrictions and wavering public support (as Lily Briscoe's relationship to painting in Virginia Woolf's *To The Lighthouse* suggests); as we shall see in the coda to this study, even late-twentieth- and early-twenty-first-century woman artists haven't entirely succeeded in throwing off the ideological chains which also bound their nineteenth-century foremothers.

V.

Any public debate concerning women artists in the Victorian era (and beyond, as my coda suggests) was forced to tackle the problem of the visible female body and the erotic charge which seemed inevitably to accrue in the vicinity of women who paint. The traditional erotic structure of aesthetic experience might be reductively expressed as "male artist paints beautiful female object for the delectation of a male spectator." Certainly this triangle appears often enough in history and literature to be almost invisible in its familiarity. The art object is, as any number of aestheticians and critics have pointed out, a feminized object. But what happens to the aesthetic scenario when a woman holds the brush, when she steps out of her "natural" position as the beautiful object?

The classical myth of the origin of painting suggests that even a woman holding a brush can't escape being positioned within an erotic narrative. Once upon a time, or so Pliny tells us in book 35 of his *Natural History*, a Corinthian Maid (Dibutade by name) fell in love with a beautiful young man. One day while he slept she noticed that the light cast a perfect shadow of his profile on the wall behind him. Stealthily she took a stylus and, following the line of the shadow, traced the outline of his profile on the wall, knowing that he would soon wake and leave her, but that she would then have an image of him to adore in his absence. This image was the first "painting." Art was in this tale born out of a *woman's* desire and a *man's* beauty; the erotic potential which we will see again and again attributed to the woman artist in Victorian culture thus has a surprisingly long history. Eighteenth-century painters loved this story and reproduced it frequently, although its popularity declined sharply after the Romantic period (ironically just as the number of women entering the art world began to rise most sharply) and was only revived by Pater in *Greek Studies* as a tale of the origin of *sculpture* rather than painting. (Pater, however, shifts the focus from the daughter to the father, Butade, who, as the myth explains, filled in his daughter's drawing outline with clay, thus creating the first relief sculpture.)[22]

Public disapproval of women painters in the Victorian era shows a marked though unacknowledged unease with the Corinthian Maid's disruption of the traditional erotics of art: a woman holding a brush threatened to disrupt the proper flow of aesthetic desire, placing it in the hands of the female subject rather than relegating women to the role of desired object. The negative discourse found a common solution to this aesthetic problem: by persistently re-eroticizing the woman painter, writers attempted to reinscribe the woman painter within her proper place in the aesthetic scenario. Textual and visual dismissals of women painters in the period suggest that critics of women's involvement in the art world felt that the best way to negate a woman painter's work was to refocus attention on the woman painter herself, as a desirable and beautiful art object in her own right. If the image of a beautiful woman, as Kathy Psomiades argues, traditionally works as a marker of the "private realm" (1997, 7), then this tactic served to redomesticate the woman painter. As she writes, "Because of its private sexual connotations, femininity marks [texts and paintings with images of women] as private objects of desire rather than public agents" (ibid.). While Psomiades's argument refers specifically to British aestheticism and to paintings depicting women, it is readily transferable to other genres and modes in the Victorian period (and beyond, certainly). In Victorian periodical treatments of women painters, for example, we see a common scene of aesthetic judgment in which a male spectator attempts to reinscribe the working woman as a "private object of desire" rather than a "public agent."

A selective tour through some of the negative press (both textual and visual) gives an excellent idea of this persistent eroticization of the woman painter. An 1857 article in *Punch* offers a provocative example of the public disapproval of women painters, and the attempt to defuse their social and aesthetic power by repositioning them as what Psomiades terms "private objects of desire." *Punch* advises its readers thus:

> Those who are fond of "the society of Ladies" will rush to No. 315, Oxford Street, and there enjoy an exhibition that is the result of female handiwork. It is not an exhibition of stitching or embroidery . . . or anti-macassars, or floral smoking caps, or sporting slippers with a series of foxes running helter-skelter over the toes. It is not an exhibition of Berlin-wool work. . . . It is not an exhibition of jams, or jellies, or marmalades, or preserves . . . or any other mania that occasionally seizes hold of young ladies' fingers, and makes them, for the time being, excessively sticky to squeeze. You must not expect you are about to be invited to a choice collection of pies, or tarts, or cakes. . . . It is nothing to eat, nothing to play with, nothing to wear, nothing that you can adorn your magnificent person with. ("Let Us Join the Ladies")

The exhibition to which the decidedly male readership of this *Punch* article is invited is the first Society of Female Artists show, held in London in 1857. As *Punch* sees it, the problematic or unusual aspect of this collection of female productivity is its inability to be directly appealing to men. Antimacassars (devised to protect furniture from the ravages of men's hair oil), smoking caps, slippers with foxes, Berlin-wool work—all the items which the reviewer assures the reader he will *not* find at this exhibition—are domestic trifles (not High Art) typically produced by female fingers for the consumption of men.

That women are producing what *might* be (or become) High Art causes the *Punch* reviewer considerably anxiety. The flippant tone of the *Punch* review of the SFA exhibit is one possible way to diffuse the threat posed by such a collection of female artistic productivity. But to restore fully the normal trajectory of gendered production which the SFA exhibit threatens, the *Punch* reviewer sets to work ensuring that one thing at least can be salvaged from the exhibit for the delectation of the male viewer—the female artist's *body*. As the review continues, it becomes quite clear that what can be accessed during a visit to the exhibit—and "enjoyed," as the opening line of the review suggests—is the "lady-artists" themselves, rather than their artistic products. "Away with regrets in the presence of such delightful company!" the reviewer exhorts; "You are communing with ANNA, JULIA, KATE, AGNES, FLORENCE, FRANCES, and fifty other pretty names! Not a man's ugly cognomen is to be found in the whole catalogue." The women artists rarely, in the course of the review, receive their surnames—a surname which in the normal course of artistic attribution would supply an artist with respectable patronymic, a social position irrespective of gender. In the final paragraph of the review, where specific paintings and painters at last receive recognition, the artists *are* called by their surnames. But for the majority of the review, it is precisely the patronymic—the "man's ugly cognomen" that the reviewer rejoices not to find at the SFA—which this *Punch* reviewer denies the female artists. The names emblazoned in all caps are not simply random female names, of course, but are in fact the first names of actual exhibitors in the 1857 SFA exhibit: ANNA Blunden, KATE Swift, AGNES Bouvier, FLORENCE Claxton, FRANCES Stoddart all contributed paintings to this SFA show. But the average *Punch* reader in 1857 would be unlikely to be able to supply the missing surnames. By leaving out the last names of the artists, the *Punch* reviewer contributes to the artists' continued lack of public acclaim.

By this erasure of surnames, the reviewer also takes a remarkably personal stance toward the artists, especially in an era where the use of a first name still had social implications (as does using the "*tu*" form in French, for instance). The reviewer seems to imply by this appellation that these women's last names are, in fact, up for grabs—that the artists are young, unmarried women, available to be "enjoyed" in a marriage that would necessarily result in a transference of patronymic, a switch from the feminine "pretty name" to "a man's ugly cognomen." Why should these artists be referred to by their own last names, the reviewer seems to say, when they will all be married soon and change them anyway?

The *artworks* themselves are largely ignored, or indeed looked directly through, to better see the artist beyond. The *Punch* reviewer encourages the male viewer to

> Stand with respectful awe before that picture of the tender *Brigand chief,* for who knows, HARRIET may one day be your wife? That *Bivouac in the Desert,* which is glowing before you . . . was encamped originally in the snug parlour of LOUISA—that very same LOUISA, that probably you flirted with last week at a picnic in Birnam Beeches. Be careful of your remarks. Drop not an ugly word, lest you do an injury to the talent of some poetic creature, who at some time or other handed you a cup of tea, or sang you the songs you loved. . . . With GEORGIANA on your right, MARIA on your left; with EMMA gazing from her gorgeous frame right at you, and SOPHIA peeping from behind that clump of moon-silvered trees over your shoulder, be tender, be courteous, be complimentary, be everything that is gentle, and devoted, and kind.

Again, the reviewer refers to actual artists in his romantic scenario: the EMMA who gazes from her "gorgeous frame" is Emma Brownlow; the SOPHIA who "peeps" at the viewer is Sophia Sinnett, whose "Reading the List of Killed and Wounded" garnered special acclaim at the 1857 exhibit. Yet the scene created by the reviewer becomes not one of aesthetic judgment or appreciation of the works of these painters, but rather a romantic scenario of potential erotic attachment and courtship. Here, artworks serve only as conduits back to the physical bodies of their producers; Emma Brownlow, for example, is herself gazing from her frame, even though the picture exhibited was not a self-portrait. The women painters are positioned firmly into their "proper" social and erotic functions: wives, dispensers of tea, or coquettish flirts. The reviewer substitutes a traditional courtship narrative—a narrative set in motion by the hint that HARRIET may "one day be your wife"—for a narrative of artistic production or aesthetic prowess. Yet the artworks named here—*Brigand Chief* and *Bivouac in the Desert*—intervene momentarily in this imagined courtship of artist and viewer. That the works appear to represent a socially radical figure of erotic fantasy (a leader of Bandits) and a foreign military scene (unless there are deserts in England of which I am unaware) suggests that the artworks under scrutiny aren't nearly as feminine and innocent as the "gentle, and devoted, and kind" reviewer attempts to be. To counter the unfeminine content of these images, the reviewer mimics and then attempts to diffuse the military terminology by refeminizing and domesticating it: the *Bivouac in the Desert* was "originally *encamped* in the *snug parlour* of LOUISA" (emphasis added).[23]

To further neutralize the danger posed by these women's works, the *Punch* writer must double the femininity present in the exhibition by insinuating that many of the "lady artists'" works are in fact pictures of other women:

> A Frenchman would nickname the Exhibition: *Les Femmes peintes par elles-mêmes*—though it must not be surmised that the painting is in the ungallant sense that a Frenchman would satirically convey. If cheeks are delicately coloured—if lips are strung into the precise shape of Cupid's bow— . . . if eyelashes are artistically penciled—the penciling and the painting are not upon their own fair features, but on the faces of others; and there is no law as yet laid down . . . by the tyranny of Man, that a Lady, though she may not colour her own adorable physiognomy, is forbidden to paint the face of another.

In addition to the satiric confusion between artist and artwork which permeates the entire review, the suggestion here that the subject matter of these women artists is "elles-mêmes" (the word can imply themselves, as in self-portraits, or one another, that is, pictures of other women) implies that women are interchangeable, that the artist and the art object are so similar as to be indistinguishable, and that the artists merely paint self-portraits or portraits of other women that can replace their own corporeal selves in the public view. In other words, women who paint are in essence painting their own bodies—even when the subject is neither the self nor another woman.[23] The small cartoon that accompanies the review (figure 1.8) reinforces this notion by raising the specter of female vanity. The woman reclines on a circular dais, wearing a stylish gown: in her hand she holds a mirror, the classic symbol of female vanity. Yet she does not look into it; rather, she looks out at the viewer, as if inviting our gaze. The woman artist wants to be admired; the review and the cartoon together suggest that women paint to incite desire rather than to express talent or for economic reasons.[24]

We see echoes of this throughout the fictional world of women painters. When Rochester, for example, forces Jane Eyre to trot out her portfolio of paintings for his inspection, he is mocking a traditional ritual of polite courtship. A young woman's artwork was regularly displayed—in addition to her performance on the pianoforte—as a display of the woman's "accomplishment," as a visible marker of her desirability as woman, which is precisely how the *Punch* article translates women's artwork. We shall see similar scenes in

Figure 1.8. Detail from "Let Us Join the Ladies." *Punch* 29 (July 18, 1857)

almost all the texts featuring an artist heroine which I discuss here; a young woman's works are viewed by her social community or by a prospective suitor as evidence of desire or as incitements to desire rather than as aesthetically viable, marketable commodities. Explorations of women's art inevitably become explorations of female desire.

Given such fascinated interest in the corporeality and sexuality of the artists themselves, no aesthetic critique of their artwork seems possible. The *Punch* reviewer writes, "The visitor involuntarily takes his hat off before so much *unknown* loveliness" (emphasis added). This "unknown loveliness" refers more to the beauty of the artistic producers than to the beauty of the artistic products, which cannot be called "unknown" as they are immediately available, visually present, to the reviewer. The woman painter, however, remains hidden behind her picture, tantalizingly evoked but invisible to the leering reviewer. The male viewer's aesthetic judgment of the artistic products is curtailed by the "haunting" of each picture by its producer; it is literally Emma Brownlow "gazing from her gorgeous frame" rather than a *picture* by that artist which the reviewer sees inside a gilt frame. The double-entendre on "frame" here makes Emma's *body* spring into view as one possible object of scrutiny. Each painting somehow doubles a woman's presence: she becomes both artist and art object. But the *Punch* reviewer attempts to streamline the dangerous multiplicity of women present in the exhibit by focusing solely on the individual artist's desirable body. The formidable artistic community of women involved in the SFA exhibit pose a threat that can be tackled by positioning the artists firmly into discrete courtship narratives; to foreclose on any complicated doubling of the female into artist and artwork. *Punch* manages to shift the balance in favor of woman-as-artwork, firmly nailing woman back into her traditional position as object-of-desire.

This *Punch* review is characteristic of the persistent eroticization of the woman artist throughout the nineteenth century.[25] It's no accident or surprise, given the nineteenth-century atmosphere, that of the four March sisters in Louisa May Alcott's *Little Women,* the one who wants to be an artist—Amy— is the prettiest one who marries the richest, handsomest man and becomes little more than a museum piece herself. The woman writer—Jo, in this case—is not so erotically represented.[26] Alcott is arguably reacting to a very prevalent cultural ideology which collapses artwork into artist; such a collapse recapitulates the overall character of the mid-century discourse surrounding women artists, a discourse which is notable for its fascinated concern for the woman artist's body, as if the public is confused over what should be the aesthetic object—the art or the artist. A cartoon from a series of drawings titled *The Adventures of a Woman in Search of her Rights* (1871) by Florence Claxton, a painter and engraver active in the battle for women's rights, offers a humorous representation of this erotic situation (see figure 1.9). The young artist in Claxton's drawing leans suggestively before her easel, her backside emphasized and her figure sexualized by a bustle and the bow from her painter's apron. The very clothing that marks her as an artist, then, also serves to heighten her femininity. The caption, which reads "What Tompkins said to Jones: 'Bother the Old Masters, Look at the young Miss-esses,'" offers multiple verbal puns: at first, of course, there is simply the slippage from the respectful "Old Masters" to the "young Miss-esses," signaling that the speaker (Tompkins) views the young artist not as an artist, but as a sexually available young woman. The second pun, of course, involves the close proximity of "Miss-esses" to "mistresses," which in the period could mean either unmarried sexual partner or the respectable Lady of the house. In either case, the young "miss-ess" in the cartoon has lost her status as aesthetic producer and has become for Tompkins

Figure 1.9. Florence Claxton, detail from *The Adventures of a Woman in Search of her Rights* (London: The Graphotyping Co., 1872), 17.

a female object, something to be looked at. "Look at the young Miss-esses," he says—not "look at the works of the young Miss-esses."

Dante Gabriel Rossetti's sketch titled *A Parable of Love (Love's Mirror)* provides yet another telling exemplar of the erotic charge inherent in female artistic production. The sketch (see figure 1.10) is thought to have been done in 1850, and while there is no firm proof of identity, the two central figures are generally taken to be Rossetti himself and Elizabeth Siddal, Rossetti's pupil, mistress, and eventual wife.[27] Few critics have discussed this sketch even in passing, and those who do mention it neglect its startling gender

Figure 1.10. Dante Gabriel Rossetti, *A Parable of Love (Love's Mirror)*, 1850? Birmingham City Art Gallery. Reprinted with permission.

implications. Lawrence Starzyk, for example, foregrounds the "parable" of the title and looks closely at the moral lesson the drawing tells. The simple message of the parable is that the artist draws only one face but the mirror "paints" a better picture—a picture of true love—by including both faces. Starzyk certainly notes the sexual tension implicit in the image; he points out that one of the women on the right side is in a pose "strikingly reminiscent of the woman's in Hunt's *The Awakening Conscience*" and argues that the two rear figures look on and suggest that the seated woman is in fact "potentially compromised sexually, psychologically, and artistically" (1999, 179).

What Starzyk fails to note, however, is that the sketch represents not a love scene but a scene in which female visual potential is literally blotted out by male power: the male teacher's hand is guiding the female student's hand to *paint out her own eye*. As Susan Casteras notes in her brief discussion of the sketch, "the degree of male control of female creativity is extreme in this example" (1992, 216). The male painter has "the upper hand" quite literally and wipes out the very organ that would enable the woman painter to paint. Love, as represented by the dyad in the mirror, is an oppressive force for the woman artist. Significantly, too, it is only the *male* painter here who sees the vision of love the mirror offers; only the male figure looks in the mirror at the pair of lovers. The female painter's gaze remains resolutely fixed on her canvas (now despoiled as it might be). Rossetti's sketch, like the *Punch* review, attempts to eradicate female visual creativity by reinstating romance and erotic desire as central to a woman's experience; Rossetti's sketch, however, at least obliquely suggests that the female painter may refuse to be complicit in this scenario.

Other male painters entered into the representational debate as well. One of the most interesting representations of the woman painter is by John Singer Sargent, whose painting *The Fountain,* painted just after the end of the Victorian era in 1907, can be read as a wonderful joke on women painters (see figure 1.11). The woman in the painting is herself a professional artist, Jane Emmet von Glehn; the man is her husband, the artist Wilfrid von Glehn. Jane was entirely cognizant of the combined satire and respect in Sargent's portrait of her; in a letter to her sister Lydia (6 October 1907) she writes:

> Sargent is doing a most amusing and killingly funny picture in oils of me perched on a balustrade painting. It is the very "spit" of me. He has stuck Wilfrid in looking at my sketch with rather a contemptuous expression as much to say "Can you do plain sewing any better than that?" He made Wilfrid put on this expression to avoid the danger of the picture looking like an "idyll on a P. & O. steamer" as he expressed it[.] I look rather like a pierrot, but have rather a worried expression as every painter should have who isn't a perfect fool, says Sargent. Wilfrid is in short sleeves, very idle and good for nothing, and our heads come against the great "panache" of the fountain. . . . Poor Wilfrid can't pose for more than a few minutes at a time as the position is torture after a while. (quoted in Hills 1986, 191)

Wilfrid is "stuck" in the painting to provide the voice of dismissive male critique (which desires a woman to be a domestic seamstress rather than a public artist), but he is also "good for nothing" and, ironically, forced to undergo "torture" to maintain his apparently languid pose. The torture seems

Figure 1.11. Detail from John Singer Sargent, *The Fountain, Villa Torlonia, Frascati, Italy,* 1907. Art Institute of Chicago. Reproduced with permission.

punishment for his "contemptuous expression" as he views his wife's artwork. Jane herself, on the other hand, has the "worried expression" of an active painter and is anything but idle; her figure in the portrait is bolt upright and focused. We should note that the painting is called *The Fountain,* which is not what the woman is herself painting but what Sargent, the male painter, makes central. In the painting itself, the woman painter is slightly off-center;

the focus is the fountain itself, shooting ridiculously and with sublimely silly connotations out of the reclining male figure's head. The lounging male's ejaculation, Sargent seems to say, is of more force than whatever the woman paints. The erotic relation is reinforced by the physical postures of the two figures: the woman is upright, the man languorous, postcoital. The placement of the fountain also disrupts what could have been a perfectly triangular composition—and the distortion seems caused by the woman painter herself. Since the erotics of art is about a kind of triangulation—male artist, female art object, male viewer—this is certainly another part of the joke. The presence of the woman artist, as we will see so frequently, has disrupted traditional aesthetic and erotic structures.

As these examples suggest, the woman painter in the act of painting was for the Victorians an object of aesthetic pleasure and scrutiny. In countless periodical reviews and in all of the novels this book examines, we find scenes in which a woman artist paints while being watched by another, almost always male, presence. This viewer then consistently attempts—with varying success—to contain the painting woman inside a frame, to turn her back into a beautiful art object. Even when the artist herself is not present (as in the exhibit the *Punch* reviewer discusses), she must be conjured, recreated to stand behind her production, as if only her female body could guarantee the aesthetic attraction of a work of art. The texts I discuss in this book take up this problem, arguing that part of the struggle for women artists must be to avoid becoming art objects themselves.

VI.

Given the prevalence of such dismissive discourse, proponents of women's involvement in the art world had a tough sell. Anyone wishing to celebrate women painters had to negotiate the dual problem of visibility and desirability so as to "excuse" women painters for their public presence, lest they be aligned with those other visually available women: prostitutes, actresses, and the like. The "association between access to public life, freedom of movement, and sexual impropriety" that Harman finds "appears insistently" both in the discourse surrounding the suffrage movement and in the detractors of female doctors and lawyers is no less present in the cultural debates over women painters (1998, 5). In fact, I would argue that the art world drew the link between public professionalism and sexual looseness in women painters even more tightly than almost any other profession (save theater and dance). The cartoon in figure 1.12, for example, singles out painters, musicians, and

Figure 1.12. George Du Maurier, "Removal of Ancient Landmarks." *Punch* 82 (June 25, 1881).

actresses specifically for their public appearances; the prim, dry governess is horrified by the thought of "Playing in *Public* or Painting for *Hire*" (italics in original), making the painter's craft sound precariously like the selling of the woman's body.

The few art historical texts from the period that offer sustained examination of women painters are forced into remarkable mental gymnastics to overcome the ideological prejudices against women painters. One of the most comprehensive nineteenth-century sources for biographical and ideological information about professional women artists from the Renaissance through the mid-Victorian era is an impressive two-volume compendium titled *English Female Artists,* published in 1876 by Ellen Clayton. That Clayton could amass information on several hundred English women artists, from the time of Charles I to the mid-nineteenth century, speaks volumes both for the history of women artists and for Clayton's extraordinary research achievements. Clayton's entries are largely biographical, often fanciful; she tells quaint stories about the early girlhoods of her artists, creating mini-narratives that attempt to position working women artists as "heroines" in a lively and romantic history. Yet Clayton begins her massive compilation with a plaintive gesture of submission and apology, desperately insisting on the invisibility of women artists:

> Artists, especially English artists, and above all, English Female Artists, as a rule lead quiet, uneventful lives, far more so than authors. In the majority of instances, their daily existence flows tranquilly on within the limited precincts of the studio, only casually troubled by anxious meditations respecting the fate of . . . minor works . . . or by the unkind slights of a hanging committee. Eminently respectable, they affect little display; they leave surprisingly few *bon mots* or personal anecdotes for the benefit of future biographers.
>
> Our native paintresses, as the old-fashioned art critics and compilers of biographical dictionaries quaintly termed them, have left but faintly impressed footprints on the sands of time. They do not glitter in the splendor of renown, like their sisters of the pen or of the buskin. It is a difficult task to obtain a sparse list of their original works, or glean any scattered remarks on their most valued copies of great masters. Even the most romantic or admired of these fair dreamers on canvas or ivory have scarce an incident beyond the commonplace in the brief record of their public or private career. (1876, 1: 1–2)

This is a far cry from the "power" seen by George Eliot in Rosa Bonheur's work. Quiet, tranquil, and respectable are Clayton's "fair dreamers on canvas," and so very different from the muscular artist imagined by Ruskin—and markedly different from authors, those "sisters of the pen" who are aligned here with theatrical women "of the buskin," and thus positioned as more radically public and of questionable respectability. As we have seen, this contrast flies in the face of much of the public discourse surrounding women painters, which represented them as more radical, public, and sexualized than women authors (who still, as plenty of critics have argued, came in for their share of harassment). Clayton insists (and arguably protests too much) that the woman artist is intently domestic, inhabiting the "limited precincts of the studio" rather than venturing into the outside world. Clayton's artist is also fragile of ego, vulnerable to "slights" (a word more suited to social interaction than aesthetic judgment), and above all remarkably *invisible* for someone involved in visual arts. Women painters are hidden within a studio; they affect "little display"; they do not "glitter"; nor do they leave behind them any mark or trace or echo of their endeavor—they are almost literally weightless and bodiless, leaving "but faintly impressed footprints on the sands of time."

Similarly, Elizabeth Ellet's enormous volume, *Women Artists in All Ages and Countries* (1859), represents women painters as gentle, quiet, nonthreatening, and above all feminine.[28] Ellet's book is a compilation of the *personal* histories of as many women artists as she can uncover in the historical record. Ellet writes, "No attempt has been made in the following pages to give elaborate critiques or a connected history of art. The aim has been simply to show what woman has done . . . and to give . . . impressions of the character of each prominent artist" (vi). Biographical information takes center stage here; there are occasional references to an artist's style, or to a particular work, but these are rare. The overall message is that these are women first and foremost—sweet, kind, loving, and feminine women who just happen to have painted for a living.

Ellet begins her book with a quotation contrasting women painters with women writers: "'Men have not grudged to women,' says a modern writer, 'the wreaths of literary fame.'" (21). An inevitable "but" is of course implied here: women might have been permitted to achieve literary success but have achieved little success in the realm of visual art. Ellet's extensive research into the lives of women painters is her attempt to suggest that there have been *some* women artists "in all ages and countries" who have excelled at their work; they simply have not been adequately celebrated. Ellet continues her introduction with an insistence that art comes *naturally* to women: women, she writes, have always loved ornament, decoration, and beauty of all sorts. Writers often tried to make women painters ideologically palatable in this way, by appealing to women's "natural" connection to the world of beauty.

What could be more natural than women's desiring to create art that reproduces and preserves such beauty? [29]

Ellet's biographical histories of women artists, like Clayton's, are so highly emotive or melodramatic as to be a kind of mild romance fiction. In her section on Angelica Kauffman, for example, Ellet writes, "All too quickly, indeed, passed the two years of her first residence in Como; and it was then with poignant regret that she left her beloved home. . . . Even this dreaded change, however, was a fortunate one; for it seemed to be appointed that Angelica's youth should glide away like a stream in the sunshine of happiness" (147). Taken as a whole, Ellet's book (again, like Clayton's) tries to make women artists into personalities—albeit ones characterized by extremely feminine traits. Elisabetta Sirani, for example, is depicted as if she were the heroine of a rather nauseating sentimental novel: "She would rise at dawn to perform those lowly domestic tasks for which her occupations during the day left her little leisure; and never permitted her passion for art to interfere with the fulfillment of homely duties. . . . All praised her gracious and cheerful spirit, her prompt judgment, and deep feeling for the art she loved. . . . Her devoted filial affection, her feminine grace, and the artless benignity of her manners, completed a character regarded by her friends as an ideal of perfection" (69).

Yet overall Ellet's book is surprisingly less personal—and less narratively melodramatic—than Clayton's. Ellet takes the artists she considers more seriously, representing them more frequently as working women. Occasionally Ellet even breaks out into something approaching feminist ire, as when she notes that the emperor refused to award the Legion of Honor to Rosa Bonheur (who was entitled to it when she won a prize for her painting "The Horse-market") "*because she was a woman!*" (277; emphasis in original). Ellet's work also makes a good introduction to the American scene, where women painters—although still facing many of the same struggles as British women painters—were treated slightly more seriously. If one contrasts Elizabeth Stuart Phelps's novel *The Story of Avis* (1877) to Anne Thackeray Ritchie's *Miss Angel,* for example, one can see the distinction clearly. Phelps's novel is much more explicitly angry over the oppressions working women were up against.

Clayton's and Ellet's persistent feminizing and softening is one common technique for Victorian women writers to make palatable the problematic public presence of the woman painter. It was also, as Julie Codell suggests, a way to include women artists in the larger category of "Victorian artist," who, as I discussed in the introduction, were increasingly constructed by popular discourse as domestic and respectable rather than transgressive (as in the Romantic or Modern periods). Codell writes, "Women artists' discretion was not only a gendered trait but also a part of the larger Victorian domestication of artists, expressed in the theme of the artist's uneventful life, circumscribed within the studio" (2003, 235). Thus, women artists were normalized on two fronts: first, they were represented as appropriately feminine; second, they were depicted as similar to their male counterparts—quiet, respectable, and hard-working.

Women painters themselves, when they wrote their memoirs, adopted similar narrative strategies for excusing their work to a possibly unsympathetic and threatening populace; they emphasized the peaceful, domestic, and quotidian nature of a woman painter's professional existence (even when that was far from their experience). In particular we find that English women painters, in their autobiographies, stress their daily domestic struggles (regularly rendered humorous) rather than focus on their dreams of fame or their aesthetic beliefs.[30] They also often focused on economic considerations, as if to represent art as a livelihood first and foremost, rather than any kind of participation in an elevated aesthetic tradition. Louise Jopling's memoir (1925) with its light, cheerful tone offers another way of representing the woman artist: as a kind of social butterfly, a popular and charming woman rather than a hard-nosed professional. Although her *Twenty Years of My Life* records its share of dismal moments (poverty, hard work, family deaths, failed marriages), the bulk of her tale is one of fashionable parties with well-known artist-guests. Indeed, even though she was the primary breadwinner for her family and worked herself to exhaustion on numerous occasions, Jopling represented herself—and was constructed in the public presses which reported artists' doings—as an elegant hostess and a graceful model rather than the bohemian, active feminist, and productive artist she arguably was.

The title of Sophia Beale's (whose name we see blazoned in the *Punch* review) memoir, *Recollections of a Spinster Aunt* (1908), may sound inauspicious for introducing a serious artist, but does serve to render her "safe" for the reading public. What have we to fear from a spinster aunt, one of those amiable creatures who doted on other people's children? But Beale was an active exhibitor at the Royal Academy and the SFA from 1860 to the 1880s, mainly as a figure painter; she was also known as an art writer, author of *A Handbook to the Louvre*, and she signed the Women Householder's Declaration of 1889 supporting women's suffrage.[31] Her memoir, presented as a "fictionalized" series of letters to a cousin, contains a lively account of the art scene in the 1850s and 1860s and provides insight into what struggling young women artists might have gone through in pursuit of education, fame, and *fortune*.

This last she considered an elusive prize for the average artist. Her characterization of "the artist" (coded male according to tradition, although she herself and all her friends are women artists) includes such qualities as the ability to live hopefully and cheerfully on the salary of a "dock-labourer," and the ability to not look on money as the end and aim of existence. "But all the same," she writes,

> filthy lucre is necessary, even for such pleasures as tea accompanied by muffins, to say naught of rent, rates, taxes, butchers, bakers and candlestick makers—though I spend little on *him*. Don't you agree that the greatest curse of this world is gold? The mere fact of one's mind dwelling upon money, or the want of it, is degrading. Was it not Dora Greenwell who said the meeting of both ends was a somewhat sad ideal at which to aim; she would like the ends to tie in a nice bow. So should I. A small, fixed income, increased by the proceeds of work . . . and a nice bow for innocent worldliness . . . is what I desire—and never shall obtain! (1908, 158; emphasis in original)

Here we see a precursor to Virginia Woolf's "five hundred a year and a room of one's own" as the necessary prerequisites for true female creativity. Yet the epistolary style allows for lightness of tone, a kind of flippancy behind which Beale hides her more serious social critiques. Beale's style also relies heavily on ventriloquizing various characters in her life; for example, Beale quotes stories told to her by a model she has hired to sit for her and transplants what is obviously Beale's own serious criticism of the art world into the model's mouth. The model is the widow of an artist whose paintings rarely sold and who like many artists suffered from the public opinion that art and money should not be spoken of in the same breath. The model recounts,

> It is droll, too, if it were not so serious, that the public looks upon money in connection with art as degrading; artists being ideal creatures who should be above such vulgar trafficking as money making; "art is not commerce," they say; but all the same it is only another sort of commerce to groceries, and unless all artists are to have an income provided by the State, I don't see how they are to live without selling their pictures. If exchange and barter were to be revived it would be very delightful; my dead husband always said we should be quite rich then as we had so many pictures we could have exchanged with the butcher and baker and grocers. (117)

The obsession with *groceries* in both Beale quotes is rather telling; throughout Beale's narrative there is a fixation on the simple acquisition of bread which serves as a reminder, amid all her discussions of famous paintings and studio parties, of the fact that artists, like other people, need to exchange money for food.

Elizabeth Thompson Butler provides a counterexample of a woman painter who played the financial and social game with success and refused to apologize for herself; in her memoir she constructs herself as a dedicated professional, unintimidated by the rich and famous with whom she regularly interacted. Butler erupted onto the British art scene in 1874, when her impressive 8-foot painting "Calling the Roll after an Engagement, Crimea" (popularly known as "The Roll Call") was accepted by the Royal Academy and hung *on the line*—that is, in the place of greatest visibility (and hence prestige) on the high walls of the Academy galleries. The work was so popular that policemen had to be hired to control the crowds struggling to get a glimpse of her picture at the R.A.—and to protect two paintings by Lord Leighton that had the misfortune of being placed at right angles to "The Roll Call" in one corner and hence were being scraped by turbulent Academy-goers eager to see Butler's work. In her memoir, Butler calls Leighton's paintings "two lovely little pictures"—a condescending remark which subtly reduces and feminizes Leighton's work, especially in contrast to Butler's huge canvas, its masculine subject, and the violent unladylike response it incited in the crowds (Butler 1922, 112).

In fact, the entire saga of Butler's artistic success dramatizes her destabilization of gender norms. Even before the official opening day of the Academy, Butler records in her memoirs, "The Roll Call" enthralled the Academicians and set in motion a politely cutthroat bidding war between various art collectors, art dealers, the Prince of Wales, and eventually Queen Victoria herself. Butler had painted the picture under commission for a Mr. Galloway, a Manchester manufacturer and art collector, for £100. Upon completion, he was so impressed he paid her £126 instead of the £100 agreed on and sent the picture to the Academy, where it kindled immediate interest. Galloway had many eager purchasers, some offering him as much as £1000 for a picture he had obtained for £126. (Butler wasn't the loser by any means; she sold the engraving copyrights to the picture for £1,200.) At last, Queen Victoria exercised her royal privilege and forced Mr. Galloway to cede "The Roll Call" to her. It is neatly ironic that this enormous picture, with its "masculine" subject but painted by a woman, is eventually sold to The Woman—the Queen. The trajectory of the picture seems to dramatize the potential for female control over the art world: not only does the Queen gain control over the painting, but Butler also gains considerable power as an artist after her fame with "The Roll Call." When Galloway insisted that Butler paint her next R.A. picture for him, and at the *same price* as he paid for "The Roll Call" (£126), Butler was no fool; she understood perfectly what her sudden popularity could mean. She writes in her memoirs:

> I had set my heart on painting the 28th Regiment in square receiving the last charge of the French Cuirassiers at Quatre Bras, but as that picture would necessitate far more work than "The Roll Call," I could not paint it for that little 126 pounds—so very puny now! To cut a long story short, he finally consented to have "Quatre Bras" at my own price, [£]1,126. (111–12)

One wonders if her setting the price at £1,126—precisely £1000 more than Galloway paid for her first endeavor—was meant as a subtle reproof for his previous radical undervaluing of her artwork.[32]

Butler's no-nonsense approach to her life and her work is unusual; the breezy or earnest styles we find in Jopling and Beale are much more common. Some Victorian women novelists share the strategies we see in these more light-hearted memoirs and in Ellet and Clayton; the woman painter is made safe by a kind of feminization that repositions her within traditional gender roles. But more frequently, as we shall see in succeeding chapters, novelists who chose to depict women painters opted for a more radical vision of their sister artists as disruptive, revolutionary, bohemian, and in general existing outside the norms and regulations of the social order—even if they are eventually represented as folded safely back into this order. As one can see from the above short history of the woman painter and the discourses that surrounded her, women writers would certainly have noted key similarities between their own experiences and those of their sister artists; barriers to success in the art world were just one part of a whole package of well-known ideological oppressions that Victorian women faced. But women painters were a particular case; their experiences highlighted and intensified key problems in the gender politics of the time, especially in terms of their erotic position in the aesthetic scenario. This intensity gave women writers ample opportunity to engage in radical gender debates. Women novelists, as the following chapters show, were highly attuned and attentive to the range of social, political, and aesthetic issues raised by the woman painter in the nineteenth century.

CHAPTER TWO

Desire and Feminist Aesthetics in Anne Brontë's *The Tenant of Wildfell Hall*

I.

THE TENANT OF WILDFELL HALL is regularly read (when it is read at all) as a kind of afterthought in the Brontë universe, something one reads when one has exhausted all the other Brontë novels and is feeling desperate.[1] The title of one of the few critical articles on Brontë's novel, "*The Tenant of Wildfell Hall:* Anne Brontë's *Jane Eyre*" (Berg 1987), gives some indication of the derivative status often accorded Anne Brontë. Twentieth-century critics were slow to embrace Anne's work; but feminist critics began at last to embrace the novel starting in the 1980s,[2] and more recent scholarship has made important inroads into redressing the balance of Brontë scholarship.[3] Anne Brontë's fiction, paradoxically, has been both sustained *and* devalued by its close association with her sisters' better-known novels. On the one hand, *Tenant* cannot be overlooked because it is a valuable (if peripheral, as some critics think) part of the Brontës' literary history. On the other, *Tenant* has often been regarded as not as "good" a novel as *Jane Eyre* or *Wuthering Heights*.

We have inherited this critical disparagement in large part from Charlotte Brontë herself, who as the sole surviving sister had great influence on the publication and reception of her sisters' works after their deaths. *Tenant* dismayed Charlotte, and although *Tenant* was well enough received after its first publication to require a speedy second edition, it was not reprinted until after Charlotte's death in 1855.[4] When Smith, Elder & Co. proposed, after the deaths of Anne and Emily, to print a definitive edition of their works, Charlotte agreed to a republication of *Wuthering Heights* and Anne's first novel *Agnes Grey* but refused to consider a republication of *Tenant*. Charlotte wrote to W. S. Williams, "'Wildfell Hall' hardly appears to me desirable to preserve. The choice of subject in that work is a mistake; it was too little consonant with the character, tastes, and ideas, of the gentle, retiring, inexperienced writer" (Wise and Symington 1932, 3: 156).

It horrified Charlotte that her "gentle, retiring, inexperienced" baby sister could write a story where drunken debauchery, verbal and emotional abuse, flagrant adultery, and physical violence figured so prominently. Specifically, Charlotte saw too many similarities between the drunk, dissolute husband Arthur Huntingdon and Branwell Brontë, whose drinking, financial instability, and moral profligacy formed a large part of the Brontë family tragedy. In her "Biographical Notices of Ellis and Acton Bell," appended to the edition of *Wuthering Heights* and *Agnes Grey*, Charlotte wrote disparagingly of Anne's "choice of subject": "She brooded over it [Branwell's debauchery and death] till she believed it to be a duty to reproduce every detail . . . she hated her work, but would pursue it. . . . She must be honest; she must not varnish, soften or conceal" (*Agnes Grey*, repr. 1988, 55).

Charlotte's problem with *Tenant* is its systematic, unflinching realism, which Charlotte significantly expresses in painterly terms—"reproduce every detail" and "she must not varnish." Nineteenth-century critics had similar responses: one periodical warned the novel's "lady-readers" against its overly raw realism; another wrote that it represented a "full and complete science of human brutality"; others condemned the novel's "vulgarity" but praised its "reality of description" (quoted by Angeline Goreau in her introduction to *Agnes Grey*, 11–12). A critic in *Sharpe's London Magazine* was horrified by the novel's "disgustingly truthful mimesis" (quoted in Jacobs 1986, 206). Anne herself, in her preface to the second edition of *Tenant*, writes that her object in writing *Tenant* was "to tell the truth," and her scenes, she insists, were "carefully copied from the life" (*Tenant*, repr. 1979, 29). An analysis of Anne's particular theory and practice of realism, and its relation to the heroine's artistic experiences and productions, is one of the overarching goals of this chapter.

Critics of *The Tenant of Wildfell Hall* have expended little energy considering the ramifications of the heroine's career as a professional painter. The oversight is surprising, considering the intense scholarly interest—particularly from feminist and historicist Victorianists—in working women of all kinds. But the intricacies of courtship, marriage, and marital abuse, alcoholism, child custody battles, and religious fervor (all of which *have* been discussed by recent critics) are registered quite clearly in the aesthetic realm: passion—be it love or anger—materializes in visual art and in language. Just as Jane's paintings in *Jane Eyre* expose critical elements of both Jane's psyche and the social situation in which she found herself (as we shall see in chap. 3), so too in *Tenant* does artwork function to represent key social and psychological events. But whereas in *Jane Eyre* painting surfaces infrequently, in *Tenant* we see the heroine Helen Graham painting at every stage of the novel's complex narrative. Unlike Jane, Helen is regularly at her easel, and her relationship to painting, which changes dramatically during the novel, offers a running narrative of female artistic development. Helen is an amateur painter at the (chronological) beginning of the novel; by the end, the novel represents art as an occupation rather than a hobby and dramatizes the difficulty women artists of the time had in finding suitable and varied subject matter, accessing materials, and entering the market. By making her heroine a professional painter, Anne Brontë enters a lively public debate concerning the social and aesthetic value of women artists and gives herself the perfect vehicle for working through her peculiarly troubling theory of mimesis.

Anne Brontë's decision to make her heroine a painter must have been based on her own (and her family's) intense commitment to art.[5] All the Brontë children were avid artists (Branwell's goal was to become a professional painter, as was Charlotte's before her eyesight failed), and the family culture included regular study of and attention to art. Anne Brontë, like her sisters, had training in drawing; many of her juvenile works remain. In one of these, a simple pencil sketch, a slim young woman stands on the edge of a rock, gazing out at a sunrise over a sea so tranquil it seems doubtful whether the sailboat in the left background could be moving at all (see figure 2.1). The sketch is the work of Anne at age nineteen, done during her first post as governess at Mirfield in 1839.

Most of the Brontë sisters' artwork consists of copies of engravings of famous paintings, images in books or newspapers, or landscape etchings used for educational purposes—but this sketch is one of the few surviving drawings that *cannot* be traced to an existing print. Alexander and Sellars suggest that this drawing is at least partially—if not entirely—the product of Anne's imagination, rather than copied from another source (1995, 406).

Edward Chitham, in his collection of Anne Brontë's poems, tells us that the *Woman Gazing* (also called *Sunrise at Sea*) sketch should be taken as a self-portrait, symbolic of Brontë's dawning maturity; he argues that in this sketch "Anne portrays herself creatively in a symbolic setting" (1979, 23). Chitham gives roughly the same meaning to a sketch Brontë did the following year, representing a young woman peering nervously out from between some trees:

Figure 2.1. Anne Brontë, *Sunrise at Sea*, or *Woman gazing at a sunrise over a seascape*, 1839. Brontë Parsonage Museum. Reproduced with permission.

this sketch he terms "a second romantic self-characterization" (ibid.). Both sketches are read as the symbolic self-expression of a girl poised on the edge of womanhood; neither sketch receives significant nonbiographical commentary. The overall tenor of Jane Sellars's discussion of Brontë's work is similar: her artwork punctuates her life like so many iconic snapshots, full of personal significance. Of the *Woman Gazing* sketch, Sellars writes, "It is refreshing to look at a drawing by Anne in which she has invested some of her own feelings" (1995, 142). Sellars clarifies these "feelings" by suggesting that the young woman in the sketch "expresses the emotion of yearning for contact with a larger world than her own"; more specifically, Sellars argues that the sketch also reflects Anne's emergent interest in her father's new young curate (ibid.). To accuse a Brontë sister of such bland and simple sentiment seems rather blasphemous, given the sharp anger and gothic brooding for which Anne Brontë's more famous sisters are known. Such purely biographical arguments are reminiscent, I will argue, of a particular nineteenth-century stance on women artists, one that privileges the personal, focusing attention on the artist herself and away from the artist's productions, much as we saw in the *Punch* review discussed in chapter 1.

The biographical reading of Brontë's artwork is even more problematic given the resolutely unsentimental and distancing force of the visual arts in Anne Brontë's second novel, *The Tenant of Wildfell Hall*, published nine years after *Woman Gazing* was completed. Critics of the sketch may argue that the thoughts that preoccupy the figure are purely emotional—the longing for a lover or the desire for a wider world experience as suggested by Sellars. Frawley, similarly, writes of the sketch, "The subject is so preoccupied with her thoughts as to be oblivious to the gaze of the viewer" (Frawley 1996, 30). However, given Anne Brontë's interest in the visual arts, a second possibility is worth considering. Notice that it is the female figure's line of sight which organizes the painting; she stands slightly to the left of center and looks out slightly to the right. Anne's sketch itself mimics this angle. The sketch then—if we squelch the desire to read each figure symbolically and biographically (the girl is Anne, the sunrise represents future potential; the distance is the wider sphere Anne wishes to attain, etc.)—is an aesthetic exercise. As a young artist Anne is practicing various elements of her art: perspective, shading (the rocks), drapery (the young woman's dress), reflection (the light on the water, the waves), and framing (the way the rocks on the left encase that side of the picture, as do the few rocks and the cloud formation for the right side). We might see the painting as an exercise in *looking,* in planning an artistic endeavor rather than in simply dreaming of love and far-off lands. The female *figure* in the drawing might be longing for something, striving to see a ship in the distance—but the young female *artist* producing the drawing is exercising technical aesthetic skills.

Tenant features a painter-heroine, Helen Graham, whose juvenile works receive aesthetic interpretation of a similarly dismissive kind as that leveled at her creator. In one scene of the novel, the young Helen is at work on what she rather audaciously considers her masterpiece. She writes of the picture in her diary:[6]

> I had endeavored to convey the idea of a sunny morning. . . . The scene represented was an open glade in a wood. A group of dark Scotch firs was introduced in the middle distance to relieve the prevailing freshness of the rest; but in the foreground were part of the gnarled trunk and of the spreading boughs of a large forest tree, whose foliage was of a brilliant golden green—not golden from autumnal mellowness, but from the sunshine, and the very immaturity of the scarce expanded leaves. Upon this bough, that stood out in bold relief against the sombre firs, were seated an amorous pair of turtle doves, whose soft sad-coloured plumage afforded a contrast of another nature; and beneath it, a young girl was kneeling . . . her hands clasped, lips parted, and eyes intently gazing upward in pleased, yet earnest contemplation of those feathered lovers. (*Tenant*, 175)

Arthur Huntingdon, the handsome young rake who stumbles into the library in search of Helen, has no trouble reading the painting's message: "Very pretty, i'faith!" he pronounces it, "and a very fitting study for a young lady—Spring just opening into summer—morning just approaching noon—girlhood just ripening into womanhood . . . Sweet innocent! She's thinking there will come a time when she will be wooed and won like that pretty hen-dove" (175). He follows up his praise with one version of what will become a refrain spoken by more than one of Helen's admirers throughout the novel: "I should fall in love with her, if I hadn't the artist before me!" (175).[7]

Huntingdon here analyzes Helen's painting iconographically, searching for particular symbolic motifs and assigning significance to various visual elements in her picture. Huntingdon fails to make the Panofskian jump from Iconography to Iconology, from cataloguing particular symbolic images to interpreting the complete symbolic horizon of a work. The next jump, toward the concern of W. J. T. Mitchell for the "idea of the image as such" (1986, 2), is well beyond Huntingdon's aesthetic power. In Huntingdon's iconographic reading, the spring landscape symbolizes "girlhood just ripening into womanhood," while the doves, predictably, stand for the erotic desire Huntingdon wishes to uncover in Helen. Huntingdon also reads biographically (another traditional art-historical mode): Helen's picture bears meaning only with reference to her own self. In fact, the girl in the picture and Helen are, in Huntingdon's mind, structurally identical. Later in the scene, in fact, Huntingdon complains that Helen, who is dark-haired, has made the girl in the picture fair; his disapproval indicates his belief that a young woman's paintings should be precisely autobiographical and contain nothing more nor less than the artist herself. To paint anything else is a risk: the fair girl in the picture becomes an auxiliary temptation, a possible replacement of Helen ("I should fall in love with her, if I hadn't the artist before me," Huntingdon says). In deviating from her own experience—indeed, from the very image and likeness of herself—Helen has erred against Huntingdon's understanding of the feminine aesthetic.

A Huntingdon-style interpretation of Helen's painting has been, oddly, the one most frequently adopted by critics of *Tenant* who tackle, however tangentially, the meaning of all Helen's artwork throughout the novel. I say "oddly" for two reasons: first, Huntingdon's iconographic and biographic interpretation applies only to what we might call Helen's "juvenile" work: he never sees her mature productions, as they are done either in secret while they are living together after their marriage, or at Wildfell Hall after her flight from him. Hence, any critical interpretation which takes Helen's first artistic attempts as *the* site from which to explore the meaning of painting in the novel ignores the very different products of Helen's later career. Second, and more importantly, it seems decidedly awry to accept the aesthetic assessment of a character whose primary role in the novel is as its villain—for Huntingdon becomes the alcoholic, adulterous, and abusive husband from whom Helen is forced to flee with her son, taking up residence at last in Wildfell Hall. Anne Brontë's point, surely, is that Huntingdon's appraisal of Helen's artwork is misguided, motivated solely by aesthetic ignorance on the one hand and sexual interest and egotism on the other. Huntingdon sees in Helen's artwork precisely what he wants to see—a young girl just coming to sexual awareness and waiting for his advances.

This is not to say that Huntingdon's reading of Helen's early painting is incorrect, for Brontë's novel is as much a treatise about how and what women should paint as it is about how men (and critics) should interpret women's artwork. The novel details Helen's artistic development from precisely such overtly sentimental, symbolic art as exhibited in her early "masterpiece" with the doves toward resolutely less self-expressive art, an art more in keeping with Brontë's commitment to mimetic realism. But we see hints of this rejection of symbolic aesthetics even in Helen's early career as a painter. In fact, it is only *Huntingdon's* judgment of Helen's painting that gives the impression that it is pure "romantic fantasy"; Helen's *own* ekphrastic description of her picture is along very different lines. By letting Helen control the ekphrasis, Brontë gives her heroine *some* control over the interpretation of the paintings. Again, Helen writes: "I intended it to be my masterpiece, though it was somewhat presumptuous in the design. By the bright azure of the sky, and by the warm and brilliant lights, and deep, long shadows, I had endeavored to convey the idea of a sunny morning" (174–75).

A "presumptuous design" hints at the intervention of the artist into the realities of nature, the presence of conscious aesthetic form rather than systematic copying from nature; likewise, the statement "convey the idea" indicates something beyond mimetic reproduction. To convey an idea is not simply to represent a landscape as it appears, but rather as it is felt or thought. Helen deals here in *ideas,* not images. More importantly, her description of the painting first in terms of color, light, and shadow—form rather than interpretable icons—also distances her reading of her work from Arthur's interpretation, which is solely based on a symbolic reading of discrete figures. When she does briefly explain the content of her painting, she refuses to draw any conclusions—any autobiographical meaning—from the figures she has created. Instead she talks of balancing the colors, shapes, and moods of the painting:

> . . . a group of dark Scotch firs was introduced in the middle distance to relieve the prevailing freshness of the rest. . . . Upon this bough, that stood out in bold relief against the sombre firs, were seated an amorous pair of turtle doves, whose soft sad-coloured plumage afforded a contrast. (175)

In Helen's reading, the birds are present simply to add color contrast to the work, not because of their symbolic resonance. Additionally, the use of the passive voice ("was introduced") seems to distance the young artist from the work under scrutiny; by depersonalizing her own relationship to the painting, she paradoxically claims for herself the position of *artist* rather than mere recorder of personal emotions. Hence, while she does not claim agency through direct authorship or personal feminine experience, she does claim authority through the fitness of the work, the perfect balance of its form with the effects that she wants to produce.

Critics of *Tenant* have expended little energy considering the ramifications of Helen's career as a painter, and those who do consider Helen's artwork follow Huntingdon's lead, consistently assigning her paintings the narrative role of blatant iconographic symbolism. In one of the few critical essays on *Tenant* that considers Helen even briefly as an artist, Margaret Mary Berg writes of the young Helen's artworks: "In these scenes, 'self-expression' . . . is trivialized, reduced to the embarrassingly naive representation of romantic fantasies" (1987, 14). Berg's reading (like Huntingdon's) sees in Helen's paintings only the expression of the desire of the self—a naive self at that. I wish to argue here that, to the contrary, Helen's art cannot be considered mere background to the novel nor as the simple expression of adolescent desire.[8]

In *Tenant*, painting never simply works symbolically to express character or signal narrative events. Scenes of painting in *Tenant* are less concerned with individual character or the character of fiction than with the complex public dramas which arise when a woman's artistic production—the actual act of painting—is considered. A static ekphrasis is not Brontë's main mode in *Tenant:* her concern is not with the aesthetic artifact but with the scene of a woman painting as a gendered cultural event with wide-ranging significance. Even in her ekphrastic description of her turtledove painting, Helen's word choice is active, descriptive of the process of producing the painting rather than its final appearance. It is *painting* as a verb, not painting as a noun, which is at issue here. We must see the scenes of painting in *Tenant* as barometers for the novel's radical view of women's role as creative producers during a particularly complex art-historical moment. The novel's many scenes of painting provide its readers with detailed, if oblique, guidelines for proper aesthetic production and interpretation. Most particularly, such a reevaluation of the role of painting in the novel resolves a central critical debate over the novel's problematic narrative structure.

II.

In a passage that figures prominently on many paperback versions of Anne Brontë's novels, the fin-de-siècle novelist and critic George Moore claimed that Anne Brontë's first novel, *Agnes Grey*, was "the most perfect prose narrative in English literature" (1924, 257). But *Tenant* too came in for its share of praise from Moore, due to what he called Brontë's "quality of heat," by which he seems to mean a powerful but unfulfilled sexual or religious passion which is transmitted or represented without loss of intensity. Heat is an "almost animal emotion" (255), rare enough in the real world but almost unknown in fiction. But Moore qualifies his praise of *Tenant* because of what he sees as a seminal structural failure of the novel, a failure to which many subsequent critics also called attention—and which almost all recent criticism has concerned itself with justifying. Moore writes that while the "weaving of the narrative in the first hundred and fifty pages of *The Tenant of Wildfell Hall* reveals a born tale-teller," in the second half of the novel "Anne broke down" (253). The first hundred and fifty pages to which Moore refers contains a narrative in the first person by Gilbert Markham, who has settled himself down on a rainy afternoon to write a letter to his brother-in-law in which he will detail what he calls "the most important event of my life" (*Tenant*, 34), namely, his meeting with Helen Graham, the "fair recluse" who moves into the derelict old Wildfell Hall with her young son. The first half of the novel tells the story of Helen and Gilbert's meeting, their gradual and fraught friendship, and Gilbert's eventual passionate attachment to her.

So far, so good, at least as concerns the "quality of heat." Gilbert's frantic and intent pursuit of Helen and her painfully restrained avoidance of him set up an erotic tension which evidently pleased Moore. But the breakdown of this heat, as Moore sees it, occurs at the moment midway through the novel when Helen hands her diary to Gilbert as a way of explaining her inability to return his affections. At this point the narrative shifts from Gilbert's voice to Helen's, and we read in her diary the story of her past, of her starry-eyed courtship and dismal marriage to the dissolute, alcoholic, and abusive Arthur Huntingdon. Helen, we now discover, is not the widow the townsfolk have taken her for, but is in fact still married and hiding from her husband at Wildfell Hall under an assumed name. The diary takes us from the saga of her courtship with Huntingdon through her marriage and to the point when Helen, escaping from Huntingdon, arrives at Wildfell Hall and meets Gilbert; and there the diary breaks off. Gilbert now resumes his narrative, telling the rest of the story (Helen's eventual return to her ailing husband, his death from alcoholism, and finally Helen and Gilbert's reconciliation and marriage) and providing the other edge of the frame for the internal narrative in Helen's diary.

This nesting narrative structure has drawn frequent complaint from critics, whose negative opinions may have helped position the novel where it is today, resting uneasily on the borders of the nineteenth-century canon. Winifred Gerin, who writes the introduction to the 1979 Penguin edition of *Tenant,* shares Moore's view of Brontë's narrative "breakdown" and considers the novel marred by "the clumsy device of a plot within a plot" (13).[9] The multiple narration, then, is the problem; it serves to lessen the intensity and *presence* of the fiction. Moore writes that "the diary broke the story in halves" and in doing so cooled off an otherwise hot narrative. Gerin, in her introduction, quotes Moore's animadversions and follows up with the words, "How right was Moore! By the device of the diary the drama . . . is seen at one remove, not in the heat of the action" (14).

Much of modern criticism of the novel seems just a footnote to George Moore, who first put his finger on the sore spot of the novel's structural organization. It has been the goal of almost all recent critics of *Tenant* to justify Brontë's technical decision to include Helen's diary, and their accounts have been, to my mind, overwhelmingly successful. Juliet McMaster (1982, 363) defends the diary by insisting that it is immediate, rather than passive;

the diary records Helen and Huntingdon's relationship and its deterioration more powerfully than if Gilbert had recorded Helen's verbal telling of the tale. N. M. Jacobs argues that *Tenant* shares with *Wuthering Heights* a reliance on the "gothic frame-tale" to deal with an unconventional or socially unacceptable subject matter. The frame narrator—Gilbert, in *Tenant*—reports or relays the shocking story of events that occur outside (narratively and literally) the respectable reality of the narrator's world. Jacobs's point is that in both Brontë sisters' novels, the framing narrative and the framed narrative are like "competing works of art, or outer rooms in a gallery, or even the picture painted over a devalued older canvas" (1986, pp).[10] The frame and content both demand equal attention and are of equal narrative value. This revaluation of the nested narrative, according to Elizabeth Langland, allows for a radically feminist reading of the novel in which Helen's diary diffuses Gilbert's narrative rather than (as critics have argued) being subsumed by it. Langland argues that the two narratives interact as exchangeable narrative currency with a "transgressive economy that allows for the paradoxic voicing of feminine desire" (1992, 112).

More recently, Elizabeth Signorotti (1995) has offered a caution to Langland and other critics who see Helen's diary as liberatory; Signorotti suggests that Gilbert's use of Helen's diary within his letter to his brother-in-law is Brontë's way of dramatizing male control over Helen. Her essay displays Gilbert's duplicity throughout the novel and lays out very compelling reasons why Gilbert is not the noble hero he pretends to be. The novel becomes, then, in Signorotti's reading, a much bleaker account of Helen's inability to resist masculine control in any way, even narratively—and the nesting narrative is Brontë's elegant way of dramatizing Helen's complete binding by masculine authority. In contrast to these arguments, Rachel Carnell has recently opened up a way to rethink this structural division: by pointing out that most analyses of the bifurcated narrative rely on the overly simplified and historically inaccurate doctrine of separate spheres, Carnell offers a reading of the novel in which "Helen challenges the separate gendered spheres by offering herself as one of the rare enlightened women who could claim a voice in public debate" (1998, 11). The dual narrative, then, becomes a way for Brontë to undermine any static confinement of women or men into separate cultural realms.[11]

III.

My goal here is not to prove yet again that Brontë's decisions regarding the structural makeup of her novel were valid—the critics discussed above have, I believe, amply justified Brontë's technical decisions. I wish instead to suggest that any criticism of the novel that takes Moore's dismay over the structure of the novel as a starting point should consider the reasons behind this dismay. Moore's argument about *structural* mistakes was in fact a masquerade, a cover-up for his real problem with the novel, which involves the sexual politics of spectatorship and is incarnated in the profession of the heroine. As a painter, Helen Graham is a creative producer in her own right, rather than an aesthetic object; *this* is where the real "heat" of the novel is—in Helen's painting and the ideological arguments arising from it. Helen's position as creative producer is what truly distresses Moore, beneath all his complaints about narrative structure. Listen to how he articulates his (ostensibly technical) denunciation of *Tenant*'s structure: he writes that Brontë's structural mistake stemmed

> not from lack of genius but of *experience*. An accident would have saved her, almost any *man of letters* would have *laid his hand upon her arm* and said: You must not let your heroine give her diary to the young farmer. . . . Your heroine must tell the young farmer her story, and an *entrancing* scene you will make of the telling. . . . The *presence of your heroine*, her voice, her gestures, the questions that would arise and the answers that would be given . . . would preserve the atmosphere of *a passionate and original love story*. The diary broke the story in halves. (1924, 253–54; emphasis added)

The "man of letters" in Moore's little romance of intervention must physically touch the woman writer, must lay his hand on Anne Brontë and save her from the narrative blunder of allowing her heroine disembodied speech.[12] Both Moore and Gerin (and other critics who share Moore's disapproval of the nested narrative structure) mourn the absence of Helen's *physical* presence in the central framed portion (the diary) of the novel. Just as Moore envisions the man of letters enjoying tactile contact with the "inexperienced" woman writer, so must the hero of the novel remain in physical contact with the heroine for the erotics of the novel to function properly in Moore's eyes. Gilbert must be able to lay his hands on Helen for the traditional erotics of a "passionate love story" to be maintained; women's bodies must not be separated from their narrative productions but must be present, tangible, and visible.

But Anne Brontë had other ideas. To begin with, the novel is not designed as a love story at all—at least not of the type Moore evidently desired.[13] Rather, the novel explores a sophisticated feminist aesthetic that finds its narrative expression in the profession of the heroine. Her social role as aesthetic producer makes it impossible for her to remain herself an artwork that could be ever-present for Gilbert's (and Moore's) delectation; as an artist, Helen is necessarily separated from her productions during the course of the novel. Helen's resistance to embodiment ultimately frustrates Moore; he objects to precisely her incarnation as an artist, a creative producer whose artworks (her diary here stands metonymically for her other visual art productions) are necessarily separate from her own body.

Helen's artistic production places her outside the traditional aesthetic scenario (male viewer/female object) and in fact provides a sort of screen behind which Helen can hide. Brontë stages this several times within the novel: at one point during her first marriage, for instance, one piece of her artist's kit—a palette-knife—is pressed into service to protect her virtue from an encroaching admirer (362–63), and other paraphernalia of the artist work similarly to symbolize Helen's self-reliance and autonomy through art. Similarly, when Helen begins to "speak" for herself in the diary portion of the novel, she once again shifts from artwork (tangible appreciable object) to artistic producer; *this* is Moore's essential complaint with the structure of the novel. Once again, Helen seems to be transposing a product of her aesthetic production (her diary) between her body and her male viewer or reader. Significantly, Moore can never bring himself to mention that Helen is a visual artist, and many twentieth-century critics of the novel share his refusal to see the tremendous ramifications of the heroine's profession. In *Agnes Grey* the heroine is a governess—a properly feminine and submissive social position—and so *Agnes Grey* garners nothing but praise from Moore. But Helen Graham in *Tenant* paints for a living, and in doing so encroaches on a field of endeavor most dear to Moore, who himself trained as an artist in his youth and wrote art criticism throughout his career. In Moore's most important work of art criticism, *Modern Painting* (1898), a chapter called "Sex in Art" lays out his views on women in art, which can be summarized succinctly in Charles Tansley's words from *To the Lighthouse:* "Women can't paint." Women might be able to write, as *Agnes Grey* demonstrates, but in Moore's estimation they certainly cannot paint. Moore detested—there is no other word for it—women visual artists, primarily because of the relation he envisioned between sex and art. For Moore, "sex" is related to "heat": he defines "sex" as "the concentrated essence of life which the great artist jealously reserves for his art, and through which it pulsates" (1898, 222). Women, on the other hand, cannot reserve their sexual desire for their art but expend it too freely in their daily life: "The natural affections fill a woman's whole life, and her art is only so much sighing and gossiping about them. . . . In her art woman is always in evening dress; there are flowers in her hair, and her fan waves to and fro, and she wishes to sigh in the ear of him who sits beside her" (223). Moore believes that women are fundamentally incapable of visual invention precisely because of their relation to the erotic[14]—and here, perhaps, Anne Brontë might see his point. *Tenant* offers us an exploration of how profoundly erotics gets in the way of female aesthetic production.

IV.

Helen Graham arrives on the narrative scene as a fully formed, professional painter, defined by her relation to her artistic production. When Gilbert pays his first call on Helen, he and his sister are shown not into the parlor but into Helen's studio in the derelict Wildfell Hall:

> To our surprise, we were ushered into a room where the first object that met the eye was a painter's easel, with a table beside it covered with rolls of canvas, bottles of oil[15] and varnish, palette, brushes, paints, etc. Leaning against the wall were several sketches in various stages of progression, and a few finished paintings—mostly of landscapes and figures. (68)

Etiquette dictates that Helen apologize to her guests for not receiving them in the proper space of the sitting room, and her apology sets her priorities on the table. The parlor is out of the question, she explains, because it has no fire; she has chosen instead to heat only the studio, a space of work rather than leisure. This is literally a Victorian "drawing room"—rather than a "withdrawing room." The workspace must make room for guests, although this is difficult: Gilbert reports that Helen must "disengag[e] a couple of chairs from the artistical lumber that usurped them" (68). In Gilbert's reading, it is the "artistical lumber" that "usurps"—that is, physically occupies without sanctioned or appropriate authority—the place of polite company. As the scene progresses, however, it becomes clear that it is society, in the persons of Gilbert and his sister, who are the "usurpers" in this space. When her guests have been seated, Helen returns to her seat behind her easel: "Not facing it exactly, but now and then glancing at the picture upon it while she conversed, and giving it an occasional touch with her brush, as if she found it impossible to wean her attention entirely from her occupation to fix it upon her guests" (68).

Gilbert's use here of the term "occupation" should draw our attention. All the interconnected connotations of the term—professional occupation, occupation of land or space, and occupation as something that captures the attention—come into play in this scene. Helen has a professional *occupation*, and she *occupies* Wildfell Hall, but as a "tenant" rather than one legally in possession of the space.[16] Furthermore she is *occupied by* her painting to the exclusion of her company; the easel remains Helen's focus here, just as the easel was for Gilbert "the first object that met the eye" when he entered her domestic space. This bit of "artistical lumber" stands centrally throughout the narrative, attesting to Helen's authority as artist. The palette-knife, as mentioned earlier, distances Helen from one unwelcome lover, while the easel in this scene with Gilbert forms a physical barrier against his admiring gaze and claims the attention he feels should be focused on himself.

Forbidden from staring at Helen by her manner as well as by the intervening easel, Gilbert instead examines the picture of Wildfell Hall on which Helen is working, and we learn that Helen is a talented painter when Gilbert surveys the picture on her easel "with a greater degree of admiration and delight than [he] cared to express" (68). Gilbert's observation of the picture on the easel further reveals that Helen signs her paintings with initials that are not her own and labels the image of Wildfell Hall with the false name "Fernley Manor, Culberland." Helen explains that she must engage in this bit of subterfuge because she is in hiding and because those from whom she is hiding "might see the picture, and *might possibly recognize the style*" (69; emphasis added). That Helen's paintings have a recognizable style is crucial; taken together with Gilbert's serious aesthetic commentary on her paintings it suggests that Brontë wishes us to understand that Helen is not merely an amateur. The false initials, read metaphorically, further separate Helen from any personal, emotional involvement with her art; she has entirely severed the *affective* connection between artist and work as well as the semiotic/mimetic connection between name and place.

We also learn in this scene that Helen paints for *money*, further marking her as a professional artist and making it quite clear that the paintings will leave Helen's physical presence, rather than remain to become conduits through which admiring visitors such as Gilbert might approach her. When Gilbert asks why she does not intend to keep the picture, she replies briefly, "I cannot afford to paint for my own amusement" (69). Helen's young son pipes up to tell the company that "Mamma sends all her pictures to London, and somebody sells them for her there, and sends us the money" (69). Helen, like many nineteenth-century women painters, does not sell her products directly, but requires masculine intervention in the market.

The paintings which Gilbert sees in this scene are our first introduction to the mature Helen's artworks, and they make an interesting contrast to the symbolic turtledove picture. Gilbert reports that one of the paintings represents a "view of Wildfell Hall, as seen at early morning from the field below, rising in dark relief against a sky of silvery blue, with a few red streaks on the horizon." Lest we imagine that these red streaks denote Turneresque abandon, Gilbert insists that the painting is "faithfully drawn and coloured, and very elegantly and artistically handled" (68). Helen's chosen genre is primarily realist landscape painting, but with a strong tinge of idealism, a hyper-reality which suggests that Brontë may have meant Helen's paintings to be in the manner of John Martin (whose works were a strong influence on all the Brontës).[17] Gilbert's description of Helen's style as characterized by "freshness of colouring and freedom of handling" (69) may alternately suggest her alignment with the landscape styles of Constable or the traditional drawing masters like Gilpin or the early Ruskin.[18] We see Helen "studying the distinctive characters of the different varieties of trees in their winter nakedness, and copying, with a spirited, though delicate touch, their various ramifications" (50); obviously the impulse toward naturalism is there, but always modified by an independent style: "spirited" and "delicate" rather than mechanical or duplicate.

The change from minute detail, imaginary landscape, and symbolic elements which characterized youthful paintings to the more original, "fresh" handling of actual landscapes in her mature art mirrors, in part, the sort of art education young women—like Anne Brontë herself—might have undergone in the early 1800s. The Brontë girls, like other girls of their age and class, were taught to draw by copying engravings (see Alexander and Sellars 1995, 37–59). The goal was utter accuracy; the engravings copied were generally landscape scenes of sentimental or picturesque style. But Brontë suggests that Helen has progressed artistically well beyond such endeavors. Helen's early picture of the young girl and doves was minutely copied from the life in two respects only: it represented mimetic precision with respect to the trees and leaves (although it was not drawn *en plein air* as are her mature works) *and* with respect to the artist's feelings. An older, aesthetically wiser Helen has moved away from such slavish copying; her physical freedom from Huntingdon translates into aesthetic liberty.

Helen's artistic freedom is further expressed spatially, by the crucial fact that she has a studio of her own. Before her marriage she paints in the public parlor; during her marriage to Huntingdon, Helen must paint in the library to be effectively hidden from him and his debauched cronies: the library is "a secure retreat at all hours of the day, [for] none of our gentlemen had the smallest pretensions to a literary taste" (359). When she flees Huntingdon and arrives at Wildfell Hall, one of her first concerns is to set up a studio, and she is pleased with its "professional, business-like appearance" (397). Both adjectives—"professional" and "business-like"—attest that this space is not a place of amateur amusement, nor a room allotted for any activity other than painting. This was rare for women in the nineteenth century; only women from artistic families or at the top of their profession might have studio space of their own. Laura Alma-Tadema and Henrietta Ward both had studios—but both were the wives of professional painters. Elizabeth Thompson Butler found herself a studio only *after* the phenomenal success of her battle painting, *The Roll Call*.[19] Women who had studios were forced to feminize them: Louise Jopling, who became a well-known painter after her husband's death, used her studio as a space in which she could be both an elegant hostess and a professional artist. The Ladies Column of the *Illustrated London News* complimented Jopling's creation of an elegant *salon*-type environment: "Her studio parties are always interesting and she knows so many people who are always somebody in literature and art" (quoted in Cherry 1993, 89). Jopling's art is not mentioned; instead, she plays a proper feminine role as hostess and social coordinator.

Women who could not afford, or who were not permitted, studio space of their own were forced to make space within the domestic sphere for their painting. This was not an easy venture. For example, Mary Ellen Best's painting, *An Artist in Her Painting Room* (figure 2.2), depicts with quiet irony the place an artistic woman could command. This so-called painting room shows abundant evidence of being in fact a general sitting room. There are enough chairs for multiple people to sit; the arrangement suggests the room is organized for conversation. Family portraits and decorative china give further suggestion of a common room. The artist looks up from her work as if interrupted by an unwelcome arrival. Finally, the room is spotless—painting accouterments cover a tiny portion of the available space.

A similar scene appears in Jessica Hayllar's *Finishing Touches* (figure 2.3), which depicts a young woman painting in a corner of what appears to be an entry room or large hall—certainly not a studio. A screen serves to cut off—or hide—the woman from the rest of the elegant domestic space.[20]

In *Tenant*, the positions are reversed; the studio must unwillingly make space for the duties of the parlor. Brontë represents Helen not in the feminine role of hostess but in the decidedly unfeminine role of preoccupied and grumpy genius, toiling away at a painting with no time for society. The entire chapter in which this scene with Gilbert takes place—a chapter called simply and pointedly "The Studio"—forges a radical professional female identity for Helen: she paints in a recognizable style and for money; has a studio of own; and evinces a commitment to art, not to the self or the social. But the scene also articulates, through the shadowy presence of the "someone" who comes to take pictures to market, the *problems* of female professionalism. Here Brontë literalizes the problem many women had in their painting careers—how to "hide" their artistic endeavors from a disapproving husband or a repressive

Figure 2.2. Mary Ellen Best, *An Artist in her Painting Room*, 1837–39. York City Art Gallery. Reproduced with permission.

Figure 2.3. Jessica Hayllar, *Finishing Touches*. Originally displayed at the Institute of Oil Painters, London, 1887. Present whereabouts unknown. Source: Deborah Cherry, *Painting Women*, plate 7.

economic system which discouraged women from publicly selling their wares. Professional women artists faced particular legal complications if they were married, as Helen is.[21]

The historical inspiration for Helen's marital difficulties—at least as regards her rights to her artistic property (and its lucrative proceeds) and her son—came from the notorious career of Caroline Norton, whose explosive marital battles led to the eventual institution of numerous laws protecting married women and their children. In particular, Norton's experience brought to the public attention the problem of women's access to the financial rewards of their creative labor. Caroline Sheridan—granddaughter of the Whig statesman and dramatist Richard Sheridan—became Caroline Norton in 1827 when she was nineteen. Her husband, George Norton, was a Tory M.P. and a lawyer with little income; Caroline Norton began writing novels and poems and editing women's magazines to augment the couple's meager finances. She became enormously successful in her literary endeavors but in her married life was not so lucky. In 1836 George Norton abducted their three children, refused to let his wife see them, and began divorce proceedings on the grounds of his wife's alleged adultery with the Whig prime minister, Lord Melbourne. The sensational divorce trial ended abruptly: the jury, without even leaving the courtroom for deliberation, proclaimed Mrs. Norton not guilty and the divorce could not go through.

Matters did not end there. Since she was still married (and, since Norton's divorce proceedings had failed, now irrevocably so), Mrs. Norton was effectively a legal nonperson. At the time married women had virtually no rights; by the common law principle of coverture, married women were "covered" by their husbands. Hence, everything married women "possessed" or "owned" was in fact *entirely* the property of their husbands: money, clothing, land, and children. Wives' nonperson status under the law served, also, to eradicate a married woman's ability to bind herself to any contract or to make an independent will. Husband and wife, the saying went, were essentially one person—and that person was the husband. Mrs. Norton, separated from her husband but not divorced, was nonexistent; she had no legal right to see her children, and no legal right to keep the earnings from her continued literary efforts. When a Tory newspaper accused her—yet again—of having an affair, she could not even sue for libel: her husband would have had to sue in her stead (and in any case, any money received if she won the case would have been her husband's property).

The Nortons' quarrel raged—in the courtroom and in the public press—until his death in 1875.[22] The saga of the Norton marriage—so widely publicized, so entangled with the politics of the day (when the Tory Norton accused his Whig wife of adultery with the Whig Prime Minister Lord Melbourne, many people believed it was a Tory plot to discredit the Whig government)—was enormously influential throughout the nineteenth century and became an effective rallying point for the emergent feminist movement. In 1837, Caroline Norton began to campaign for law reform, publishing pamphlets, giving speeches, writing letters, and urging well-connected friends to help effect changes in Parliament. In the same year she wrote *Observations on the Natural Claim of the Mother to the Custody of her Infant Children, as affected by the Common Law Right of the Father*, a political pamphlet which she distributed herself. Her first foray into practical politics was successful: in 1839 the Infant Custody Bill was passed. The bill provided that a mother whose children were in the custody of their father (or someone appointed by the father) could apply to the Court of Chancery to appeal that custody. If the children were under seven, the court could either grant the mother custody of the children until they reached seven, or provide the mother with a court order allowing her to see the children at regular intervals. In *Tenant,* Helen's child is, significantly, just six years old when she escapes with him to Wildfell Hall. Even if she could have received a court order for custody or visitation rights, those rights would end as soon as young Arthur reached seven—thus the need for secrecy and concealment.

Mrs. Norton's other legal battle involved married women's possession of property and income. Again, because she was married, Mrs. Norton could not legally keep her earnings from her literary work, nor could she collect the annuity she had been left in her father's will—it too belonged to her husband. So Mrs. Norton was dependent financially on an allowance her husband rarely agreed to pay her—with the ironic result that *he* was often sued by creditors for *her* debts (for a wife's debts, too, were the property of her husband). In 1854 she published another pamphlet, *English Laws for Women in the Nineteenth Century,* one of the earliest explicitly political and legal-minded tracts of the emergent feminist movement, and one which had a profound impact on the budding young feminist (and painter) Barbara Leigh Smith (later Bodichon). Smith's exposition of the legal status of women, *A Brief Summary, in Plain Language, of the Most Important Laws concerning Women,* was published later in the same year. The multiple profeminist bills and acts proposed in Parliament from the first Married Women's Property Bill, introduced by Mrs. Norton's friend Lord Brougham in 1857 (and not passed until 1870), through the various divorce reform bills (the so-called Matrimonial Causes Acts and others) all harked back, implicitly or explicitly, to the very public scandal of the Norton marriage.

The personal experiences of women such as Caroline Norton inspired not only Anne Brontë's depiction of a married woman's plight in *Tenant,* but another tale of an artist heroine whose indigent husband leaves her with no recourse but to support herself (and pay his debts) by painting.[23] "Margaret von Ehrenberg, The Artist-Wife" is a novella in William and Mary Howitt's collection of *Stories of English and Foreign Life,* published in 1853 (five years after *Tenant*); it tells the tale of another woman painter whose troubles stem from her being both an artist *and* a wife in an era when married women had few legal rights. Mary and William Howitt were prominent members of the Victorian literary scene. In the 1840s they met Anna Jameson and other celebrities in the European art world. William (1792–1879) and Mary (1799–1888) were writers, editors, and translators, both writing extensively for the periodical press as well as producing translations, children's books, and mediocre three-volume novels. They were, at various times, Quakers, Unitarians, and spiritualists—but at all times they believed firmly in the principle of equality between the sexes. Socially, they moved in the Pre-Raphaelite circle;

politically, Mary Howitt was actively involved in agitation for women's rights and the abolition of slavery. Her eldest daughter, Anna Mary Howitt (whose novella "Sisters in Art" I consider in chap. 4), became friends with the Pre-Raphaelite painter Elizabeth Siddal and with Barbara Leigh Smith; exhibited her works in the Society for Female Artists shows; and occasionally contributed to Leigh Smith's feminist periodical, *The Englishwoman's Journal*.[24]

Given this family history, it is not surprising that the Howitts' novella is an impassioned plea for artistic freedom and gender equality. Margaret, an Englishwoman and a talented painter, marries a charming but slippery German, Baron von Ehrenberg, who encourages Margaret to concentrate solely on portrait painting (portraiture brings in more ready cash, and the Baron is broke), while refusing to acknowledge her much more extraordinary talent in producing historical and allegorical landscapes. He hides from her the great success of two anonymous pictures on historical subjects that she has sent to the great art exhibit in Munich, while exaggerating her reception as a portraitist.[25] Early on in the tale the baron skips town, leaving Margaret to pay his enormous debts herself. In Germany, a wife is held accountable for debts in a husband's name (and vice versa), and our heroine narrowly escapes imprisonment for her husband's profligacy. Margaret asserts to the men who come to arrest her, "The debt is not mine: what possible right, therefore, can exist for your seizing upon my person." And one of the men replies:

"The right which is given us by the law of the Land, Lady Baroness. The debt is your husband's: it is equally the same as if you yourself had contracted it. I should suppose you know . . . that marriage makes man and wife into one flesh and bone—so it matters little which half of the married pair endures the penalties of the law!" (80)

After great pleading, Margaret is permitted to become a prisoner not in jail but in her own home; she pledges repayment of the debt by the proceeds of her art and, evincing prodigious strength, refuses to rise from her easel until the last debt is paid. Rather than having the artistic freedom to practice her skill in the "higher" art forms, Margaret, for money's sake, becomes an extremely popular portrait painter. Her devotion to her art triumphs at least in the material arena—her debts are cleared, her future is secure. Meanwhile the baron has traveled to England with the intent of ingratiating himself with Margaret's wealthy but estranged relatives and succeeds in wheedling himself into the position of beneficiary in the matriarch's will. Conveniently, the baron dies fighting in the 1848 revolution in Paris just days after reaping the financial benefits of his trickery—and Margaret, benefiting at last from her legal status as the baron's wife, inherits the lot.

Similarities to *The Tenant of Wildfell Hall* are arresting. In both texts, profligate husbands become the driving force for the onset of artistic professionalism in their long-suffering spouses. Both Helen and Margaret paint before their respective marriages, but both become fully fledged *professional* women directly because of their husbands' economic tyranny. What was once a matter of amusement becomes a matter of financial importance: as she plots to escape her abusive husband, Helen writes in her journal, "The palette and the easel, my darling playmates once, must be my sober toil-fellows now" (358). Art, in both texts, serves as the representative of "married women's property," and the "artist-wives" (a paradox in itself, for how can a married woman truly exercise any profession, if the fruits of her labor do not belong to her?) must struggle to keep control over their artworks. Though the artworks might be considered as properly belonging to her who *creates* them, Brontë and Howitt show us that the law decrees otherwise. Hence, art must be painstakingly wrested out from underneath the husband's rule.

In *Tenant,* one scene dramatizes the incredible power a husband has over his wife's property, a scene which culminates in his complete control over her artistic productions. Before Helen can flee Huntingdon, he comes upon her one evening as she writes in her journal (the very journal Gilbert Markham, and the reader, is reading). He says, "With your leave, my dear, I'll have a look at this," but his request for permission is ironic, as he then "forcibly wrests" the journal from Helen. What he reads incites him to investigate his wife's apartments: "I'll trouble you for your keys," he tells her, "the keys of your cabinet, desk, drawers, and *whatever else you possess*" (370; emphasis added). Even keys, Brontë seems to say, cannot keep safe anything a married woman might "possess." Just as her private journal is open to her husband, so too her entire material inner life—suggested by the symbolism of the trio of "secret" spaces Arthur Huntingdon plans to investigate (cabinet, desk, drawers)—is open to her husband's eyes. In her desk he finds the money she has earned by secretly selling paintings; when he returns the key to her he tells her,

> There! You'll find nothing gone but your money, and the jewels—and a few little trifles I thought it advisable to take into my own possession, lest your mercantile spirit should be tempted to turn them into gold. I've left you a few sovereigns, which I expect to last you through the month—at all events, when you want more you will be so good as to give me an account of how that's spent. I shall put you upon a small monthly allowance, in future. (372)

If he has taken her money, her jewels, and her "trifles," one wonders what exactly might be left to Helen. The husband's containment of his wife is here explicitly financial: what he wishes to control is her "mercantile spirit" rather than, say, her intellect. Brontë echoes the case of Caroline Norton most powerfully here: Mrs. Norton's punishment for being an independent wife was similarly to be economically constrained.

Huntingdon winds up his harangue in language which makes the sexual nature of his actions clear. He gloats, "It's well I wasn't overfull [drunk] tonight, now I think of it, or I might have snoozed away and never dreamt of looking what *my sweet lady* was about—or I might have lacked the sense or the power to *carry my point like a man,* as I have done" (373; emphasis added). To confiscate one's wife's possessions is to be properly "manly," while "my sweet lady" is put in the position of skulking sneak: the scenario Huntingdon envisions pits a plotting, devious wife against a noble, manly seeker after truth. The sexual innuendoes of this scene should be noted as well: rifling Helen's desk can be read as a form of physical or sexual assault on a woman's "private spaces"—in fact, in the BBC video version of *The Tenant of Wildfell Hall,* Arthur literally rapes his wife after he has emptied her desk. Arthur's boast that his plundering of Helen's possessions is acting "like a man" further affirms the sexual nature of his abduction of Helen's material property.

After thus taking possession of her money or those things—like jewels—which stand directly in for money, Arthur then proceeds to *burn* all Helen's art supplies—canvases, palettes, paint, brushes, everything. This, also, is within his rights, for legally he has simply burned his own possessions. Much of the power of the novel derives from the suppressed rage with which Helen receives these actions. She knows she has no immediate defense against him; instead, her revenge comes in the form of representation (as did Caroline Norton's)—that is, in the diary which makes his iniquities known. Arthur's burning of Helen's artistic paraphernalia registers his understanding that her artwork, like her jewels, is a *marketable commodity* and hence taints his wife with the color of trade: "And so, you thought to disgrace me, did you, by running away and turning artist, and supporting yourself by the labour of your hands?" he asks her after burning her canvases. The disgrace of his wife's becoming an artist seems to outweigh the disgrace of merely running away. Huntingdon fixates on the *physical* marks of such a profession in his concern for Helen's "hands," and again when he continues: "And you though to rob me of my son too, and bring him up to be a dirty Yankee tradesman, or a low, beggarly painter?" (372). Again, it is the physical disgrace of trade or of art as a profession that dismays Huntingdon, rather than the loss of his son.

The class problematic which Helen's profession brings to *Tenant* is overlooked by Terry Eagleton, who like most other critics of *Tenant* finds the novel weaker than those by the other Brontë sisters. Eagleton sees in Anne Brontë's novel a triadic class structure: "a pious heroine is flanked by a morally lax upper class man on the one hand and a principled hero on the other"

(1975, 122). Eagleton is most distressed that neither Helen nor Gilbert can be taken as symbolic of a whole social order and that "the dreariness of Wildfell Hall is symbolic merely of one individual's suffering, not, as with Wuthering Heights, the hardy endurance of a whole class" (152). Helen fails to become a "representative" character along the lines of Catherine or Heathcliff or Hindley; Gilbert too remains more an individual than a marker of one position in the social order. Yet Arthur Huntingdon, who is such a marker, is dismissed as "little more than a stereotype of the traditional wicked aristocrat" (133).

Part of Eagleton's dismissal of *Tenant* as "slighter" than *Jane Eyre* or *Wuthering Heights* stems from the lack of distance in the lovers' social positions: Helen and Gilbert are simply not far enough apart, classwise, for Eagleton to discover a "myth of power" within the narrative of *Tenant*. I would suggest, however, that he is looking in the wrong place. The novel seethes with power struggles, power dynamics—they happen to regard the nexus of *gender* and class, rather than merely social class alone, and issues of gender are alarmingly absent in all Eagleton's work.[26] When Eagleton makes the outrageous claim that Helen's "final union with Gilbert Markham has no representative social significance" (1975, 133), he must have overlooked the remarkable fact that in this courtship scenario, Helen—a woman and now extremely wealthy—proposes to Gilbert, a man of lower-class standing. Any historically inflected reading of the text must take into account the significance of gender, on the one hand, and Helen's distinct and problematic social position as an emergent professional artist.

Similarly, in the Howitt's novella Margaret's social position is also an issue. Paradoxically, Margaret is accepted as an artist in Germany because she is foreign (i.e., English) and hence not bound by the codes of gender behavior expected of other women in the novella—yet simultaneously her relatives in England blame the influence of German mores for Margaret's errant professionalism. These English relatives, unable to accept her "profession," have effectively disowned her; it is only as a stranger in a strange land that Margaret can become an artist. Margaret's Englishness becomes a social and artistic stigma (her paintings are often described by the German spectators as "really clever, but too English, too English!") but also a mark of exemption, of excuse—something that permits her to be eccentric, to be an artist at all. The rigid English disapproval of women artists is exemplified by a young English printseller, who sees Margaret's self-portrait in the exhibit and embarks on an immensely contradictory bit of artistic and cultural criticism:

> Just the thing to engrave for my next volume of the "Beauty"! These foreigners are a deuced deal cleverer than us! Where's an Englishman, say nothing

of an Englishwoman, who would strike you out such a thing as this? Just suit the English taste, too: portrait-like, yet not *like* a portrait; and still without any nonsensical allegory, which these Germans . . . are a deuced deal too fond of! (3; emphasis in original)

This portrait comes, he assumes, from the brush of a German artist—the signature on the painting reads simply "Baroness von Ehrenberg"—even though the style itself is English. As a miscegenated work of art, then, it becomes highly desirable: the German woman artist can be excused both her gender and her nationality because she has been sensible enough to paint according to "the English taste." But when the baron, eager to court the young man's patronage, remarks in his broken English, "All the world will declare the English lady have done something quite *magnifique*," the Englishman shouts in horror: "ENGLISH LADY! ENGLISH LADY! How so, sir? By George! Sir, what do you mean?" When the baron explains that his wife is English, her countryman replies, "That's an unlucky accident, sir, allow me to inform you, a *very* unlucky accident, her ladyship's English birth; it quite alters the aspect of this matter of business" (3). A German woman artist painting in the English style is one thing, and quite marketable—a real live Englishwoman painting in the English style is impossible. Englishwomen cannot be involved in a "matter of business."

V.

Both Margaret's and Helen's eventual successes highlight the possibility that female artists, no matter their personal and legal struggles, might achieve some kind of professional independence. And while the language of painting allows for an aesthetic of independence in these texts, in *Tenant* it also provides a way of articulating female desire. Desire in *Tenant* stems from artistic production: whoever holds the pen or brush generates desire. When, for instance, the various key characters in *Tenant* go together on a picnic excursion to the seashore and Helen tries to slip away to paint, Gilbert cannot help but follow: "I felt myself drawn by an irresistible attraction to that distant point where the fair artist sat and plied her solitary task—and not long did I attempt to resist it" (87). He follows, and as he watches her paint he easily writes her into the position of desirable art object:

[She] sketched away in silence. But I could not help stealing a glance, now and then, from the splendid view at our feet to the elegant white hand that held the pencil, and the graceful neck and glossy raven curls that drooped over the paper. "Now," thought I, "if I had but a pencil and a morsel of paper I could make a lovelier sketch than hers, admitting I had the power to delineate faithfully what is before me." (88)

By the end of this study, such scenes will become extremely, even tediously, familiar. We will hear countless variants of the phrase, "I could have made a lovelier sketch than hers..." made by numerous other male characters as they admire women artists. In Anne Brontë's version, art and artist threaten here to merge entirely: the "view at our feet" melts into Helen's hand, which becomes an aesthetic extension of the pencil; her curls, drooping on the paper, seem to flow into the scene she draws. So far, we have a scene of visual appropriation quite similar to those in which Huntingdon claimed visual authority over Helen's artwork and her self; Brontë shows us that it is Helen who is the beautiful art object in Gilbert's eyes. This scene neatly encodes precisely the danger for women of what Adorno, Siegel, Mitchell, Agamben, and others term the "turn" in nineteenth-century aesthetics from the art object to the artist: in this case the increasing interest in the figure of the artist causes, for women artists, a reabsorption *back* into the role of art object.

Brontë shows her awareness of these aesthetic dangers but also offers ways out of the bind. Helen, when watched by Gilbert in the scene by the shore, remains steadfastly oblivious to this attempt at visual appropriation; Gilbert must report that her first words to him after finishing her sketch are, "Are you still there, Mr. Markham?" Actively painting rather than being painted, Helen becomes, in this scene at least, immune to his aesthetic appropriation. This intent concentration on art has profound benefits for Helen; professionalism allows her to begin short-circuiting the erotic structure of the aesthetic experience such that the woman-as-object can become the woman-as-subject. Similarly, during a conversation about painting with Gilbert, Helen remarks, "I almost wish I were not a painter. For instead of delivering myself up to the full enjoyment of [the delightful touches of nature] as others do, I am always troubling my head about how I could produce the same effect upon canvas; and as that can never be done, it is mere vanity and vexation of spirit" (104–5). The phrase "troubling my head" is usually one of condescension spoken to young girl or woman—as in "Don't trouble your pretty little head about it." Here instead it is made a marker of excess professional thought, an inability to stop the process of aesthetic mediation which in part defines an artist.

But other instances in the novel show that Helen cannot entirely cloak herself in her professionalism; painting is still a dangerously sexy activity, and

Brontë insists that the focus on the artist figure has inextricably troublesome effects on women artists. In another scene, as Gilbert watches Helen sketch, his erotic evaluation of her body again overtakes his aesthetic evaluation of her artworks: "I stood and watched the progress of her pencil: it was a pleasure to behold it so dexterously guided by those fair and graceful fingers" (74–75). I shall merely point to the possible phallic implications of a woman playing with a pencil and go on to note that Helen, this time, does not find it so easy to ignore Gilbert's presence: "Erelong their [the fingers'] dexterity became impaired, they began to hesitate, to tremble slightly, and make false strokes, and then suddenly came to a pause, while their owner laughingly raised her face to mine, and told me that her sketch did not profit by my superintendence" (75). When Helen "raises her face" to Gilbert, one almost expects a kiss to follow, rather than a dismissal. The trembling and hesitation which ostensibly refers to artistic production slides easily into an erotic register. During the course of *Tenant,* Helen (and the reader) learns that painting—because it always seems to require the *presence* of the female body in close proximity to the male viewer—is remarkably dangerous.[27]

VI.

While painting offers Anne Brontë the ultimate test case for negotiating the trials of female aesthetic production in the public sphere, it also allows her to work through a tricky and complex theory of realism and representation. Helen's artwork, as we have seen, teaches us to read the novel's structure; it can also offer insight into just what sort of realist novel Brontë was attempting to write. The prevalence of letters and journals as the raw materials for the novel suggests that Brontë aims at absolute realism, a "true story" feeling. Human artifacts—Helen's diary, letters from Helen to her brother, Gilbert's letter to Halford, and others—tell the tale in place of an omniscient narrator.[28] Anne's preface to the second edition begins by accusing critics of the first edition of being uniformly excessive, both in their praise ("greater than it deserved") and their blame ("it has been censured with an asperity which . . . is more bitter than just"). A defense of her grim realism follows. Brontë insists on her allegiance to faithful mimesis of unpleasant truth over the "delicate concealment of fact" which she claims characterizes her age. As if to counter this tendency toward concealment, the preface is riddled with the language of uncovering, discovery, and depth.[29] Truth is conceived as *aletheia,* the unveiling or making present what has been hidden, in which case "mimesis is the representation necessary to this process, the doubling which enables something to present itself" (Culler 1982, 186). She attempts to make this mimesis as immediate as possible—even though the narrative is a document of memory (Gilbert's letter to Halford), it is also marked insistently with statements of authenticity (Gilbert says he refers to his journal to compile his epic letter; Helen's story told in diary form)—hence the mimesis is as uncorrupted by memory as possible. This reinforces Brontë's urgent desire to present the unvarnished truth of vice, truth uncorrupted by memory or polite euphemism.

She insists that her intent in writing *Tenant* has been "to tell the truth," unsoftened by fictional fantasy:

> I maintain it is better to depict [vice and vicious characters] as they really are than as they would wish to appear. To represent a bad thing in its least offensive light is doubtless the most agreeable course for a writer of fiction to pursue; but is it the most honest, or the safest? Is it better to reveal the snares and pitfalls of life to the young . . . or to cover them with branches and flowers? Oh Reader! If there were less of this delicate concealment of facts . . . (30)

It would seem, then, that Anne Brontë strives for absolute mimetic realism—the faithful delineation of scenes, no matter how distasteful. Critics from both the nineteenth and the twentieth centuries have concurred, praising the novel's "remarkable reality of description" or its "total dedication to truth" (quoted in Goreau 1988, 11–12). But the problem with reality or truth, as Brontë's preface also makes clear, is that it is both elusive and covered with slime:

> But as the priceless treasure [truth] too frequently hides at the bottom of a well, it needs some courage to dive for it, especially as he that does so will be more likely to incur more scorn and obloquy for the mud and water into which he has ventured to plunge, than thanks for the jewel he procures; as, in like manner, she who undertakes the cleansing of a careless bachelor's apartment will be liable to more abuse for the dust she raises, than commendation for the clearance she effects. (29)

The extended simile crosses gender lines abruptly here—we begin with a universal "he" who plunges into the mud after a jewel called truth, and end with a very particular "she" who tidies like a whirlwind through a bachelor's flat. In the one case, a daring male seeker discovers a specific, tangible object of value; in the other, a female servant (the apartment belongs to a bachelor, hence the woman who cleans cannot be his wife, but is most probably hired help) finds truth, strangely, in "clearance"—a nothingness, a blank. Is truth, then, a precious jewel or an empty apartment? When one considers that Brontë's aim in writing *Tenant* was to "depict [vice and vicious characters] as they really are," the image of Brontë as housekeeper becomes more and more comprehensible. Domestic mess is precisely the issue throughout *Tenant:* from Helen's makeshift inhabitation of Wildfell Hall to the debauched lifestyle led by her husband in their marital home, houses contain filth that must be eradicated.

It is also central to this extended metaphor that truth and its attendant slime are often indistinguishable, even interdependent. Truth hides beneath layers of grime which are, to the public eye, indistinguishable from the treasure itself. That is, truth and mud or dust are discovered simultaneously, and the latter seems to outweigh the former in the public opinion. Anne Brontë tropes this inherent duplicity of truth again in the body of the novel, this time in visual form. During Helen's initial courtship with Huntingdon, he amuses himself with Helen's portfolio during an evening's entertainment in the drawing room (the other unmarried young lady, Miss Wilmot, plays the piano for the assembled company; we see similar scenes in which women's amateur art and music are used as social amusement and courtship advertisement in many nineteenth-century novels). While looking at her sketches, Huntingdon discovers his own face drawn on the *reverse* of another (more socially appropriate) drawing. He reexamines all the drawings in Helen's portfolio and discovers that she has (as Helen puts it in her diary) "disfigured the backs of several with abortive attempts to delineate that too fascinating physiognomy" (171). Only one drawing, which Helen calls "an eternal monument to his pride and my humiliation" (173), is completely visible; the others are mere shadowy hints, echoes of "abortive attempts" at portraiture which Helen had subsequently rubbed out. But, as she again says, "The pencil frequently leaves an impression upon cardboard that no amount of rubbing can efface" (171). Huntingdon gloats over his findings, remarking to Helen, "I perceive, the backs of young ladies' drawings, like the postscripts of their letters, are the most important and interesting part of the concern" (172). This scene rings changes on the truth-and-mud metaphor from the preface; Helen's desire for Huntingdon might be said to be the "truth" of these portraits, just as her desire is also the "truth" of the picture with the turtledoves I discussed at the beginning of this chapter. But this truth is distasteful, as the terms "disfigured," "abortive," and "humiliation" make clear (certainly this desire leads directly to Helen's miserable and abusive marriage). Like fiction, visual art offers a way to present unvarnished, but dangerous and distasteful, truths.

Gilbert and Gubar read Helen's double-drawing (one proper picture for public consumption on the front of the sheet, one secret tracing of illicit desire on the back) as a simultaneous self-repression and self-expression: "She produces a public art which she herself rejects as inadequate but which she secretly uses to discover a new aesthetic space for herself" (2000, 81). They also argue, "Whether Helen covertly uses a supposedly modest young lady's 'accomplishments' for unladylike self-expression or publicly flaunts her professionalism and independence, she must in some sense deny or conceal her own art, or at least deny the self-assertion explicit in her art" (ibid.). Gilbert and Gubar then make this scene allegorical and argue that women artists in general (and writers in particular) "withdraw behind their art even while they assert themselves through it, as if deliberately adopting Helen Graham's duplicitous techniques of self-expression" (82). Certainly, Helen's double-drawing can be read as a simultaneous withdrawal-behind and assertion-through art. However, in *Tenant,* as in many of the other novels of the period featuring women artists, the withdrawal is explicitly, even aggressively, critiqued and rejected. Again, in *Tenant* we must return to the narrative structure of the novel to make this clear. Because of the reverse chronology of the frame narrative, we see Helen "publicly flaunt her professionalism and independence," in Gilbert and Gubar's words, well *before* we see her as a young woman who must resort to hiding her desires on the back of her sketches. Furthermore, in her adult, professional life, Helen is attempting to almost literally overturn the sexual and aesthetic "mistakes" of her younger self. Brontë makes it quite clear that the young Helen's withdrawal behind art leads directly to disaster.

Just as the sketches of Huntingdon haunt the backsides of other work in her portfolio, so too does the formal painted portrait of him done early in their marriage haunt Helen after she flees to Wildfell Hall. When she unpacks her paintings at Wildfell, Helen discovers that her maidservant Rachel has inadvertently packed the portrait; Helen writes, "It struck me with dismay . . . when I beheld those eyes fixed upon me in their mocking mirth, as if exulting, still, in his power to control my fate, and deriding my efforts to escape" (398). She says, significantly, that "the frame, however, is handsome enough; it will serve for another painting" (398), suggesting that she has some kind of artistic control (she is the "frame narrator" of this portrait at least) over the raw material that is Huntingdon's portrait (this distinction between frame/form and raw material will become important again in a moment). But, surprisingly, Helen refuses simply to destroy the painting—not for sentimental reasons regarding its subject, but rather because she needs it as a template against which to measure the development of her son: "I have put it aside," she writes, "chiefly that I may compare my son's features and countenance with this, as he grows up, and thus be enabled to judge how much or how little he resembles his father—if I may be allowed to keep him with me still, and never to behold that father's face again" (398). In Anne Brontë's terms, the portrait is the "truth" that should not be hidden, no matter what slime attends it.

We can usefully align Helen's concern for the appearance of her son with her artistic production. It's nothing new to consider the products of creativity as metaphoric children, of course, but Brontë deepens this comparison by implicating Arthur Junior in the textual negotiations of mimesis. Huntingdon complains that his wife is raising their child to be *girlish*—that is, in her own image. Huntingdon's attempts to give his son an early taste for wine, women, and song show the father's impulse to equally create his son in *his* own image. The battle over their son becomes a battle over mimesis. Marie-Hélène Huet claims that the theory of generation "has always been a theory of art" (1993, 95), all the way back to Aristotle, who believed that conception was essentially a man having an idea in a woman. The man is idea, form, stamp—the woman is receptacle, matter, flesh. Thus in Aristotle's model, children are copies of their *male* parent—his "stamp" should be apparent on the flesh of the child, as it should also be on a work of art. Any child that didn't resemble its father was a monstrosity; furthermore, writes Aristotle, "The first beginning of this deviation is when a female is formed instead of a male" (*Generation of Animals* 4.3.401; quoted in Huet 1993, 223). According to this model, the father is the true parent, the one who imprints the child, while the mother performs the function of container, the unformed material which receives this imprint passively. Occasionally, a woman transgressively stamps the child in her own image. Renaissance theories of monstrosity, for instance, blamed the mother's "impressionable and desirous imagination for imprinting the embryo with an image other than the father's" (namely, her own image) (ibid. 4).[30]

Helen's obsessive concern that her child betray no likeness to his father (which shows up throughout the novel in numerous ways) indicates the extent of Brontë's manipulation of the traditional association of form with the masculine. The last we see of Arthur Junior suggests that Helen has won this battle: Gilbert remarks that when he has grown into a young man he has "his mother's image visibly stamped upon his fair, intelligent features" (479). Helen succeeds in rearticulating the Aristotelian and traditional dynamic of both aesthetic and sexual generation by claiming the right to be the master framer and form-giver rather than the passive vessel. By the end of the novel, Brontë has put Helen in control of her son, her artwork, her now deceased husband's property (which originally came from Helen's family anyway), and her erotic life: she proposes to Gilbert in the final chapter. The scene involves a symbolic statement by Helen that brings us right back to her earlier turtledove painting: to make it clear that she wants to marry Gilbert, Helen reaches out the window to grab a rose that is blooming bravely amid the snow. She hands it to him, saying, "This rose is not so fragrant as a summer flower, but it has stood through hardships none of *them* would bear. . . . Look, Gilbert, it is still fresh and blooming as a flower can be, with the cold snow even now on its petals. Will you have it?" (484). Gilbert's blockheaded lack of comprehension of this gesture (she has to tell him point-blank "The rose I gave you was an emblem of my heart" [485]) is certainly annoying but can be interpreted as a positive trait in comparison with Huntingdon's earlier immediate interpretation of Helen's painting as emblematic of her younger heart. An older, wiser Helen has chosen a new partner who doesn't interpret *everything* as emblematic of the female body.

The Tenant of Wildfell Hall, then, traces a movement away from what we might call a body-based aesthetic; Anne Brontë urges her artist heroine gradually away from a self-expressive mode of art—a mode which has brought her nothing but trouble. As we shall see in chapter 3, Anne's sister Charlotte also saw painting as a form of personal rebellion for women but offers a more positive spin on self-expressive art. In *Jane Eyre,* painting becomes a positive conduit for female self-expression as well as a locus for social critique.

Chapter Three

Ekphrasis and the Art of Courtship in *Jane Eyre*

I.

CRITICS MORE OFTEN think of Jane Eyre as a reader than as a painter; she has proved a central example of the Victorian "reading woman" discussed by so many recent scholars. Reading for Jane is dangerous and empowering simultaneously; Charlotte Brontë's representation of Jane's experience of reading participates in the dominant cultural discourse on women readers, which saw in the reading process evidence of a possibly radical subjectivity for women. In her study of the cultural meaning of the woman reader in the period 1837–1914, Kate Flint (2000) argues that the self-absorption of the reading woman hinted at a dangerous interiority, potentially disruptive of social codes of femininity; Flint sees visual and textual representations of women reading as consistently negotiating this possible interiority. Within the scene of reading, the woman reader withdraws into herself, just as Jane withdraws into the curtained recess at Gateshead. The scene of reading in literature and art becomes, in the words of Mary Jacobus, a "temporary form of madness" which is necessarily both frightening and potentially empowering (1997, 13). Reading becomes a space that "involves concepts or unconscious phantasies of inner and outer, absence and boundaries" (9). Jane's reading does precisely this: at the opening of the novel, it introduces a heroine whose imaginative interiority is nothing if not socially disruptive. Mark Hennelly writes that Jane's reading is a "retreat from life"; reading becomes "an act of individualism and imaginative rebellion against the confining circumstances of her life" (1984, 695). Similarly, Patrick Brantlinger argues that Jane's reading is an escape from the Reed family (1998, 116). Sicherman argues in general that reading was a way for women to exempt themselves from social obligations and gender norms (1989, 201–2), and Golden concurs that Jane "indulges in independent reading, a delicious but dangerous act" (2003, 53).

Yet even if Jane is the woman reader *par excellence,* Brontë still insists on making Jane a viewer of images in the novel's opening pages and, later, a producer of images as well as a reader of texts. Gayatri Spivak, in her essay famous for its exposé of Imperialism in women's fiction, offers a brief analysis of the curious presence of the visual in *Jane Eyre.* Spivak notes that while supposedly "reading" Bewick's book in the novel's first scene, Jane's attention is actually more focused on the pictures in the book she holds: "She cares little for reading what is *meant* to be read: the 'letterpress.' *She* reads the pictures." Spivak terms this practice of reading only the pictures a "singular hermeneutics" and links it to Jane's study of the outside scene beyond the glass: both ways of "reading" "can make the outside inside" (1985, 246).

Numerous critics have picked up on Spivak's hint and traced a wealth of visual references in the novel. Before Spivak's landmark essay, Gilbert and Gubar's equally seminal reading of the novel focused attention on the blinding of Rochester, an event generally now read as Brontë's radical demolishing of masculine power troped as sight.[1] *Jane Eyre* is in fact shot through with the language of vision; the verbal texture of the novel is built on references to sight perception, both in its literal manifestation as bodily vision but also metaphorically in the sense that the entire novel might be read as a justification of Jane's "point of view." During Jane's roof-walk in chapter 12, she articulates a powerful statement of the metaphorical force of seeing: she looks out across the fields beyond Thornfield and says, "Then I longed for a power of vision which might overpass that limit; which might reach the busy world" (*Jane Eyre,* 95).[2] Since her eyes cannot *physically* see beyond the farthest hill, however, Jane turns her steps inside and her sight inward: "My sole relief was to walk along the corridor of the third story . . . safe in the silence and solitude of the spot and *allow my mind's eye to dwell on whatever visions rose before it*" (95; emphasis added). In this same scene, Jane articulates her loudest feminist manifesto, beginning, "Women feel just as men feel; they need exercise for their faculties and a field for their efforts" (96). The vision of equality seen in Jane's "mind's eye" becomes, as her autobiography progresses, increasingly fulfilled; her marriage results in her becoming quite literally Rochester's "mind's eye," his only access to the visual world.

Saying that *Jane Eyre* is a visually rich novel—both in its stylistic content and its thematic obsessions—is nothing new; its strong pictorial quality is one of the things that early critics liked best about it. George Henry Lewes, in his review of *Jane Eyre* in *Fraser's Magazine* (1847), was but the first of many critics to note the strong visual elements of Brontë's novel. More recently, Lawrence Starzyk has argued for "the centrality of the pictorial in the development of [Jane's] world view" and insisted with good cause that the entirety of *Jane Eyre* is a "verbal exegesis of the mute images stored in Jane's museum of memory" (1991, 289). Similarly, Christine Alexander, in her productive research into Brontë's early artistic endeavors, found sources for Brontë's "fondness for the vignette, her method of analyzing a scene as if it were a painting, and her tendency to structure the novel as if it were a portfolio of paintings" (Alexander and Sellars 1995, 56). Alexander writes of Charlotte's intense fascination for the visual arts: "It is not too strong to say that Charlotte Brontë had a fetish for pictures" (37). Elizabeth Gaskell reports that Charlotte's school friend Mary Taylor said of Charlotte, "Whenever an opportunity offered of examining a picture or cut [woodcut engraving] of any kind, she went over it piecemeal, with her eyes close to the paper, looking so long that we used to ask her 'what she saw in it.' She could always see plenty, and explained it very well" (Gaskell 1996, 109). Charlotte's juvenilia reveal, too, her early fascination with pictures, portraits in particular. It seems unsurprising, then, that her novels would be—as they are—so filled with pictures. *Jane Eyre* in particular offers us a wealth of works of visual art.

Several of the artworks in *Jane Eyre* have been thoroughly discussed by critics, who have not overlooked the novel's opening fascination with the illustrations of Bewick nor failed to see in Jane's three strange and surreal paintings in chapter 13 a microcosm of themes and images from the rest of the novel. Bewick's illustrations and Jane's three watercolors are not, however, the only instances where pictures matter, although they have received the bulk of critical attention. Jane also produces a self-portrait in charcoal, an ivory miniature of Blanche Ingram, pictures of Georgiana and Eliza Reed, a sketch of Rochester, four more eerie sketches while visiting Mrs. Reed's deathbed, and a formal portrait of Rosamund Oliver.

Jane's artworks are generally, and I think correctly, read as symbolic manifestations of her psyche. Alison Byerly writes, "To represent an inner reality that might otherwise remain hidden . . . the fantastic watercolor pictures painted by Jane Eyre, though not realistic in the sense of reproducing the physical world, are psychologically true to Jane's state of mind" (1997, 93–94). Likewise Jane's charcoal sketch of herself when confronted by the imminent arrival of Blanche works as an indicator of Jane's self-critical mood, as does her picture of Rochester drawn from memory during her visit to Gateshead at Mrs. Reed's death. But I wish to argue here that Jane's paintings can be read as more than symbolic monuments. Just as Helen Graham's work in Anne

Brontë's *The Tenant of Wildfell Hall* has significance beyond the biographical, so too does Jane's work. Art in Charlotte Brontë's novel is an expression of the heroine's psyche, certainly, but it also works to perform a powerful social and aesthetic critique.

Charlotte Brontë would have been heavily invested in the cultural politics of women and the visual arts. She herself wished to be a painter before her eyesight failed and she turned to writing. But even after her decision to give up painting, Charlotte and all the Brontë siblings were thoroughly knowledgeable about the visual arts, a fact attested to by the frequent appearance of scenes of painting in Charlotte and Anne Brontë's novels. As children the Brontës had access to numerous engravings of famous paintings, as well as several drawing masters; in her adult life Charlotte regularly visited galleries in London. Being a painter was, for Brontë, an unfulfilled fantasy; giving her heroine success in this realm was certainly one way to explore missed opportunities for self-expression. The power of the painter, however, comes not only from her ability to express herself in paint; it also comes from the curious ability of paintings as objects to reconfigure certain social situations. By looking at the scenes in which paintings occur (rather than simply reading the paintings iconographically), I will try to suggest ways in which Brontë uses her heroine's artworks to comment on gender and class politics. Persisting in symbolic or allegorical readings leads us to miss the intense social and historical ramifications of painting that Jane's artwork allows Brontë to explore; pictures are conduits through which Brontë makes substantive commentary not only on Jane's psyche but also on issues of gender, class, representation, and aesthetics. Critics who read the paintings as mere conduits to Jane's "real" inner self fetishize the pictures, worshiping them as stand-ins for Jane's ultimately inaccessible true self (as Rochester, at one point, does).[3] I attempt here to consider the whole aesthetic package—the picture, its circumstances of production, and the scenarios of consumption, viewing, interpretation, and judgment which Brontë offers—to suggest that women's art not merely reveals private vision but instead participates in a public exhibition in which a female artistic force (embodied by Jane) must grapple with the dangers of sexual objectification, social disenfranchisement, and aesthetic regimentation.

I also argue that Brontë endows Jane with the power of ekphrasis, a specifically narrative power. *Jane Eyre* thus functions as a powerful defense of ekphrasis as a literary mode particularly suited to articulate female power. If ekphrasis, as I discussed in the introduction, is traditionally a way of controlling a female image, Brontë radically rewrites this to allow her heroine control over both the production *and* the description of the image.[4] We must always keep in mind the fact that it is Jane describing her paintings; these paintings are in a sense ekphrastic exercises rather than visual artworks. In other words, the narrative voice knows that we, the readers, cannot see the artworks in question, and she seems to relish her power of stopping the narrative to describe them to our verbal vision. In *Jane Eyre*, she who sees and paints is also she who describes, giving the heroine an unprecedented consolidation of representational power. Since Jane's paintings become such important texts, Jane's descriptions of her own artworks serve to replicate Jane, to multiply the textual sites which "envoice" (to use Heffernan's [1993] term) Jane. In masculine ekphrastic texts from Homer to Keats, the "feminine" art object is effaced (if incompletely) by the voice of the masculine ekphrastic subject, whose ability to describe something Other (the artwork) confers a kind of power of possession or knowledge. In *Jane Eyre*, Jane's ability to describe—and she is the only one who can—her *own* artwork gives her a double power: to create and to recreate in words. The relationship between word and image never becomes paragonal; rather, the two become necessary partners in the construction of an all-powerful female subject.

The scene of painting and ekphrastic description which is played out again and again in the novel foregrounds Jane's role as a *producer* of visual artifacts, a maker of things that are seen.[5] The various pictures Jane produces are moments—indeed, monuments—in a trajectory toward visual independence that requires Jane to *generate* visual images rather than simply reproduce them. Given the preponderance of visual productions that Jane offers, the much-noted emphasis on the visual in *Jane Eyre* should not be limited to metaphors of eyes or vision or to pictorial representations of landscapes or interior scenes. Rather, in *Jane Eyre* a woman's point of view emanates from behind the brush, so to speak; at critical moments throughout the novel, Jane represents herself as a representer, as one whose power depends on her prowess at visual representation. And Charlotte Brontë—like her sister Anne—imagines as an extraordinarily seductive medium, although Charlotte celebrates this seduction rather than offers it as a warning. This power is then compounded by the ekphrastic power that Jane wields when she translates her own works of visual representation into words, thereby controlling their interpretation.

II.

Near the end of *Jane Eyre*, Jane (living now as Jane Elliot in her own cottage near her cousins' house and working independently as a schoolteacher) paints a miniature portrait of Rosamond Oliver, the beautiful daughter of the local squire. Unlike all of Jane's previous artwork, this portrait has been formally sat for by the subject; it is not generated by fantasy or memory. Furthermore, it is painted (again unlike her previous artwork) explicitly for others, and possibly (although Brontë does not tell us so explicitly) for financial gain. Before finishing the portrait and giving it to Rosamund's father, however, Jane amuses herself by perversely torturing St. John Rivers with it, forcing him to let down his defenses and admit his desire for the portrait's original. Seeing his close attention to the image, Jane offers to paint him a "careful and faithful duplicate" (327); when he avers that this would not be "judicious or wise," she remarks bluntly that it would be "wiser and more judicious if you were to take to yourself the original at once" (328). Jane's insistence that Rosamund loves Rivers causes him to indulge in a brief fantasy (precisely timed by his watch); he muses,

> I see myself stretched on an ottoman in the drawing-room at Vale Hall, at my bride Rosamond Oliver's feet: she is talking to me with her sweet voice—gazing down on me with those eyes your skilful hand has copied so well—smiling at me with these coral lips. She is mine—I am hers . . . Hush! Say nothing—my heart is full of delight—my senses are entranced—let the time I marked pass in peace. (328)

One can certainly understand Plato's point of view on the danger of the visual arts. The portrait of Rosamond Oliver functions here as a traditional kind of seduction; it is a stand-in for a real object (a beautiful woman in this case) which elicits erotic desire and leads the viewer (Rivers) momentarily away from the path of truth (not Plato's truth in this case, but Rivers's Christian truth). Jane's advice to "take to yourself the original at once" tells us that she wants the image to function as a conduit for desire, a conduit running from the original through the image to the viewer. The scene is reminiscent of a more farcical one in Jane Austen's *Emma,* where the heroine's attempt to create desire for Harriet Smith in Mr. Elton by painting Harriet's portrait fails spectacularly—Mr. Elton turns his attention not on the image's original (namely Harriet), but on the image's producer (Emma). In *Jane Eyre,* too, desire fails to accrue to the image but adheres instead to the woman artist.

To rouse himself from the sensual reverie inspired by the portrait, Rivers draws a sheet of paper over the portrait, covering temptation—and in the process sees, on the covering sheet, Jane's real surname: Eyre. The portrait of Miss Oliver becomes the way Rivers discovers Jane's true identity, and hence her relationship to himself and her eventual legacy. Brontë suggests that art's final purpose is not to provide an object for male delectation or masculine ekphrasis but, rather, to function as a carrier of female identity. The scene thus works as a short parable of Brontë's views on the purpose of women's art: something that leads back to the self rather than (as in *Tenant*) works as a protective shield. The portrait elicits all the elements of a traditional ekphrasis of an image of a beautiful woman: first, both Jane and Rivers perform the stock idealizing "blazon" with the image, breaking Miss Oliver down into component parts by detailing her lips, hair, and eyes in sequence (326–27).[6] Next, Rivers's ekphrasis transforms explicitly into *enargia*, a kind of rhetorical ekphrasis which uses detailed sensory description to make an object appear alive for the reader; Rivers says of the portrait, "It smiles!" (327) and goes on to detail the very physical effects it has on him. The portrait also perfectly expresses the gender politics of classic ekphrasis: the image smiles and seems to be given a voice by those describing it—yet it is eventually silenced and rejected by the viewer. In Brontë's narrative, however, this is not simply because the voices doing the ekphrasis are exercising their masculine control over the image (although in both Rivers's and Jane's cases this is indeed true). Rather, Brontë suggests that the image is silenced because the *artist* who created it takes over and speaks through the image. For all the power the image possesses, Jane and Rivers are able to indulge only momentarily in the fantasy of art as a field of seduction in which the viewer is sated by the depicted *object*. Rivers rejects both the image of Rosamond and the woman herself; when he does wish to take a wife, it is Jane whom he asks. Not, certainly, for love or desire, but for those qualities that make her a good artist and would make her a good missionary. Rivers says explicitly, "There is something brave in your spirit, as well as penetrating in your eye . . . I honour endurance, perseverance, industry, talent . . ." (330). What the portrait of Rosamund finally "says" about Jane is not just that Jane is a good artist and hence would make a good missionary's wife. Rather, this portrait's most critical job is to announce Jane's name—which becomes her direct ticket to wealth and family. The portrait proclaims her social position, not her psychic identity.

Similarly, Jane's three wild watercolor paintings—the focus of the bulk of critical attention given to artwork in the novel—can be read as part of a social game rather than a psychological one. Readers first "see" these watercolors during Jane's first formal meeting with Rochester (not their more unconventional first meeting outside when he falls from his horse), who has summoned his new governess to appear before him in the drawing room upon his return to Thornfield. During the course of the evening he catechizes Jane thoroughly, forcing her to display her skills in music and art. He asks her first to play the piano for him, and after dismissing her playing with "Enough! You play a little, I see, like any other English schoolgirl" (109), he demands to see her "portfolio" of artworks.

Three of the items in the portfolio catch his attention: three watercolors with eerie subjects. I do not intend to offer a close reading of the paintings themselves, but it is, I think, necessary to remind the reader of the content of Jane's pictures, so I quote the description in full:

> While he is so occupied I will tell you, reader, what they are: and first, I must premise that they are nothing wonderful. The subjects had, indeed, risen vividly on my mind. As I saw them with the spiritual eye, before I attempted to embody them, they were striking; but my hand would not second my fancy, and in each case it had wrought out but a pale portrait of the thing I had conceived.
>
> These pictures were in water-colors. The first represented clouds low and vivid, rolling over a swollen sea: all the distance was in eclipse; so, too, was the foreground; or, rather, the nearest billows, for there was no land. One gleam of light lifted into relief a half-submerged mast, on which sat a cormorant, dark and large, with wings flecked with foam: its beak held a gold bracelet, set with gems, that I had touched with as brilliant tints as my palette could yield, and as glittering distinctness as my pencil could impart. Sinking below the bird and mast, a drowned corpse glanced through the green water; a fair arm was the only limb clearly visible, whence the bracelet had been washed or torn.
>
> The second picture contained for foreground only the dim peak of a hill, with grass and some leaves slanting as if by a breeze. Beyond and above spread an expanse of sky, dark blue as at twilight: rising into the sky was a woman's shape to the bust, portrayed in tints as dusk and soft as I could combine. The dim forehead was crowned with a star; the lineaments below were seen as through the suffusion of vapour; the eyes shone dark and wild; the hair streamed shadowy, like a beamless cloud torn by storm or by electric travail. On the neck lay a pale reflection like moonlight; the same faint lustre touched the train of thin clouds from which rose and bowed this vision on the Evening Star.
>
> The third showed the pinnacle of an iceberg piercing a polar winter sky: a muster of northern lights reared their dim lances, close serried, along the horizon. Throwing these into distance, rose, in the foreground, a head,—a colossal head, inclined towards the iceberg, and resting against it. Two thin hands, joined under the forehead, and supporting it, drew up before the lower features a sable veil; a brow quite bloodless, white as bone, and an eye hollow and fixed, blank of meaning but for the glassiness of despair, alone were visible. Above the temples, amidst wreathed turban folds of black drapery, vague in its character and consistency as cloud, gleamed a ring of white

flame, gemmed with sparkles of a more lurid tinge. This pale crescent was "The likeness of a Kingly crown" what it diademed was "the shape which shape had none." (212)

Once quoted, the paintings cannot pass entirely without comment. To my mind, the most striking thing about these paintings is that each one hints at the representation of unrepresentable things. All the pictures gesture toward things below the surface, things outside the realm of visual representation. Jane can paint only the unsubmerged half of the "half-submerged mast," yet her verbal description of it focuses on what is *beneath* the surface—submerged icebergs and sunken ships. Similarly, though she paints clearly only that part of the drowned corpse which is above water, she makes it equally clear that there is more that floats below ("The fair arm was the only limb clearly visible . . .") but that this has not been painted (because it cannot be). Likewise, in the next painting, the body of the evening star is drawn in detail only from the bust up, while the "lineaments below were seen as through the suffusion of vapour." In the third painting, the vision of the "pinnacle of an iceberg" suggests inevitably the bulk of ice that lies hidden below the surface—and the "colossal head" that rests against the iceberg must have a body attached to it, also below the surface.[7]

Given the repeated visual fascination with things below the surface, it is not surprising that these paintings are regularly taken as evidence of Jane's subconscious mind—her own submerged emotions.[8] But rather than persist in this kind of undeniable symbolic reading, I would suggest that the obsession with things hidden can also direct the reader toward investigating what is hidden in the scene as a whole; we should not let the strangeness of the images shunt us away from the business of Rochester's interview with his governess. What narrative work do the paintings do in this meeting with Rochester? A portfolio of drawings or watercolors like the one Jane opens for Rochester was something all eligible young women of the time (and of a certain class, to which Jane does not belong—but more on that in a moment) needed to be able to trot out for prospective suitors, in much the same way as young women played piano for the entertainment of visitors. We see dozens of such scenes across nineteenth-century literature, scenes in which women show off their "accomplishments" in music or art for the benefit of prospective lovers. In *The Tenant of Wildfell Hall,* for example, Helen records an evening party in which she and her rival for Huntingdon's affections were as a matter of course expected to display their accomplishments to the company:

> In the course of the evening, Miss Wilmot was called upon to sing and play for the amusement of the company, and I to exhibit my drawings, and,

though he likes music, and she is an accomplished musician, I think I am right in affirming that he paid more attention to my drawings than to her music. (*Tenant*, 171)

Here accomplishment is linked directly to desirability: the "he" in this passage, Arthur Huntingdon, registers his desire for one woman over another by his response to their aesthetic production. This scenario enables women to remain the "real" objects of desire; aesthetic activity is anesthetized, becoming a conduit through which women are visible as sexual partners. When the heroine of *Tenant* writes that Huntingdon "paid more attention to my drawings than to her music," she is saying, in essence, "he paid more attention to *me*." As Ann Bermingham writes, "Accomplishments provided an occasion for women to display themselves while denying that this was, in fact, what was happening. Men, in turn, could look while seeming to listen, or size up a woman while appearing to judge a drawing. Accomplishments were intended to arouse masculine desire, yet desire could now be masked and displaced as a detached aesthetic judgment" (2000, 184).

In *Jane Eyre*, the traditional art-as-courtship scene of *The Tenant of Wildfell Hall* is radically and ironically rewritten; Charlotte Brontë offers a decided twist on a stock scene.[9] Rather than viewing her portfolio in a parlor scene redolent with the potential for courtship, Rochester here views Jane's "accomplishments" with an eye to their marketable use in her role as a paid governess. We might first consider the word "portfolio," which in its most common meaning refers to a "receptacle for keeping loose sheets of paper, prints, drawings ... or the like" (*OED*). While "portfolio" in the economic sense of a "collection of securities" did not come into common use until the 1930s, the word nevertheless possessed a secondary, business connotation in the early 1800s: a portfolio was a "receptacle containing the official documents of a state department" (*OED*), and this scene with Rochester has an inescapably businesslike component. Jane brings out her portfolio of accomplishments for her employer's judgment: as with her piano-playing, Rochester is evaluating Jane's qualifications for the position of *governess*—not, as in *Emma* or *Tenant*, a prospective sexual partner.

By linking courtship with a job interview, Brontë highlights the fact that courtship is, in essence, a financial transaction—a scene like the one in *Tenant*, for instance, cannot escape being a business transaction in which men look at women and decide whether or not to "buy" them—that is, marry them. Rochester already has experience in the art of love-as-business: his first marriage with Bertha Mason was essentially a financial transaction arranged by his family.

So a traditional scene of courtship is rewritten as a business deal, where the old roles of male suitor and young woman are replaced by employer and employee. Yet Brontë's manipulation of the art-as-courtship scene does not end with this social critique. For Rochester *is* evaluating Jane as a future sexual partner. The scene is doubly ironic, because a young woman's art accomplishments *do* succeed in seducing a suitor. Jane's artistic style may not be particularly suitable for a proper Victorian governess, but it certainly catches Rochester's (erotic) attention. Significantly, we never see Jane teaching Adele to draw or paint; skill in these may be part of the professional qualification of a governess, but either Adele is too young yet to study them or Rochester decides that drawing drowned corpses or hollow-eyed colossal heads is not appropriate for his ward.

While Brontë transforms a traditional courtship scene to critique popular conceptions of the role of women's artwork in an economy of courtship and desire (as well as in narrative itself), she also repudiates prevailing aesthetic models by making Jane's artwork stem from Jane's imagination rather than from external models. When Rochester sets the paintings before him and questions Jane, their dialogue raises in sequence other key elements of Jane's revision of the traditions of female art:

> "I perceive these pictures were done by one hand: was that hand yours?"
> "Yes."
> "And when did you find time to do them? They have taken much time, and some thought."
> "I did them in the last two vacations I spent at Lowood, when I had no other occupation."
> "Where did you get your copies?"
> "Out of my head."
> "That head I see now on your shoulders?"
> "Yes, sir."
> "Has it other furniture of the same kind within?"
> "I should think it may have: I should hope—better." (109–10)

Rochester takes Jane's paintings as part of her "mental furniture," as part of an interior space in which she lives.[10] Rochester has assumed that her artworks, like those of most schoolgirls at the time, were replicas of drawings in public circulation, but Jane's come "out of [her] head." Standard art education for young women involved first tracing and then copying a standard series of engravings or prints of famous artworks or landscape drawings. Charlotte Brontë did a lot of this copying; the Brontë museum exhibits several of her sketches of various churches and buildings alongside almost identical ones by

Charlotte's classmates—hence one assumes all the students copied from one print. Only after a student was proficient in copying would she be allowed to take the next step: drawing from nature. Popular drawing manuals of the time followed similar patterns. After copying from sketches of trees and ruined cottages, Ruskin's *Elements of Drawing* (1857) introduces you to nature by asking you to painstakingly draw a *rock* for weeks at a time. Absolute fidelity to nature was the main tenet of amateur art education. But Brontë rejects this kind of training for Jane.

Rochester reacts to the unusual subject matter of Jane's art by acknowledging that "the drawings are, for a schoolgirl, peculiar. As to the thoughts [which inspired the drawings], they are elfish" (112). It is not the first or the last time Rochester will refer to Jane as an elf, sprite, goblin, or another *small* otherworldly creature, but the drawings offer him visible proof of Jane's radically unusual interior. Rochester's description of Jane's thoughts as "elfish" and her person as small (he repeatedly makes reference to her size) is countered by the *colossal* nature of Jane's paintings: huge birds, icebergs, an enormous head. Jane's own head has provided subject matter that rejects her own external appearance as well as what is seen as proper for women in the nineteenth century.

That a woman might get her copies "out of her head" posed a considerable threat to aesthetic models. That champion of precise drawing from nature, Ruskin, writes in 1857 to Anna Blunden—a Victorian woman artist, active contributor to galleries and exhibitor in the Royal Academy, and one of Ruskin's disciples—after she has exhibited a piece which, in his mind, came a little bit too much out of her own head (or in this case, heart):

> As far as I know lady painters they *always* let their feelings run away with them. If you were my pupil . . . I should at once forbid all sentiment for a couple of years and set you to paint, first,—a plain white cambric pocket handkerchief—or linen napkin, thrown at random on the table, and *kept there*—till finished—taking about a week's hard work to said pocket-handkerchief. Then a coloured one, with a simple pattern. Then an apple. Then a child's cheek—perhaps two inches of it—if you were very good—I would give you a bit of lip—as much as would take half a smile. Then a curl or two of golden hair—putting you back to bricks the moment I saw you getting sentimental. If you won't do this I can't much help you—but I should think that you would be able to please many people by your pretty feeling for expression. (Ruskin 1972, 90–91; emphasis in original)

The slow process of drawing—from handkerchief to apple to cheek to lip—

seems to tantalize us with the promise of more and more *body* if we are "very good." The *OED* records 1821 as the earliest instance in its records of the slang sense of "giving lip" to mean "saucy talk or impudence"; certainly what is at stake here is Blunden's talking back to the great master and his rather violent ("putting you back to bricks") reaction to her sentimental art. Ruskin's critique of feminine art is that it is too self-expressive: "lady painters . . . *always* let their feelings run away with them" (emphasis in original) rather than focusing on painting basic, tangible reality in the form of apples and bricks.

Ruskin would definitely put Jane "back to bricks." By making Jane's artwork radically nonrealistic and overly self-expressive, Brontë overturns prevailing aesthetic models for women, particularly those that attempted to prescribe the subject matter of women's art. Still lives, detailed nature painting, portraits of children or animals, and domestic scenes were considered suitable for women artists; large-scale history paintings, nudes, and imaginative art of any sort were unacceptable—and, indeed, quite rare. In Ruskin's letter to Anna Blunden, we see this narrow focus on natural objects (apples), domestic interiors (a napkin on a table), and portraits (the child). Similarly, the *Athenaeum* review of the second Society for Female Artists exhibit in 1858 assesses the character of women's art at mid-century:

> Summing up the characteristics of female art, we find it tender and refined, but essentially unimaginative, restricted, patient, dealing chiefly with Blenheim spaniels, Castles of Chilon, roses, firstborns, camellias, ball-dresses, copies and miniatures. As to truth, detail, patience and love, it is capable of every triumph, but it can never reach the robust or the exalted.[11]

"Truth, detail, patience and love" are precisely what Ruskin demands of Anna Blunden, and he offers just such a constricted series of subjects for women to paint. The litany of subject matter detailed by the *Athenaeum* reviewer throws the strangeness of Jane's paintings into further relief; pictures of drowned corpses and colossal ghostly heads leaning on icebergs were simply not exhibited by women in mid-century Britain. Nor, if we recall the *Punch* article discussed in chapter 1, would such subjects fit neatly into the ideological system that critics developed to account for women's art.[12]

Jane's paintings, as well as separating her out from the accepted traditions of female artistry, also write her into an unusual class position. Genre realism—pure representation of everyday events—was considered considerably less highbrow than, say, history-painting (which in theory required education and an elevated mind to appreciate). Charles Eastlake, nephew of the R.A.

president of the same name, writes in his introduction to *Hints on Household Taste* of the universality of realist art: take, he suggests, an average-educated man "who had never chanced to reckon a painter among his intimate friends" and take him to a

> second-rate modern exhibition, and afterwards to the collection of old masters which now forms our National Gallery. Can anyone doubt that he would prefer the most literal representations of contemporary life to the ideal treatment of the classical schools? The cheapest form of sentiment embodied in a modern picture, so long as it seemed to realize scenes, incidents and actions which he was accustomed to see about him, would at once appeal to his imagination and interest his eye. (1868, 2)

Realism was seen as something "for the masses," certainly, but more particularly for the *uneducated* in art. Art is not something people were imagined to have an innate feeling for but must be taught to enjoy. (Eastlake's book, which I discuss more thoroughly in chapter 4, is a contribution to the education of taste in interior design.) By representing Jane's art as decidedly not "the most literal representations of contemporary life"—and by tracing Rochester's positive response to the unusual watercolors—Brontë marks Jane and Rochester as members of an exclusive class of art appreciators.

Rochester's judgment of Jane's paintings marks, then, Jane's deviation from her class (as orphan and governess) and her gender. In addition, Jane's verbal retelling of the scene of painting that produced these odd artworks perverts contemporary beliefs surrounding the purpose of art for women. On the surface, Jane's way of painting seems innocuous enough. She reports that she painted them "in the last two vacations I spent at Lowood, when I had no other occupation" (109). But when Rochester asks her, "Were you happy when you painted these pictures?" she replies, "I was absorbed, sir: yes, and I was happy." For a woman to paint in her "spare time" was precisely the use to which an artistic education was expected to be put; making money or expressing genius were discouraged. Sarah Ellis writes of the benefits of painting:

> Among these advantages, I will begin with the least. It is quiet. It disturbs no one; for however defective the performance may be, it does not necessarily, like music, jar upon the sense. It is true, it may when seen offend the practiced eye; but we can always keep our productions to ourselves. In addition to this, it is an employment which beguiles the mind of many cares . . . drawing is of all other occupations *the one most calculated to keep the mind from*

brooding upon self, and to maintain that general cheerfulness which is a part of social and domestic duty. (1848a, 149; emphasis added)

Jane, we assume, is properly quiet while painting; if her vacations at Lowood were anything like the painfully solitary school holidays spent by Jane's fictional sister Lucy Snowe in Charlotte Brontë's *Villette,* then one can be certain that Jane "disturb[ed] no one," because all those more fortunate would be visiting family or friends. Further, if Jane recalls that painting the pictures "was to enjoy one of the keenest pleasures I have ever known" (109), then painting served well to "maintain that general cheerfulness" which Ellis sees as paramount to social and domestic life. However, drawing decidedly does *not* keep Jane's mind from "brooding upon self." Because her paintings serve as self-expression, they encourage self-absorption and self-awareness rather than the self-denial that Ellis encourages.

During this holiday, Jane, like countless other eighteenth- and nineteenth-century heroines, suffers from lack of occupation, though only at infrequent intervals. Thus Jane is able to work at her paintings "from morning till noon, and from noon until night"; as she bluntly says, "I had nothing else to do" (109). But rather than painting serving primarily (as Ellis suggests) to prevent "brooding," in Jane's case painting requires Jane's ardent attention. Jane's paintings, because they do not derive from copies or nature, *require* brooding upon self for inspiration.[13] "I saw them with the spiritual eye," says Jane of her watercolors, a statement that makes her painting closely aligned with Brontë's writing: both try to reproduce the "bright pictures" that Imagination shows them. George Lewes praised the novel's ability to *paint* reality, to represent what he calls "the material aspect of things":

> We have spoken of the reality stamped upon almost every part; and that reality is not confined to the characters and incidents, but is also striking in the descriptions of the various aspects of Nature, and of the houses, rooms, and furniture. The pictures stand out distinctly before you: they *are* pictures, and not mere bits of "fine writing." The writer is evidently painting by words a picture that she has in her mind. (1847)

Lewes's praise for the novel is based on its "deep, significant reality," its adherence to truth—he admires it because, in essence, he sees it as a realist novel. "The authoress is unquestionably setting forth her own experience," he writes, and the "house, rooms and furniture" of which he speaks are in his mind part of the author's concrete experience. At those narrative points where Brontë strays from the path of realism, Lewes complains of "melodrama and improbability," particularly in connection with "the mad wife and all that relates to her."¹⁴ Yet when Lewes writes that the pictures Brontë paints are "in her mind," he raises the possibility that the nature Brontë copies is not external reality but an internal vision; Lewes suggests that "realism" can be truer to some internal experience than to external reality. And in fact Brontë wrote rather bluntly to W. S. Williams in response to Lewes's praise of her novel's realism, "Mr. Lewes is not always right. I am afraid if he knew how much I write from intuition, how little from actual knowledge, he would think me presumptuous ever to have written at all."¹⁵ Lewes assumes that the realism of *Jane Eyre* arose from the writer's mimetic retention of various aspects of reality and her subsequent re-vision of these things on paper. But Brontë makes us take literally Lewes's phrase, "painting by words a picture that she has in her mind"; that is, she makes it clear that the pictures in *Jane Eyre* were productions of her *imagination* rather than images taken into the writer's memory from external reality. She writes to Lewes,

> You advise me, too, not to stray far from the ground of experience, as I become weak when I enter the region of fiction; and you say "real experience is perennially interesting, and to all men."
>
> I feel that this also is true; but, dear sir, is not the real experience of each individual very limited? . . . Then, too, Imagination is a strong, restless faculty, which claims to be heard and exercised: are we to be quite deaf to her cry, and insensate to her struggles? *When she shows us bright pictures, are we never to look at them, and try to reproduce them?* (*Letters,* 6 November 1847; emphasis in original)

Imagination here shows the writer pictures which the writer then "reproduces" in a different medium, in language. The visual images that Jane and Brontë reproduce come not from external nature but from *internal* galleries of art.

This reproduction of the internal is not entirely successful for Brontë's heroine, again suggesting an obsession with things that remain hidden and cannot be represented visually. Later Jane confesses to Rochester, "I was tormented by the contrast between my idea and my handiwork: in each case I had imagined something which I was quite powerless to realize" (110–11). Rochester's erratic and irate answer to this is worth quoting in full, as it contains several conflicting explanations of why Jane's aesthetic project might have fallen short of its aim:

> Not quite: you have secured the shadow of your thought: but no more, probably. You had not enough of the artist's skill and science to give it full being: yet the drawings are, for a schoolgirl, peculiar. As to the thoughts, they are

elfish. These eyes in the Evening Star you must have seen in a dream. How could you make them look so clear, and yet not at all brilliant? And what meaning is that in their solemn depth? And who taught you to paint wind? There is a high gale in that sky, and on this hilltop. Where did you see Latmos? For that is Latmos.[16] There,—put the drawings away! (111)

On the one hand, it is Jane's "artist's skill" which is insufficient to capture the pictures which Imagination has shown her; yet on the other hand, her representational aims are enormous. For not only does Jane paint nonrealistic things (the Evening Star, colossal heads), she tackles unrepresentable things as well. When Rochester asks, "And who taught you to paint wind?" he points to yet another unrepresentable element in Jane's work. Wind is not a force that lends itself readily to representation; like things under darkened water, wind can be suggested but not literally depicted. Wind is a visual enigma; because it defies graphic depiction, wind can stand for the failures of representation, and wind becomes a seduction for the artist because it stands at the limit of what can be painted.

By asking where Jane learned such a skill as painting wind, Rochester implies first of all that she cannot have learned the artist's skill by herself, naturally, but was "taught" it by someone—which, for Rochester, may be another taunt. But Jane has set him straight once before, when he asks of her watercolors, "I don't know if they were entirely of your doing: probably a master aided you?" She insists that her painting is entirely her own work, which is probably accurate, for the only person (speaking art-historically) who might have been able to teach Jane to paint wind is Leonardo da Vinci—who did try to paint wind. Ruskin tackled clouds, but not wind specifically. The graphic depiction of air movement was actually a philosophical as well as a technical problem for the Renaissance; Leonardo's notebooks are full of drawings and textual passages detailing how wind is created, and how wind relates to waves, flame, and unmoving air. A quick glance at any of his attempts is enough to make one understand, as Leonardo did, that you can't actually capture wind on paper—you can only trace its lines of force, motion, or influence. You know it only through its effects (1998, 9.5). You can see, in waves, that there is wind; or the "serried clouds" that Jane paints might make you understand that wind whipped the clouds along. But actual wind cannot be painted. To accuse Jane of successfully painting wind—that most unrepresentable of nonthings—suggests then that Jane's artwork achieves something dangerously close to representing the unrepresentable. Which is one of the reasons they are such powerfully seductive images, for Rochester and for us.

That Jane paints *wind* curiously reverberates with other issues in the novel. Just as you can know wind only by its effects, so, often, do we know

Jane through the effects she causes on others. Elizabeth Rigby (Lady Eastlake) finds fault with the novel on precisely this ground of the disparity between cause (Jane) and effect. In her famous review of *Jane Eyre* in the *Quarterly Review*, Rigby writes,

> The error in *Jane Eyre* is, not that her character is this or that, but that she is made one thing in the eyes of her imaginary companions, and another in that of the actual reader. There is a perpetual disparity between the account she herself gives of the effect she produces, and the means shown us by which she brings that effect about. (1848, 167)

According to Rigby, Jane's positive effect on Rochester or the Riverses cannot be made to harmonize with the picture Jane paints of herself—she cannot be, as she says she is, meek and mild and insignificant if she shows herself, in her actions, to be a figure powerful enough to confess her affection to her employer or to hurl insults at Mrs. Reed. Similarly, Jane's "self-eulogiums on the perfect tact . . . with which she is gifted" are contradicted by the fact that "every word she utters offends us . . . with their . . . pedantry, stupidity, or gross vulgarity" (167). Rigby insists that Jane "is not quite so artless as the author would have us suppose" (170).

In the quotation above, Rigby complains of Jane's machinations in dealing with Rochester (which Rigby terms "the arts of coquetry"), but Rigby connects the discrepancy between cause and effect in the personality of Jane to a similar discrepancy in Jane's *drawings*. Rigby writes, "There is not more disparity between the art of drawing Jane assumes and her evident total ignorance of its first principles, than between the report she gives of her own character and the conclusions we form for ourselves" (176). On one side of the equation, Rigby places Jane's drawings and Jane's report of herself (suggesting that Rigby, like twentieth-century critics, sees Jane's drawings as part of her autobiography, as evidence of Jane's interior self); on the other, the "first principles" of art and the readers' opinions of Jane. Rigby, an accomplished artist herself, and the wife of Royal Academy president Charles Eastlake, takes Jane's deviation from the principles of art to be indicative of her similar deviation from morality, religion, and social etiquette; in both realms, Jane has set up a distasteful and dangerous (according to Rigby) series of principles at odds with traditional systems.

III.

Jane's three watercolors, then, manage successfully to topple multiple aesthetic, sociohistoric, genre, and gender traditions. The watercolor scene also provides a twist on the expected narrative use and gender politics of ekphrasis. To critique the tradition, Brontë first sets up ekphrasis as an explicitly seductive narrative technique. Jane's paintings are flagrantly offered to the reader in minute ekphrastic detail; we are given absolutely no choice but to want to interpret the images. And of course, as numerous critics (and countless readers) have found, the images offer ample scope for symbolic reading (as do the Bewick images that Brontë introduces in the first pages of the novel). The images are offered as rather easy narrative riddles—easy in the sense that their symbolic interpretation is on one level relatively obvious. Caroline Levine has argued that both the public riddle of the identity of the Bell "brothers" and the numerous narrative enigmas, mysteries, and withholdings of truths in *Jane Eyre* are strategies of suspense that Brontë uses for "political ends, overturning widely held convictions about femininity" (C. Levine 2003, 66). In general, suspense in Victorian literature functions as subversive, Levine argues, because it makes readers "hesitate in [their] convictions" (74); it "invites us to nurture a skepticism about maxims and generalizing representations, to test sweeping principles against the evidence" (75). Suspense in *Jane Eyre* "emerges as a powerfully subversive tool" that empowers Jane and Brontë simultaneously (66); Jane's dismissal of accepted conventions and her relentless curiosity make her narrative a model of suspense in this sense. Jane's paintings are a key moment in this kind of narrative suspense—not suspense of plot, but suspense of *interpretation.*

Certainly Brontë knows that her readers will mine the ekphrastic descriptions for symbolic evidence of Jane's psyche; the passage is obviously so heavily larded with symbols as to make such a reading inevitable.[17] But she also complicates this reading in several ways, disrupting the ekphrastic tradition in doing so. First of all, she makes it too easy—Jane's drawings are so alarmingly, almost embarrassingly, symbolic that one cannot but assume that their very symbolic overabundance is the point of the passage, rather than the symbolic content itself. In other words, Brontë is telling us that ekphrasis itself inevitably functions as a seduction, an invitation to interpretation and attention. Part of my overall argument in this book has been that painting *always* becomes a seduction when women are involved, and that this can often be a disastrous trap for women. Here, Brontë's harnessing of ekphrasis enables this erotic charge to work to the heroine's advantage. If ekphrasis is traditionally about controlling a female image, in *Jane Eyre* it is about controlling the representation of the female image *yourself,* and thereby attracting the kind of attention you choose.

Ekphrastic moments like this one in *Jane Eyre* are often considered narrative blocks; they disrupt the flow of story in favor of description. In this context we can look at Heffernan's discussion of Aeneas and Dido in the *Aeneid*. Aeneas is seeing the murals depicting the destruction of Troy on Dido's temple, sacred to Juno (lots of femininity around). He is transfixed by them, and this puts him in danger:

> In spite of the masculine ferocity of what most of them portray, they are silent and seductive; they offer themselves to be consumed by the gaze of a man who is thereby threatened with emasculation. That their entrancing power soon gives way to the beauty of Dido suggests that she is herself a work of art, the most beautiful picture—*pulcherrima forma*—to be seen in all Carthage. But Aeneas cannot remain transfixed by her; the imperatives of his mission—the inexorability of the narrative that drives him onward—compel him to forsake her.... (1993, 28)

Narrative momentum is here troped as male; the arresting image as female. This dovetails neatly with the early history of aesthetics as articulated by such practitioners as Baumgarten, who felt the need to justify the "weak" genre of aesthetics against the more masculine rational philosophic discourses. Even in the eighteenth century, when the spectator was explicitly male, the whole business of looking at art was dangerously feminized; and Heffernan tells us why in his reading of Aeneas: if you sit around looking at paintings, even ones that depict blood and guts and dying horses, you might not get on with the job of founding empires.[18]

Brontë overhauls this tradition, transforming paintings into texts that are as important to the story as the story "proper." The images are part of the story; they actively carry the action forward because they come *from the same voice* as the story proper. Ekphrasis is not an obstruction originating from outside the narrative but an integral part of the narrative action. Brontë slyly hints at this when she has Jane introduce her ekphrasis by saying, "While he is so occupied I will tell you, reader, what they are." Rochester is arrested, certainly; what is static in this scene is the viewer of the "real" images (namely, Rochester) rather than the subject of the ekphrasis (the paintings). Jane's pictures fail to become static, feminine, mute artifacts in a traditional gendered model of ekphrasis; they function instead as embodied scenes of Jane's narrative power. There might be drowned corpses in the paintings, but the paintings themselves are certainly not dead artifacts.

Other artworks described by Jane extend this argument. When Jane returns to Gateshead to attend Mrs. Reed on her deathbed, she sketches (among other things) a portrait from memory of Rochester. Jane writes,

"One morning I fell to sketching a face: what sort of face it was to be, I did not care or know" (205). This vague apparition soon begins to look decidedly familiar; almost of its own accord, a portrait of Rochester emerges, feature by feature.[19] What emerges in language is a remarkable blazon with the gender roles reversed. Jane says her portrait of Rochester is a "speaking likeness," which is delightfully ironic considering the gendered tradition of ekphrasis Brontë would have been referencing. In this scene Rochester is never given the chance to speak; he remains a mute object, subject entirely to Jane's representational power with word *and* image. While Jane the artist draws each feature in turn, Jane the narrator describes them with emotive additions:

> Soon I had traced on the paper a broad and prominent forehead and a square lower outline of visage: that contour gave me pleasure; my fingers proceeded actively to fill it with features. Strongly marked horizontal eyebrows must be traced under that brow; then followed, naturally, a well-defined nose . . . then a flexible looking mouth . . . then a firm chin . . . some black whiskers were wanted, and some jetty hair. . . . Now for the eyes: I had left them to the last, because they required the most careful working. . . . "Good! But not quite the thing," I thought as I surveyed the effect . . . I wrought the shades blacker, that the lights might flash more brilliantly—a happy touch or two secured success . . . I looked at it: I smiled at the speaking likeness; I was absorbed and content. (261–62)

We might call this "ekphrasis with addenda"; her ekphrasis here emphasizes the process of painting rather than the product. On the one hand, ekphrasis here proceeds alongside the production of the sketch; the two are chronologically coterminous, and one gets the sense that the verbal description is necessary to the production of the visual image. Second, the description focuses on the artistry involved as much as or more than on the image created; Jane spends as much time telling us *how* she is painting and what she thinks of it as she does describing what she is painting.[20]

If we return to the description of her watercolors, we see something similar happening. At first appearance, the ekphrasis of the three paintings seems largely to focus just on what is depicted on the paper. But the description is in fact heavily sprinkled with references to Jane's artistry, her *production* of the images. She writes, for example, that the gems on the bracelet were "touched with as brilliant tints as my palette could yield, and as glittering distinctness as my pencil could impart." Jane the artist is not to be forgotten in this ekphrastic moment; again, this is not a static narrative roadblock but an active part of the story. And these constructions using the word "as" in comparative mode, all of which serve to reinforce Jane's artistic presence in the passage, echo the passage's many similes that likewise rely on "as" to carry the weight of a comparison. Jane cannot describe her artworks without similes: "as if by a breeze," "as at twilight," "as through a suffusion of vapour," "like a beamless cloud," and so on. The weight of all these similes (and numerous metaphors as well) also strengthens Jane's interpretive presence here; a simile is an interpretive statement, after all. To describe these three visual images, Jane must resort to figurative language. But the flood of similes in this ekphrastic passage demonstrates that language must resort to visual metaphors; each of the metaphors or similes Jane uses is drawn from the visual realm, based on color or shape rather than (say) on touch or sound. Word and image here work in tandem: to express herself, Jane needs to paint; to describe her paintings, Jane needs language; to succeed in description, language must reference the realm of the visual.

Jane's use of ekphrasis to emphasize her presence as artist (rather than to bring the art object to the fore) surfaces most powerfully and curiously in her descriptions of her self-portrait and the portrait of Blanche Ingram. Early in her sojourn at Thornfield, Jane reprimands herself for her growing affection for Rochester by calling herself a "Blind puppy!" and setting herself the following artistic task:

> Listen, then, Jane Eyre, to your sentence: to-morrow, place the glass before you and draw in chalk your own picture, faithfully, without softening one defect; omit no harsh line, smooth away no displeasing irregularity, write under it, "Portrait of a Governess, disconnected, poor, and plain."
>
> Afterwards take a piece of smooth ivory . . . take your palette; mix your freshest, finest, clearest tints; choose your most delicate camel-hair pencils; delineate the loveliest face you can imagine; paint it in your softest shades and sweetest hues, according to the description given by Mrs. Fairfax of Blanche Ingram: remember the raven ringlets, the oriental eye . . . the Grecian neck and bust; let the round and dazzling arm be visible, and the delicate hand. (190–91)

Again we see Jane more interested in describing the *process* of creation, down to the technical decisions (tints and pencils and media) than the product. But what is most striking about the brief ekphrasis of Blanche's portrait is that it describes a portrait *not yet painted* of a woman Jane has *not yet seen*. This admonitory ekphrastic exercise is prescriptive rather than descriptive; when the portrait of Blanche is completed, Jane merely writes, "It looked a lovely face enough" (191). Both images are valued not for their final appearance but for their emotive effect (in this case as deterrents to emotion) on the artist.

By making ekphrasis Jane's main discursive strategy, Brontë positions Jane as an active creator in two mediums, language and visual art. Ekphrasis is a foundational technique of Brontë's novel that yokes the power to represent things visually to the ability to narrate at all; stories, Brontë shows us, cannot be revealed without pictures for words to work on. Given Jane's obsession with the visual, we can justifiably read *Jane Eyre* as Brontë's manifesto for women's vision, as a "powerful defense against the exclusion of women from visual pleasure and authority" (Gezari 1992, 89).[21] As we saw in chapter 2, this is also a particularly apt description of *The Tenant of Wildfell Hall* and might indeed serve as one connecting point among all the texts discussed in this book. Novels with artist heroines exploit the visual component of painting in order to illustrate precisely this "exclusion of women from visual pleasure and authority" and to dramatize ways women might break into the realm of the visual and reconfigure what Jane Kromm calls "scopic custom," the "customary, gendered patterns of looking and being looked at which dominated Victorian society" (1998, 369). *Jane Eyre* takes the defense of vision and the critique of scopic custom to extremes.

Brontë's interest in paintings and in what Kromm calls "scopic custom" is not limited to *Jane Eyre*. Like Jane, Lucy Snowe in *Villette* is also a determined viewer. Her trip to the museum and her scathing interpretations of both the "improper" Cleopatra painting and the "proper" *La vie d'une femme* series have been the subject of much commentary; critics generally read the scene as a concise articulation of Lucy's rebellion against social gender norms (Gilbert and Gubar 2000, 403; Kromm 1998, 387; Matus 1993; Millett 1970, 143). Lucy's dismissal of the male-produced images stems from their false mimetic claims, their inability to truthfully represent either woman's experience or her physical presence. As Kromm writes, Brontë "emphasizes the ways in which mimetic illusionism itself is central to a certain kind of male pictorial practice and spectatorial preference" (1998, 391). Jane certainly shares Lucy's critique of masculine visual hegemony; Jane's experience is filled with examples of men exercising tyrannical visual power (for example, Brocklehurst unjustly punishes her by making her stand at length before her peers; Rochester scrutinizes her work and her self continually and is blinded in symbolic response). However, Jane is a visual producer as well as a visual commentator; she exercises her right to see not just by critiquing the visual world (as does Lucy) but by intervening directly in it and producing visual images to tell her story for her. Jane's paintings are narratives almost literally; just as in her early reading of Bewick she insists that "each picture told a story," so too do Jane's own pictures; each image becomes a condensed moment of intense narrative significance.

Chapter Four

Making a Living
Howitt, Eliot, Oliphant

I.

IN HER BOOK *Women and Work,* Barbara Bodichon writes, "One great corresponding cry rises from a suffering multitude of women, saying, 'We want work'" (1857, 2). Echoing the sentiment, if not the tone, Thomas Purnell wrote in 1861 in *Art Journal,* "What share of the ordinary avocations of life may fairly be assigned to woman, is unquestionably one of the most difficult social problems of our times" (107). Traditional ideology held up the nonworking married woman as a middle-class ideal: to have "made it" financially meant that a man could afford to support an idle wife, much of whose housework and maternal work would be done by servants. Such an ideal, obviously, was impossible for the majority of Victorian families; many women were forced by economic necessity to work and many women *wanted* to work. But the prejudice against working women was extreme, and few lucrative options were open to women.[1] Bodichon's feminist treatise *Women and Work* argues vehemently against the paucity of employment open to women: "At present the language practically held by modern society to destitute women may be resolved into Marry—Stitch—Die—or do Worse" (17). The "worse" was, of course, prostitution—an evil with which Bodichon threatens any society which does not provide adequate employment for women.

The art world offered one reasonably respectable means of employment for women. Because the practice of making and selling art or art objects was not (and still is not) regulated by the need for legal certificates or licenses—as were law, medicine, the church, or other professions—women could at least enter the field with relative ease and make a decent living if they were talented, diligent, and lucky. One Victorian periodical writer insists, "With a very large class of feminine artists the great object is not to become famous, but to early earn a livelihood, for girls are beginning to tire of the drudgery of teaching at servants' wages, and marriage is a remote chance with a large proportion of women. . . . New careers must be made for women, and art opens a wide field to her" (L. Scott 1884, 99). Not all women artists were expected to become history or landscape painters—or even *painters* at all. "Art" as a profession encompassed a wide variety of options: "It is by no means necessary for her to confine her efforts to mere water-colours and oils. She may etch, and draw on wood. She may design chintzes and wall-papers . . . paint on china in a porcelain manufactory; paint tapestries for hangings." (ibid., 99).

This chapter considers three fictional representations of women who work in the less prestigious artistic fields of popular portraiture, illustration, engraving, or design (for textiles, pottery, china, wallcoverings, and the like). These women artisans come into the art market publicly and for financial reasons; they are represented as professional working women whose livelihood depends on a complexly structured market economy, and whose social position rests on even more precarious ideological beliefs about the proper role of women and art. In particular, I ask why George Eliot, Margaret Oliphant, and Anna Mary Howitt might wish to use in their fiction a woman working in the so-called "low arts"; if the novel as a genre was often threatened with devaluation in the hierarchy of arts (especially if written by a woman), what might it mean for fiction to represent—favorably, in these cases—women who embrace not History painting but rather illustration or textile design? I suggest that these women writers were trying to effect a reevaluation and recuperation of these art forms; the social and narrative positions of the artist-characters in their novels call into question the Victorian artistic hierarchies. These texts argue that the so-called "low arts" can provide women artists with a kind of feminist artistic utopia not possible in the cutthroat High Art arenas. As one Victorian writer argued,

> We shall be suspected of no disrespect to Art by confessing ourselves to be not of those who are disposed to consider it as something sacred. . . . It is only second rate minds that go into ecstasies about Art, or any other calling, for its own sake. . . . The best men have ever considered it as only a means to an end; and none surely but will acknowledge that end a noble one which has for its object the amelioration of the condition of women. (Purnell 1861, 108)

The three texts discussed in this chapter represent the so-called low arts as rich in potential for the "amelioration" of women's social condition. I first consider an idealized vision of a successful band of "sisters in art" in the painter Anna Mary Howitt's novella "Sisters in Art." I then explore the successful if muted artistic life of the Meyrick family in Eliot's *Daniel Deronda;* the Meyrick women work at home in a potentially utopian space that offers a curious counterpoint to the very different artistic ambitions or romantic experiences of the novel's more widely discussed female characters (Gwendolyn, Mirah, and the Alcharisi). In both *Daniel Deronda* and "Sisters in Art," we are offered visions of female artistic utopias: spaces of productivity in which artistic pleasure and economic gain coexist and which provide a locus of resistance to traditional gender expectations. In *Miss Marjoribanks,* the third text I consider, the woman artist voices her *desire* for just such a utopia, but Oliphant's message here is that women's social circumstances in Victorian culture make this admirable desire impossible to fulfill. In Oliphant's novel, the rich young heroine's struggles to find adequate occupation for her time are contrasted rather darkly with the professional struggles of Rose Lake, the drawing master's daughter, whose utopian fantasy of an artistic life never materializes. These three texts give us three visions of female artistic utopia on a sliding scale: the fantasy perfection of "Sisters in Art"; Eliot's more reasoned portrayal of successful artistic sisters in *Daniel Deronda;* and Oliphant's dismal depiction of the way social circumstances conspire to kill a woman artist's dream of artistic community. All three of these texts explore the ideological tensions that arise when women attempt to engage in economically profitable aesthetic activity as declared professionals. For Howitt and Eliot, what makes the women artists' success possible is precisely their decision to work in the "low arts" of design and illustration; their professional choices are then their ticket, so to speak, out of certain oppressive, heteronormative gender positions. Oliphant's take, however, is less positive; even humble ambitions cannot save her young artist from succumbing to the pressures of Victorian gender norms.

II.

Anna Mary Howitt, the daughter of Mary Howitt, whose "Margaret Von Erhenberg, Artist-Wife" was discussed in chapter 2, was for many years a professional painter. Along with Bodichon and Bessie Rayner Parkes, Howitt formed part of the unofficial Pre-Raphaelite sisterhood, a forum for the members' writing and painting; she was also a member, with others in the Pre-Raphaelite Brotherhood, of the Folio Club, "a project in which a folder passed around the members, each adding a piece of work to it as it came through their hands" (Nunn 1987, 22). Howitt was involved in the founding of the Society of Female Artists and was a regular exhibitor there and at the Royal Academy until her marriage in 1859 to Alaric Watts, after which she had a mental breakdown, turned to spiritualism, and painted no more.[2] Her second major work, *An Art Student in Munich* (1854), is a slightly fictionalized memoir of Howitt's art education in Germany. It details a blissful, free, productive life abroad among a community of artistic women (Barbara Bodichon and Jane Bentham Hay appear as "Justina" and "Clare"). The memoir offered the English public a glimpse of what women's art education could be in England, if the quality of art schools improved.

The feminine and feminist artistic utopia is even more clearly drawn in her novella "Sisters in Art." Serialized across eight issues in *The Illustrated Exhibitor and Magazine of Art* (later known simply as *The Magazine of Art*) beginning in July 1852, "Sisters in Art" comes at the beginning of a boom in women's art education and production. Though the story is published anonymously, Pamela Gerrish Nunn and other critics justifiably believe the work to be Howitt's—certainly "Sisters in Art" shows many similarities with *An Art Student in Munich*.[3]

"Sisters in Art" tells the story of Alice Law, an orphan who comes to study in London at "Mr. C's Art School," probably based on Cary's famous art school in London, one of the few that accepted women students in the 1850s. Alice boards with her aunt and uncle, the Silvers, who twenty years previously had cast out Alice's mother for refusing to marry a very old but very rich art dealer who owned two fine paintings by Rubens that Silver was desperate to get his hands on. Mr. and Mrs. Silver run an art and decorative goods shop and have become prosperous. Their name, "Silver," however, suggests that though they may have gold, they are still in themselves inferior metals. Mr. Silver is a cynical, avaricious man who tries to cheat his tailor out of sixpence and can welcome the idea of his niece's visit only by imagining her as a salesgirl in his shop: "We'll make her useful; a Sevres jar or Dresden plate will tempt best in pretty hands, I dare say" (215).

Mr. Silver's "sovereign idea upon worth and art" may be summarized in his own words: "so it's costly, so it's rare, that's the thing" (239). He cares nothing for form, design, or beauty, being in the art trade purely for profit—for "sovereigns." His counterpart in the narrative is old Guiseppe, a poor Italian artist who makes plaster casts of famous sculptures to sell to art schools or individuals. Mr. Silver insults Guiseppe's medium, denigrating plaster as not as valuable as marble; but Guiseppe's motto is "no matter what the substance is, so the form is beautiful" (239). Guiseppe, who is befriended by Alice and her "sisters in art," stands for the ancient European traditions of art and design which Mr. Silver, as a nouveau riche, blasphemes by his materialism.

The story becomes a parable of the importance of design in beautifying the world of "others"—the poor, the foreign, the wealthy and materialistic. Alice, as representative of English leisured whiteness (she is an orphan, but with a small income that enables her never to have to work, but to study art), befriends a collection of non-English or non-leisure-class individuals who find their pleasure or their livelihood in design: Lizzy the tailor's daughter; Mrs. Cohen the rich Jewess (who has transformed her home into a palace of art treasures, most of them purchased from the Silvers' shop, and whose religion figures her as foreign in the novella); and Guiseppe, the poor Italian plaster-cast maker.

If the story can be said to have a narrative secret or denouement of any sort, it involves the Silvers' mysterious lodger, a Doctor Falkland, of whom the Silvers live in trepidation lest anything should annoy so lucrative a dweller. The doctor has made absolute privacy a primary condition of his paying a very high rent to the Silvers; hence Mr. Silver guards the doctor's rooms as if his life and his fortune depend on it. Alice asks at one point why she has never been shown his rooms, and Mrs. Silver answers, "I do know what is proper for a young girl of your years. I should no more introduce you into the doctor's rooms, where there are skulls and skeletons, and heavens knows what, than I should burn your hand." To which piece of wisdom Alice mildly replies, "I have drawn the skeleton, both whole, and in portions . . . and more, too, for in our academy we draw the undraped figure" (262). Anatomy, thinks Mrs. Silver, is an improper study for a young girl, whose modesty must be shielded from knowledge of things in a "doctor's rooms." But Alice has intimate knowledge of the human figure, both with its skin and without it; she apparently attends one of the few London schools that permitted women to draw from "the life," that is, from the nude figure. (If Alice's "Mr. C's" does indeed refer to Cary's art school, Alice could have received such training, for Cary's was one of the only private art schools where young women could draw from a nude model of either sex, but most frequently female.)

One evening Alice and Esther find themselves in need of an anatomical model of a hand; Dr. Falkland is absent from his rooms, and the two convince Mrs. Silver to sneak them in. Of course the doctor arrives at his lodgings to catch them, but his appearance is rather a narrative letdown; rather than erupting into some kind of Gothic rage, he does not seem to mind the presence of people in his rooms, but merely asks them quietly for some privacy as he has important letters to write. When Dr. Falkland does suddenly cancel his lease (for reasons totally unrelated to the intrusion), Silver explodes in fury, heaping insults on Alice, who—though in general a perfectly mild Victorian miss—righteously gets up and leaves the house. The scene in which the girls enter the doctor's forbidden study to draw from the model of the hand can be read as a parable of women's search for the sources of art, the foundational models for design and drawing. Their search offends the "old school" of ideas about women and art, represented by the mercantile Silver, and forces them to set out on their own.

But it is the old school that must provide the economic support for younger generations and their (literal) new school: when Silver, on his deathbed, makes a will leaving a substantial fortune to Alice, he makes possible her desire to start a Woman's College of Art right on the site of Silver's shop—a college which teaches exactly those skills Alice and Esther had to skulk into the forbidden study to acquire. Silver's hoard of marble, bronze, and ivory treasures becomes an object of study for women students, rather than merchandise. Mrs. Cohen likewise leaves her magnificent house, gardens, and collection of china as a gift for the college. Dr. Falkland, too, makes plans to leave his anatomical collection to the college, and all of Guiseppe's plaster casts will make their home there, as models for students; by the end of the tale, all material wealth is absorbed into the cause of women's art education.

The curriculum of this artistic school involves intensive study not only in the fundamentals of art and design but also in *all* branches of knowledge: languages, anatomy, mathematics, and botany. It is, the narrator tells us, "a true school of art in relation to design" (364) because it is based on the principle that "art is the corollary of many forms and departments of knowledge, instead of being as heretofore considered in the common art-schools of the country, as consisting of nothing more than in the objective use of the brush" (364). As well as being holistic, the school teaches collaborative production. The utopian artistic community of Alice and her friends is held together because of a traditional aesthetic *sensus communis,* a common, innate sense of taste that binds members of a society together without force—or such was the fantasy of many eighteenth-century aestheticians.[4] In "Sisters in Art," however, this *sensus communis* has important individual variations. That is, the community is in perfect harmony *not* because all members have the *same* aesthetic pleasures, but because they have different but complementary ones and work together. Alice tells the head of the Belgian firm that brings them a prize that their work is but

> the simple result of our several tastes, or readings of art, brought to bear upon one object. The larger outlines . . . are mine . . . gathered from the great field of nature; the geometrical curves . . . are Esther's . . . [who] draws her truths

from such fields of nature as anatomy and the noble one of science . . . whilst the filling up in detail, the stray flower, the rounded boss, the delicate touches . . . are those of [Lizzy]. (334)

Their endeavor is here collaborative, the antithesis of Romantic models of artistic solitary genius.

As with utopian fiction more generally, Howitt's novella allows her to comment on the current state of art education for Victorian women. As the sisters in art lay out their plans for the college, an admirer tells them, "Till education is made to form a correlative of art, art will not advance, nor half the sources of design be laid open . . . yes, do this for England,—for considering the undoubted talent she has to deal with, her Female School of Design is a national disgrace" (335). The Female School of Design that the friend calls a disgrace was founded in London in 1842 and taught design, textile work, or other artisan fields rather than painting or sculpture; its mission was to improve ornamental design in England, to help working- and middle-class women earn money, and to improve the level of design for industry and manufacture in England (which lagged behind other countries in the quality of their artistic design). As a contemporary art critic writes, the School was founded "partly to enable young women of the middle class to obtain an honorable and profitable employment, and partly to improve ornamental design in manufacturers, by cultivating the taste of the designer" (Purnell 1861, 108). In its early years, the Female School of Design shared space and often class time with the Government School of Design at Somerset House in London, established in 1837 for male artisans. Local schools along the same model began to pop up in manufacturing districts and major population centers soon after; in Oliphant's *Miss Marjoribanks,* the fictional Carlingford boasts such a school (that Carlingford has a School of Design suggests that it is a center of industry rather than, say, of education).

Women learned the lessons of design quickly and embarrassingly well. Female students at the first coed Schools of Design, for example, performed so well that it became necessary to institute two sets of prizes, male and female, to save male students from embarrassment. In 1847, under questionable circumstances, the separate Female School of Design was forcibly moved by Government decree to grimy quarters in the dubiously respectable Theatre District; the move almost killed the school, since what respectable father would now permit his middle-class daughter to attend? This is the "national disgrace" spoken of in Howitt's novella. In 1852 (the date of "Sisters in Art"), however, the school was renovated, changed its name, and increased its membership by including young women who merely desired art education as a genteel accomplishment; enrollment rose sharply. From 1852 to 1861, more than 690 young women took classes at the school (Purnell 1861, 108). In 1862, after being threatened once again with dissolution, the school came under the patronage of Queen Victoria and became known as the Royal Female School of Art. The school still continued to offer women skills for professional employment, but a large portion of women attending had no need for financial gain. In 1862, of the 118 students enrolled, only twenty did so with a view to support themselves.[5] Young women who sought to make a living from their art could and did now attend numerous other government schools, private art schools, foreign ateliers, and non-London schools. Women involved in any of the numerous art schools faced a great deal of public scrutiny and possible disapproval, largely because the schools were considered (and often rightly so) to be hotbeds of emergent feminist thinking. Such is certainly the case with the young women in "Sisters in Art."

The network of Schools of Design attempted to improve English taste, English goods, and English manufacture; the creation and maintenance of the schools were a matter of national pride and concern. Many writers of the time echo Leader Scott, who recommended "training in art as an admirable means of refining the national character" (1884, 98). Imperial expansion brought Indian, Chinese, Japanese, and African textiles, pottery, furniture, and jewelry into England, thereby highlighting her deficiencies in design. In addition, the nineteenth-century fascination with medieval art and architecture heightened the public's awareness of the dismal aesthetic qualities of their material surroundings. Hence Schools of Design were charged with raising the quality of English material culture by bringing its furniture, fabrics, and china into accordance with the most elegant and uplifting aesthetic principles. In addition to the Schools of Design, a spirited discourse of design improvement sprang up in England after the Great Exhibition of 1851 and the Paris Exhibition of 1867 made it clear that British design was vastly inferior to the products of other countries.[6] (Much of the rhetoric of the Pre-Raphaelite artisans is part of this design reform movement in England.) While technical schools attempted to rectify the situation from the production end, numerous books attempted to train English consumers in the art of design *appreciation*. The goal of Charles Eastlake, for example, in *Hints on Household Taste*, is to "suggest some fixed principles of taste for the popular guidance of those who are not accustomed to hear such principles defined."[7] The book contributes to the discourse encouraging "improved taste in objects of modern manufacture" among "our art-loving public" (xxi). Published in 1868, Eastlake's book attempts to lay down "fixed principles" for interior design—both in the manufacturing of objects and in the choosing and arranging of them in the home.

Largely, though not overtly, his text is a diatribe against women as consumers, who he believes have no innate taste and no proper training. Eastlake writes, "The faculty of distinguishing good from bad design in the familiar objects of domestic life is a faculty which most educated people—and women especially—conceive that they possess. . . . The general impression seems to be, that it is the peculiar inheritance of gentle blood, and independent of all training" (8). Hence,

> In the eyes of Materfamilias there was no upholstery which could possibly surpass that which the most fashionable upholsterer supplied. She believed in the elegance of window-curtains . . . which had been sent to the Duchess of——, and concluded that the dinner service must be perfect which was described as "quite a novelty." (3)

Women need to be educated out of their false conceptions of what is "good"; they need to demand true aesthetic quality rather than simply be swayed by fashion.

Eastlake also argues strenuously for an intimate connection between High Art and manufacture: "There is an intimate connection between this falling off in the excellence of our manufactures, and the tame vapid character which distinguished even our best painters' work in the early part of the present Victorian age" (5). He continues:

> National art is not a thing which we may enclose in a gilt frame and hang upon our walls, or which can be locked up in the cabinet of a collector. To be genuine and permanent, it ought to animate with the same spirit the blacksmith's forge and the sculptor's atelier, the painter's studio and the haberdasher's shop. (5)

Increasing taste in interior decor, he reasons, will eventually cause a concomitant rise in artistic quality in all media. His project, therefore, involves training a certain "class of young ladies," as well as the general public, in the "established principles" of good taste in domestic decoration. These principles are, he insists, the same ones that should govern all areas of aesthetic judgment: The graceless clothing and extravagant "appointments of the modern boudoir" are "mirrored on the modern canvas" (7). Eastlake blames this on the prevalence of realism in art: "The most natural instinct of the painter's mind is, after all, to depict life as he finds it. . . . We can hardly hope then to sustain anything like a real and national interest in art while we tamely submit to ugliness in modern manufacture. We cannot consistently have one taste for the drawing-room and another for the studio" (8).

Howitt's novella insists that the sorry state of English design, which Eastlake likewise bemoans, can be remedied by women; in fact, the novella depicts women and the feminized foreigner as the *only* individuals in a crass and materialist England to have a natural instinct for artistic beauty. Howitt further renders artistic talent as a powerful spiritual and social force located in women that can counteract the materialism of the wealthy British middle class. But by making women the only ones attuned to beauty, Howitt is not simply following the traditional ideological conception of women as keepers of the emotional, moral, or aesthetic realm. Rather, women in Howitt's tale are not just appreciators of beauty but the only successful producers of it as well. The novella is obsessed with art as an active vocation for women, rather than as a spiritual calling. As one critic puts it, "For all her emphasis on artistic and spiritual perfection, the author of "Sisters in Art" constantly intruded upon the narrative to offer details about money" (Gillett 1990, 185). Similarly, for all her discussion of the glory of High Art, the author is much more concerned with design and with the manufacture and retail of decorative objects. Even though Alice attends "an academy where our attention is chiefly directed to the living figure and anatomical drawing" (that is, not a Female School of Design), it is still pottery, busts, and figurines that fill the narrative rather than any reference to painting. The College of Art that the women start is similarly focused on design rather than history or landscape painting.

Painting in fact exists only as the memory of a failed financial transaction: twenty years previously, the mercenary Mr. Silver cast out his wife's sister because she would not marry a wealthy art dealer, "though he'd sixty thousand pounds—and two Rubens' that were worth five more." Mr. Silver bemoans regularly, "Ah! Those Rubens'; I never made such a miss before; for if the girl would but have married the old man, I should have got 'em for a hundred or so apiece!" (215). Other well-known paintings hover on the periphery of the narrative but never enter fully into the story. Instead we are in a world where high art is impractical—both economically and spiritually—for the majority of individuals in a modern industrial city. Alice, for all her aspirations, repairs pottery for Mr. Silver, and after their estrangement, makes extra money by similar jobs in design. We hear that Esther, Alice, and Lizzy have been "the successful competitors for a design advertized [*sic*] for by a Belgian firm" (334); and Guiseppe, for all his elevated aesthetic ideals, thinks he has done more for society by popularizing famous sculptures by casting them repeatedly in plaster and spreading them throughout society.

The working world of these artisans also allows them a way out of heteronormative narratives. The story ends by reporting coyly that "it is rumored" that all three sisters in art are engaged to various men—but this rumor never materializes into action; as the story ends, all three women are living and teaching together in their college of art and design. Like the Meyrick sisters whom we shall examine in Eliot's *Daniel Deronda*, these "sisters in art" are not forced by the narrative into the proper life of heterosexual marriage; instead, they remain in their utopian artistic space, working and wealthy. Both Howitt and Eliot offer examples of ways art might provide economic and emotional support for Victorian women in a woman-only environment.

III.

A surprising number of characters in George Eliot's *Daniel Deronda* follow—or want to follow—various branches of art as a profession: the novel is filled with musicians, singers, actresses, engravers, painters, textile workers, and others. *Daniel Deronda* is Eliot's "art" book, much in the way that *Middlemarch* is often read as her "science" book because Ludgate's profession seems to bleed out into the narrative so thoroughly. In the case of *Daniel Deronda*, the language of art structures the narrative. All the sympathetic characters, though they are not "working class," nevertheless *work* at something, and most of them are artists of one kind or another. Most of them are women artists, except for Klesmer and Hans Meyrick (who is significantly not a success); in Eliot's other fiction, women who work professionally are rare, but in *Daniel Deronda* they proliferate. The novel seems to offer not only Judaism[8] but also the life of hard work as a retreat from the evils of gentile English life (as represented by Grandcourt and Gwendolyn), especially for women. Although this artistic labor is not the "working class" labor of the mill or domestic service, it is not a middle-class existence either—the life of the artist offers women a social position outside the traditional hierarchies.

The art which has, perhaps justifiably, received the most attention in the novel is music, the medium that Klesmer, Mirah, and the Alcharisi practice. Yet as obsessed as it is with music and theatricality,[9] the novel nevertheless contains a powerful undercurrent of the visual arts. Eliot's knowledge of art history was extensive—she saw and studied numerous paintings in art galleries and churches both in England and Europe; when Eliot and George-Henry Lewes traveled, they regularly toured private galleries, and even private studios.[10] Eliot was also close personal friends with the painter Barbara Bodichon; Eliot traveled to see Bodichon's one-woman exhibit in France, and the two corresponded frequently about painting and literature as well as feminist concerns. Eliot and Lewes were also acquainted with other painters of the time: Burne-Jones, Morris, Rossetti, Holman Hunt, Cruikshank, Leighton, and others (Witemeyer 1979, 16). Eliot read Ruskin's *Modern Painters* avidly and reviewed volumes 3 and 4. *Daniel Deronda* is certainly filled with references to painting; critics have noted that the art referred to in the part of the novel which deals with Daniel and Mordecai is mainly by Titian, Rembrandt, or other great masters while the art in the part of the novel focused on Gwendolyn is generally genre scenes by Sir Joshua Reynolds or other popular portraitists. This hierarchy forms part of the metaphoric structure of the novel, which influences our judgment of the two worlds in the novel: Gwendolyn's world is wealthy, vulgar, and filled with the "false" arts of tableaux and portraiture, while Mordecai's world is the world of high art, timeless art.[11]

But there is another strain of art history represented in *Daniel Deronda*, which introduces us to a third and ignored "artworld" within this novel: the domestic, Dutch-style painting of the Meyrick women. The novel offers us a vision of a strangely peaceful realm run by these female visual artists who offer a quiet but no less profound argument for women's productive capacity. One critic insists that "Alcharisi is the only woman in all George Eliot's fiction who finds a vocation and sticks to it" (Barrett 1989, 167), and another writes that in the Alcharisi "Eliot represents for the first time in fiction the figure of a professional woman artist" (Booth 1991, 119). Yet the main representative of working women artists in *Daniel Deronda* is not, as critics have insisted, the Alcharisi—that powerful female figure who shows up only at the end of the novel to be dramatic and make disclosures. Much more central to the narrative are Mrs. Meyrick and her daughters Kate, Amy, and Mab, artisans working in various branches of visual and textile arts for their living. Kate draws illustrations and makes engravings for publishers; Amy, Mab, and Mrs. Meyrick do fancy embroidery work—satin cushions, ornate fabrics, and the like—for "the great world," as they call it. They live entirely independent of male assistance: their brother Hans, who might in the normal Victorian way of things be expected to provide for a widowed mother and three unmarried sisters, is encouraged by his female kin to follow his "natural" if utterly unprofitable bent toward becoming a painter.[12]

The character of Kate Meyrick, the eldest and most artistic sister who is an illustrator, may be based on the artist Helen Allingham née Paterson. William Allingham was a close friend of Eliot and her partner Lewes; when she heard the news of Allingham's marriage to Helen Paterson, she wrote to Barbara Bodichon (another woman artist with whom Eliot maintained close personal ties) on 23 September 1874, "I rejoice in . . . the indications that his bride is an accomplished industrious woman" (Haight 1954–78, 6: 84). Helen Paterson was a prolific and well-known (and well-paid) illustrator—she illustrated Hardy's *Far From the Madding Crowd* for *Cornhill* in 1872 (see Cherry 1993, 176); she also illustrated Anne Thackeray Ritchie's novel *Miss Angel* (discussed in chap. 5) when it was serialized in *Cornhill*. She worked for *Once a Week* and *The Graphic* and other periodicals, as well as illustrating for the Cassell's children's book series (Clayton 1876, 2: 1–5). After her marriage in 1874, Helen Allingham stopped illustrating regularly for the public press and started painting watercolors—at which she was phenomenally successful. She was arguably one of the three most famous English women artists in the last decades of the nineteenth century (Kate Greenaway and Elizabeth Thompson Butler were the others), giving one-woman shows at the Fine Art Society throughout the 1880s and 1890s (Nunn 1987, 215). It was Allingham whom Eliot suggested as an illustrator for the "cheap editions" of her novels; she evidently believed in supporting women in this line of endeavor. She wrote to her editor, John Blackwood, on 30 January 1877, "If an illustrator is wanted, I know one whose work is exquisite,—Mrs. Allingham" (Haight 1954–78, 6: 335). It is possible that Eliot had Allingham's illustrations of *Miss Angel* in mind, since those were among the last periodical press illustrations Allingham did before turning to watercolors. In a letter to the artist's husband, Mr. Allingham, Eliot wrote on 17 May 1860, "I hope . . . your dear wife is by your side preparing to make us all richer with store of new sketches" (ibid. 3: 255–56). Rather than hoping his dear wife is by his side making domestic bliss for him, Eliot turns the tables here and hopes the wife is by Mr. Allingham's side being *publicly* productive. Nevertheless, Mrs. Allingham remains at his side; illustrating and engraving was one public work a woman could do in a domestic setting, as the Meyricks prove.

Eliot paints a similarly cozy domestic portrait of the interior of the Meyricks' abode—with its emphasis on bright windows, subjects absorbed in artistic occupations, and comfortable domestic furniture—that might come right out of Vermeer. We know from Eliot's famous manifesto of realism in *Adam Bede* that Dutch painting is Eliot's touchstone for realist art. In that novel, Eliot praises Dutch painting for a "rare, precious quality of truthfulness that I delight in" (*Bede,* 176). She continues: "I find a source of delicious sympathy in these faithful pictures of a monotonous homely existence, which has been the fate of so many more among my fellow-mortals than a life of pomp or of absolute indigence, of tragic suffering or of world-stirring actions."

The Meyrick household is just such a place: monotonous and homely. (It is because of this stasis that Deronda feels he can place Mirah in the Meyrick's care after he has saved her from drowning herself in the Thames.) On the outside, the Meyrick house is shabby and "grim-walled"; on the inside, it is a haven for "culture . . . spotlessly free from vulgarity" (*Deronda*, 166). The house is a monument to art; on the walls hang pictures for which Mrs. Meyrick has scrimped so as *not* to have to sell them; the narrator calls them later in the novel a "glorious company of engravings" (312), and the engravings tell a "world-history in scenes and heads," which forms the basis for the daughters' education. Eliot's description seems static and confining at first, even silent: the first words of the chapter which introduces us to the Meyrick house are "Mrs. Meyrick's house was not noisy." Eliot then introduces the Meyricks themselves as a domestic miniature painting: "Seeing the group they made this evening, one could hardly wish them to change their way of life. They were all alike small, and so in due proportion to their miniature rooms" (167). All four of the Meyrick women, remarks the narrator, "if they had been made of waxwork, might have been packed easily in a fashionable lady's traveling trunk" (167). This extraordinary image of the Meyricks as waxen dolls crammed into a lady's trunk has its gruesome side—as if the women, because of their modest means, their professions, and their physical stature are themselves disposable kinds of waxwork art which are in grave danger of being swept away by the unconcerned upper classes. Yet their size also serves to separate the Meyricks from the world of such rich ladies as Gwendolyn, whose physical presence Eliot depicts as overbearing. The narrator reminds us that the fashion at that time "would have demanded that four feminine circumferences should fill all the free space in the front parlour" (167)—that is, the hooped and petticoated dresses of fashionable women invaded domestic space and left no room for domestic life to proceed smoothly.

Eliot's own narrative style falls on the Meyrick side of things, so to speak. A review of *Daniel Deronda* published in the *Academy* in 1876 praised the novel's "exquisite cabinet pictures to which George Eliot has accustomed us" (Saintsbury 1876, 114). The *Oxford English Dictionary* quotes from an 1859 source which states, "Cabinet pictures are so named because they are so small in size as to be readily contained in a cabinet." Like the Meyricks, who are small enough to be readily contained in a lady's trunk, certain moments in Eliot's fiction are likewise diminutive—precise, detailed, and momentary, like the brief picture Eliot paints of the small Meyrick family.[13] Eliot may have had a reputation as a painter of grand canvases, but those canvases are made up of small-scale elements like the Meyrick family. Crucially, Eliot represents their diminutive stature as liberating rather than oppressive. If the Meyrick household is first represented as confined to a traveling trunk, the description soon opens out into a utopian discourse of open space: "There was space and apparatus for a wide-glancing, nicely-select life, open to the highest things in music, painting, and poetry" (167). From being "miniature rooms" with ancient furniture, the Meyrick house *expands,* almost literally, under the influence of such phrases as "wide-glancing" and "open to the highest." Eliot figures this movement from a confining *material* interior (a house) to an unconfined intellect and spirit by likening the Meyricks' *minds* to "medieval houses with unexpected recesses and openings from this into that, flights of steps and sudden outlooks" (167). Mental space and domestic space are at once at odds and productive of one another: the Meyricks' cramped quarters force them into the "wide-glancing" life of art. They do not strive to produce High Art, yet Eliot treats them with incredible respect. Within the economy of the novel, the Meyricks are both a narrative disruption (nothing happens to the Meyrick sisters, as we shall see, and so they stop the flow of plot) and a place of stasis and rest—they are like a large peaceful rock in the middle of a rushing stream. Deronda, Mirah, and Gwendolyn are carried around them on torrents that never disturb the central space. In Suzanne Keen's terms, they are a strange kind of "narrative annex," a space outside the main plot in which "impermissible subjects" can be represented; these annexes then work to "reveal Victorian novelists' creative responses to the capacities and limitations of their form" (Keen 1998, 1). In Keen's analysis, such impermissible subjects are generally not nearly as seemingly innocent as the Meyrick sisters (Keen focuses mainly on nonrealist elements, fantastic moments that "disfigure the structure" of novels). Yet I would argue that the "Meyrick annex" (which is almost literally an annex in the spatial sense) is Eliot's way of allowing herself to comment on the limitations of the realist novel that insists on confining women within traditional romance narratives.

The figure of the Alcharisi—Deronda's mother, a singer and actress who rejects her father and her religion, motherhood and love, for life on the stage—is often cited as Eliot's argument against such traditional romance narratives. Art for the Alcharisi provides a radical outlet from traditional social norms—radical in one sense because it confers on her a social rank outside that which she would deserve from her masculine connections (fathers or husbands). Women who were artists after the manner of the Alcharisi can say with Klesmer, "My rank as an artist is of my own winning" (*Deronda,* 212). Similarly, in Eliot's long poem *Armgart* (Leighton and Reynolds 1995, 227–48), inspired by Mme de Staël's "Corinne" and Elizabeth Barrett Browning's "Aurora Leigh," about an Alcharisi-like opera singer who chooses her profession over love, then loses her voice and repents in an excess of womanly humility, the heroine tells her rejected lover, "I am an artist as you are a noble: / I ought to bear the burthen of my rank" (lines 83–84). The lover retorts, " . . . A woman's rank / Lies in the fulness of her womanhood" (lines

88–89). Here the heroine claims art as a "rank"; the noble lover attempts to deny any woman the right to a rank outside her destiny as a wife and mother. The poem, writes one critic, "like *Daniel Deronda,* poses the incompatibility of love and art for the artist who is a woman" (Blake 1995, 82). In *Daniel Deronda,* the Alcharisi sets out this incompatibility when she tells Daniel, "Had I not a rightful claim to be something more than a mere daughter and mother? The voice and the genius matched the face. Whatever else was wrong, acknowledge that I had a right to be an artist, though my father's will was against it. My nature gave me a charter" (570).[14]

In calling on her "nature" as that which gives her the right to be an artist, the Alcharisi borrows language from the ideologies of aristocracy and femininity: both discourses used "nature" to support their beliefs. Aristocrats were born not made; women were one thing "by nature." Alcharisi turns the tables: if nature is to be crux of the matter, then nature made her an artist. Klesmer, a male artist, gets his romance along with his professional career, but women artists have to choose: Mirah gives up her art for Deronda; the Alcharisi gives up love for art.

But the Meyricks offer a surprisingly positive alternative to the Alcharisi's story. The Meyrick sisters represent the working woman artist who plods along and does her job *outside of narrative,* almost in the narrator's shoes; the Meyricks offer a striking example of what a woman's life might be like if she had productive work to do. Eliot heroines are noted for needing something to do—Dorothea Brooks, Maggie Tullliver, and Gwendolyn Harleth (in *Middlemarch, Mill on the Floss,* and *Daniel Deronda,* respectively) are all desperately attempting to exercise overactive intelligences within the restrictive possibilities of Victorian middle- and upper-class womanhood. The Meyrick sisters offer the novel's only view (and perhaps the only view in Eliot's fiction) of contented, productive female existence—a sort of utopian state outside the turmoil of a heroine's traditional narrative existence, which involves passion and trial and marriage and death and all the rest of it. Above all, the Meyrick sisters are immune to passion and the narrative confusions that arise from passion. They reject an erotic plot which would culminate, as it does with Mirah, in the woman's complete absorption into her husband's existence (Mirah's short-lived "career" as a singer vanishes without a murmur upon her engagement to Deronda). The sisters see Deronda only as a mentor and artist's *model,* never as desirable man. Mab cries out, "No woman ought to want to marry him. I never should. Fancy finding out that he had a tailor's bill, and used boot-hooks, like Hans. Who ever thought of his marrying?" To this her sister Kate replies, "I have. When I drew a wedding for a frontispiece to [a book] I made a sort of likeness of him for the bridegroom" (562). Significantly, it is only as a model for a *picture* of a bridegroom that Deronda sparks interest for the Meyrick girls—never as a flesh-and-blood man.

In *using* Daniel thus—as a model—rather than seeing him as an individual, the Meyrick sisters exhibit the same tic we see in the narrator: the likening of all characters to pictures. The world of *Daniel Deronda* is a world where famous artists and paintings are mentioned on almost every page. Gwendolyn, for example, is referred to as the "Vandyke Duchess" by Hans Meyrick, and a stranger says of Deronda, "He puts me in mind of Italian paintings" (281). Our first introduction to the Meyricks shows them instantly at work in this kind of art historical characterization: after first meeting Daniel, the youngest Meyrick sister, Mab, immediately sets to work painting him as Prince Camaralzaman, a heroic figure from the *Arabian Nights* (156). The sisters refer to him after that as Prince Camaralzaman; when they meet Mirah they cast her, too, as various historical figures, and Hans begins a series of paintings with her as the model for Berenice, the Jewish woman who lived with the Roman emperor Titus.[15] The narrator follows the Meyricks' lead. We hear of Mordecai that "he commonly wore a cloth cap with black fur round it, which no painter would have asked him to take off" (405), and that Mirah's face could look so happy that "a painter need have changed nothing if he had wanted to put it in front of the host singing 'peace on earth and goodwill to men'" (312). Likewise Deronda "might have been a subject for those old painters who liked contrasts of temperament" (137) or "when he was thirteen he might have served as model for a painter who wanted to image the most memorable of boys" (141). In the Meyricks' world, then, people are pictures.[16] And they are the only characters within the novel who share this worldview with the narrator, for whom people are also pictures.

The Meyricks thus provide an alternative to the martyred women in other Eliot novels—and in nineteenth-century novels in general—for whom femininity and creativity cannot be contained in the same body. Although the Alcharisi does put aside traditional marriage and motherhood for art (she marries a man she can control utterly, and she passes her son, Deronda, over to Sir Hugo to raise), she appears to us in the novel only in shattered form, her voice, health, and beauty in ruins, and lacking the strength to continue fighting against her father's influence: she feels compelled, at long last, to meet her son and disclose to him the secret of his birth. But the Meyricks are not drawn along such melodramatic lines; they do not follow a traditional heroine's path. Alison Booth—borrowing from Nancy Miller borrowing from Freud—lays out two possible plot lines for a heroine's story: the plot of ambition, which takes the heroine into the world, or the erotic plot, which leads to the private world of marriage and childbearing (1991, 114). Gwendolyn, when her family loses its money, wants to sign on for the plot of ambition,[17] but opts instead for the marriage plot—which does not prove a resounding success. The Alcharisi chose the plot of ambition, but she too, though a success as an artist, fails in the end to maintain her distance from the private demands of family. The Meyricks fall outside both these narrative structures: within the bosom of an all-female family, ambition and creativity can blossom, if only to a mild extent. Yet mild is the key term. Their existence may be utopian in certain ways, but they are not raging artistic successes. They are neither geniuses nor *public* art figures—like Klesmer, the Alcharisi, or Mirah—or Eliot herself. They are not revolutionary models for successful artistic women; rather, they are models for the only way Eliot seems to envision that nineteenth-century society might let women live as artists and be happy: poor, unmarried, and anonymous. The Meyricks preserve a pristine feminine modesty yet work actively for their living from within the quiet confines of the domestic sphere. And yet from within that sphere, they are able to critique and to escape the tumults of the plot around them.

IV.

If Howitt and Eliot offer us views of female artistic utopias, Margaret Oliphant offers a more poignant story of a woman artist in which the tumults of plot (in the form of heteronormative, traditional gender roles) prove insurmountable barricades erected by the social order between a woman artist and her artistic inspirations. *Miss Marjoribanks* is regularly cited as Oliphant's best novel, out of an impressive lifetime production of more than ninety novels.[18] The novel is part of Oliphant's well-known five-volume Chronicles of Carlingford series detailing the domestic, religious, and political life of a cathedral town, Carlingford, near London. *Miss Marjoribanks* has been called an "ironic comedy about power" (O'Mealy 1966, 46); it should also be considered a rather painful satire on women's work, something Oliphant knew all too much about. Oliphant's writing provided the main financial support for her husband and their children; after his early death she became the sole financial support for her three children, her two brothers, and several of her nieces and nephews. In addition to writing novels, Oliphant augmented her coffers by producing numerous volumes of history, biography, and travel writing; she was also a regular literary reviewer and general contributor for the prestigious *Blackwood's* magazine. There wasn't much Oliphant didn't know about the life of a struggling middle-class working mother in Victorian England. In *Miss Marjoribanks,* Oliphant explores the question of women's work through two female characters: the heroine, Lucilla Marjoribanks, and a young artist, Rose Lake.

We are introduced to Lucilla Marjoribanks at the moment when her mother dies. The death of Mrs. Marjoribanks occasions little grief but much concern over *occupation*. Mrs. Marjoribanks's maid is heard to say, "I can't abear to think as I'm to be parted from you all, miss. I've lost the best missus as ever was, and I shouldn't mind going after her" (*Marjoribanks*, 6). The narrator, however, makes it quite clear that what is truly distressing the maid is the loss of her job rather than her mistress. But this garners no real disapproval; the narrator remarks that "the weeping handmaiden . . . naturally saw her own loss in the most vivid light" (6). The maid's concern for her occupation is then echoed by Lucilla's own earnest desire that the death of her mother will allow her to leave school and find "work" as a "comfort for dear papa."

Her desires for immediate occupation are thwarted, however, when her father insists on sending her back to school. Lucilla's acceptance of her father's dismissal is couched in terms of sovereignty and battle: "Thus she consented to postpone her *reign* . . . and retired with the full honours of *war*. She . . . re-arranged all the details, and settled upon all the means possible of preparing herself for what she called the *charge of the establishment* when her final *emancipation* [from school] took place" (11; emphasis added). The language of government, of reign and rule and kingdom and dominion, permeate the novel; Lucilla's struggles to become the Queen of Carlingford are allegorized into a mock-heroic narrative, turning the domestic space into a public arena for metaphoric battles. In preparation for her "reign" as mistress of her father's house and monarch of the town, Lucilla returns to school and demands to be taught political economy, "to help me manage everything" (11). This course in political economy becomes Lucilla's battle cry, as she believes she now knows how society should be arranged: "It is all put into a system of political economy, you know. It is very funny before you get used to it; but you know there has to be a balance in everything, and that is how it must be" (242).[19]

In the three years she remains at school after her mother's death, Lucilla is "conscious of having had a career not without importance" (14). This "career" involves amiable dictatorship over the other schoolgirls and continued preparation for her chosen profession as "a comfort to dear papa." Once home, Lucilla embarks on what Oliphant consistently terms a "career" and consistently represents in the language of labor, work, or occupation. Lucilla's work centers on her intention to redesign Carlingford's social environment by effecting what she sees as great changes in the way her "subjects" run their lives. Lucilla has often been called the "Victorian Emma," and for good reason: "handsome, clever, and rich, with a comfortable home and happy disposition" (Austen, *Emma*, 3) could as easily describe Lucilla as it does Emma, and both heroines share a domineering, meddling tendency. But while Emma expends her energy matchmaking, Lucilla meddles in both politics and social mores; her goal is not to marry everyone off but to bring about a "revolution of tastes and ideas" (*Marjoribanks*, 33). Lucilla differs from Emma in that her (Lucilla's) machinations are more clearly marked as material production; one might say that the creative impulse that Emma exercises upon Harriet's person (by trying to turn Harriet into a more elegant woman) is extended, in *Miss Marjoribanks,* to an entire town.[20] Everyone in Carlingford is fodder for Lucilla's social experimentation; people were "simple material for Miss Marjoribanks's genius, out of which she had a great result to produce" (62).

Lucilla's campaign to create an elegant and well-disciplined society begins with her redecoration of home. Dr. Marjoribanks and his nephew discover Lucilla one evening "in the act of pacing the room—pacing, not in the sentimental sense of making a little promenade up and down, but in the homely practical signification, with a view of measuring, that she might form an idea of how much carpet was required" (44). Her father reads her actions incorrectly and asks, "What were you doing, Lucilla? Re-hearsing Lady Macbeth, I suppose" (44). Dr. Marjoribanks's response to Lucilla's domestic interests brings out one common use for nineteenth-century drawing rooms: amateur theatricals. A wealthy young woman of leisure like Lucilla might be expected to indulge in such pleasures to while away her time. The reference to acting also foreshadows the tenor of the "Evenings" Lucilla plans to hold in her newly carpeted drawing room: they will be, in every sense of the word, stage-managed by Lucilla. Every movement of every guest will be monitored, every entertainment carefully chosen for the appropriate effect.[21]

Casting Lucilla as Lady Macbeth exposes the more ferocious side of Lucilla's personnel management; both women share a strong manipulative impulse and neither wastes much concern on the people they must make use of in their quest for queenship. Lucilla's father recognizes this latent power in his daughter but cannot understand it. Although a professional man himself, the doctor does not seem to understand the need for female activity and cannot comprehend his daughter's desire to be "doing something," although he does acknowledge that with her energy and intelligence she would have made a much better professional worker than any of her male relatives. (Lucilla's desperate desire for active work connects her with other nineteenth-century heroines such as Emma or Dorothea Brooke, who chafe at the lack of opportunities for financially secure middle-class women in the century.)

Lucilla's mock-professionalism is set against the real and financially necessary professional artistic aspirations of Rose Lake,[22] the local drawing master's second daughter; this contrast is made all the more powerful as Oliphant consistently tropes Lucilla's "career" in society in artistic terms, as when she writes that Lucilla's social goals involve "the grand design of turning the chaotic elements of society in Carlingford into one grand unity" (157). We hear in the first chapter, in the most offhand manner, that Rose Lake has lost her mother at the same time as Lucilla; but the aside marks a world of difference between the two families:

> A painful heaviness possessed him [Dr. Marjoribanks] when he became aware how little real sorrow was in his mind, and how small an actual loss was this loss of his wife, which balked before the world as an event of just as much magnitude as the loss, for example, which poor Mr. Lake, the drawing-master, was at the same moment suffering. (6)

That the Lake family is brought forward first in a clause introduced by "for example" highlights the social insignificance of the drawing master and his brood: they are merely used in contrast to the more socially prominent Marjoribanks family. The narrator seems to tell us that, if Mrs. Marjoribanks had not died at the same time as Mrs. Lake, we might never have heard of Mrs. Lake at all. Rose is introduced into the narrative in much the same way, as an addendum to Lucilla—and Rose, like her father, is given the epithet "poor." Rose Lake attends the same school as Lucilla, but instead of paying for schooling Rose gives the younger children drawing lessons in exchange for her education; the narrator tells us that she "was not at all badly off in her inferior position" (17). Rose's artistic career—teaching, art production, helping her father to run the local School of Design—contrasts sharply with Lucilla's more metaphorical "career" as the prominent hostess and social arbiter in Carlingford. Rose and her elder sister Barbara (whose musical talents become crucial for the success of Lucilla's "Thursday evenings") appear initially in the novel as pure use-value.

Rose is valued and used by Lucilla and society at large (Rose is called "twice as serviceable" as her sister, 125), for her ability in design, which has brought her very mild prominence in the artistic community:

> Her design for a Honiton-lace flounce, a spirited composition of dragons' tails and the striking plant called teazle, which flourishes in the neighborhood of Carlingford (for Mr. Lake had leanings towards Preraphaelitism), was thought by the best judges to show a wonderful amount of feeling for art. (17)

Because of her skill, after her graduation Rose is placed in charge of the female pupils of the School of Design. The "flounce" which wins Rose such acclaim returns to the narrative again and again; Rose speaks of it as a great work in progress. The narrative voice, however, is more satirical on the subject, as when Rose attributes the polite bowing of some gentlemen in the street to their appreciation for her artistic talent—when in fact the young Rose Lake is rather pretty. She tells her sister, "Of course I was pleased [at the attention]; but then I knew it was my design he was thinking of—my Honiton flounce, you know" (95). The ironic twist of the very word "flounce," suggesting as it does a flirtatious way of feminine movement precisely antithetical to Rose's demeanor, appears utterly beyond Rose's comprehension; for the young artist, her material "flounce" (the art object) is what garners her fame, rather than any personal physical trait. The narrator's description of Rose's "Preraphaelite" design suggests additional irony: the intertwining of fanciful dragons and a common plant symbolizes both the young artist's ludicrous fantasy life (treated with pathos by the narrative, as we will see) and its inevitable choking by the pressures of family and social life.

Rose and Barbara Lake are, in Lucilla's mind, as much a part of the available raw materials for her great social plan as are her drawing-room furnishings. But because the Lake sisters are artists, they resist manipulation and muck up the wheels of Lucilla's social machine. Barbara's "flashing" good looks and beautiful voice attract Mr. Cavendish, who had been paying his attentions to Lucilla. The first volume of the novel traces a surprising series of failures for Lucilla's reign—that is, we see a sequence of scenes where various men are considering proposing to her but transfer their affections to other women, all of them professional, working women: Mr. Cavendish turns from Lucilla to Barbara Lake, who begins as a singer and eventually becomes a governess; the new archdeacon, whom the town expected to court Lucilla, discovers in Mrs. Mortimer, a local schoolteacher, the beloved of his youth; and the general becomes enamored of Rose Lake, our young artist and teacher, whom he mistakenly assumes is Lucilla.

The disruptive potential of the artisan class is best articulated by Rose Lake. She repeatedly dismisses social hierarchy and announces, "But the true strength of our position is that we are a family of artists. We are everybody's equal, and we are nobody's equal. We have a rank of our own" (147). We see something similar in Ritchie's *Miss Angel* when the narrator says, "Angelica started off with this high company [the ambassadress], dressed in her shabby dress, timid yet resolute—the compeer of any lady in the land. No thought of any difference of rank discomposed her" (*Angel,* 18). Similarly, in *Daniel Deronda,* Herr Klesmer the musician announces to the Arrowpoints, who have told him angrily that he shall have none of their fortune if he marries their daughter: "But understand that I consider it out of the power either of you or of your fortune to confer on me anything that I value. My rank as an artist is of my own winning, and I would not exchange it for any other. I am able to maintain your daughter" (*Deronda*, 212). Klesmer echoes little Rose Lake's more vehement assertions of the distinct separateness of the artist or artisan class. Both artists give voice to the transformation of the artist class during the nineteenth century in England.

Rose, like Lucilla, sees herself as a "queen," as a ruling force in her small corner of the world. On her way to visit Lucilla, Rose walks through town with "her bright eyes regarding the world with that air of frank recognition and acknowledgment which Rose felt she owed as an artist to her fellow creatures. They were all good subjects more or less, and the consciousness that she could draw them and immortalize them gave her the same sense of confidence . . . as a young princess might have felt whose rank protected her" (*Marjoribanks*, 144). That Rose calls the people of Carlingford "good subjects" plays on the dual meaning of "subject"—for Lucilla, Carlingford's populace are good subjects under her authority, pledging allegiance to her reign. For Rose Lake, the people are good "subjects": they are all potential subject matter for Rose's artworks.

Rose's status as an artist gives her a rank of her own, she thinks; it also desexes her and provides her with freedoms not normally given to her sex. This is one reason why women as artists caused such social commotion: they broke down both gender *and* class barriers. "We are artists," wrote a nineteenth-century French woman artist, "for whom the ideal should be something sacred, to elevate themselves above distinctions of sex, in the same way they have already placed themselves beyond prejudices of class and to honor the chisel which produces masterpieces without looking to see if the hand that guides it belongs to a man or a woman."[23] Thus Rose can walk alone on the streets of Carlingford (Lucilla walks with her maid) because her artisan class exempts her from the traditional regulations of gender.

The meetings between Rose and Lucilla often have something of the flavor of a stand-off between warring politicians, each set so firmly on their chosen path that their conversation fails to be dialogue and remains instead two monologues which must pause for breath occasionally to admit the other. Each young woman has an aim and a set of beliefs; neither comprehends that the other's "career" is of any social value. Lucilla remarks to Rose, "I can't think why you never came to see me before; as for me, you know, I never have any time. Poor papa has nobody else to take care of him." To which Rose replies, "I have a great deal to do too, and then all my spare moments

I am working at my design. Papa always says that society accepts artists for what they can give, and does not expect them to sacrifice their time." Lucilla immediately thinks that "society was utterly unconscious of the existence of the Lake family" (145) but that young Rose could be an "effective instrument" for Lucilla's social improvements: Lucilla proposes that Rose become one of the evening "entertainments" for Lucilla's social gatherings, now that Barbara Lake had deserted Lucilla. Rose replies:

> "Barbara ought to have been some rich person's daughter, with nothing to do. She would not mind being of no use in the world. It is a kind of temperament I don't understand," continued the little artist. All this, it is true, was novel to Miss Marjoribanks, who had a kind of prejudice in favour of the daughters of rich persons who had nothing to do. (146)

The narrator's brief ironic remark about the idle rich momentarily elevates the young Rose; her status as a working woman seems a cut above Lucilla's unproductive occupations. Miss Marjoribanks, however, is not to be outdone by Rose Lake—Lucilla pounces on the "little artist" and ropes her into coming in place of the sulking Barbara to be the entertainment at the next "evening." And so Rose promises to come and display her portfolio for the interest and amusement of the idle rich. Rose feels a tingle of "pride and excitement and pleasure and a kind of pain" (146) at the thought of being displayed in public as an exemplar of "the artist."

The evening party, however, does not provide Rose with the kind of excitement she had in mind. Perhaps the most curious thing about the scene is how much Oliphant chose to contract it in her revisions from serial to book form—and in doing so, how much she radically altered and diminished the character of Rose Lake. The novel was first published in *Blackwood's* from February 1865 through May 1866. Blackwood and Sons publishers then brought out a three-volume edition in 1866; Oliphant herself undertook the revisions for this publication. The majority of the revisions are stylistic, but Oliphant chose to make heavy changes in one particular place: chapters 18 and 19 from the original magazine have been significantly cut and revised to become chapter 18 of the three-volume novel. The bulk of the two magazine chapters focuses on Rose Lake's experience at Lucilla's party and builds a startlingly angry critique of public art appreciation.

In the magazine chapters, Rose's experience at the party is "a disenchanting process" (appendix to *Miss Marjoribanks*, 538). She arrives at the party with her sister Barbara, who proceeds to display publicly her misery over Mr. Cavendish's disappearance from town; the party members avoid her, laugh at her, and hold her in disgust. Rose attempts to talk her sister into acting with dignity but fails and stands forlorn in her inappropriate dress. Rose has little to spend on her clothes, so she has attempted to create for herself a red and black outfit "made with quaint little slashings at the shoulders and round the waist of an architectural character" (537) which sounds exceedingly Pre-Raphaelite and which Lucilla and the other women (dressed all in simple white evening dresses) mock. She has brought her portfolio of designs and sketches with her in the expectation that art would be a main topic of conversation among such elegant company, but no one shows the least interest:

> All of them [the company] might have seen the portfolio had they liked, and yet they went on talking about the most unimportant matters;—where they were going, and what they were to wear, and what new amusements or occupations had been planned for the morrow—which two words indeed seem to mean the same thing according to the Carlingford young ladies. As Rose Lake stood and listened, a few of her childish illusions began to leave her. In the first place, nobody said a syllable either about art, literature, or even music, which gave the lie to all her previous conceptions of conversation among educated people—and then it began slowly to dawn upon Rose, that a life like her own, full of work and occupation, which she had been used up to this moment to think a very good life, and quite refined and dignified in comparison with most of the lives she knew of, was in reality a very shabby and poor existence, of which a young woman ought to be ashamed when she came into society. . . . She who had thought of the Female School of Design as of a Career, and considered herself a little in the light of one of the pioneers of society and benefactors of her kind! But in Miss Marjoribanks's drawing-room the Career seemed to change its character. (538)

Oliphant continues for several paragraphs in this vein, getting (through a free indirect discourse representing Rose's thoughts) angrier and angrier. It is a rare moment in Oliphant's work, a moment where social beliefs are decried with a rage similar at times to Jane Eyre's diatribe against the emotional and intellectual confinement of women. Oliphant rarely flies this far off the handle, and it is significant that this outburst should occur during a discussion of art and society. In their introductory essay to the volume *Politics and Aesthetics in the Arts,* Kemal and Gaskell write, "Anger is so prevalent, whether explicitly or implicitly, whenever politics, aesthetics and the arts are discussed together that it [anger] is almost always implicitly a fourth concept" (2000, 2). All the women writers I discuss in this book display this anger when tackling women's relation to art; in Oliphant's case the anger becomes more visible because of the generally placid backdrop of her novels.

And it gets worse. This is only Rose's first moment of disillusion at the party, and it happens while only the women are in the room; Rose must first undergo the realization that she is utterly different from other women in her world. Then the gentlemen return from their separate postprandial drinks and Rose must undergo a new degradation, this time directly related to her artworks. This moment of the reintroduction of the sexes is always the most difficult for Lucilla to manage at her parties. Lucilla lives in horror at the "circle of black coats" which tended to consolidate away from the womenfolk; she must exert herself to overcome the inertia which results, in Carlingford, in the complete social segregation of men and women. At this particular "Thursday Evening," she drags the Archdeacon Mr. Beverly out of the circle of men and brings him across the room to Rose, who is then asked to display her portfolio of drawings.

To get the ball rolling, Lucilla reaches into Rose's portfolio to grab one sketch at random—she chances on the one sketch in the portfolio which was actually done by Rose's brother Willie. The sketch, though not (the narrator tells us clearly) better than those by Rose, happens to suit Archdeacon Beverly, who begins to praise it highly without ever giving Rose a chance to explain that it is not her work. Mr. Beverly, in his lordly manner, delivers his encomiums, qualifying them because of his (mistaken) belief that the creator is a woman: "There is a great deal of very fine feeling. . . . There is a freedom in that leg, for example, which is extraordinary for a lady—" (appendix to *Miss Marjoribanks,* 542) Rose, who has been "half frantic" all the while, finally bursts out "But it is not a lady!" The archdeacon, however, misunderstands her and (pointedly looking at her dress) believes her to mean that she herself is not a "lady"—that is, a woman of leisure and quality. Rose, with her mild manner and meek voice, never succeeds in making him understand his mistake. But Oliphant describes her behavior and emotions in extraordinary language. Rose is first "trembling with impatience and a kind of feminine rage" (541). She wants "to box and pinch him into listening" (ibid.) and after Mr. Beverly has stopped talking she is "palpitating with vexation and impatience, and keen feminine rage" (543). The "impatience" and "feminine rage" are repeated, but the second time have gained new force—first Rose is "trembling" but later she is "palpitating," and first the rage is qualified by the phrase "a kind of" but later it is bluntly "keen."

The narrator steps in at this point to offer an extended Homeric metaphor linking Lucilla's use of Rose to a great Monarch's use of footsoldiers in battle: "If a great monarch was to count how many soldiers would be killed every time it was necessary . . . to fight a great battle, what would become of the world?" (544). Lucilla has, in her own mind, simply made use of Rose and Barbara for society's greater good; but Oliphant's tone is close to brutal as she explains that "Miss Marjoribanks had made use of them as society generally makes use of art" (544). The Lake sisters retreat in dismay, and Oliphant remarks, "And thus the two representatives of the arts went home in their wounded condition, after having served their purpose" (ibid.). Rose and Barbara stand in for all of art—including, presumably, novel-writing—and the scene becomes a stark depiction of art's devaluation at the hands of society.

All of this is cut from the final three-volume version of the novel. In that version, Rose simply comes to the party with Barbara, and we hear only that Lucilla "left the Archdeacon . . . beside the Lakes and their portfolio of drawings" (*Marjoribanks,* 156). The portfolio becomes the joint property of "the Lakes" (when in the periodical version it is only Rose's) and we hear of neither Mr. Beverly's approbation nor Rose's anger. The now much shorter party scene is entirely Lucilla-focused. Why would Oliphant have chosen to cut the chapters? In the three-volume novel version, Rose Lake seems an oddly incomplete figure. She is introduced at key moments but says very little; her artistic labor and aesthetic creed act as weak counterpoints to Lucilla's mock-heroic social activities. Yet the two serial chapters represent Rose as a relatively noble woman with a rich interiority who is undergoing a painful social awakening, and the chapters come across as painful commentaries about a woman artist's devaluation in the world. The chapters in their earnestness and anger almost unbalance the tone of the rest of the book; they are a serious indictment of Lucilla's world and worldview. Not that Lucilla is particularly mean to Rose—but, in contrast to Rose, Lucilla becomes momentarily *uninteresting* when put in conjunction with the much larger-scale philosophical, social, and aesthetic revelations Rose experiences. Suddenly Oliphant introduces into her narrative a possible countervoice, a figure who could (if Oliphant let her) become a narrative center for serious critique. Rose *could* become Oliphant's alter-ego—and in the serial chapters does for a brief moment. Rose articulates Oliphant's anger over the woman artist's position in society, as well as a more general fury at how society people "make use" of art. But this unbalances the book, turns it into a very different sort of text. The three-volume novel version removes Rose from this position of power and centrality, returning her to the periphery as just one other of Lucilla's satellite instruments.

That Oliphant felt the need to remove the pages suggests that such aesthetic and gender commentary was too radical for the kind of fiction Oliphant generally produced. And throughout the final version of the novel, Oliphant refuses to follow through with the socially disruptive or utopian possibilities of Rose's artistic philosophy. Rose is always "the little artist"; her aspirations surrounding her flounce are made absurd. The portfolio is neglected by society, and eventually Rose must give up her dreams of art to become a proper domestic woman. After the death of Mrs. Lake, and after Barbara has run off to become a governess after her romantic "disappointment," Rose is forced to give up her career in art to take care of the Lake household, her father, and younger siblings. Although Barbara deserves no such sacrifice and certainly no sympathy, Rose says of her eldest sister, "'She has suffered so much here; how can any one ask her to sacrifice herself to us? And I am quite happy.... It is her *heart*, you know; and it is only my Career'" (328). Rose represents the fragility of such "careers," their inability to hold up under the onslaught of material life.

Such experience was common; it was a rare woman who could carry on a family life and—as Rose always capitalizes it—a Career. The few who did so were as famous for their domestic heroism as for their artworks (or, in Oliphant's case, literary production). Artistic training did not fit one for becoming a good housewife. Lucilla's training in "political economy," however, *does* fit her for her eventual "career" of matrimony. Rose Lake's vision, on the other hand, has been ruthlessly abandoned. It seems odd that Oliphant, herself a working woman, should have so cruelly denied Rose her artistic career. Because Oliphant did not consider her own fiction to be "High Art" any more than Rose considers her designs to be such, the crumbling of Rose's career in design seems doubly strange. Why not simply let Rose become a designer, if not a practitioner of high art? Rose Lake's punishment keeps her from becoming another Oliphant-like figure; instead of her being permitted to be a first-class producer of "second-class" art, Rose Lake's career is cut off entirely. Oliphant's message seems to be that such a life is impossible, at least in fiction, where a woman artist's ideology would unsettle the central heroine's more conservative narrative. Rose at novel's end is bitter and disillusioned; she says of art: "I am not so sure about the moral influence of Art as I used to be—except High Art, to be sure; but we never have any High Art down here" (429).

Working women, Oliphant implies, are not the stuff of fiction. Oliphant's unusual *Autobiography* echoes this notion, and allows us to see Rose's plight as a reflection of Oliphant's own dismal meditations on the quality of her own literary productions. In her *Autobiography,* Oliphant writes,

> ... I should rather like to forget it all, to wipe out all the books, to silence those compliments about my industry, &c., which I always turn off with a laugh.... I suppose this is really pride.... When people comment upon the number of books I have written, and I say that I am so far from being proud of that fact that I should like at least half of them forgotten, they stare—and yet it is quite true.... They are my work ... though they are never so good as I meant them to be. (1899, 5–6)

Oliphant's dour self-effacement is well known; she considered herself something of a hack writer, not a true artist (like Eliot, against whom she explicitly measured herself). Rose Lake's disappointment in art can easily be seen as voicing Oliphant's own opinion of her literary productions. But what emerges from reading Oliphant's *Autobiography* is a kind of anger against a social order that made it *impossible* for her to become a writer of Eliot's caliber. As Virginia Woolf wrote, Oliphant "sold her brain, her very admirable brain, prostituted her culture and enslaved her intellectual liberty in order that she might earn her living and educate her children" (Woolf 1966–67, 166). Woolf believed that Oliphant *could* have written more erudite and polished novels but for her dismal personal situation, which Woolf argued stemmed directly from gender concerns. Woolf saw Oliphant as a victim of Victorian patriarchal culture, too worried about making a living to have time to worry about making art. Oliphant echoes this when she writes in her *Autobiography*:

> I don't quite know why I should put this all down. I suppose because George Eliot's life has, as I said above, stirred me up to an involuntary confession. How I have been handicapped in life! Should I have done better if I had been kept, like her, in a mental greenhouse and taken care of? . . . It is a little hard sometimes not to feel . . . that the men who have no wives, who have given themselves up to their art, have had an almost unfair advantage over us who have been given perhaps more than one [dependent] to take care of. Curious freedom! I have never known what it was. I have always had to think of other people, and to plan everything. . . . I have not been able to rest, to please myself, to take the pleasures that have come in my way, but have always been forced to go on without a pause. (1899, 5–6)

Similarly, at the start of her *Autobiography*, she writes:

> I have been tempted to begin writing by writing George Eliot's life—with that curious kind of self-compassion which one cannot get clear of. I wonder if I am a little envious of her? I always avoid considering formally what my own mind is worth. I have never had any theory on the subject. I have written because it gave me pleasure, because it came natural to me, because it was like talking or breathing, *besides the big fact that it was necessary for me to work for my children.* . . . I feel that my carelessness of asserting my claim [to being a great novelist] is very much against me with everybody. It is so natural to think that if the workman himself is indifferent about his work, there can't be much in it that is worth thinking about. (4–5; emphasis added)

Eliot, who was lucky enough to have the time, money, and support to give her work careful attention, represented the kind of artist Rose Lake and Oliphant herself could not be due to circumstances. At one point in her *Autobiography* Oliphant writes in despair, "No one even will mention me in the same breath with George Eliot" (7). This chapter attempts to assuage Oliphant's feelings somewhat, by doing just that. Certainly the difference between the two writers is clear—and here I am not making a qualitative comment. While Eliot (and Howitt) could imagine a female artistic utopia in which women artists could practice an unexalted but nevertheless successful art—similar perhaps in its hierarchical position to domestic fiction—Oliphant had no such faith. Her own artistic experiences were anything but utopian, and in Rose Lake we can hear Oliphant's angry (and forlorn) critique of the social pressures that restrain women artists.

Chapter Five

The Afterlife of Angelica Kauffman

I.

IN ONE OF THE MOST famous articles in the annals of feminist art history, Linda Nochlin asked the crucial question, "Why Have There Been No Great Women Artists?" Feminist art historians have spent the last several decades trying to answer that question; their recovery work on forgotten women artists and their reevaluation of those few women artists who found precarious reputation on the fringes of history has salvaged much of women's art, both literally and figuratively. But this is not a new endeavor; Victorian women writers were similarly interested in discovering and reevaluating a lineage of women artists, as models for contemporary Victorian women who struggled to find their place in the history of art and as rebuttals to the many dismissals of women's artistic capacities. This chapter considers Victorian representations of Angelica Kauffman, a prominent eighteenth-century painter whose life history offers an unusually good example of the struggles faced by women painters. I focus in particular on Anne Thackeray Ritchie's fictionalized account of Kauffman's life titled *Miss Angel and Fulham Lawn* (employing a nickname used in Kauffman's lifetime by Reynolds and others), published in 1876. Ritchie's work dramatizes with particular clarity the difficulty a woman artist had in balancing her physical existence with her creative life. Other Victorian writers on Kauffman echo this problem; Victorian art critics or historians rarely bothered to mention Kauffman's paintings, so fascinating did they find her personal and sexual history. Kauffman becomes a startling embodiment of a woman painter's absolute inability to shed her skin.

Angelica Kauffman was born in Switzerland in 1740; after a childhood spent studying art in Italy, she moved to London in 1766 and became a prominent figure in the London art scene. She was friends with Sir Joshua Reynolds and other influential artists; her patrons were elite and numerous. She was best known as a History painter (an unusually elevated genre for a woman), although her portraits gained her wealth and access to the highest (even royal) circles. Most of her Academy work was classical History painting based on modern and ancient history as well as mythological, biblical, or literary narratives. She came to England just at the moment when the English art theorists and practitioners were distraught at the lack of a noble British tradition of History painting (considered by aestheticians, if not the viewing public, to be the highest genre of painting) and were importing Continental and American artists (Kauffman and Benjamin West were the best known) to fill the absence. Kauffman was an astute businesswoman; many of her history paintings appealed to her adoptive country's national pride by featuring subjects from British history, literature, and mythology. When the Royal Academy was founded in 1768, she was one of two female members (the only women so honored until well over one hundred years later in 1922), a fact Victorian women artists never forgot during their numerous campaigns for inclusion in the august institution.

One might think that her fame, financial success, and election to the Royal Academy made Kauffman a natural candidate for idealization by Victorian women looking for past examples to emulate and celebrate. However, Kauffman's Victorian legacy is anything but idealizing. The historical record paints an intensely contradictory portrait: Kauffman is alternately represented as a success and a failure, a respectable professional woman and a hopeless coquette. However varied the representations, one thing stands out: Kauffman's problem, during and after her lifetime, is the inescapable presence of the visible female body. Claxton's cartoon in figure 1.9 ("BOTHER the old masters, look at the young mis-esses") could easily stand as a condensed allegory of her life as an artist. Kauffman was a well-known figure in her own day and remained popular into the Victorian era not only because of the quality and quantity of her work but also because of her sensational personal history and—most importantly—the legacy of her physical beauty, which is touted with depressing regularity whenever her name arises in art-historical documents. This obsession with the personal details of women artists (both specifically physical and more generally biographical) like Kauffman does not end with the Victorians; the tendency has been remarkably slow to disappear and perverts a surprising number of artists' histories. For example, the recent explosion of interest in the Renaissance painter Artemesia Gentileschi has emphasized again and again her rape (or seduction, depending on the rendition) rather than her artwork.[1] Kauffman receives similar treatment, as the entry under "Angelica Kauffman" in the first (1970) edition of the *Oxford Companion to Art* demonstrates:

> ANGELICA KAUFFMAN (1740–1807)
> Swiss decorative painter. She traveled with *her father J. J. Kauffman* from an early age in Switzerland and Italy; on her later visits to Rome she was greatly impressed by the Neo-Classical vogue and on this she formed her style. . . . She came to London in 1766 where her work and *her person* were greatly admired. She was a friend of Reynolds and became a foundation member of the Royal Academy. . . . In 1782 she settled in Rome. She *married her second husband,* the decorative painter Antonio Zucchi, R.A. in 1781. (Osborne 1970, 622; emphasis added).

The entry is filled with irrelevancies, all of them erring on the side of the personal: Kauffman's father need not be listed, but seems important here only to prove that she did not (Heaven forbid) gallivant about Europe on her own. The reference to her physical appearance ("her person") is particularly appalling, as even a cursory glance through the biographies of male painters in the same volume reveals that "the person" of male painters is nowhere mentioned; a reference to beauty is reserved for the female artist. Equally curious is the fact that none of the biographies of male painters in the *Companion* list the names of their wives or the dates of their marriages—not even Diego Rivera's entry, which stunningly fails to mention his wife, the artist Frida Kahlo (who does not appear *at all* in this edition of the volume). In the entries on female artists, however, personal information is regularly offered. Kauffman's fellow Royal Academy founder Mary Moser's entry is listed only as part of her father's entry (Artemisia Gentileschi's entry is a similar appendage rather than an entry in its own right). Moser's entry reads:

> His daughter MARY MOSER (d. 1819) was a flower painter. . . . She exhibited at the Society of Artists 1760–8 and was a foundation member of the Royal Academy; at the Academy's troubled presidential election of 1805 her name was irresponsibly put forward as a candidate . . . in 1793 she married Captain Hugh Lloyd as his second wife. (1970, 749)

Although there might be an argument for including the name of Kauffman's husband, Antonio Zucchi (because he was a fellow artist), the fact that he does not merit enough acclaim for his own entry makes it seem irrelevant data for Kauffman's biography. Moser's biography is even more shocking: first, that her name was put forward "irresponsibly" as a presidential candidate is the personal opinion of the author of this entry in the *Companion* rather than proved historical fact; second, "Captain Hugh Lloyd" has no connection whatsoever with the art world and need not be mentioned at all. Finally, why on earth do readers need to know that Moser was his "second wife"? Are we to understand that she is therefore somehow "second best"? The entries for Kauffman and Moser consistently belittle the artists by these repeated references to their private lives. These are "women," the entries are telling us—women with personal lives filled with husbands and fathers. They aren't *artists*.[2]

The explicit link drawn between "her work and her person" in the entry for Kauffman in *Oxford Companion to Art* is more poignant when one realizes that it is, unfortunately, an accurate depiction of Kauffman's experience as an artist in the late eighteenth century. She was consistently and ruthlessly viewed by the art public as a desirable woman first and an artist second. Kauffman did not hesitate to exploit her appearance, recognizing it as a selling point; she did this both by cultivating her beauty and charm (so contemporary sources tell us) as well as (so the art historical record suggests) by repeatedly presenting the viewing public with elegant images of her self. Not only did she produce numerous self-portraits that were well known, but Kauffman also produced numerous symbolic images representing female figures as some aspect of Art (Design, Imitation, Colour, Invention, Fame, and Painting) using herself as the model. In one case she created a *Self-Portrait* (1788) using the same pose and paraphernalia as an earlier symbolic image (*Allegory of Imitation,* ca. 1780–81). These pictures become *both* self-portraits and allegorical texts; the female artist's body is simultaneously real (based on Kauffman) and imaginary (used to evoke a concept).

In two of her best-known paintings, Kauffman sets her "real" self alongside allegorical female figures. In *Self-Portrait in the Character of Painting Embraced by Poetry* (1780–81), we see Kauffman as the figure of "Painting" seated with a drawing portfolio and stylus in her hands; close beside her sits the figure of Poetry holding a lyre (see figure 5.1). Kauffman's image looks straight at the viewer, while Poetry, her head half in shadow, tilts her head to look at Kauffman (or "Painting").

If we didn't know that the figure of Painting was in fact a self-portrait of the painter herself, this would be a much more straightforward image: simply two female figures clothed in neoclassical garb standing in for two concepts (Painting and Poetry). But because we do know (and Kauffman made sure viewers did know by labeling the work a Self-Portrait) that the allegorical

Figure 5.1. Angelica Kauffman, *Self-Portrait in the Character of Painting Embraced by Poetry*. The Iveagh Bequest, Kenwood. Source: *Angelica Kauffman: A Continental Artist in Georgian England*, ed. Wendy Wassyng Roworth. Published by Reaktion Books in association with the Royal Pavillion, Art Gallery and Museums, Brighton, 1992.

figure of Painting is in fact a portrait of the "real" person of the artist, the tenor of the painting changes; the interaction between the two figures becomes more complex. No longer simply two unknown, unnamed, and impersonal "figures" for concepts, the two female bodies—or at least one of them—must also be seen as both more and less than mere allegory. Kauffman's image is at once herself and a symbolic idealization; furthermore, viewers must be constantly aware that the painter behind the canvas is also Kauffman herself. The image becomes saturated with Kauffman's presence; no matter how you look at it, she *is* Painting.

Almost ten years later, Kauffman produced a twist on this image titled

Figure 5.2. Angelica Kauffman, *Self Portrait: Hesitating between the arts of painting and poetry*. Nostell Priory, W. Yorks. Source: *Angelica Kauffman: A Continental Artist in Georgian England*, ed. Wendy Wassyng Roworth. Published by Reaktion Books in association with the Royal Pavillion, Art Gallery and Museums, Brighton, 1992.

Self-Portrait: Hesitating Between the Arts of Music and Painting (1791) (see figure 5.2). In this later picture, the figure representing Kauffman need not stand for anything: she is Kauffman, whereas the other two figures remain symbols of Music and Painting. If we compare the faces of the women in both portraits, we can see the development of Kauffman's thinking. In the earlier *Self-portrait in the Character of Painting Embraced by Poetry*, both figures look like portraits (Kauffman's more than the figure of Poetry, but both are still marked by individualized features). In the latter image, only the figure of Kauffman appears to be a portrait; the other two are extremely alike, almost stylized representations of classical features. Kauffman seems to be consciously separating the figure of the woman artist from the more bland symbolic images of Woman.[3] In both paintings, Kauffman is invested in using the real (her own face) to point toward multiple layers of allegory. If we look at her *Self-Portrait* from 1788, in which Kauffman represents herself in the same pose as her earlier symbolic *Allegory of Imitation* (which is not a self-portrait), we can find echoes of this development. By updating the impersonal allegory, Kauffman suggests that "Imitation" (here read positively, as one key aspect of Artistic production) is embodied in a real woman painter, who can be at one and the same time a beautiful real woman and an idealized symbol.

Kauffman's interest in representing the female figure in the symbolic guise of a series of aesthetic concepts was balanced by her determination to include herself as a real example of these vague concepts. Kauffman's paintings, which so often foreground her own body, therefore anticipate the bulk of writing on her during the Victorian era, which focused obsessively on her physical appearance. It's as if Kauffman knew that her legacy would be based in part on her own physical self and wanted to leave as many visible reminders of this as possible. Yet those reminders also insist on a certain measure of distance from the woman artist's body: in her paintings she is both a visually delectable sight and a symbol pointing *away* from herself toward an aesthetic truth. Victorian representations have a much more difficult time looking away.

II.

Anne Thackeray Ritchie's *Miss Angel and Fulham Lawn* might fittingly take for its motto Virginia Woolf's well-known statement in *A Room of One's Own* that "We think back through our mothers if we are women" (53)—more fittingly because Woolf was Ritchie's niece. Woolf, of course, had writers (including her aunt) in mind when she wrote this: she needed to imagine a vibrant female literary ancestry to understand her own literary aspirations and struggles. Ritchie, however, wrote not about her literary foremothers but rather about a previous woman *painter*—a real, historical individual rather than an imaginary character. As we have seen, writers who invent fictional painters use these characters to voice complex and contested arguments about gender, aesthetics, and the social order; women writers like Ritchie who reimagine historical painters make their real subjects do similar work. But "real" is a gray area in Ritchie's text; Ritchie's Kauffman is certainly based on historical data, yet as we shall see, absolute adherence to the facts of history is often much less important for Ritchie than the articulation of ideological beliefs about the impact of gender on aesthetic tradition or about women's position in the art world.

Ritchie was the daughter of the novelist William Makepeace Thackeray, for whom she acted as amanuensis and unofficial biographer, but she also became an author in her own right. Her first work appeared in *The Cornhill Magazine* (of which Thackeray was editor); she soon branched out to less nepotistic venues. Ritchie wrote numerous novels, essays, and short stories; toward the end of her life she turned to writing memoirs of famous

Victorians—particularly her father. After his death she wrote lengthy and remarkable "introductions" to his novels; taken together these almost become the biography Thackeray forbade anyone to write. At her death in 1919, Ritchie's niece Virginia Woolf—who in her work arguably "thought back through" Ritchie in numerous ways[4]—wrote Ritchie's obituary in the *Times Literary Supplement*.

Critical reception of Ritchie was ambivalent during her lifetime (although her 1873 novel *Old Kensington* garnered considerable praise) and after her death; with the exception of her introductions to her father's novels, none of her works has remained consistently in print. In the late 1990s several of her novels (*The Story of Elizabeth, Old Kensington,* and *Mrs. Dymond*) were reprinted with excellent introductions by Esther Schwartz-McKinzie. Critical attention has subsequently begun to revive, in part because feminist scholars have found Ritchie's treatment of women's issues unusual and compelling. As one critic argues, "She relied on a positive representation of women as the rhetorical strategy that allowed her to question . . . dominant ideologies while avoiding radical feminist statements" (Mourao 2000, 75).

Ritchie's biographer Winifred Gerin writes that "sympathy with her subject" is one of the most profound elements of the narrative voice in *Miss Angel*. Gerin argues persuasively that Ritchie's interest in Kauffman was based strongly in the familial and personal; Gerin writes that Ritchie was attracted to Kauffman's story because of "some similarity to her own predicament at the moment of writing" (174). Ritchie was still suffering from a loss of direction after her famous father's death a decade earlier and was trying to find (as Kauffman does) solace in her art.[5] But I would argue that familiarity does not always mean sympathy: Ritchie's relationship with her fictional heroine is intensely complex; the narrative voice is often sympathetic, certainly, but at times it is catty and on occasion downright cruel. Furthermore, Ritchie's rare forays into aesthetic theory suggest that she does not always hold Kauffman *as an artist* in high esteem, even if she sympathizes with her as a public woman. Ritchie's depiction of Kauffman's troubled life should be read not simply as Ritchie's working out of personal problems (as Gerin argues) but also as a manifesto for Ritchie's very ideological complaints about the difficulties encountered by women artists in their public life. Ritchie's *Miss Angel* can be read as a lamentation for the imprisonment of a woman artist in a publicly visible and sexually desirable body and as an exposé of the negative impact this kind of public vulnerability can have on a woman's artwork. The book offers a critique of the social system that engenders (in multiple senses of the word) this plight.

As such, *Miss Angel* is in keeping with much of Ritchie's other work. As Mackay writes, "For Ritchie, hatred—taking shape as anger—seems largely directed at social unfairness, often . . . focused on women" (1988, 119). To represent and contain this anger, Ritchie uses what Mackay calls *espieglerie*, or prankishness: a kind of whimsy that involves apparently chaotic prose structures ("playing with reality and illusion, as well as time travel") and intermittent but intense focal scenes around which emotions coalesce (ibid., 124). This whimsical style is very much in evidence in *Miss Angel*, although it often crosses the line into melodrama, which the narrator views ironically. In other words, the characters in the novel launch into melodramatic monologues of despair, but the narrator remains quietly amused by the outbursts. And there is certainly evidence of the narrator's quiet anger directed at the characters around the heroine: Lady W., for her selfish, aristocratic use of Angel; Count de Horn, for his scandalous behavior; even Angel's father receives a few blasts for his failure to protect his daughter from the predators in her social milieu. Indeed, the only character at whom the narrator doesn't direct anger is Antonio Zucchi, Kauffman's friend, fellow artist, and second husband, who is himself so permanently enraged by everything and everybody he sees in Angel's world that he makes a good candidate for a narratorial mouthpiece. Antonio, like the narrator, is generally (although not always) in sympathy with Angel and therefore angered on her behalf by the impediments society places in the way of her artistic career.

Miss Angel should also be read as part of Ritchie's larger lifelong project to recover a female artistic tradition, very much as her niece Virginia Woolf did several decades later. Even a brief look through Ritchie's varied writings makes it clear that the assessment and perpetuation of such a tradition was of seminal importance to her. Her novels focused almost solely on "the woman question," and her nonfiction essays, as Mourao argues, "contribute to the consolidation of a female writing tradition" (1997, 81). Ritchie's volume *The Book of Sibyls*, for example, contains chapters on the late-eighteenth- and early-nineteenth-century writers Amelia Opie, A. L. Barbauld, Maria Edgeworth, and Jane Austen. Continuing in this vein, Ritchie also wrote essays, introductions, reviews, or speeches on such women writers as Felicia Hemans, Elizabeth Gaskell, George Sand, the Brontës, Margaret Oliphant, George Eliot, Charlotte Yonge, Mary Elizabeth Braddon, Mrs. Humphrey Ward, Rhoda Broughton, and Mary Cholmondeley, among others (Mackay 2001, 79). *The Book of Sibyls*, as Anthea Trodd writes, "is an early attempt to construct a women's tradition of writing" (2000, 195). Numerous other Ritchie scholars have noted her "growing sense of a female literary tradition" (Mackay 2001, 56).

Yet although she devoted *A Book of Sibyls* to fellow women artists, there is little in the work that might deserve the name feminist; as Mourao writes, "Ritchie's claim for the artistic value of their [the writers discussed in *Sibyls*] work is more often than not subtle, if not muted, as her choice to write essentially biographical essays indicates, and she is careful to represent the authors as sufficiently decorous and domestic to be acceptable to Victorian readers" (1997, 81). Mourao continues later in her essay: "As a result of this strategy, the essays can be disappointing for contemporary feminist readers who might expect Ritchie to be able and willing to articulate more clearly the unfair assessment of women's intellectual capacities, as well as their unequal access to opportunities of self-fulfillment outside the domestic role" (83). *Miss Angel* can in part fill this desire for a more explicitly feminist manifesto, even while it partakes of the historical tendency to consider Kauffman more as a woman than an artist. Certainly Ritchie's *The Book of Sibyls* shares its central goals with *Miss Angel;* both are recovery projects designed to celebrate a female artistic tradition. But the obvious differences allow Ritchie greater freedom in *Miss Angel* to articulate stronger claims for women's artistic power. First, *Miss Angel* is historical *fiction,* which, while largely based in fact, still offers scope for fictional restructuring and interpretation. Second, Kauffmann is not a writer but a painter, and a foreign-born one at that; Ritchie can and does indulge in a critique of Kauffman that she could never have done with a British writer (like the already sainted Austen). All these instances of "othering" give Ritchie much more liberty to critique rather than blandly celebrate her sister artist. Ritchie has serious moral and aesthetic criticisms of her heroine and of the art world of Kauffman's time. Kauffman, as we will see, is both condemned and admired by the narrative voice. Curiously, the condemnation allows for a stronger feminist reading that simple admiration might generate.

The preciousness of the work's title, *Miss Angel,* demonstrates immediately its fictional bent and the familiarity with which Ritchie treats her subject. But if one expects a typical historical novel, one is quickly disappointed. In truth, *Miss Angel* is extremely hard to characterize generically. Ritchie's novel might be considered an example of one subset of historical fiction.[6] Harry Shaw divides historical fiction into three categories: first, what he calls "history as pastoral," in which "history has provided an ideological screen onto which the preoccupations of the present can be projected for clarification and solution, or for disguised expression" (1983, 52). Tennyson's "Idylls of the King" is an example of this use of history. The second involves the use of history as a kind of "drama" behind a fictional story, as in the case of Dickens's *A Tale of Two Cities.* The third category, exemplified by large parts of *War and Peace,* contains fiction which takes history itself as a subject. Works of this final category explore the historical process itself through the guise of fiction.

Ritchie's novel fits none of these categories clearly, certainly not the final two. However, *Miss Angel* does bear resemblance to the first category, history as an "ideological screen." In oblique ways, Ritchie uses Kauffman's story to comment on contemporary Victorian issues. The 1870s—the decade in which Ritchie published *Miss Angel*—saw an increase in interest in the eighteenth century for just this purpose. After 1868 a "spate of eighteenth-century novels started to be reissued" (Jay 2004, 102), and Margaret Oliphant embarked on a series of essays on eighteenth-century figures for *Blackwood's Magazine* (the series was later to be published in book form as *Historical Sketches of the Reign of George II*). Victorian opinion of the eighteenth century was of course extremely varied, but in general there seems to have been a rejection of eighteenth-century values and culture during the first half of the Victorian era and then a reassessment during the later part of the nineteenth century. As Fairer writes, "Some Victorians, most noticeably from the 1870s on, were finding in eighteenth-century culture elements of classical strength and clarity that their own age was perceived to lack" (2004, xiii). Although she was undoubtedly tapping into the market for eighteenth-century fiction and history, Ritchie's interest in Kauffman stems less from her historical position as an eighteenth-century subject than from her personal history—indeed, Ritchie spends so little time laying out Kauffman's historical context that if the reader wasn't already aware that the book's events do in fact take place during the reign of George II, one could easily forget all historical specificity. Historical personages do appear regularly—Sir Joshua Reynolds, Queen Charlotte, and others—but they are never represented as historically inflected. That is, they are more literary characters than historical individuals—they eat and talk but do not do anything which history specifically records that they have done.

Miss Angel might also be called fictionalized biography—*highly* fictionalized in terms of its attribution of emotions and thoughts to historical individuals, but based on facts (as Ritchie was able to gather them. The accuracy of her sources—some of them highly romanticized themselves—is a separate issue.) But if "the characteristic Victorian biography was not only a story about a life, but was also about the times which molded the life" (Amigoni 1993, 1), then *Miss Angel* is definitely not a characteristic biography. Certainly the modes and manners of eighteenth-century artists and art patrons are of passing interest to Ritchie, but they are not her subject in any way. As I argued above, Ritchie is not attempting to recreate a period, to offer a sense of the age, or to theorize history. To make a fitting analogy to painting, Ritchie's novel is a portrait of *just* a head—there is no historically correct costuming, no significant background landscape or cityscape. The book is also unlike a biography in that it offers few dates and places but provides lots of dialogue and even more interior monologue. Although the basic plot outlines of Ritchie's *Miss Angel* are based largely on biographical data gathered from various sources (particularly the 1810 biography of Kauffman written by the sculptor Giovanni de Rossi, 1762–1839), the book is resolutely nonbiographical in its tone; its narrative structure, dialogue, and sentimental description align it more closely with the *novel* than the biography.

But it is not entirely a novel, either. It doesn't have a strong novelistic shape: it has a story (a series of events) but no real plot (with rising and falling action, denouements, suspense, etc.). It is, rather, a composite form, part romantic biography and part sentimental fiction, and as such unusual and perhaps unprecedented.

III.

Miss Angel begins with a kind of "ghost story" which is in many ways similar to the one with which Ritchie begins *The Book of Sibyls,* where she sees and tries to communicate with the almost articulate apparition of Anna Barbauld walking in the street.[7] This "potential communication between two women" (Trodd 2000, 197) is again seen in the opening passages of *Miss Angel,* where the narrator details her experience with an engraved portrait of Kauffman. The first page of the novel contains a description of this portrait of Kauffman, seen by the narrator in a Victorian printshop. The narrator (a disembodied explicitly Victorian voice who occasionally brings herself and her era to our attention) uses the print as the occasion for an extended ekphrasis of Kauffman's appearance that slowly transforms first into character analysis, then into a larger discussion of eighteenth-century culture, and finally into an unusual and oblique statement about women's relationship to knowledge. The description that begins *Miss Angel* follows an objectifying pattern we have seen before: it first presents Kauffmann as a pretty woman rather than an artist. Ritchie's only concession in this early scene to the profession of her heroine is to briefly note that Kauffmann's face is "peculiar"—a term which, in the context of the personal description of the passage, hints at the possibility of something unusual in the life of the figure depicted. Ritchie also displays a flash of wit when she remarks that the "little head" in the print is "charmingly set upon its frame" (*Angel,* 1). The use of the word "frame" here obviously points to Kauffmann's professional identity, yet we see here—and we shall see in the entirety of the book—that Kauffmann herself is metaphorically enclosed within a frame rather than free to produce artworks and define herself.

The specific description of the portrait-print gradually gives way to larger concerns; by the end of the paragraph the narrator remarks, apropos of portraiture in general, that "there is some secret understanding transmitted, I do believe, from one set of human beings to another, from year to year, from age to age, ever since Eve herself first opened her shining eyes upon the Garden of Innocence and flung the apple to her descendants" (2). It seems an odd ending to the paragraph, and an odd introduction to this pseudo-novel. On the one hand, the notion that portraits "speak" to us across time is a traditional and convenient trope that allows Ritchie to claim a certain validity for her historical fiction. With the more unusual final reference to Eve, however, Ritchie suggests that this transmission of understanding is both dangerous and possibly scandalous or sinful (as the reference to the apple implies) and very much a woman's game (as the slippage from general "human beings" to Eve specifically implies). Ritchie seems to be claiming for herself, as a woman writer, a privileged position as a "descendant" of other Eve-like women artists of the past. Kauffman therefore occupies the role of Eve, flinging the apple of knowledge to her descendant, Ritchie. The knowledge Kauffman transmits seems to be the knowledge of what a trial it is to be a woman artist.

The rest of *Miss Angel* largely fulfills the expectations set up in this early paragraph; we see the same three main impulses at work. First, Angelica the visible woman is more of interest than Kauffman the artist; her personal appearance and emotional passions receive considerably more space than her artistic endeavors. Second, Ritchie's narrative mode is sentimental, continually making affective statements and judgments about Kauffman's actions rather than objectively offering an account of her life. Finally, the novel as a whole raises the question of woman's role as a creative producer, the possible destruction and despair this might bring both to her and to those around her—yet balanced with a simultaneous insistence on the potential *legacy* of women artists. The woman artist remains an Eve-like figure, both a creator and destroyer, and very much oppressed by the fact of her female body.

The plot proper of *Miss Angel* opens with Angelica in her late teens, dreamy and romantic, living in Italy and copying the works of the great masters. We follow her as she embarks on what the novel sees as the most important move in her life: to England. The bulk of *Miss Angel* focuses on Kauffman's social and romantic life there: her brief, unsuccessful (and historically unsubstantiated) romance with Sir Joshua Reynolds, her election as one of the founding members of the Royal Academy in 1768, and then her brief (and in the novel implicitly unconsummated) marriage to the mildly villainous impostor Count de Horn, which forms the central tragedy of the plot. De Horn convinces Angelica to marry him under false pretenses and largely against her wishes; Ritchie suggests that his main motivation for the marriage is his hope that her fame and ties to the aristocracy will ensure his safety when his crimes are revealed. After de Horn is unmasked and flees the country, the story quickly passes over ten years in a paragraph or two, only to pick up again in the final chapters with Kauffman's acceptance (in 1781) of a marriage proposal from Antonio Zucchi, her lifelong friend and fellow R.A. painter, and Angelica's permanent departure from England.

The text presents us with a very familiar series of what we should by now recognize to be stock "pretty woman painting" scenes that consistently privilege the female body over the visible artwork. Prospective suitors and appreciative friends repeatedly make remarks about Kauffmann's physical appearance as she paints. A viewer of one of Kauffman's early copies of Renaissance masterpieces remarks, "You must allow me, madam, to envy the fortunate possessor of such a picture, copied by so fair a hand" (10). The words hold particular significance because this admirer is Count de Horn, the opportunistic impostor and scoundrel who becomes Angelica's first husband. The fairness of the hand is what attracts the Count (as well as the fact that Angelica's social prominence will gain him amnesty for his crimes), and the slippage from "possessor" of the painting to "possessor" of the woman herself is implicit. The Count says something similar in a later scene when he exclaims, "'Good heavens, what genius!'" while "scarcely looking at the picture but at the blushing painter" (184). Another admirer, her eventual second husband Antonio Zucchi, consistently sees Angelica herself as a painting: as he watches her he thinks,

> How well he knew every shade and light of that sweet living picture. How often he had watched it, at home, in the strange galleries where she painted all day long. . . . Only yesterday . . . he had seen her standing as now with her palette in her hand. He could have drawn each line and curve of the light figure. (13)

This scene with Zucchi continues with more of the same, until Ritchie pulls a remarkable stunt: Zucchi's persistent objectification of Angelica (note that she is an "it" at the start of the above quote) may turn her into a painting, but it also then allows Angelica to enter *into* a painting, to understand and experience art from within. Ritchie writes, "So there she stood . . . presently her heart began to beat, and the colour came into her cheeks as she forgot her own insignificance. . . . Some fancy came to her that she was one of the women in the crowd looking on with the amazed Apostles [in the painting she is copying]" (13). Angelica enters *into* the artwork and glories in its colors and shapes for a while, then is recalled "to life" by the voice of her father. That Ritchie signals Angelica's movement out of Antonio's metaphoric and oppressive "love-painting" and into the literal painting of a Renaissance master by *animating* her ("presently her heart began to beat") makes the transition one from confinement or death to liberation and life. While Zucchi objectifies her, her heart presumably is not beating; when Ritchie sets her free to join the figures in the painting, Angelica comes alive.

Art continues to be for Angelica a space of mental and physical freedom that contrasts sharply with the numerous attempts by male figures in her life to control and contain her within metaphoric frames. Early in the book Angelica counters any attempt at romance by insisting that "I am married to my brush . . . I want no other husband" (26) and that "my love is for Titian, for the great Veronese, for Tintoret" (27) rather than for mortal man. And when asked by her early patron Lady W. if she has a sweetheart, Angel replies, "Mine is a cold heart, I fear . . . I have to earn money for our home, and to take care of my father in my mother's place. My interests are too great to leave place in my heart for love" (27). When Kauffman moves, alone, into her own home and studio, Ritchie continues the trope by writing that "no bride coming to her new happy home for the first time could have felt more proudly excited than this little, impulsive, well-meaning, foolish creature, who had, by sheer hard work and spirited determination, earned a right to this paneled nest" (139).

But as this quote suggests, by calling Angelica a "little . . . foolish creature," Ritchie is not content to let Angelica simply become a strong-minded successful heroine. The text shifts abruptly back and forth between representations of Angelica as a powerful and independent woman and scenes that show her to be weak, incompetent, or thoughtless. Her relationship with Sir Joshua Reynolds—one on which the historical record is largely silent—is a case in point. Ritchie shows Angelica to be worthy enough as a painter and as a woman to catch the "great man's" professional and personal eye, yet Ritchie also blasts her heroine with unbelievably negative scenes. When Reynolds and Kauffman first meet, for example, Ritchie writes: "'Will you honour me by permitting a visit to your studio to-morrow morning?' said the great painter to the quivering, smiling, charming little painter in her pretty quaint dress" (94). Kauffman couldn't be more trivialized or reduced to feminine qualities than that. Similarly, when Angelica rejects Reynolds's marriage proposal (a historical conjecture, but widely believed then and now), Ritchie has her heroine acting "woman-like" (190), which in this scene clearly means coy, cruelly saucy, and secretly pleased by her power over men.

Why the inconsistency? We will encounter the like again when we come in chapter 7 to the work of Mary Ward, who allows her painter-heroine freedom, success, and independence and yet punishes her repeatedly for such unfeminine behavior by making her *negatively* feminine—that is, endowing her with negative characteristics that are traditionally coded as feminine. Ritchie's final words on Angelica's marriage to Zucchi at the end of the novel reinforce this sense of tentative punishment: Ritchie writes that in marrying him, Angelica was "free to peaceful bondage, free to accept his tender care and domination" (318). The tension we hear between on the one hand "free," "peaceful," and "tender" and on the other hand "bondage" and "domination" is consonant with the tensions vibrating throughout the text. Significantly, however, in *Miss Angel* negative representations of Kauffman *decrease* in frequency as the narrative progresses; it is only when Angelica is actively involved with romantic interests that Ritchie seems to punish or condemn her (as did the British public).

In Ritchie's novels, her ambiguous representation of marriage is where she most clearly articulates a position that critiques the dominant ideology of domestic femininity. "Unlike many of her contemporaries," writes Mourao, "Ritchie depicts marriage at least as often as courtship, and she refuses the uncritically celebratory stance that some take on it" (2000, 75). Mourao notes that in an alternate unpublished ending for her first novel, *The Story of Elizabeth,* Ritchie planned to keep her heroine single and happy—an unusual ending for domestic fiction of the time. Early manuscript versions of *Old Kensington* also show that Ritchie had at several points planned a very different novel in which marriage was represented as destructive to woman's happiness (ibid. 78–80). Even in that novel's final version, the heroine's happy marriage comes only after she has decided, with contentment, to remain unmarried. And in Ritchie's modernized revision of the fairy tale of Sleeping Beauty, she further critiques marriage by allowing her narrator to say that she and her companion "uncharitably counted up, I am ashamed to say, no less that six Bluebeards" among their acquaintances (Ritchie 1868, 22). In her nonfiction essay "Toilers and Spinsters," published anonymously in *Cornhill Magazine* in March 1861, Ritchie argues that marriage is not and should not be women's only source for personal fulfillment. Ritchie parodies the image of the miserable spinster and blames patriarchal ideology for making spinsters *unhappy;* she does not blame population imbalances, economic depression, emigration, or other common reasons offered by Victorians for the increasing number of unmarried women in the period. The number of spinsters is not the problem for Ritchie; their oppression by an unsympathetic social system *is*. Ritchie's own marriage was not particularly successful (Gerin 1981, 211–17), and she, like Margaret Oliphant, continued to work and write throughout marriage and motherhood. It may have been Kauffmann's own early disinclination to marry, as well as her troubled marriage with the Count, which attracted Ritchie to her real-life heroine: Kauffman's life story offers a ready-made critique of marriage, particularly for artistic women.

Ritchie represents the romantic tragedy as heightening Angelica's physicality: after the debacle of her first marriage became public, Angelica retreated into a solitary depression: "It was not all imagination on Angelica's part when she thought that people were looking at her, counting her poor heart-throbs, scanning her lonely tears. She was a well-known character" (277). Here we sense the frustrations Ritchie feels with the enforced corporealization of the woman artist: the public eye focuses not on her work but on her tears and heart—bodily realities but also symbols of feminine emotionality. It is only after her romantic adventures are detailed and the public has forgotten them that Ritchie can go on to narrate the founding of the Royal Academy, of which Kauffman was elected as a founding member. Once the obligatory love scenes with Reynolds and the Count are safely put behind her and Angelica is on her own again, Ritchie can say of her heroine, "She was but a woman, but she too could paint, could rule light and space, call harmonies of colour to her service" (238). In classic *Künstlerroman* fashion, Angelica must be made to undergo a debilitating emotional experience so that she can emerge on the other side as an artist. Before the romantic crisis, critics are reported as saying her work is too "rose-coloured" (278); after it, the narrator insists that she "never painted better" (287).

IV.

It is only after her suffering that Angelica is permitted, however briefly, to articulate her views on aesthetic theory; it is almost the only time in the story where the real Kauffman makes a sustained appearance in her artistic persona (rather than her female one), albeit with significant historical revisions. One might expect to be able to focus on ekphrastic moments in the novel, places where Ritchie describes Kauffman's visual productions. Yet oddly, *not one* of the real Kauffman's pictures is described in any detail in the novel. Ritchie mentions in passing several copies, an unnamed symbolic landscape, and a portrait of the sculptor Mrs. Damer (who was outspoken on women artists' rights, as the emasculation fear displayed in figure 5. 3 suggests),[8] but nothing else. One might expect that telling the tale of a *real* woman painter, who after all produced real and visible artworks that one could actually interpret, would necessitate ample ekphrastic description and attendant discussion of aesthetic principles. But even the female art historians I discuss later in this chapter, who compiled enormous treatises on women artists through the ages, rarely if

Figure 5.3: "Damerian Apollo." "Studies from Nature: A Model to Make a Boy." Anonymous engraving, 1789. British Museum. Reproduced with permission.

ever comment on the aesthetic character of the artworks produced by women artists or engage in more general aesthetic debates.

In *Miss Angel,* Ritchie indulges in aesthetic discussion just once, near the end of the novel, when Kauffman, Mrs. Damer, and Reynolds debate the proper way to create art:

> "Surely," cried Mrs. Damer, "surely an impression, however conveyed, is more valuable to the artist than mere imitation. I can often work better . . . from my own mental recollections than by merely copying something which does not after all represent my idea."
>
> [Reynolds replies,] "That is precisely what I must ask leave to contradict. . . . With all your great gifts, your sweet impulsive industry, and admirable feeling, it is only the study of Nature that can give any of us that mastery which we must all desire . . ."
>
> "You mean that in Art, as in other things," said Angelica, blushing, "it is by submitting most completely to the laws of truth that we best discover her intentions? Do you know," she went on, "I seem sometimes to have found out of late that obedience is best?" (*Angel,* 296–97)

The rest of the scene authorizes Angelica's "obedience" to Nature, to side with Angelica and Reynolds in this age-old debate between interpretation (or impression) and imitation. Reynolds closes his side of the argument by insisting, "I must hold to my guiding principle, and seek for a calm and even pursuit of facts as they appear to me" (298), with which Angelica agrees wholeheartedly. In this scene, Ritchie is radically revising both Reynolds's and Kauffman's aesthetics, putting oversimplified mid-Victorian ideas and ideals in their mouths. On the one hand, this is a rather obvious attempt by Ritchie to "Ruskinize" her heroine, to bring her in line with the most popular aesthetic doctrines of the day.[9] But I want to suggest that Ritchie's revision of the aesthetic doctrines of her characters is undertaken not simply as a patronizing updating of what she evidently perceived as archaic eighteenth-century aesthetic values, but with a particular goal in mind: to alleviate some of the intense focus on Kauffman as a woman and encourage consideration of her as an artist. If Angelica is obedient to nature rather than to her own impressions or fancy, she has a chance at objectivity, at removing herself from the equation and being judged as an artist rather than a woman.

Let us first take a look at precisely how Ritchie is revising eighteenth-century aesthetic ideology, as represented by the historical Reynolds and Kauffman. The debate Ritchie introduces here—that of how much subjective interpretation is desirable when representing nature (be it in a leaf, a landscape, or a human face)—is absolutely central to the history of eighteenth- and nineteenth-century art, as well as central to Ritchie's biographical project itself. Should the artist—or the biographer—strive to copy precisely, even minutely, what he or she sees, or is there some scope for transmutation and interpretation? How much change is too much? Such questions, and the more general battle over the function, value, and status of mimesis in art, go back of course to Plato. Aestheticians have always argued whether art should be primarily imitative or primarily idealizing or some blend of both. As Stephen Halliwell argues, during the mid and late eighteenth century (when Reynolds and Kauffman were active), the term "imitation" had a positive spin—art was thought to imitate a higher reality by representing nature in an idealized form. Halliwell points out that Samuel Johnson, for example, in his preface to his 1765 edition of Shakespeare, uses "imitate," "represent," and "copy" interchangeably, and all with a positive meaning to describe Shakespeare's ability to transform life into literature (2002, 349).

The historical Reynolds (in contrast with Ritchie's version) had a similar take on the term and concept of "imitation." Reynolds's theory of art was, taken all in all, much closer to that offered by Mrs. Damer in Ritchie's scene. In his *Discourses* (his best-known work, and one with which Ritchie would probably have been familiar), the term "imitation" is used favorably to mean copying the old masters, which was extremely crucial to Reynolds's theory of art education. The imitation of nature, on the other hand, did not constitute great art. In Discourse 3 he warns, "Nature herself is not to be too closely copied" (1992, 102), and argues that the painter must "improve [Nature] by the grandeur of his ideas" (103). His most anti-nature sentiment comes in Discourse 13: "Painting . . . is, and ought to be . . . no imitation at all of external nature" (286). In Discourse 13 he argues that the best painting should approach the condition of poetry, whose "very existence . . . depends on the licence [*sic*] it assumes of deviating from actual nature" (286).

As many critics have pointed out, however, Reynolds's *Discourses* are not known for their coherence or consistency (see Wendorf 1996, 229). In the later discourses, Reynolds does insist that the study of nature is important for the aspiring artists, but never does he fail to follow such statements with one of two qualifications: First, the study of the old masters is more important than the study of nature. "Study nature attentively," he insists, "but always with those masters in your company" (Discourse 6, 173). Similarly, he writes, "The daily food and nourishment of the mind of an Artist is found in the great works of his predecessors" (Discourse 12, 273). Only if you replaced the word "predecessors" with "Nature" could you bring such a philosophy in line with Ruskin. Second, Reynolds follows all discussions of Nature with the caveat that Nature is simply not enough to make great art. An artist must improve nature with his own "intellectual nature" (Discourses 8, 205). He writes in Discourse 11 that "we are not always pleased with the most absolute possible resemblance of an imitation to its original object"; a "complete impression" is better than a detailed copy. Following the Neoplatonic tenets of Neoclassicism, he also argues that "ideal beauty [is] superior to what is to be found in individual nature" (2: 103).

It must be remembered, too, that Reynolds is almost always arguing—explicitly or implicitly—for the primacy of history painting rather than (as Ruskin was to do later) landscape painting. Reynolds's aesthetic theory was grounded firmly in the very eighteenth-century notion that art should encourage the moral virtues of the public man—hence History painting was key, since it articulated social ideas. As John Barrell has argued, eighteenth-century aesthetics, particularly that articulated by Reynolds and others involved with the very nationalistic venture of the Royal Academy, argued for the political value of art as a means to promote public virtue. Of Reynolds, Barrell writes, "What remains constant [in the *Discourses*] is the notion that art has a political function which it fulfills when it impresses us with an awareness of our common nature, an awareness whose ultimate end is that we should recognize that our true nature is discovered only as we are members of a political society" (1986, 72). History painting—with its allegorical force and representation of commonly known scenes and events—was thought to best achieve this.

The nineteenth century saw a profound transformation in this aesthetic. Hazlitt, for example, broke completely from the notion that art should motivate public virtue. As Barrell writes, Hazlitt saw the "necessity of a complete separation of the republic of taste from the political republic." Rather, Hazlitt insisted that "the satisfactions offered by painting are offered to us as we are private individuals, not public citizens" (315). This focus on the private goes hand in hand with an emergence of an aesthetic that insists on absolute fidelity to nature; art should be an "immediate imitation of nature" (Hazlitt 1934, 301). He argues that it is only "as the mind advances in the knowledge of nature [that] the horizon of art enlarges" (296). In fact, Hazlitt—contrary to almost all other art historians and critics—argued that the great Greek statues were *not* idealized representations of humanity but faithful portraits of real individuals—who were perfectly beautiful because the ancient Greeks were naturally that way (see Barrell 1986, 318). Later Victorian writers on art, such as Sir Edward Poynter, director of the National Gallery (1894–1904) and president of the Royal Academy (1896–1919), held similar (and hopelessly old-fashioned from the point of view of his contemporaries, the Aesthetes) beliefs that "the imitation of nature is the principal object" of art and that artists must "study nature as to receive and retain the most complete and distinct impressions" and not let "ideas run away with us in art" (Poynter 1885, 169). Poynter criticized the French mode of painting in his time for being incapable of focused attention to the real: "Their conception of ideal beauty is not that it is to be found by looking for it in nature, but rather by adding something to nature of their own devising . . . which is absolutely devoid of any real and inherent beauty" (119).

Ruskin is well known for a similar view of the absolute importance of faithful attention to nature; he is also committed to the belief that art has essentially a private effect. "For Ruskin, modern painting is inevitably the place of privacy, of private freedom," writes Barrell (1986, 339), and this certainly holds true for almost all of *Modern Painters* and *Elements of Drawing*. Later works may have been more explicitly political, but even in his early works, art must first have a private impact on the soul of the creator or viewer before it can have any public impact whatsoever. But Ruskin was explicitly against the *imitation* of nature; in an early chapter in volume 1 of *Modern Painters* he argues that imitation is "contemptible" (if pleasurable) because it sets out to deceive the viewer rather than to inspire "high or noble emotion or thought" (1873, 1: 93). Ruskin is here making "imitation" mean a slavishly accurate copying of nature; in the early volumes of *Modern Painters* he (like

Reynolds and Ritchie's Damer) argues that *thought* matters more than detail or precision of mimesis (see 1: 81–83).

Yet *Modern Painters* is full of digs at Reynolds, whose aesthetic philosophy Ruskin found entirely inaccurate. Ruskin explicitly rejects the idealizing impulse of the Grand Style that Reynolds advocates (1: 147, 154) even as he argues that truth in painting comes more from impression than from imitation (1: 159). But for Ruskin, impression is decidedly not the same as idealizing; a true impression of nature is achieved only after lengthy, detailed, and minute study of nature. After all, huge portions of *Modern Painters* are devoted to precise, near-scientific delineations of different kinds of clouds, mountains, rocks, and plants. In volume 2, he argues that a perfect picture must have both thought (impression) *and* fidelity to nature (2: 212). In volume 3, he argues that although art must be imaginative (that is, express an impression of nature rather than a precise copy of it), it can be good art only if it focuses on the *specific* rather than the general. Ruskin blasts Reynolds for believing the opposite, that great art expressed the general and avoided the particular (3: 22, 43). In his explanation of the "pathetic fallacy," Ruskin moves further away from any acceptance of idealization or symbolic representation of nature and closer to an argument that precise fidelity to nature (even to the extent of what we might call copying) is what makes a great artist.

In fact, as *Modern Painters* progresses—and indeed as Ruskin's thinking progresses over time in other works—he comes closer and closer to Ritchie's rather flat statement that "obedience is best" (*Miss Angel,* 296–97). If we look at his drawing manual, *Elements of Drawing,* published in 1857 (volume 1 of *Modern Painters* was published in 1843, volume 2 in 1846, volumes 3 and 4 in 1856, volume 5 in 1860), we can see Ruskin set out some of his most straightforward statements as to the precision of imitation required by artists. Granted, *Elements of Drawing* is meant as a beginning guide for amateurs and the general public, but that very fact makes it crucial in understanding what we might call "received Ruskin": the ideas that members of the general Victorian public, like Ritchie, would have had of Ruskin's philosophy of mimesis. One of the exercises in *Elements of Drawing* well exemplifies the manual as a whole: Ruskin asks his reader/pupil to draw a rock. He writes,

> Now if you can draw that stone, you can draw anything; I mean, anything that is drawable. Many things (sea foam, for instance) cannot be drawn at all, only the idea of them more or less suggested; but if you can draw the stone rightly, everything within reach of art is also within yours. . . . For all drawing depends, primarily, on your power of representing Roundness. . . . Look your stone antagonist boldly in the face. . . . Now, remember always

what was stated in the outset, that everything you can see in Nature is seen only so far as it is lighter or darker than the things about it, or of a different colour from them. . . . If you will not look at what you see, if you try to put on brighter or duller colours than are there, if you try to put them on with a dash or a blot, or to cover your paper with "vigorous" lines, or to produce anything, in fact, but the plain, unaffected, and finished tranquility of the thing before you, you need not hope to get on. Nature will show you nothing if you set yourself up for her master. *But forget yourself, and try to obey her, and you will find obedience easier and happier than you think.* (1857, 36–38; emphasis added)

This sounds almost identical to the pronouncements of Ritchie's Kauffman and Reynolds, even down to the common term "obedience." In chapter 3 we saw a similar Ruskin insist that Anna Blunden forgo imagination and go "back to bricks"; in both cases he insists on an obedience to the visible world and a firm squelching of any subjective artistic intervention or interpretation.

Where did the historical Kauffman enter into this debate? Ritchie has her side with Reynolds, but we have seen how inaccurate that portrait is. Unfortunately, Kauffman left no treatises on her aesthetic principles; she left only her work, and the bulk of her history painting shows her to be deeply invested in the neoclassical idealization of the human form. Her paintings are not naturalistic: the scenes she chooses and her representation of human and natural forms are markedly idealizing rather than realist. For the historical Kauffman, "Imitation" was something one could easily allegorize as a woman in Greek costume rather than the faithful representation of the natural world.

Yet Ritchie, we must remember, clearly had Angelica voice a doctrine of complete obedience to nature, not one of interpretive impression or allegorical idealization. What do we do with this seeming disparity between the "facts" of Kauffman's work (and the standard aesthetic principles of her era and artistic community) and the fictional Angelica's views? We can choose to brush it aside by saying that Ritchie was simply taking an aesthetic with which she was familiar—a simplified Ruskinian view—and forcing it on her characters. But this overlooks the fact that this scene with Damer and Reynolds must be taken in context with the few hints at aesthetic theorization that crop up at other points in the novel. Ritchie's Angelica has not always (as indeed she implies in this scene) held this doctrine of obedience. The young Angelica is represented as living in her own world of imagination and allegory—a world much more like that depicted in the historical Kauffman's works. Ritchie describes the young Angelica (favorably, it should be noted) as living half in a "world of her own creating" (*Miss Angel*, 37); it is only after her arrival in England and her entry into the carousel of romance, aristocratic parties, and Academy politics that she falls from grace and is forced to temper her imaginative power with obedient realism. As with Helen Graham in Anne Brontë's *Tenant of Wildfell Hall*, the young artist in her innocence can make what she wants of nature; after heartache and maturity, however, the woman artist turns to fidelity to nature for solace and safety.

Safety is key here. We saw in chapter 2 that Helen, whose landscapes were of recognizable scenes around her, was forced to sign her work with a false name to escape detection: but still she chose a kind of landscape realism for her style. Why do this, when surely painting imagined symbolic scenes like her earlier work with the girl and doves (painted without models) would be entirely safe? Anne Brontë, I argued, suggested that a lack of idealism and visual symbolism was inevitably necessary for Helen to mature as an artist and a woman. Ritchie, too, seems to be arguing that after Angelica's heartbreaks she too turns to objectivity in art rather than her earlier "rose-coloured" scenes.

But we must grapple with one remaining paradox: why does Ritchie have her heroine voice a doctrine—fidelity to nature—of which Ritchie approves yet does not follow in her own narrative? Ritchie is interpreting rather than imitating the "facts" of Kauffman's life in *Miss Angel;* she is far from obedient to the laws of truth, taking numerous liberties with biographical fact and making no apology for doing so. The scene between Damer, Reynolds, and Kauffman thus becomes more complex when we realize that the aesthetic problem under debate—the appropriate amount of mimetic exactitude required by art—is precisely the problem Ritchie faces as she constructs her "biographical novel." Theorists, writers, and critics of biography during the nineteenth century held, unsurprisingly, diverse views on the scope, form, content, and ethics of biography. (One thing seems to be undeniable: as a form, it was extremely popular.) Two main debates characterize discussions of biography in the period; both are versions of the question "how much is too much?" First, biographers grappled with the problem of the appropriate *quantity* of facts: should every last detail be recorded? If not, what selection process should be used? What aspects of a life should be considered in greatest detail? Most critics considered complete reportage undesirable:

> For there can be no question that the most common defects of biography are useless repetition and provoking redundancy. The more earnestly the biographer throws himself into his task, the more indispensable does each trivial detail appear to him. In working out the features and the figure of his subject,

he is slow to reject anything as inconsequent or insignificant. (Anonymous, "Contemporary Literature . . ." 1879, 483)

It is important to note that the language of visual portraiture is very near the surface here, in the mention of the "features" and the "figure" of the subject. Indeed, as Richard Wendorf has argued apropos of portraiture traditions in Stuart and Georgian England, "visual and verbal portraits often shared similar assumptions about the representation of historical character" (1996, 4). Such similarities extend into the nineteenth century as well; Hazlitt wrote that "portrait-painting is the biography of the pencil" (quoted ibid., 7). Portraiture in the Victorian era has received scant critical attention, and a book-length interart comparison of the two arts (biography and portraiture) during the Victorian era would be extremely valuable.[10] But what is important for my discussion of Ritchie is simply the fact that in both painting (in general as well as portraiture specifically) and biography, *selection* of facts (visual or historic) was a seminal debate. The question of selection must have been highly relevant for Ritchie. What "facts" of Kauffman's life should she include, and how should she weight them? Ritchie certainly leaves out numerous details of Kauffman's life which we find included in other biographers; she also gives greater narrative space to certain parts of Kauffman's life that are treated scantily in other biographers.[11]

If the quantity of facts was one problem, what to do with *distasteful* facts was the second, more pressing problem. Margaret Oliphant, who wrote dozens of biographies during her extremely productive literary career, felt that biographers should gloss over or omit altogether any immoral or otherwise repellent acts done by the subject under consideration (1883, 78–82). Far more theorists of biography, however, had grown tired of the hagiographic impulse and advocated a more revealing approach to a subject's life. In "A Suggestion for a New Kind of Biography," Robert Goodbrand argues that writers must include the "broken angles and flaws" (1870, 26) of the biographical subject; only in that way can the biography proceed with "mingled tenderness and truth" (24–25). The Ritchie of *Miss Angel* was a steadfast proponent of this "new kind of biography." As we have seen, Angelica is drawn as a highly flawed figure—at times weak, foolish, ignorant, incompetent, or vain.

Yet for all her flaws, Kauffman is Ritchie's analogue in many respects, and Ritchie seems well aware of this. Like the historical Kauffman, Ritchie's art idealizes (not always in its positive sense) historical individuals and scenes; she chooses narrative moments not for their fidelity to nature but for their symbolic potential. At the end of *Miss Angel*, Ritchie explicitly admits that the real has gotten away from her, and she celebrates rather than laments this lapse. In a return to the vaguely supernatural language with which Ritchie began the novel (reminiscent of *A Book of Sibyls*), she writes at the end of the novel, "I have been trying to tell a little story, of which the characters and incidents have come to me through a winter's gloom so vividly that as I write now *I can scarcely tell what is real and what is but my own imagination*" (319; emphasis added). Coming as it does after the three artists' discussion of imagination versus imitation, a discussion which seemingly sided with imitation (that is, a fidelity to nature), how are we to take this admission that the narrator cannot tell the real from the imaginary? The final paragraph gives us more to work with and suggests that Ritchie's "imagination" is less a fantasy than a representation of something intangible or otherwise inaccessible: "One day, not long ago," writes the narrator, "a little boy in a passion of tears asked for a pencil and paper to draw something that he longed for and could not get. The truth of that baby's philosophy is one which strikes us more and more as we travel on upon our different ways" (322). The slippage between drawing and reality is powerful here; the boy draws that which he cannot get, but by drawing he does in some manner come to possess it, and thus the imagined becomes the real.

Here Ritchie makes an oblique claim for the power of literature. If the imaginary (literally the image, that which the boy draws) can stand in for the real, by analogy and extension the text can substitute for the "real" life that cannot be literally accessed. Ritchie's claim seems to be that her fictional Angelica has become as real (or more so) than the historical individual—or at least real enough to satisfy someone (like the child) who cannot get the real one. In this rather unusual take on realism, Ritchie comes once again in line with Ruskin. In *Modern Painters,* as I have discussed, Ruskin set out a complicated theory of realism based not on precise imitation of the visible world but rather on a more vague fidelity to the closely perceived essence of nature. This theory, in particular the extreme arduousness of the labor of perceiving correctly, can be read as profoundly revolutionary. As Caroline Levine writes, "Conventional ways of seeing dangerously cloud and corrupt our vision, and thus Ruskin exhorts us to work assiduously to counteract their influence. We must seek to cast off the weight of established traditions and received judgments in favor of a more faithful relationship to the world" (2000, 78).

Ritchie's little scene with the boy and his drawing suggests that mimetic realism can get you what you want, or at least substitute successfully for something that cannot be articulated. This, I think, is what Ritchie wants for her Angelica, and why she places such un-neoclassical words in her mouth. The world has proven a dangerous place for Angelica; Ritchie sees her salvation in a kind of Ruskinian obedience to nature—not a soul-killing obedience but a submersion of the self (her self has after all brought Angelica nothing but trouble) and a negation of societal conventions (which have likewise done her little good) in favor of an intense encounter with the natural world. For the woman artist, this kind of realism can have radically liberatory potential.

V.

Victorian nonfiction writers approach Kauffman very much as Ritchie does: as an artist whose physical, sexual, female body intervenes in her attempts at artistic production. For some writers, this is Kauffman's fault: as a woman, she should simply know better than to try to paint. For others, the insistent presence of Kauffman's gender is seen as socially reinforced and something to be much mourned. Among the former, the title of John Oldcastle's article on Kauffman in the *Magazine of Art* (1883) tells you everything you need to know: "The Love Affairs of Angelica Kauffman." The article details in turn the numerous men who were "deeply smitten" with Kauffman (33). At one point Oldcastle criticizes with remarkable (and unperceived) irony the workings of an idealized figure called "Gossip" who "could not let a maiden, so lovely and so much admired, quite alone" (33). Nowhere in the article does he mention more than the titles of her artworks; his sole aesthetic commentary is that she could not have been a good artist because she was too attractive and desirable a woman. He goes so far as to wonder "if she really painted, without [Reynolds's] considerable help, the magnificent portrait of himself which is credited to her brush" (33).

Other art critics took Kauffman more seriously but still concentrated on her physical appearance (and its repercussions) rather than her artistic products. Kauffman appears in Elizabeth Ellet's *Women in All Ages and Countries* (1859) as a more successful, professional woman than the weak fluttery sensitive depicted in both Ritchie's *Miss Angel* and Ellen Clayton's *English Female Artists* (1876). Ellet is aware of the highly contradictory nature of Kauffman's legacy: phrases like "at the same time" (158) and "on the other hand" (156) appear regularly in Ellet's prose as she records opinions of Kauffman's appearance, works, manners, and actions. Although she never says so explicitly, it is clear that Ellet's overall take on Kauffman is that the people around her—critics, admirers, fellow artists, even family members—were instrumental in impeding her work, ruining her good name, and generally mucking up her life because the public simply could not accept a high-profile woman painter who was simultaneously attractive, foreign, cultured, and talented.

Ellen Clayton's section in *English Female Artists* on Kauffman is much indebted to Ellet's work (which is listed in Clayton's opening list of sources). But the tone has been changed slightly; it is more romantic, less positive. Clayton decides not to retell an attempted rape story (detailed in Ellet with great disapproval, 1859, 153–54) and heightens the de Horn saga instead (as does Ritchie). Clayton also tells of romances with Henry Fuseli and Nathaniel Dance, both artists themselves, which Ritchie chooses to leave out of her narrative. Clayton's work makes a kind of bridge from the relatively serious (although by no means art-historical) account in Ellet to the full-blown melodrama of Ritchie's treatment of the story. Ritchie's novel was serialized in *Cornhill* between January 1874 and January 1875 and then published in single-volume format in 1876; Clayton's work was published in 1876. There is, then, the strong possibility that Clayton could have read Ritchie's serialized novel while writing her own history. But whether or not there was direct influence, Clayton drew on many of the same sources for her work as did Ritchie and Ellet: *Vita di A. Kauffman* by Giovanni de Rossi, the first and most prominent Kauffman biography, and various memoirs and letters of artists contemporary with Kauffman—all of which foreground the beautiful woman over the professional artist.

But Clayton, for all her romanticizing, still (like Ritchie) has moments where she offers her subject some support. For example, Clayton begins her chapter on Kauffman with a reference to Joseph Kauffman, Angelica's father, which reads like a direct, if anti-chronological, riposte to the editors of the *Oxford Dictionary of Art:* "He was not endowed with more than very mediocre talents; indeed, he never attained the dignity of being honoured with a separate line of remembrance from the compilers of biographical dictionaries" (1876, 1: 233). And Clayton does briefly talk about Kauffman's style: "Grace, elegance, and suave harmony were the chief qualities she aimed at, with delicate effects of chiaroscuro, and classical beauty, and dignified refinement. Perhaps if she had had a more capable master, she would have gone a better way to reach those front ranks to which she so eagerly pressed" (1, 240). Clayton also tells stories of Kauffman's unbelievable drive—of working alone, morning til night, with no thoughts of love ("Strangely enough, unlike most girls, her thoughts rarely turned to the magnetic subject of love" [ibid.]). Overall, the moral of the story seems similar to the message in *Miss Angel:* Angelica Kauffman, though gifted with rare talent and industry, was impeded in her artistic ambitions by an ideological system that privileged her desirable female body over the products of her brush.

Two final representations—visual ones this time—of Kauffman offer a recapitulation of these conflicted Victorian views of the artist. In 1892, the

Figure 5.4 Margaret Dicksee, *'Miss Angel'—Angelika Kauffmann, introduced by Lady Wentworth, visits Mr Reynolds' studio*. Royal Academy, 1892. Current whereabouts unknown. Source: Fine Art Photographic Library. Reproduced with permission.

painter Margaret Isabel Dicksee exhibited *'Miss Angel'—Angelika Kauffmann [sic] Introduced by Lady Wentworth, Visits Mr. Reynolds' Studio* at the Royal Academy (see figure 5.4).

The painting shows Kauffman standing before a canvas in Reynolds's studio; her head is arched gracefully away from the easel, however, and she appears to be gazing off into space rather than focusing on any of the figures or objects in the studio. Reynolds looks rather tenderly at Kauffman, while Lady Wentworth, Kauffman's early patroness, lounges in an ornate costume of obvious expense and fans herself. Susan Casteras has argued that Dicksee's representation of her artistic predecessor is "degrading and fails to acknowledge Kauffman's creative side" because Kauffman is presented as overly feminine, coy, and insipid in her appearance and mannerisms (1992, 218). Casteras writes that the painting "depicts Kauffman more as a frivolously dressed coquette than as a serious practitioner of the arts" (ibid.); Dicksee's representation of Kauffman visiting Reynolds's studio and viewing his painting (rather than the other way around) places Kauffman in a subservient role.

Yet Casteras's reading, although compelling, needs to be complicated. Although it is certainly true that Kauffman's physical appearance is elegant and feminine, she is not necessarily meant to appear frivolous simply because of her dress; Reynolds, too, wears ruffs and frills and a curled wig. Deborah Cherry argues that although the painting "undoubtedly plays into the myths, fabricated by the artist herself, of her youth, beauty and vulnerability," the image is still subject to more feminist readings (2000, 180). In Dicksee's painting, for example, Kauffman is boldly differentiated from Lady Wentworth; Kauffman's upright pose and less ornate attire (she wears no hat and no jewelry, unlike Lady Wentworth, and the fabric of her dress is simpler) suggests her greater artistic seriousness, as does her position in the painting: her head is precisely on a horizontal par with Reynolds's, and she stands closer to the canvas, physically aligned with the medium that was her livelihood.

Dicksee was primarily a history painter, as was Kauffman; she was also an ardent supporter of female suffrage and, one might expect, a supporter of women's right to profess art.[12] Similarly, Helen Patterson Allingham (discussed briefly in chapter 4) was an artist who combined marriage and a career as a painter and illustrator while steadfastly supporting women's rights to work, vote, and participate in the artistic community (she was the first woman to achieve full membership in the Royal Watercolour Society, in 1890). Her engraving from 1875, *Angelika Kauffmann in the Studio of Joshua Reynolds* (see figure 5.5), shares many similarities with Dicksee's picture. In Allingham's image, an elegantly dressed Kauffman holds her head and eyes at a coy angle, refusing to look either at Reynolds or his artwork. Her hands are demurely crossed and she holds a closed fan. Reynolds himself is obviously more concerned in this image with his lovely visitor than with his own artwork. These conflicted images of Kauffman as both subservient (visiting another artist's studio rather than in her own; reliant upon a wealthy patron) and yet directly involved in the world of art suggests that Dicksee and

Figure 5.5. Helen Paterson Allingham, *Angelika Kauffmann in the Studio of Joshua Reynolds*, 1875. Wood engraving; whereabouts unknown. Source: Pamela Gerrish Nunn, *Victorian Women Artists*, 111.

Allingham, like Ritchie, found their artistic predecessor to be a troublesome figure—worthy enough to be immortalized in the historical record, but with serious criticisms. How many of these criticisms are directed at Kauffman herself, and how many at a social environment that relentlessly objectifies the woman artist, remains difficult to judge.

Chapter Six

Disfigurement and Beauty in Dinah Craik and Charlotte Yonge

> My back's bad and my leg's queer.
> —Jenny Wren, in *Our Mutual Friend*

I.

JENNY WREN'S double deformity—a bad back and a queer leg—neatly encapsulates in one body the individual physical disabilities of the artist heroines discussed in this chapter. The eponymous heroine of *Olive* by Dinah Craik[1] has a hunchback; Geraldine Underwood in *Pillars of the House* by Charlotte Yonge[2] has a crippled foot that is eventually amputated. We have seen in previous chapters how women artists received unusual physical attention during the nineteenth century; their bodies become works of art and receive the same—or greater—scrutiny as their actual artworks. In this chapter I explore how the physical disfigurements of these two artist heroines provide liberation (if only temporarily) from the pressure of physical scrutiny. Physical deformity separates the young artists from the normal category of "woman," thereby permitting them certain transgressive freedoms—one of which is the freedom to produce art in relative peace. Olive and Geraldine are exempt from the aestheticizing gaze directed at their fellow female artists; we never see them being stared at by desiring men while working—they work unhampered by the necessities of heterosexual narrative. They can become artists because their deformity exempts them from the traditional expectations of womanhood.

This chapter is much indebted to and in dialogue with the recent proliferation of studies in the cultural representation (fictional and otherwise) of disabled people. In the past few decades, "disability studies" has at last entered the critical scene in the humanities (it has long been a subject of discussion in medicine and sociology). Rosemarie Garland-Thomson explains that this new field

> conceptualizes disability as a representational system rather than a medical problem, a discursive construction rather than a personal misfortune or a bodily flaw, and a subject appropriate for wide-ranging cultural analysis. . . . From this perspective, the [disabled] body becomes a cultural artifact produced by material, discursive and aesthetic practices. (2000, 181)

Within literary studies, analyses of disabled characters in literature have been enriched by this new interdisciplinary perspective. Works like *Narrative Prosthesis* by Mitchell and Snyder (2001), Garland-Thomson's *Extraordinary Bodies: Figuring Physical Disability in American Culture and Literature* (1996), and *Woeful Afflictions* by Mary Klages (1999) explore the representation of disability in American literature and culture; Martha Stoddard Holmes's *Fictions of Affliction* (2004) explores the same in British Victorian literature. While offering myriad arguments about disability and literature, these texts share a fundamental assumption that the discourse of disability has a profound impact on the stylistic and generic aspects of literary texts. In other words, disabled characters in literature do narrative work, forcing texts into new shapes.

In the Victorian era, as Stoddard Holmes points out, physical disability was used as a fictional strategy in specific generic ways. She writes, "Victorian discourses of disability, and the texts that convey them, are overwhelmingly melodramatic" (2004, 4). Mary Klages makes a similar argument about American literature of the same period. Physical disability or deformity, Stoddard Holmes suggests, was commonly included in Victorian literature as a way to add heightened pathos to a story (think of Tiny Tim, for example). Physically disabled female characters, however, were often more complex. Plots that feature disabled women "of marriageable age," in Holmes's terms (5), are less likely to simply write the disabled female character off as a convenient plot device to heighten pathos. In Dickens's *Our Mutual Friend,* for example, the disabled Jenny Wren is allowed, in Helena Michie's words, to turn her disability into "narrative power" (1989, 200).

Jenny's physical ailments are her path to self-knowledge and, significantly, give her a kind of safe haven from which to view rationally and sympathetically the romantic experiences of other characters (particularly Lizzie and Eugene). As Holmes writes, characters like Jenny are placed "parallel to 'normal' lives" to "critique and erode ability and normalcy" (2004, 15).

Similarly, in *Olive* and *Pillars* the disabled female characters become windows through which the reader can view the ideological problems of being a woman and a woman artist in Victorian England. As Stoddard Holmes and Garland-Thomson suggest, the disabled female character is particularly useful in serving as a safe place from which writers can critique the cultural position of "women in general"—safe because the disabled woman is almost always represented as asexual, removed from the normative marriage plot. Yonge and Craik make use of Geraldine and Olive in just such a fashion. However, by making their disabled characters *artists,* Yonge and Craik add a further dimension to the cultural debate. Disability becomes not just a freedom *from* (from the marriage plot) but a freedom *to:* to create, express, and work for profit. And the discourse of disability becomes a kind of narrative irony in these texts as well, a way for Yonge and Craik to critique the cultural connection between women and beauty. Craik and Yonge reject the normative ideology which insists that women themselves be beautiful objects; rather, in these texts the disabled (and hence not traditionally beautiful) woman herself creates beautiful objects, and in the process becomes subject rather than object.

On one level, then, female deformity in these two texts works like a cloak, hiding the wearer from sight and enabling her to then exercise her sight as an artist. This invisibility is regularly neutralized, however, given Victorian culture's fascination with physical deformity and the prevalence of exhibitions displaying just such "oddities" as hunchbacks or cripples. "Freak shows"—public exhibitions of dwarfs, cripples, "monstrosities," and perfectly normal individuals of foreign extractions (Aborigines, Hottentots, Fakirs, etc.)—were hugely popular entertainment during the early and mid-nineteenth century, as Richard Altick demonstrates in *The Shows of London* (1978; see especially chaps. 19 and 20). An 1847 cartoon from *Punch* with the caption "Deformo-mania" records this cultural obsession; the cartoon depicts a crowd of well-dressed spectators cramming into exhibition halls with signs claiming "THIS is the ne plus ultra of hideousness" and "Hall of Ugliness: The Greatest Deformity in the world within" (see Altick 1978, 254). As the century progressed, however, public interest in deformity became less a matter of spectacle and more a matter of scientific representation and debate; as Lisa Kochanek argues, the freak was "reframed" as science rather than as sideshow (1987, 227–30). In *Olive* we see uncomfortable echoes of the culture's earlier tendencies when the heroine, at age five, is formally "exhibited" by her nurse to her father for the first time (he has been away in the Colonies). He covers his eyes with his hands, aghast—but later forces himself to return to her nursery to look at her in a kind of horrified fascination. And "as though arming himself for a duty—repugnant, indeed, but necessary—he took his daughter on his knee, and kissed her cheek" (*Olive*, 29). Later in the novel, the racially other Celia Manners is narratively exhibited in a similar fashion: she is portrayed reclining on a sofa, dying in her dingy apartment, grotesque with starvation and consumption but with a fierce beauty and temper. (This exhibit of a mad West Indian woman invites comparisons with the scene in *Jane Eyre* in which some of the wedding guests are invited to view the "freak show" of mad Bertha clawing around in her cell.)

Such fascination with deformity has a long history, with intimate relations to gender. Aristotle writes in the *Generation of Animals* that the human male is the pinnacle of perfection; one huge evolutionary step below him comes the human female, whom Aristotle says represents "the first step on the road to deformity" (*Generation of Animals* 4.767b). Thus, according to Greek tradition, the female is *already* deformed, just by virtue of being female.[3] That this idea persists is one of the threads running through Thomas Laqueur's influential *Making Sex* (1990), which traces the language and images used to represent male and female genitalia throughout history. For much of scientific history, the female body was considered incomplete, deviant, or even monstrous in comparison with the "perfect" male form.[4] As we have seen in previous chapters, women artists—or indeed any working women—were regularly considered doubly monstrous because of their participation in the masculine realm of art.

Craik and Yonge make visible and somatic the psychic disfigurement that was so regularly attributed to artistic women.[5] Olive and Geraldine are thus not just disfigured, they are doubly, even trebly so. First as women, always already deformed; next as deformed physical bodies; then as artists in a culture that feared women's imaginative capabilities.[6] The cartoon in figure 6.1 from the *Illustrated London News* gives evidence of this. In the center is a small image of a delicate young woman holding a drawing pad (but not actively at work); around the edges are sketches of various other women at their easels—and all of these women are in some way "disfigured." One is wearing a rather loud Scottish patterned dress and has an angular masculine face (the Victorian prejudice against the Scots as vaguely barbaric comes into play here); the next squints up close to her canvas. A third stands with decidedly unladylike, almost hunchbacked, posture; below her is an elderly woman in spectacles and a matronly cap and apron; the final woman's backside spreads out considerably upon a box. None of the women in the peripheral images appear beautiful or ladylike. Together, and in contrast to the central "beauty," they form a powerful statement about the public belief of women artists' unacceptable *bodily* presence.

Figure 6.1. "Lady Students at the National Gallery." *Illustrated London News* 87 (November 21, 1885).

It is oddly fitting that visual artists receive visual marks of their talent—the physical deformities of the female artists serve in these two novels as diacritical marks, separating the women from normative social codes. Both novels—by writers espousing very different ideological views (Craik was an ardent, politically active feminist; Yonge opposed suffrage and advocated traditional religiously inflected gender norms)—act to materialize an already present but subtle ideological belief that professional women artists, even more so than women in general, were *already deformed* in multiple ways, both because of their gender and, more importantly, because of their entrance into a male professional world. But both Craik and Yonge make this multiple disfigurement into a powerful opportunity for women to escape normative gender roles and succeed in the world of art.

II.

Dinah Craik's little-known novel *Olive* is generally read as a revision of *Jane Eyre* with heightened concern for the issues of racial hybridity. Both Cora Kaplan, in her introduction to the Oxford edition of *Olive,* and Sally Mitchell, in the only recent book-length study on Craik, consider *Olive* in dialogue with *Jane Eyre*—and for good reason. Both novels feature a "plain" heroine who must transform her physical imperfections into an asset; both heroines are forced to make a living without family support; in both novels an explosive, rakish man (Rochester; Olive's father) introduces a considerably more explosive West Indian woman (Bertha; Celia Manners) into a supposedly sacrosanct English society; both novels contain a tightly wound icy minister (St. John Rivers; Harold Gwynne); and both novels are strongly concerned with the highly charged issues of female independence and racial otherness.

But where Charlotte Brontë made painting a hobby (albeit a significant one) for her heroine, Craik puts the profession of painting center stage,[7] and it is from this vantage point that I wish to consider the novel, with emphasis on the ways in which the heroine's profession and her physical deformity are made structurally similar. In Craik's novel, the hunchbacked Olive is born into a family whose physical beauty is legendary. The mother and father have an almost psychopathic devotion to physical beauty; the knowledge that Olive is deformed causes her mother, Sybilla Rothesay, to faint and cease all interest in the newborn girl. The child is an affront to the bloodline: Angus's pride in his Scottish background is shattered by her deformity, and Sybilla's vacuous adoration of beauty in all forms (especially in her own form) is likewise besmirched by the presence of this disfigured child. Yet Olive's deformity hints at something in their blood, some taint within their lineage. Her deformity means that something is rotten *within* the line of outwardly exquisite Rothesays.

That something rotten derives implicitly in the novel from the mixing of bloodlines. In considering Anne Brontë's *Tenant of Wildfell Hall* in chapter 2, we saw the almost parthenogenic upbringing of Helen Graham's son, and I outlined briefly the tradition of the discourse around the relative contributions of mother and father to an offspring. In *Olive*, this discourse comes into play again, but with a significant twist: it is not merely a child's character or appearance for which origin is sought, but a child's deformity. Although Olive has both a mother and a father, the father's line is theoretically "pure"—his Scottish nurse recalls generations of physically godlike Rothesays. Olive is explicitly coded within the novel as the product of miscegenation, a mésalliance which results in this deformity; Sybilla's unknown and mongrel English heritage plays havoc with the pure proud Scottish blood of Angus Rothesay.

Olive's genesis foreshadows the more radical miscegenation that occurs later in the novel between Angus Rothesay and his quadroon West Indian mistress, Celia Manners. Their offspring, Christal Manners—Olive's half-sister—appears externally perfect (and perfectly white), but internally all is not well. The *psychical* deformity of Christal's character and Olive's *physical* deformity are literally "related"—that is, they are of the same blood. The product of imperial miscegenation—Christal—and the product of miscegenation within England—Olive—appear equally flawed. Christal, to overcome her innate rage, must eventually take the veil to remove herself from society, an action structurally similar to Olive's decision to become a professional artist, which produces an equally inviolate celibacy (at least for a time).[8]

In compensation for her missing beauty, and indeed because of her physical deformity, Olive possesses immense spiritual and artistic depths, and after the death of her father manages to support herself and her now blind mother by selling paintings. Her artistic talent is both a compensation for her deformity and the result of it: Craik suggests both that Olive paints *instead of* leading a "normal" woman's life and that Olive paints *because she is exempt* from that confining existence. The same deformity that exiles her from one sphere of existence proves her introduction to another. In doing so, the deformity explicitly becomes a blessing. Olive's hunchback, though it repulses her parents, carries with it the suggestion of vestigial—or nascent—angel wings, crushed inside a physical restraint. She is repeatedly described as otherworldly: her complexion has a "colourless transparency," which gives "a spectral air to her whole appearance" and she is likened to an elf, "supernatural, yet fraught with a nameless beauty" (*Olive*, 23). (In this blending of deformity and otherworldliness we see yet another connection to Jane Eyre, who though not deformed physically is similarly elf-like.)

Craik's view that art is a compensation for physical difference does not work just for Olive. Olive's art teacher, Michael, though not physically deformed, shares with Olive an equally problematic exterior: "You probably would not see an uglier man twice in a lifetime," reports the narrator; "Gigantic and ungainly . . . coarse in feature, he certainly was the very antipodes of his own exquisite creations. And for that reason he created them . . . he had said, 'Providence has created me hideous; I, with my hand, will continually create beauty'" (111–12). This paradox—the ugly creates the beautiful—repeats itself in Olive, who herself was paradoxically begotten from beautiful parents. When Michael is waxing rhapsodic on the nature of art, he says,

> They who embrace Art, must embrace her with heart and soul, as their one and only bride. And she will be a loving bride to them—she will stand in the place of all other joy. Is it not triumph for him to whom fate has denied personal beauty, that his hand—his flesh and blood hand—has power to create it? (231)

At this Olive drops at his feet and cries, "I, too, am one of these outcasts; give me then this inner life which atones for all! Friend, counsel me—master, teach me! Woman as I am, I will dare all things—endure all things. Let me be an artist" (132).

Here the disfigured woman will wed her bride, Art, and gain an 'inner life' to replace the outer life of erotic love. The "inner life" of a woman is thus to be built around artistic images of beauty that her outer image cannot supply. Michael speaks of sublimation; he suggests that because he cannot marry, he paints, and Olive adopts this transformation of libidinal energy into artistic creativity, likewise claiming Art as her "bride." But this marriage between two female figures raises interesting problems for Craik's portrayal of Olive's gendered identity, which is perpetually in flux because of her deformity and now is further complicated by her artistic "marriage." Michael's figuration of the artist and his art sounds like a version of the Pygmalion myth: the artist embraces Art, which comes alive (metaphorically speaking here) at the touch of the artist's "flesh and blood hand" and returns the artist's love. But Olive's entrance into the world of Art transforms this traditional myth.

To create a properly feminine myth of Art for Olive casts the narrative momentarily into crisis. On the one hand, Olive stands outside traditional gender codes because she is unattractive and because she is the head of the household, financially independent, and a working woman. On the other, Olive's gender theoretically precludes any possibility of artistic genius; the narrator insists that

> no woman can be an artist—that is, a great artist. The hierarchies of the soul's dominion belong only to man, and it is right they should . . . let him take the preeminence. But among those stars of lesser glory, which are given to lighten

> the nations, among sweet-voiced poets, earnest prose writers, who, by the lofty truth that lies hid beneath legend and parable, purify the world, graceful painters and beautiful musicians, each brightening their generation—among these, let woman shine! (126)

The distinction here seems to be between those geniuses who are for *all* time and those who have positive social effect ("lighten the nations") during their lifetime, their "generation." Craik's novel bears out this statement: Olive becomes a painter who pleases the populace, who earns money and makes a name for herself—but she never earns the appellation "genius"; whereas Michael, whose paintings never sell, is represented as a misunderstood artistic genius whose works may be appreciated some day, but only by the artistic elite. Yet the novel explicitly values having positive impact on one's generation over the faint possibility of future fame. What begins in the above passage as a giving of power and potential to men alone—men are first in creation and hence first in art—winds up entirely eradicating men from the social art world. By the end of the passage, women become the poets, writers, painters, and musicians whose works can be communicated to the social body. A similar fluctuation occurs when the narrator continues:

> But [woman's] sphere is, and ever must be, bounded.... Nature, which gave to man the dominion of the intellect, gave to her that of the heart and affections.... He, strong in his might of intellect, can make it his all in all, his life's sole aim and guerdon. A Brutus, for that ambition which is misnamed patriotism, can trample on all human ties. A Michelangelo can stand alone with his genius, and so go sternly down unto a desolate old age. But there scarce ever lived the woman who would not rather sit meekly by her own hearth, with her husband at her side, and her children at her knee, than be the crowned Corinne of the Capitol. (126)

This passage takes some unraveling, so tightly wound are the subtle ironies and contradictions. To begin with, the intellect that ostensibly gives men dominion is misguided and even "misnamed"—Brutus has only ambition rather than the more noble patriotism, and Michelangelo's honored name is sullied with the rather shocking word "desolate." And the final insistence that there "*scarce* ever lived" a woman who would prefer Art to a husband and children opens up the possibility that there *are* some few who decidedly do prefer Art, and the reference to the "crowned Corinne of the Capitol" reinforces this possibility. Corinne, Mme. de Staël's poetess-heroine, was one of the models across the nineteenth century for the woman artist—though her story was tragic, it was embraced, as Linda Lewis argues, as an inspiration by creative women who were desperate for any representation of a successful female artist. De Staël's Corinne and Sand's Consuelo Lewis argues, a kind of founding myth (Western culture offering none) for women artists, which subsequent women writers embraced in order to represent their own artistic desires. As Lewis writes, "the female *Künstlerroman* [developed] parallel to but separate from its male counterpart and . . . literary matriarchy proved to be nurturing—not an anxiety of influence—to literary daughters creating their own fictions of female genius" (Lewis 2003, 4).

"Corinne of the Capitol" is also the title of a poem by Felicia Hemans, the popular early nineteenth-century poet.[9] Much of her poetry, like Craik's novel, is "obsessed by fame, both its cost and its attraction to women" (Leighton and Reynolds 1995, 1); poems such as "To a Wandering Female Singer," "Woman and Fame," and "Properzia Rossi" (on the celebrated Italian female sculptor) explore the seductions and hazards of female involvement in the art world. Hemans would very likely have been an influence on the young Craik; Hemans's "interest in the contradictions of power and womanliness, fame and modesty, self-expression and self-denial . . . gave later generations a characteristic topos . . ." (ibid., 2). In "Corinne of the Capitol," that "characteristic topos" emerges as a vacillation between the glory of fame and the sweetness of woman's domestic duty. After five and a half stanzas extolling the poetic gifts of the "Radiant daughter of the sun," the poem ends with a rather typical reversal:

> Happier, happier far than thou,
> With the laurel on thy brow,
> She that makes the humblest hearth
> Lovely but to one on earth. (lines 45–48)

The same tacked-on "turn" occurs in every stanza of "Woman and Fame"; each stanza begins by offering some benefit of fame (immortality, social impact, etc.) which is then rejected by the female speaker, who prefers instead affection, a flower, or "home-born love." Similarly, in "Properzia Rossi," the heroine, dying of unrequited love, bemoans that all her artistic talent still could not equal the certain pleasures of domestic bliss. And yet, particularly in "Properzia Rossi," the rewards of artistic renown that Hemans appears to deprecate become potent enough to ensure lasting fame that supplants heterosexual love. Creative power, though it is a "fruitless dower" (line 37), is yet the means by which Rossi can say "I leave my name" (line 132), rather than taking a husband's name.

Like Hemans, Craik is similarly ambivalent about the possibility of a woman becoming a practitioner of High Art. But Craik wants to have her cake and eat it too: just as Olive is both deformed and beautiful, so too is she both a lowly woman *and* a successful artist. In fact, Craik's narrative threatens to overturn her own moral homily on the bounded nature of women's creative powers, as Olive grows in skill and ambition as her artistic career progresses and prospers. As she does so, gradually her sex seems to slough off her; Michael, for example, gradually "learned to view his young pupil *as* a pupil, and never thought of her sex at all. Under his guidance, Olive passed from the mere prettinesses of most woman-painters to the grandeur of sublimer Art. Strengthened by her almost masculine power of mind, she learned to comprehend and to reverence the mighty masters" (*Olive*, 127). The progression Craik traces here suggests that Olive must pass through having no sex at all so that she can liberate her "almost masculine" mind; in this transition, of course, Olive's deformity plays a key role. Just after heralding Olive's masculine qualities, Craik writes, "That sense of personal imperfection which she deemed excluded her from a woman's natural destiny, gave her freedom in her own" (127). And further, "Olive could do many things with an independence that would have been impossible to beautiful and unguarded youth" (127). Her deformity permits her to study unchaperoned with Michael, to study alone at the British Museum, and to be initiated into the immodest mysteries of anatomy. The de-sexing of deformity further makes possible Olive's metaphoric marriage to the bride of Art; that is, only her deformity can make her un-female enough to be masculine enough to embrace the "loving bride" of Art. Real-life women artists, like Rosa Bonheur, borrowed from the characteristics and wardrobe of masculinity to set themselves apart as artists. Other artists, like Marie Baskertshiff, Angelica Kauffman, or Louise Jopling, did the opposite: they capitalized on their femininity in publicizing themselves as artists. Craik lets Olive choose another path. And yet, at the end of the passage that first praises Olive's masculine mind and then credits her deformity for liberating her from "woman's natural destiny," Craik comes full circle with Olive's gender identity: "And wherever she went, her own perfect womanliness wrapped her round as with a shield" (127). Can Olive be at once feminine, masculine, and genderless? Craik's answer seems to be yes, because some alchemy arising from the mixing of physical disfigurement and art transfigures gender.

Olive's de-sexing is not unsensual, however, for Craik renders this marriage of artist and Art as explicitly *physical;* as Olive listens to Michael expound the glories of his bride, an "ardent enthusiasm . . . dilated her whole frame while listening" (125). Likewise the paradox I spoke of earlier—the ugly creating the beautiful—becomes for both Olive and Michael an erotic (almost an autoerotic) pleasure. The marriage to Art provides Olive with her second pseudosexual awakening, one whose object falls outside the heterosexual domestic paradigm set down for young Victorian women. Olive's *first* erotic attachment is to a lovely young woman, Sara Derwent. The two strike up "that romantic friendship peculiar to sixteen" (57); the narrator speaks eloquently on the subject for some pages:

> There is a deep beauty—more so than the world will acknowledge—in this impassioned first friendship, most resembling first love, whose faint shadowing it truly is. . . . Many a mother with her children at her knee, may now and then call to mind some old playmate, for whom, when they were girls together, she felt such an intense love. How they used to pine for the daily greeting—the long walks, fraught with all sorts of innocent secrets. Or, in absence, the . . . positive love-letters, full of "dearests" and "beloveds" and sealing-wax kisses. Then the delicious meetings—sad partings, also quite lover-like in the multiplicity of kisses and embraces—embraces sweeter than those of all the world beside. (58)

The homoeroticism of the girls' relationship reaches a peak at a party during which Olive, unpartnered because of her deformity, asks Sara to dance with her. The two dance, and afterward Olive, overhearing Sara tell another girl that Olive will never have a lover, demands of Sara the reason. Olive, whose parents have avoided speaking of her deformity, has no real knowledge of it—she knows merely that she is slight and awkward, and strangely distasteful to some people. Sara gently lays her arm across Olive's humpback, and tells her, "I assure you, dear, it does not signify to me, or to any of those who care for you; you are such a gentle creature, we forget it all in time. But perhaps with strangers, especially with men, who think so much about beauty, this defect—" (67). Olive responds, "I see, as I never saw before—so little I thought of myself" (67). The realization is capped when, a short time later, Olive attempts to control her drunken father and he bursts out, "My daughter! how dare you call yourself so, you white-faced, mean-looking hunchback" (76). The two experiences combine to form the novel's "coming of age" scenario for Olive, who unlike Sara or other girls, enters into womanhood only by contraries: she becomes a woman by realizing that she is not a "woman," that is, not able to participate in the traditional events of Victorian middle-class womanhood.

The realization disrupts the romance between the two girls; Sara's statement, "especially with men," thrusts Olive from blissful homoeroticism into heteronormativity, one predetermined for her to end in failure. Sara leaves Olive to enter heterosexual marriage with Harold Gwynne, a young curate. The marriage is unhappy (it resembles the Rothesay union: drawn together when young and beautiful by sexual passion, the two find themselves utterly incompatible after the honeymoon) and after a time Sara dies. Eventually Harold enters Olive's orbit when he demands repayment for a debt her dead father owed him. When eventually Harold takes Olive as his second wife, Olive's young love for Sara reemerges, transmuted into love for Sara's husband. On a simple level, this triangle can be read as similar to the triangle in *Jane Eyre*, in which the "bad" first wife (Sara is no Bertha but is still represented as flighty and frivolous) must be eliminated before the second "good" wife can be properly installed. But a more radical reading—and one which the novel overtly encourages—positions Harold as a figure passed "between women" (to evoke the work of Eve Sedgwick [1985], with a difference) who desire *each other* rather than himself. This reading fits more closely with the cross-gendered character of Olive's other erotic experience, as *husband* to a feminized Art. As Denis Denisoff suggests, art allows Olive the space for same-sex passion; Olive cathects only on beautiful and *female* object choices (see 1999, 165–67). Even Olive's relationship to her lovely mother is couched in the same homoerotic terms: "No lover ever gloried in his mistress's charms, no painter ever delighted to deck his model, more than Olive loved to adorn and to admire the still exquisite beauty of her mother" (*Olive*, 50).

But for all the romance surrounding art in the novel, Olive in fact becomes an artist for financial reasons. This is a common theme in novels featuring women painters; the practical aspects of the art world consistently figure prominently—more prominently in novels with female artists, it should be noted, than in those with male artist figures (where the need for money is explicitly rejected, often, in favor of the idealized spiritual drive to art—and where the male artists are generally supported financially by female relatives, as is Hans Meyrick). Olive needs money to repay her dead father's debt to Harold; when she first sees Michael's artwork, she asks immediately, "Do people ever grow *rich* as artists?" (118). Michael's sister Miss Meliora cites Sir Joshua Reynolds and Sir Thomas Lawrence as evidence that occasionally people *do* become rich as artists. Miss Meliora adds that women, too, have been well-known painters: "There was Angelica Kauffman, and Properzia Rossi, and Elizabeth Sirani. In our day, there is Mrs. A— and Miss B—, and the two C—s" (118).[10]

"And so," breaks in the narrator of *Olive*, "though this confession may somewhat lessen the romance of her character—it was from no yearning after fame, no genius-led ambition, but from the mere desire of earning money, that Olive Rothesay first conceived the thought of becoming an artist" (119). This proclamation echoes much of what we saw in chapter 4 in the works of Eliot, Oliphant, and Howitt and will see again in chapter 7 in the novels of Mary Ward: women often considered art as a means to make a living rather than as a sacred vocation. In *Olive,* the materialist view of art is used—ostensibly—to denigrate Olive's pretensions to art: it "lessen[s] the romance of her character." Ironically, however, lessening the romance is precisely what Craik is trying to do, at one level: she wants to remove the woman artist from the typical heterosexual romance narrative. And Olive's economic motivations actually strengthen the "romance of her character" in another, nonsexual, direction. Olive desires money so as to make her mother comfortable, and to clear her father's name: art, and the money that comes from it, thereby strengthens Olive's representation as a loving daughter.

The male artist Michael, on the other hand, ignores his devoted and adoring sister, exploits her labor, and fails to mourn her death; Olive represents a more humane side of art. Foregrounded throughout Craik's novel, and again in Yonge's *Pillars of the House,* is the contrast between male and female art. In *Olive,* we have on the one side Michael and his High Art (images of historical, classical, or biblical subjects): he paints, for example, a scene from the story of Alcestis, who agreed to die for her husband, Admetus (her story is told in a play by Euripides). By implication, this kind of art is shown to be empty of life, value, or popular appeal. On the other hand, Olive's art—sentimental, morally uplifting, and popular—represents woman's art. We never "see" Olive's paintings; there are no detailed ekphrastic descriptions of her subjects, and none of her style. We are told that her first sketches—before formal training from Michael—have raw power and illustrate scenes from Romantic poetry (Olive favors Byron, whose own physical deformity contributed greatly to the romance surrounding his character) or are portraits of her mother. As with all the women artists we have met so far, Olive's material is limited: the only subject matter available is her sole family member and imaginative scenarios from literature or history. She also paints children: her only large-scale picture is named "Charity," and the wealthy patron who purchases it does so because "the two little children in the background resemble [his sons]"; the same patron asks Olive to add the family horse and greyhounds to the allegorical painting (141). This meager information is enough to tell us that Olive is not moving in the high art circles but caters instead to a wealthy public—the same public that began in the 1850s (*Olive* was published in 1850) to flood the art market, making the fortunes of artists. It also tells us that Olive's paintings were considered not untouchable masterpieces, but works that could be altered with impunity on the whim of the purchaser. But nevertheless, in contrast to the cold and unpopular High Art of Michael, Olive's paintings are celebrated for their sentimental appeal, their moral value (with titles like "Charity"), and their intelligibility.

Other than these hints, Olive's paintings remain a kind of narrative secret, a way for Olive to enter the public world yet remain free of the kind of controlling, masculine ekphrastic gaze which (as I discussed in the introduction) was so common in the nineteenth century. Her paintings are not present in the narrative as repositories of emotional or psychological truth; Craik does not use Olive's paintings as indicators of her mental state (as in *Jane Eyre*) but as manifestations of and commentaries on her social position as a working woman. Just as Olive's own body is allowed—because of her deformity—to escape the visual attentions of male members of society, so too do Olive's paintings remain "unseen" by the general public within the novel as well as the reader outside it; her works enter the marketplace quietly, privately, femininely, without public display. When the time comes for Olive to put the finishing touches on her first major painting (we never know the subject) and send it to the Royal Academy for possible exhibition, Mrs. Rothesay falls ill. "Passing it was, and not dangerous, but to Olive's picture it brought a fatal interruption" (135). Daughterly duty supersedes the demands of art, and the painting is not sent. And at last April rolls around—the traditional time in which viewers and purchasers visit artists' studios to see paintings before they are sent to the Royal Academy—and Olive misses the opening of the R.A. "season," which as I discussed in chapter 1 was a highly public, social event. Olive would have been among the throngs at the Royal Academy (as is Geraldine, in *Pillars of the House*) had her painting been sent and successfully admitted. Instead, she nurses her ill mother and assists Michael on "Picture Sunday"—the day in April where art patrons, friends, and other artists would invade studios to see pictures before they were sent to the R.A. for selection. It is during this alternate, more domestic form of exhibition that Olive's unfinished picture, standing in Michael's studio, attracts the attention of a wealthy art patron. Ironically, then, Olive's picture is sold anyway (while those of her master Michael, though accepted at the R.A. show, remain unsold). Craik cannot permit her heroine to exhibit publicly with the enormous institution of the Royal Academy; instead, Olive's first painting is sold from a private space, and the financial transaction is entirely between men—the first Olive hears of the sale is when Michael's sister pours a handful of coins given to her by Michael into Olive's lap. Money therefore passes from the male patron to the male artist (Michael), who then passes it on to his sister—who is the only one permitted to pass it to the woman artist. But this bubble of privacy immediately bursts as Olive takes up her first earnings and, businesslike, mails them off to her father's creditor, Harold Gywnne. Even if her paintings do not enter the market, the proceeds from them decidedly do.

Olive's eventual marriage to Harold, who has given up his ministry and become a scientist, effectively ends her artistic career. In another revision of themes in *Jane Eyre*, Olive receives two marriage proposals; the first is from Michael, her art master, who is about to move to Rome. He tells her, "I ask you—not for my own sake, but for that of our noble Art . . . I cannot give you love, but I can give you glory . . . I can make of you such an artist as no woman ever was before" (158). Just as St. John Rivers tells Jane, "you are formed for labour, not for love. You shall be mine; I claim you—not for my pleasure, but for my Sovereign's service" (*Jane Eyre*, 354), so too does Michael "claim" Olive for his "sovereign"—Art. Unlike St. John, however, Michael offers Olive artistic *equality* rather than a pure immolation of self. But she refuses him, arguing as did Jane when she refuses St. John that to marry without love would be immoral.

When Olive does marry, Craik tells us that "it was a natural and a womanly thing that in her husband's fame Olive should almost forget her own" (325). The "almost" here is telling, as is the implication that Olive too has some measure of fame already. To complicate matters further, the economic substructure of the marriage is unusual and further undercuts Harold's domestic superiority. It is after all Harold's financial claim that originally motivates Olive toward art and stimulates her artistic "genius" to emerge. As we have seen, the money Olive makes through art goes to Harold. Curiously, then, Olive's marriage reunites her with the economic fruits of her labor: when she marries Harold, she can once again enjoy the money she sent him in repayment of her father's debt. Significantly, before their marriage all of Olive's initial interactions with the man who will one day be her husband are *financial;* in an ironic revision of lover's courtship, Olive carefully saves his responses to her *business* letters. Similarly, by marrying Harold Olive is "reunited" with a family legacy that by rights should have been Olive's. (This trajectory should remind us of previously discussed financial transactions surrounding Married Women's Property.) By marrying, Olive forfeits all claim to her income; yet here, marriage appears the only way for her to regain that income, albeit circuitously.

In addition to making possible such aesthetic and social critiques, Craik, like other novelists I have discussed, uses her discussions of painting to act out her own beliefs about prose fiction. Simply put, Craik's novelistic vision of the world is heavily impacted by the pictorial. The novel's relentless pictorialism on the one hand suggests that Craik's aesthetic mode is directly mimetic, that she sees prose fiction as a means of reproducing pictures from life. On the other hand, Craik's pictures—like Olive's—tend always toward the Ideal and hence lose much of their potency by being merely stereotypical. Craik's conflict is between High Art or the Ideal on the one hand and the quotidian complexities of character, emotion, and event on the other. Olive's troubled but ultimately successful passage from "the mere prettinesses of most woman-painters to the grandeur of sublimer Art" is the same path Craik *wishes* to take in the realm of novel-writing—yet the generic requirements of the kind of novel she constructs (a *Künstlerroman* married to a sentimental romance novel) do not lend themselves as easily to her endeavors as she might have hoped.

On the stylistic level, however, Olive's career rubs off, so to speak, on Craik's fiction with greater success. Scenes in *Olive* progress like word-paintings—paintings that are very much like those we see Olive producing. If Olive's pictures are stock scenes, representing moral types (Olive's great masterpiece is called "Charity," and depicts an idealized, moral parable in images), Craik follows her heroine's lead and paints in words a series of allegorical, stock scenes that might wear such typical names as The Loving Mother, The Faithful Sister, The Artist, and so on. As Olive's mother fades toward death, for instance, Craik writes:

> Let us draw the picture which lived in Olive's memory evermore.
>
> Mrs. Rothesay sat in a little low chair. . . . She did not wear an invalid's shawl, but a graceful wrapping-gown of pale colours . . . which suited well her delicate, fragile beauty. Closely tied over her silver hair . . . was a little cap, whose soft pink gauze lay against her cheek . . . Her eyes were cast down . . . but her mouth smiled a serene, cheerful holy smile, such as is rarely seen on human face. . . . Her little thin hands lay meekly crossed on her knee, one finger playing, as she often did, with her wedding-ring, now worn to a mere thread of gold. (202)

The picture of the dying mother, complete with its symbolism of worn ring and angelic face, is but one such portrait in Craik's gallery. We are offered portraits of Mother and Child clinging together, and of Olive's serene face after her mother's death. Other portraits are less positive and powerfully represent pain, degradation, or anger. When Olive first meets her father's West Indian mistress Celia Manners, the portrait Craik draws of Mrs. Manners has a suppressed power quite unlike the more calm pictures of Olive and her mother:

> She was indeed a very beautiful woman, though her beauty was on a grand scale. She had flung herself, half-dressed, upon what seemed a heap of straw with a blanket thrown over. As she lay there, sleeping heavily, her arm tossed above her head, the large but perfect proportions of her form reminded Olive of the reclining figure in the group of the "Three Fates."
>
> But there was in the prematurely old and wasted face something that told of a wrecked life. (129–30)

Just as Olive likens Celia Manners to a picture, so too does Craik use the lexicon of painting to describe the reclining figure: "grand scale," and "perfect proportions." Similarly, when Christal arrives at the Rothesay's home unexpectedly in the midst of a storm, both Christal and Olive are offered symbolic portraits of their unacknowledged sister. Christal, first, arrives at the door and sees inside the framed image of Olive and her mother huddled together: "Thus they showed, in the faint glimmer of the lightning, a beautiful picture of filial love—to the eyes of a stranger, who that moment opened the door" (148–49). Olive then has her opportunity to observe Christal, as that young lady stands in the kitchen drying herself off from the storm:

> She stood, a picture less of girlish grace, than of such grace as French fashion dictates. Her tall, well-rounded form, struggled through a painful slimness.... Nay, there was something in the very tie of her neck-ribbon which showed it never could have been done by English fingers. She appeared, all over, "a young lady from abroad."
>
> ... She had one beauty—a proud, arched, column-like neck, gliding into a well-set head, which she carried loftily. (149)

This second picture—which we might give the name Craik suggests, "A Young Lady from Abroad"—contains within it all the elements the reader needs to place Christal in her narrative place in contrast to the "portrait" of Olive and her mother on their domestic hearth. Christal's portrait is coded with multiple references to her difference from her half-sister Olive: Christal is alone where Olive has her mother in her arms; Christal is marked by multiple references to her foreignness ("never have been done by English fingers," "from abroad"); and finally, Christal's neck, straight and proud, stands in striking contrast to Olive's "elevation of the shoulders" which resulted in a "shortening of the neck, and [gave] the appearance of a perpetual stoop" (23).

Through similar scenes of word-painting, the novel tackles enormous and historically topical issues: race, miscegenation, religious doubt, physical deformity, adultery, and women's professionalism—as well as taking on *Jane*

Eyre. At the same time, it sets itself up as a moral parable, with Olive as a kind of "everywoman" savior figure. On the one hand, Craik is trying to write "just" a novel; on the other, she is trying to produce something (as she says of Olive's painting) "not of the passing hour, but for all time" (127). Just as Olive is both beautiful and deformed at the same time, Craik's novel tries to be two seemingly incompatible kinds of prose fiction—domestic and political. The two narrative impulses, at war, may unsettle the novel (as many critics have argued), but also give it its continued pertinence.

III.

Just as Craik's representation of her heroine's artistic career is constructed of conflicting aesthetic and ideological values, so too does Yonge's treatment of Geraldine Underwood in *Pillars of the House* vacillate wildly between endorsement of and punishment for her artistic talents. Geraldine is one of a dozen children in the Underwood family, whose crowded history Yonge details in more than seventeen hundred pages. In the five-volume novel Yonge introduces a complex class drama in which the various Underwood siblings represent an array of positions along the social spectrum. The novel traces the family fortunes from high to low and back again—but each sibling, depending on when he or she reaches maturity, absorbs a different character of a different class. Mr. Underwood began his married life with the expectation of a lucrative clerical living together with the estate of Vale Leston (described as "a tolerably good estate, enough to qualify the owner for the dangerous position of 'squareson'" *Pillars,* 1: 10), but both living and estate are snatched away by a greedy relative who exploits a flaw in the will. Mr. Underwood thence removes his growing family to Bexley, where the unhealthy climate and the failing family fortunes are registered by Geraldine's diseased foot. After the deaths of both Mr. and Mrs. Underwood, the dozen children begin their slow, uphill climb toward prosperity with Felix, the eldest son, at their head and Wilmet, one of the eldest daughters, as their surrogate mother.

Felix and Wilmet must necessarily declass themselves, sacrificing the values and behavior of the class into which they were born to the economic necessity of their present lot. Felix becomes a clerk in a bookshop; Wilmet develops a sharp eye for a bargain and eventually marries a young sailor. Successive siblings do rather better for themselves materially, though none equal the moral authority of the eldest son and daughter. Wilmet's twin Alda opts out of the family's poverty by marrying a vapid peer entirely for his money; another sister becomes a valued governess in a noble household. One son becomes—or tries to become, as we shall see—an artist; another becomes a clergyman, and so on. The younger siblings are largely unaffected by the turbulent family fortunes; by the time they are in their early teens, the combined efforts of Felix's industry and a convenient death in the family have reinstated the family at Vale Leston.

When we first meet Geraldine during the narrator's account of the various children in the Underwood family, we are told:

> To begin at the bottom—here sat on a hassock, her back against the wall, her sharp old fairy's face uplifted, little Geraldine, otherwise Cherry, a title that had suited her round rosiness well, till after the first winter at Bexley, when the miseries of a diseased ankle-joint had set in. . . . She was, as might be plainly seen in her grey eyes, a clever child. (15–16)

She is not, however, "at the bottom" of the family in terms of age—which the passage seems to suggest even as it describes her as already aged (an "old fairy"). Instead she *physically* occupies that space as the lame sibling, though she is in fact the fifth of the twelve children. With her deformed foot (which is eventually amputated), Geraldine is situated in a noble lineage of crippled feet that starts with Hephaistos, runs through Oedipus and Philoktetes, and ends, in the generation before Yonge, with Byron. Like some of her disabled predecessors, Geraldine has "genius" of the artistic variety; when compounded with her physical deformity, her talent serves to distance Geraldine from the traditional paths of femininity. Her appearance, for instance, is lamented: as shown above, she began with "round rosiness" which the "diseased ankle-joint" eliminates. Yet the narrator is careful to tell us that Geraldine *could* be beautiful if she were not so intelligent and talented—traits which disrupt her femininity as much as does her amputated foot. When describing one of the younger siblings who is surprisingly beautiful, the narrator remarks that she is "much what Geraldine might have been with more health and *less genius to change those delicately-molded features and countenance*" (3: 126; emphasis added). Genius explicitly *disfigures* Geraldine; it literally "changes" her features.

Geraldine dismisses the traditions of domestic femininity in favor of aesthetic considerations; Yonge makes it clear that the lame artist finds no joys in traditional female activities such as those her sister Wilmet enjoys. The narrator seems to know that Wilmet's domestic economy deserves praise, but the proceedings receive no such praise from Geraldine:

> She might have admired to see Wilmet's perfect knowledge of articles and

> their value . . . while her scorn and indignation at an encounter with a Cheap Jack were something rich. But though Cherry could describe such an expedition [to the shops] with humor that threw Felix and Lance into a convulsion of merriment, it was very wearisome to her; and the more she knew it ought to be instructive, the more it depressed her. . . . She longed wearily at times for the sight of something beautiful. (3: 16–17)

Wilmet's skills in social femininity are based on her knowledge of "articles and their value"—but Geraldine prefers aesthetic value. The two women's fields of knowledge are set at odds here: the one knows foods, clothing, and household items while the other longs for "the sight of something beautiful," which the scenes of domestic femininity cannot provide.

Apropos of Yonge's earlier and better-known novel *The Clever Woman of the Family* (1882), which also features a disabled character, Martha Stoddard Holmes argues that Yonge makes disability into a positive trait, because it generates both emotion and human dependency. In *The Clever Woman of the Family*, Yonge "represents disability and mutual dependency as pervasive social goods, those which promote both the homosocial and more generally the social. . . . The novel amply affirms the power of infirmity to draw people close" (2004, 52). In *Pillars of the House*, however, Geraldine's disability is *not* represented as the emotional glue that cements the social. The difference cannot be the presence of Geraldine's artistic talent, since in *The Clever Woman of the Family*, the disabled character is also a woman artist (Ermine Williams, a writer) who is certainly represented as promoting positive mutual dependence. Geraldine's dependence, however, is of a different sort. She is rarely represented as in need of physical assistance (only twice in five volumes, in fact—once significantly during an art exhibition, discussed later in this chapter); rather, what she needs is artistic freedom, which translates into the need for financial stability. Geraldine is fettered not because she is disabled but because the family is poor. Geraldine's struggles to achieve professional success are never attributed to her lameness—instead, her lameness symbolically materializes the unfortunate fact of her gender and her family's economic situation. She has no drawing teachers; she must make do with inferior supplies and materials; she has no access to museums, no intercourse with artistic society, or *any* society for that matter—until her paintings are accepted by the R.A. and a new world opens for her. But before this, the family home is bleak; there is no Romantic nature for her to escape to and learn instinctively from, as did Olive in Craik's novel. In the passage quoted above in which Geraldine watches Wilmet bargain, Geraldine longs "wearily . . . for the sight of something beautiful" which the grim manufacturing town to which the parentless Underwoods have moved cannot provide her. In volume three of *Pillars* we are told, "Her aspiring compositions and her studies in drawing she almost laid aside in a fit of hopeless disgust, and she applied herself to what was less improving, but more immediately profitable" (3: 18)—which is the manufacture of Christmas cards, another instance of a woman artist putting her talents into the service of the domestic economy. Geraldine's productions provide the income which her sister Wilmet spends—neatly collapsing the Victorian sexual division of labor in which men produce income and women spend it.

As in *Olive, Pillars* too has a male artist figure whose devotion to High Art contrasts with the female artist's necessary production of sentimental or popular art. In *Pillars,* Geraldine must rely on her elder brother Edgar for all her artistic information; he lives a bohemian life in the London art world while she remains at home caring for the younger children. Edgar's letters home to Geraldine are her only formal art education:

> Edgar's criticism alone was worth anything to her aesthetic sense . . . his not coming home was a great loss to her art, as well as to her affection and intellect. Those windows that he opened to her of all lovely scenes and forms in nature or art, his brilliant stories of artist society and foreign manners, could not but be greatly missed as she lived her monotonous life. (3: 17)

His absence leaves Geraldine with only her native skill, perseverance, and her family as subjects. Edgar's career, unlike Michael's in *Olive,* follows a typical ne'er-do-well artist pattern like that which we see in Branwell Brontë or in Henry Gowan in Dickens's *Little Dorrit.* Edgar works intermittently, indulges in nameless debaucheries, and produces art so avant-garde that only his devoted sister admires it. His intended masterpiece "Brynhild" fails dismally at the Royal Academy exhibition, while Geraldine, on the other hand, achieves stunning artistic success by painting what she knows—family portraits. Even though the narrator relates that Geraldine's name appeared "a good way further on" in the R.A. catalogue than Edgar's, her paintings still achieve the success which his cannot. As in *Olive,* Yonge dramatizes a battle between male and female art in which male art is aligned with an unintelligible high cultural tradition, while the art of women is seen as morally uplifting, true to life, and popular.

Edgar's "Brynhild" is "in the second room, rather below the line," a snub which infuriates Edgar, who is full of tales "of injustice suffered by whomever [*sic*] did not belong to favoured cliques" (3: 182). The painting's subject is hard to discern from Yonge's ekphrasis (intentionally so): it has a "cocoon shaped glow of yellow flame" in its center, a "Turneresque whirl of flame and smoke around the sleeping Valkyr" juxtaposed with a "Pre-Raffaelitism" in the detail work; one viewer describes it as a "glaring red and yellow thing" (3: 183). Geraldine, who sees Edgar's finished painting for the first time at the R.A. exhibit, is profoundly disappointed; she makes only positive comments on it to Edgar's face but the narrator gives us full insight into Geraldine's brutal aesthetic judgment of her brother's painting. Within Geraldine's judgment lies Yonge's own conservative aesthetic; Edgar's painting explicitly follows two nineteenth-century art traditions (Turner and Pre-Raphaelitism), neither of which meets with Yonge's approval. Geraldine, staring at Edgar's painting and attempting to control her features, thinks to herself that his work "wants majesty," and more severely that its figures are entirely out of proportion. She then muses that "the Pre-Raffaelitisim" of Sigurd's armor was "too like worsted stockings." By thus turning masculine armor into winter clothing, Geraldine's comment domesticates and feminizes the extreme detail-work characteristic of Pre-Raphaelite painting.

Edgar's painting fails to "reach" its viewers; Yonge shows us that the viewing public cannot *recognize*, let alone understand, the subject matter of Edgar's painting: one viewer tells another that the picture represents "that French queen who was torn to pieces by wild horses" (3: 183). Brynhild is, in fact, a Valkyrie central to the Scandinavian prose cycle, the Volsunga Saga. She is engaged to Sigurd (Siegfried in later tales), who is given a potion of forgetfulness and marries another woman. He subsequently tricks Brynhild into marrying one of his brothers-in-law. She has surrounded herself with a ring of fire that any prospective suitor must cross, believing that only Sigurd can do so. He does so, but in his brother-in-law's form; when she discovers the trick she has him killed, then commits suicide. From Yonge's scattered clues, Brynhild surrounded by the ring of fire seems to be the subject of Edgar's painting.

Not a subject which would find much favor with the traditional and religious Yonge, certainly, with its implications of heathen goddesses, magic, and sex. Yonge critiques Edgar's choice of subject and style by having Geraldine come to appreciate Edgar's picture only *after* he has systematically pointed out to her its beauties and tried to short-circuit her judgment. When she tells him, for instance, "I had imagined it quite different," he replies scathingly, "Oh, if you came with a preconceived notion . . ." When she says the painting is smaller than she thought it would be, he mocks her with, "All ladies go in for 'igh hart on the Zam zummin scale" (3: 183; cf. Deut. 2:20). It is only when he talks her into seeing it "as it ought to have been" (but not, significantly, as it actually is) that she comes to believe it "so great and deep a work of art that study alone could appreciate it" (3: 182–83). And so it becomes Geraldine's *imagination* that creates the work of art as it should be, rather than Edgar's brush.

It is not merely Edgar's subject matter that receives Yonge's disdain. As Yonge represents it, Edgar's aesthetic is at fault because it fails to accurately represent everyday human experience. When Geraldine first sees "Brynhild," she immediately notes that the central figure is "like Marilda" (a cousin), while "Sigurd is Ferdinand" (a family friend). But Edgar, instead of making likeness his central theme, has merely *made use* of these two real individuals as artistic models. Geraldine's art, on the other hand, makes the likeness of real individuals a primary concern. She fuses stylistic faith to nature *and* the strong moral component which Ruskin—and Yonge—saw as essential to art. The narrative validates Geraldine's aesthetic judgment of Edgar's paintings by making her own paintings the object of considerable public praise, both from casual untrained eyes and from seasoned experts. Once Edgar's painting has been viewed, Geraldine and Edgar proceed into the Watercolor room, where a crowd is gathered around Geraldine's paintings. The Royal Academy has accepted five of her watercolors: four are collected into one frame, each representing a young girl during different domestic activities: "The Lesson," "Hearing a Story," "With the Kitten," and "Listening to Music." The other work is a watercolor called "The Faithful Acolyte," which depicts the boyish devotion of a young church server.

The young girl represented in the group of four watercolors is Stella, the younger sister who has the beauty that Geraldine's intelligence removes from her. The subtle irony here is that Yonge allows Geraldine to achieve fame by painting representations of the very beauty she *could* have, if she *didn't* have that deforming genius for representation. The portraits have been caught "entirely without consciousness on Stella's part," and hence they achieve a great freshness. The verbal description of the pictures oozes sentimental femininity:

> She had caught Stella's sweet little head four times over—in the seriousness of lesson-learning, with eager parted smiling lips with which she listened to a story, with her tender caressing expression towards the kitten she was nursing, and with the rapt dreamy gaze that her brother's music would bring over her countenance. (3: 185)

Although the "Constellation," as the Underwood family call this series of four views of Stella's fair face, seems to position Geraldine firmly within the "lady-like art" genre (domestic, feminine, sentimental), Geraldine's "Acolyte" turns the tables on this judgment. The painting details the interior of a church—dark, the colors dim and shady, subdued yet rich in color—and exhibits perfect mastery:

> The . . . perspective vaultings, arches, and tracery, were perfectly drawn, *knowing where they were going and what they meant* . . . the Altar hangings, richly patterned . . . were kept back in spite of all their detail, throwing out the "flake of fire" and the glitter reflected on the gold ornaments . . . while in the fragment of the east window just seen above, glittered a few jewels of stained glass touched by rising sun, and to which the subdued colouring of the rest gave wonderful glory. (3: 185; emphasis added)

The wonderful phrase, "knowing where they were going and what they meant," suggests Geraldine's complete control over the techniques of art. In this painting, Geraldine's attention to the details of the altar hangings ("richly patterned") is balanced by the overall structure of the painting (the cloths are "kept back in spite of their detail"); Yonge shows us here that Geraldine has mastered the balance between realism (of detail) and idealism—both significantly gendered categories in aesthetic theory. One of the major debates in aesthetics has been what relationship between the general and the particular is proper to art; the detail falls on the side of the troublesome particular. In *Reading in Detail: Aesthetics and the Feminine,* Naomi Schor outlines the persistent "over-determination of the woman–detail association in idealist aesthetics," tracing the "anti-particularist aesthetic" which rose to prominence in the late eighteenth century (1987, 5). The detail, as Schor sees it, tends to "subvert an internal hierarchic ordering of the work of art which subordinates the periphery to the center, the foreground to the background" (20). Too many details mean, for idealist aestheticians, too much realism and not enough attention to the whole, the abstract, the general. Even in the great age of realism, details had to be screened out of art, lest the structure of the whole be lost. Baudelaire writes:

> An artist . . . will find himself at the mercy of a riot of details all clamouring for justice with the fury of a mob in love with absolute equality. All justice is trampled under foot; all harmony sacrificed and destroyed; many a trifle assumes vast proportions; many a triviality usurps the attention. The more our artist turns an impartial eye on detail, the greater is the state of anarchy. (1995, 16)

Not only, as this passage screams, does the detail become aligned with the lower classes ("the fury of the mob"), but, as Schor shows, much of the detail's problematic status derives from its persistent association with the feminine: women, deemed for centuries incapable of abstract thought, produced and appreciated only the particular—in Baudelaire's terms, "trifles" and "triviality."[11] Yonge's point in this scene seems to be that Geraldine's painting has an appropriately feminine level of detail, yet those details are "kept back," restrained like the altar hangings to make way for a idealized message of religious glory. Edgar, however, is no master of detail—he strives only for a (masculine, in Schor's paradigm) idealism that must fail because he has no ability to represent the details faithfully (his knight's armor looks like "worsted stockings" rather than true armor).

Geraldine's picture earns for its artist the following compliment from an Academy-goer: "There's so much power as well as good drawing and expression, that I should not have thought it a woman's work." The narrator calls this piece of flattery "the most ambitioned praise a woman can receive." Geraldine is further demeaned when the narrator remarks, "both Geraldine and Edgar agreed in the belief that she was on a level with the public taste, while he soared too high beyond it" (3: 184). But Yonge follows this condescending remark with a subtle angry backlash: in describing Geraldine's painting she writes: "Her paintings had a strength of colouring unusual in inexperienced artists, perhaps owing to the depth of hue she used . . . and thus the paintings asserted themselves, and were not killed by their neighbors, *but rather committed slaughter all around*" (3: 184; emphasis added).

Here any possibility of ambition or aggression in Geraldine is shunted off onto her artworks, which take on a physical strength denied the artist herself. The products of Geraldine's frail body become powerful forces eliminating any competition from surrounding paintings, whereas Edgar's painting had been *subsumed* by its surroundings. This language of force seems then to alarm Yonge; as if in apology for this outburst of unfeminine aggression, Yonge immediately reemphasizes Geraldine's physical frailty. As she is standing with her brother in front of her paintings, Geraldine is dangerously crushed by the crowd around her own paintings. She becomes suddenly "the little lame girl" (3: 186) again, aflutter, frightened by the admiring crowds that threaten to hurt her at the very scene of her accomplishment. The entire scene of aesthetic appraisal thus fluctuates through different perceptions of female artistry; Yonge remains ambivalent about her heroine's success.

The indecision is neatly exemplified within the contrasting meanings of the word "press" which Yonge uses to describe Geraldine's danger from the encroaching crowd. Geraldine grows "nervous at the press" of people around her and her pictures, and while "to press" in this context literally means to squeeze or bear down on, it also evokes the specter of publicity: "the press," those whose job it is to make public the lives of artists. This fear of publicity is clearly marked in the scene: Geraldine stands before her paintings anonymously, as just another viewer; when a fatherly friend of the family appears beside her, he is "too considerate to utter a name that would instantly have brought all eyes upon the little lame girl" (3: 186).

If we return to the *Punch* article that I discussed in chapter 1, we recall that the reviewer of the Society for Female Artists exhibit sought to reestablish the woman artist's self as aesthetic object to the exclusion of the woman artist's production. Yonge here rewrites this narrative slightly: there is still only room for one object here (artist or artwork); the presence of both producer and produced causes a momentary intense physical crisis, narrated by Yonge almost in terms of a rape. Geraldine must be rescued by her brother from a strangely aggressive crowd of culture seekers who appear to be trying to force the woman artist right back into the frame of her own pictures (which are significantly portraits of her own double, Stella). However, here in Yonge's novel the artist's production is what remains, rather than her marriageable body (as in the *Punch* article). Geraldine's artwork appears too powerful for invisibility, even while her body must be disciplined and subjected to a public humiliation.

Though Geraldine's success at the R.A. necessitates a backlash from Yonge, Yonge still understands the power of ambition and (unlike Margaret Oliphant) allows her young artist continued success within a particular and well-defined genre of art. Yonge appears to be genuinely contemptuous of Art with a capital A. Edgar's failure stems from his trying to produce art that goes beyond the realm of moral, narrative realism—and this is also Yonge's commentary on narrative fiction. Geraldine's paintings are simplified parables, safe and sweet. Her narrative fate seems both a reparation for her missing foot and a prize for her production of this kind of art. Geraldine may begin the novel as the helpless lame one, but as the novel progresses she becomes more and more central to the family, until the marriages of her eldest sisters and the death of her eldest brother leaves her as the remaining "pillar of the house": sole mistress of the family's newly recovered estate and accompanying wealth. In the final scene of the novel, we see her standing with her crutch on the wide steps of Vale Leston, receiving visitors as the unmarried mistress of a wealthy estate.

In her success, Geraldine functions as a counternarrative to Yonge's frequently mentioned conservatism. Although her letters, novels, and religious tracts all speak to her commitment to traditional gender roles, Yonge occasionally surprises us with moments of feminist sensibility. Yonge's earlier novel, *The Clever Woman of the Family* (1865), offers this tension again. Rachel, the "clever" woman of the title, attempts to live a life of work and independence, but her actions have disastrous consequences (the death of a child) and she ends up a pathetically dependent and meek housewife. But the novel features another disabled female character—Ermine Williams—as a counterpoint to Rachel. An explosion has burnt Ermine's legs past repair; she is confined to a wheelchair. Her disfigurement has caused an early disappointment in love—the family of her suitor refuses to countenance his marriage to a cripple and Ermine nobly breaks her engagement. She becomes a quintessential example of what one might call the irony which disability introduces into a narrative. Ermine, who appears so "useless" and helpless, turns out to be the novel's true artist: she writes well-known books under a pseudonym. As with Geraldine, Ermine's artistic career arises from her inability to pursue a more traditional gender position. Ermine does eventually marry her once-rejected suitor, but only after her literary career is well established.

There seems to be a steady progression in Yonge toward independent artistic women. Ethel May in *The Daisy Chain* (1856) gives up poetry to take care of her father and siblings; she does not return to her artistic career. In *Dynevor Terrace* (1857), Isabel Conway gives up her poetic aspirations for her once-neglected husband and children—whereupon she is immediately rewarded by the narrative with great success as a poet. Ermine Williams (from *Clever Woman,* 1865) similarly gets to have literary success *and* domestic bliss. Geraldine in *Pillars* (1873) is given artistic acclaim and economic security—without the hassle of a romance plot (nor does the novel ever even hint that she pines for one).

The physical deformities of both Geraldine and Olive motivate a variety of narrative constructions. Their disfigurement is at once a visible, somatic experience of difference and a symbolic marker of cultural marginality. The physically "other" woman painter is used by both Craik and Yonge to demonstrate ways women can circumvent the heteronormativity and economic oppression of the social order. Disfigurement also functions as a deconstructive practice whereby women writers reveal and partially dismantle or disrupt an aesthetic discourse that attempts to contain or restrain female artistic practice. Disfigurement makes visible a paranoid cultural fantasy about female artistic potential—a potential that, ironically, is tamed by the very deformity which is its marker. Finally, in both texts woman's art is implicitly aligned with the art of novel-writing, seen as expansive (both novels cast a broad net across social issues), morally uplifting, true to life, and popular. Olive's and Geraldine's art succeeds where masculine High Art (obscure, elevated, and drawing on mythological or historical events rather than quotidian, contemporary reality) fails. As with so many of the women writers this book has examined, Craik and Yonge use the actions and productions of a woman painter to safely and thoroughly negotiate the trials and rewards of novel-writing.

Chapter Seven

Painting the New Woman

Mary Ward and the Woman Artist

I.

IN HER STUDY of the female artist novel, Linda Lewis argues that "the decade of the 1890s appears to be that of the female *Künstlerroman* as defeated artist" (2003, 239); as examples, she lists Ella Hepworth Dixon's *The Story of a Modern Woman*, Mona Caird's *The Daughters of Danaus,* and Mary Cholmondeley's Hester in *Red Pottage*. To which we could add Edna Pontellier (in Chopin's *The Awakening*), Sue Bridehead (in Hardy's *Jude the Obscure*), and Elfride (in Mrs. Everard Cotes's *A Daughter of Today*), and numerous other artist heroines of various kinds, all of whom fail to achieve success in their chosen artistic fields. We might expect *some* measure of progress toward positive representations of successful female artists in fiction as the century progresses, given the steady increase in successful real-life women artists; instead we find that late-century novels offer a much more negative image of the woman artist. Why might this be? Lewis offers the sustaining influence of George Sand's Consuelo and Germaine de Staël's Corinne as at least in part responsible; mid-century women writers had a more immediate feminist legacy of successful, powerful women artists to look to, while writers at the century's end were too far away from such a tradition. Furthermore, the backlash against women that was an integral part of Aestheticism (see, for example, Psomiades 1997, 2–4), combined with the rise of Modernism and its general discontents, set up strong ideological barriers for women writers.

While there were many more successful real women painters in the fin-de-siècle period, there was also much more vicious rhetorical backlash against these women; the ideological tensions of the period, especially surrounding the New Woman, made it extremely difficult for women writers to create unproblematically positive representations of women artists. Edna Pontellier in Kate Chopin's *The Awakening* might serve as a model of the pessimistic approach taken by many fin-de-siècle women writers.

The dearth of positive models might be one reason why, in the wide-ranging and rich body of work that constitutes New Woman Scholarship, mention of women painters is surprisingly rare. Scholars working on the phenomenon of the New Woman often mention women painters but fail to follow through with detailed discussion. Lyn Pykett, for example, begins her wonderful essay on the New Woman "artist" (1999) by saying that novelistic heroines are most often one of three types of artist: writers, musicians, or painters. Pykett is most interested in writers, so they become the representative artist—but it is curious that when Pykett, five pages later, again mentions three types of artists, she lists them as musician, poet, and novelist. The painter disappears. It is certainly justifiable for scholars to focus on the female writer in New Woman novels, as a great number feature authors as heroines. But it isn't entirely fitting to consider the writer as the *representative* of all female artists of the period, since different kinds of women artists had radically different successes or problems. Furthermore, as Pykett herself writes in a later article, the term New Woman was "a mobile and contradictory figure or signifier" (2001, xi). Similarly, Sally Ledger writes, "The New Woman of the fin de siècle had a multiple identity. She was, variously, a feminist activist, a social reformer, a popular novelist, a suffragette playwright, a woman poet; she was also often a social construct, a discursive response" (1997, 1). While the New Woman was certainly all these things, she was also, in fiction and in fact, a painter. In this chapter I focus on conflicting representations of New Woman painters in the public press and in the fiction of Mrs. Humphry Ward.

Women painters of the fin de siècle certainly reaped the benefits of earlier British women painters' efforts to open avenues for women in various realms of art: training (especially "life classes"), patronage, a share of the art market, gallery space, and so on. But this is not a tale of inexorable progress, and the paths of women painters at the turn of the century were not entirely smooth. Women painters active during the fin-de-siècle period got as much (and arguably more) negative public commentary as did earlier practitioners.[1] The great public debate over New Women seems unfortunately to have given critics of women painters a language in which to voice criticism. In fact, one of the loudest voices against the New Woman in general, Eliza Lynn Linton, singled out painters for particular disapproval. In her essay "The Wild Women as Social Insurgents" (1891), Linton moans:

> Everyone who has a gift must make that gift public. . . . The enormous amount of inferior work which is thrown on the market in all directions is one of the marvels of the time. Everything is exhibited. If a young lady can draw so far correctly as to give her cow four legs and not five, she sends her sketches to some newspaper, or more boldly transfers them onto a plate or a pot, and exhibits them at some art refuge. (600)

As we see in previous decades, the quality of women's art is certainly at issue here. However, Linton is most deeply troubled by the fact that women dare to exhibit their work (and, by extension, their bodies). Linton raises the additional specter of the market; women's entrance into the economic sphere is yet another part of the crisis which the professionalization of women's art initiates.

Other writers found different issues distasteful when it came to women's artwork. Male art critics were dismayed at the subject matter and style of many turn-of-the-century women painters; the title of a 1924 review of the painter Marie Laurencin by Anthony Bertram is telling: "The Unfemale Feminine." Bertram writes that Laurencin's art shows "Woman related only to herself." He continues,

> We see woman, not as our opposite who attracts us, but as our equal, living her own separate life. It is interesting, but not entirely pleasing, an unfinished symphony, lacking the last complexity and fullest splendour of natural life, the interplay of sex. I am not piqued at being omitted from Marie Laurencin's world, but disconcerted at this cleavage of nature's harmony. . . . We come away stirred by the masterly artistic expression of femininity broken off from woman as we know and love her, and, while we fully grant the right of art to deal with what it wishes, we must, in our non-aesthetic human selves, be conscious of some little repulsion from this unfemale femininity. (quoted in Howard and Tarrant 1997, 301)

Though he insists otherwise, Bertram *is*, of course, "piqued at being omitted" from Laurencin's work—everything in his review suggests that the real problem with her oeuvre is the absence of Bertram, as a sexualized viewer as well as a subject. He is neither represented nor offered a juicy spectacle of femininity, and he cannot help letting what he calls his "non-aesthetic human self" interfere in his aesthetic commentary.

In this context we can also consider the fin-de-siècle writer and art critic George Moore's discussion of women artists' relation to the erotic; his ideas are heavily influenced by the discourses of New Womanhood that were circulating in the years during his writing of *Modern Painting*. A chapter on "Sex in Art" in this work thoroughly denigrates women's attempts at the production of art and further insists that all women's art is entirely derivative. Moore writes, "Women have created nothing, they have carried the art of men across their fans charmingly . . . and they have hideously and most mournfully parodied the art of men" (Moore 1898, 227). In quick succession he dismisses the art of most of the prominent women artists of the eighteenth and nineteenth centuries. Of Angelica Kauffman he writes, "She imitated Joshua Reynolds to the best of her ability, and did all in her power to induce him to marry her" (230). Lady Butler (Elizabeth Thompson Butler, discussed in the introduction and chapter 1) "thought she could do more than to sentimentalize with De Neuville's soldiers. She adopted his method . . . her attitude towards him was the same as Rosa Bonheur's towards Troyon; and the failure of Lady Butler was even greater than Rosa Bonheur's" (231). Lady Waterford is called "insipid . . . facile . . . painful . . . unoriginal" (231), while Annie Swynnerton's art "proceeds merely from the brain; there is hardly anything of the painter's nature in it" (232). Finally, Mrs. E. M. Ward and Mrs. Alma-Tadema are accused of "exhibit[ing] work identical in execution with that of their illustrious husbands" (233).[2]

The only female artist whom Moore admires is Elizabeth Vigée-Lebrun, because her painting of herself and her daughter is expressive of that which only a woman could know: mother love. Moore writes, "Only a mother could have designed that original and expressive composition. . . . Never before did artist epitomize in a gesture all the familiar affection and simple persuasive happiness of home" (234). Then he adds that this self-portrait and one other portrait "are, I regret to say, the only pictures of Madame Lebrun that I am acquainted with." Yet he insists, "But I doubt if my admiration would be increased by a wider knowledge of her work. She seems to have said everything she had to say in these two pictures" (234). Any argument that rejects the *unseen* works of an artist provides its own unraveling, and we can easily dismiss Moore's aesthetic opinions as so ludicrously prejudiced as to be valueless. However, Moore's attack on women painters is fascinating precisely because it turns on women's relation to the erotic, as we can see from many of the quotes above. The influence of the New Woman can clearly be seen here; one of the central obsessions of New Woman discourse (positive and negative) was woman's relation to sexuality and desire. According to Moore, women couldn't produce true, original art because they were *too* wedded to the sensual and sexual; women can't escape their need for erotic connections (or, in Bertram's terms, "last complexity and fullest splendour of natural life, the interplay of sex"). Moore's traditional woman wastes her "heat" on real life, leaving nothing left for art. Bertram seems as if he would prefer this model of femininity, rather than that presented to him by Marie Laurencin.

The Scottish artists Frances and Margaret Macdonald make excellent exemplars of the more radical type of New Woman painter; they both received the full brunt of critical treatment by the public press. The Macdonald sisters studied at the Glasgow School of Art and set up a studio together in 1896, producing "embroidered panels, metalwork, illuminated manuscripts, cartoons for stained glass and designs for posters . . . " as well as paintings in various media (Cherry 1993, 204). While there is no evidence that either Macdonald sister applied the name "New Woman" to herself, critics certainly did. Critics were predictably outraged by the sisters' refusal to conform to prevailing aesthetic principles that invested aesthetic pleasure in the visual spectacle of a beautiful woman.[3] Although the Macdonalds' style was radical, it was their representation of femininity that drew most distaste from reviewers (in fact, critics quickly considered Frances's style to be derivative of Burne-Jones's). In a review of the Glasgow School of Art exhibition in 1894, the *Glasgow Evening News* printed a satiric poem labeling the Macdonald sisters "New Women":

> Would you witness a conception
> Of the woman really New
> Without the least deception
> From the artist's point of view
> See the Art School Exhibition
> In the rue de Sauchiehall . . .
> As painted by her sister
> Who affects the realm of Art
> The Woman New's a twister
> To give nervous man a start
> Sadly scanty of fleshly padding
> And ground-spavined at the knees. (18 August 1894, 3)

"Nervous man" is here the problem; the critic/viewer is upset not because the Macdonald sisters have created bad art (value is not at issue here), but because he has nothing sexy to look at. The New Woman artist has failed to create the proper "deception" of femininity and has instead created unerotic images of women without the requisite "fleshly padding."

Figure 7.1. Frances Macdonald, *A Pond*, 1894. Glasgow School of Art Collection. Source: National Museums Liverpool. Reproduced with permission.

Frances Macdonald's work is indeed disturbing, but intentionally so; her goal was to parody female beauty of the neoclassical and Pre-Raphaelite sort. If we look at her painting *A Pond* (1894) (figure 7.1), we are troubled by the elongation of the figure, by a hint of the vagina dentata monster in the prominent jaws and open mouths.

Figure 7.2. Frances Macdonald, *'Tis a Long Path That Wanders to Desire*, 1912–15. Hunterian Art Gallery, University of Glasgow. Source: National Museums Liverpool. Reproduced with permission.

The spare skeletal figures are formed by geometric oppositions, with tonal harmonies and a flatness partly derived from Japanese prints that were widely distributed at this period and perceived as a hallmark of the modern. Macdonald embraces the principles of art nouveau and rejects academic art, representational art, and the lusciousness common in Pre-Raphaelite art. The figure's hair seems almost like a parody of Pre-Raphaelite hair: it *starts* like a Pre-Raphaelite woman's hair, then billows out into pure geometric form—a troublesome echo of Jane Morris's hair, perhaps. Another of Macdonald's paintings, *'Tis a Long Path That Wanders to Desire* (1912–15) (figure 7.2), shows an instance of the dismissal of male presence from the female artist's world (similar to that noted by Bertram in Laurencin's work). The woman in *'Tis a Long Path* seems to be asking "which" or possibly "why bother" as she considers her options—her back is turned to the two male figures behind her as if discounting their presence. The long road is behind her and she steps toward us, *away* from the road to desire, as if rejecting it.

Macdonald's paintings are unusual in many ways, but their representation of the unclothed female form is particular startling. Nude painting—of men or women, by male or female artists—was itself problematic in the Victorian era. As Nunn and others have argued, the nineteenth century saw a great deal of debate over the propriety and aesthetic value of representing the unclothed human figure (see Nunn 1995, 139–60; A. Smith 1997, 1–9). Throughout the 1870s and 1880s, women petitioned the Royal Academy schools for the right to study "from the life," but to no avail. It wasn't until 1893 that women in R.A. schools were allowed to draw from a partially draped model in a separate class (Cherry 1993, 57). Other venues, however, were increasingly available: private art schools, some run by women artists, offered women the chance to study from the nude model; women with sufficient financial means could often privately hire models from which to study; and women with means could also study in Paris, where women were offered greater freedoms in art training.

The art public worried that images of nude figures could not *but* be viewed pornographically; artists and art critics countered that the nude was a central component, if not *the* central image, in art history. Given the almost obsessive interest the Victorians had in the moral stature of the artist figure, the nude was a particular problem: a nude painting implied that a *real* painter had once stood before a *real* nude person and painted him or her. When the nude image was of a woman, and the artist was a man, this caused loud public commentary, gave rise to the general cultural stigma against female artist models, and generally caused turmoil in the public presses. When the nude image was of a woman, and the artist was also a woman, the public became at once less and more disturbed. The specter of lesbian desire seems to have been kept largely silent in the public debate over women's access to nude models; most of the public discussions during the mid century focused on women students studying from the nude *male* model. It is not until the late 1890s that women in England begin regularly to exhibit *female* nude portraits, and the debate was fierce. Artists such as Henrietta Rae, Anna Lea Merritt, Evelyn DeMorgan, and Annie Swynnerton (elected to the R.A. in 1923, the first woman so honored since the founding academicians Kauffman and Moser) were venomously attacked in the art presses for their female nudes (see Nunn 1995, 139–60; A. Smith 2002, 144, 227). In Frances Macdonald's case, her particular treatment of the female nude sparked considerable confusion. Women artists' right to depict the "classic" (i.e., High Art, and therefore theoretically beyond a woman artist's scope) beauty of the female nude was still under discussion, and here was a woman *distorting* the nude into ungraceful, unfeminine forms. She couldn't be accused of trying to incite pornographic lusts, certainly, so she had to be accused of unfemininity. Macdonald's figures, in fact, suggest barrenness, or at least a rejection of fecund sensuous beauty; they forestall desire in the viewer and utterly reject the neoclassicism of popular fin-de-siècle representations of the female nude. Rather than celebrating sexuality, New Woman painters like Macdonald opted to critique it instead.[4]

II.

Fictional New Women painters reflect with unusual clarity and verisimilitude the battles faced by real women painters. As a genre, New Woman fiction tends toward realism and blatant social commentary; the novels focus on historically specific social issues (varying from women's sexual freedom to antivivisection). A woman's right to a fulfilling professional career outside marriage is one of the social issues at stake in many New Woman novels, so it is not surprising that we should find many, and many kinds of, artists in the body of literature we call New Woman fiction. The painter heroine is a regular feature. Heroines in a surprising number of New Woman novels start to study painting only to stop and enter another artistic field, often writing. We see this progression in, among others, Ella Hepworth Dixon's *The Story of a Modern Woman*, *A Daughter of Today* by Sara Jeannette Duncan (Mrs. Everard Cotes), and Mary Humphry Ward's *Marcella* (where the heroine tries a range of artistic options before settling in to the business of courtship and politics). In other novels, the character's career in the visual arts is peripheral but significant, such as Sue Bridehead's work as an artisan which is so briefly touched on in *Jude the Obscure* that it works simply as a quick symbolic gesture (her career as a teacher is more relevant, but still peripheral). In many novels, however, the heroine's profession is a crucial aspect of the narrative structure.

Such is the case with two novels by Mary Augusta Arnold Ward,[5] who published under the name Mrs. Humphry Ward. As Linda Lewis notes, numerous Ward novels feature a woman artist—a poet, painter, actress, writer, or musician (2003, 210). In *Fenwick's Career* she uses a male painter as her hero; in *Miss Bretherton* she introduces another male painter, Forbes, as a secondary character. Lewis argues that women artists in Ward novels (she focuses on three: the actress Isabel in *Miss Bretherton,* the musician Rose in *Robert Elsmere,* and the painter Elise in *The History of David Grieve*) serve as powerful seductresses who "emasculate men to the damage of their own [the women's] souls" (242). Ward's women artists, writes Lewis, are "invariably scintillating, mesmerizing, passionate and ambitious," and Ward uses them to "explore female artistry of terrifying power and petrifying threat" (206). Lewis argues that Elise in *David Grieve,* for example, figures as "a Medusa who freezes the man who loves her, and a Salome who decapitates him" (235).

I would like to suggest a slightly less gruesome reading of Elise, in tandem with a reading of another of Ward's painter heroines, Lydia in the unfortunately named *The Mating of Lydia*. Certainly Ward's fictionalization of the woman painter reveals one thing that makes the New Woman painter so culturally problematic: her revision of the erotics of art. As Lewis argues, women artists in Ward's work "abet their creator in entertaining the most interesting questions of what price a woman must pay for art, whether love quickens or stifles it, and whether selfish egoism is an inevitable product of genius" (206). But her artist heroines also allow Ward to suggest that a woman artist's erotic effects ("freezing" or "decapitating" the men around her, for example) are the result of an unfortunate social structure that makes it impossible for a woman to shed her sexuality and achieve artistic independence. Female sexuality is, I argue, primarily a danger not to men in these texts (as Lewis's reading of *David Grieve* contends), but to women artists themselves. The two Ward novels I consider here—*The History of David Grieve* and *The Mating of Lydia*—dramatize the conflicts that arise when economic motivations coexist with affective, aesthetic goals. The two female painter figures both need and want to make money from their art; they both also glorify art and see it as a more than satisfactory substitute for emotional passion.

Ward is perhaps best known for her complicated and contradictory relationship to fin-de-siècle feminism:[6] she was a key voice *against* women's suffrage at the national level while emphatically encouraging it at the local level, as well as encouraging women to run for local office (she became one of the first female magistrates in Britain herself). She was a founder of Oxford's Somerville College for women (which later publicly renounced Ward because of her position regarding women's suffrage) and an active lecturer on the importance of education for girls and women. Ironically, Ward "remained steadfastly attached to the 'separate spheres' ideology while she served as breadwinner for her family, conversed with prime ministers and presidents . . ." (Wilt 1996, 225).

Ward makes an interesting test case for feminist concerns, precisely because her relationship to feminism is so intensely problematic. Her wavering and uneven commitment to women's rights, which makes Ward's heroines impossible to blast as "merely" cliché Victorian good girls or to embrace as models for protofeminist professionalism, is precisely the kind of stance which contemporary readers "cannot afford to admit to consciousness," to use Patricia Meyer Spacks's phrase (1994, 289).[7] As Beth Sutton-Ramspeck argues, "Ward's reputation for antifeminism stems in part from a common misunderstanding of turn-of-the-century feminism. Far from being univocal, the 'first wave' of the women's movement encompassed various, often conflicting ideas and methods" (1999, 205).

Sutton-Ramspeck continues, "Rather than being antifeminist, Ward spent her life negotiating between competing and often contradictory feminisms" (ibid.), and Ward's heroines dramatize this tension—they are often strong women, recognizably New Women, but their ideas prove to be untenable and they marry in the end, giving up their careers or intellectual passions to support husbands who are never depicted as unproblematic knights in shining armor. As in Ritchie's and Oliphant's work, Ward's artists are equally equivocal; they are neither abjectly miserable and oppressed because of their artistic temperament and femininity (which would make for good feminist criticism, as does Elizabeth Stuart Phelps's *The Story of Avis*), nor ultimately loyal to their art (as is Lily Briscoe in Virginia Woolf's *To the Lighthouse*). Nor do Ward's heroines give up art without a second glance and marry (as does Jane Eyre, for whom painting was never more than an amusement anyway). Ward's heroines, on the contrary, are perhaps most similar to Helen Graham in Anne Brontë's *The Tenant of Wildfell Hall,* a novel which modern readers, especially academic feminists, have found equally troublesome because of its unsteady commitment to cut-and-dried feminist agendas. Ward represents a highly discomforting gray area between conservative and progressive gender values, and this is most clearly seen in her treatment of women artists.

After her success in 1888 with *Robert Elsmere,* Ward wrote *The History of David Grieve,* published in 1892. Here we see Ward alternately praising and punishing the artistic woman; the history of the young painter in this novel, Elise Delaunay, is ultimately tragic, and the ideals of sexual equality and artistic ambition which Elise espouses prove to be absolutely untenable.[8] But Elise's fate is represented with a sadness which suggests that Ward is frustrated more with the social order that has prevented Elise from succeeding as a painter than with Elise's "manly" ambitions or her unconventional morality.

The History of David Grieve follows David's life from an orphaned childhood in rural England through his adult life in Manchester and Paris. David is Ward's "most fully realized working-class hero," and his intense, brooding character owes much to Ward's admiration for the Brontë sisters' life and work (Collister 1985, 419–23). The novel also follows David's rebellious and unhappy sister Louie, who eventually commits suicide after a bitter marriage and the loss of a child. We first meet the painter Elise Delaunay when David and his sister have traveled to Paris, where David has a new job as a bookseller. Elise lives alone in a studio in the same building where David has rented an apartment; when he sees her for the first time framed in the doorway to her studio, "David saw no details, only what seemed to him a miracle of grace and colour, born in an instant, out of the dark" (*Grieve,* 264). David sees her as a work of art, graceful and colorful; similarly, her living space is to David a "fairyland" described in artistic terms of color, shape, and form. Later, when he seeks her out at the Louvre, he only "glances at the great Veronese, at Raphael's archangel, at the towering Vandyke, at the 'Virgin of the Rocks'." The art objects in the Louvre do not interest him; he is more concerned to locate woman-as-object: "But he passed them [the famous paintings] by quickly. Was she here?" (280).

Ward, however, is not content to let her hero follow the traditional path and turn Elise into an art object. Elise's first response to David is to immediately liken him to Donatello's *David*—she makes *him* into art for *her* own visual pleasure. Her first word when she sees him in the light is a simple "superb!" (266), and later, when David meets her male artist friends, they joke that he should come and pose for the female students of the *atelier* where there had been "a rebellion . . . one and all declared the model was not worth drawing, and one and all left" (281). Ward implies that David is being invited to pose nude for a group of female art students (Paris *ateliers des femmes* provided this service for female art students well before English art schools consented to such activities) who, remarkably, are granted aesthetic judgment with regard to the male body; for the women artists to declare that the model is "not worth drawing" suggests that they have ideas and experience of naked men who *are* worth drawing. David's physical beauty, thoroughly discussed by Ward at various points in the novel, is here made manifestly artistic, and the tables are turned: the male body is made available to the woman artist.

Elise is outspoken in her artistic desires; she tells David, "I am Elise Delaunay. I work in Taranne's atelier. I am an artist, pure and simple, and I live to please myself and nobody else" (267). We see Elise living alone, painting at the Louvre, even smoking (which David says he's never seen an English woman do). Her character is forthright, blunt, sexually aware, artistically passionate. She has "the fierce desire to be the first in all the competitions" (273) and announces, "Well, my credo is very short. Its first article is art—and its second art—and its third is art! I believe in art—and expression—and colour—and *le vrai*" (275).

The novel uses the figure of Elise and her artistic milieu to introduce social and aesthetic debates. David's impression of the paintings he sees as he visits their studios is of "nude horrors and barbarities of all sorts" (292) and yet he is conscious always of a "goading and intoxicating freedom" (293) when he is with the artists. This freedom, for both David and his sister Louie, displays itself as a revolt against traditional narratives of gender roles. For the artists, freedom in art is freedom from traditional narratives of *any* kind. The starving young artists with whom Elise socializes and studies are resolute on the subject: traditions have no place in painting, they argue; narrative in particular is merely a sop for the bourgeois public. An evening in a local bar yields the following discussion between artists:

> "Literature, mon cher! Literature!" cries the artist, "and what the deuce do we want with literature in painting?"
>
> "Say what you like, you want something else in a picture than painting. That'll damn you, and make your fortune some day, I warn you. Now I have a picture on the easel that will make the bourgeois skip . . ."
>
> "The artist must live, and the bourgeois will have subjects. He won't have anything to do with our 'notes' and 'impressions' and 'arrangements' . . . He wants his stories and his sentiment." (301–3)

Ward's mention here of "notes" and "impressions" and "arrangements" is a reference both to the school of Impressionism and very likely to the recent scandal and aesthetic debate surrounding the *Whistler v. Ruskin* libel trial in 1877. Whistler's compilation of letters, review notices, epigrams, and reminiscences of the trial and other events in his artistic life was published in 1890 under the title *The Gentle Art of Making Enemies*. Whistler's evocative paintings were often given such titles as *Arrangement in Grey and Black* (popularly known as "Whistler's Mother") and were famously (some thought scandalously) free of narrative content.

The artists in Ward's novel, including Elise, are fighting to be free of the need for narrative structure in painting. Analogously, Elise fights to remain unbound by the bourgeois narratives of marriage and traditional femininity; she sees both as incompatible with art. When she and David fall in love, she rejects his marriage proposal but eventually agrees to an *union libre* only if he is willing "to be content that art should come first and you second" (300).

Their affair is short-lived, however, as Elise finds that her love for David interrupts her artistic freedom and focus. She tells him, "I know nothing about [love]. Art breaks all chains, and accepts none. The woman that has art is free, and she alone; for she has scaled the men's heaven and stolen their sacred fire" (321). Later Elise tells David, "When I am with you, I must be a woman. You agitate me, you divide my mind, and my force goes. There are both capacities in me, and one destroys the other. And I want—I *want* my art!" (354; emphasis in original). Thus, the New Woman painter disrupts the traditional romance narrative by deserting our hero for her art—she literally transfers her desire ("I *want*") from her lover to her profession. David thereafter returns to England to marry a "proper" feminine woman. But this traditional narrative, too, is disrupted when David's wife Lucy dies just a few years after their marriage; David then *fails* to marry the "good girl" in the novel (ironically named Dora in case readers might have missed the many intertextual allusions to *David Copperfield*) who has been in love with David all along. Ward dismantles multiple romance narratives in *The History of David Grieve* and persists in refusing, in this and in later novels, to give the reader the expected romantic resolutions.

We do not see Elise again until the end of the novel, when David, now a widower, comes upon her looking wan and tired; forced by family ties, she has married her crippled cousin. Lewis argues that Elise is "saved from herself by marriage . . . because she eventually serves love and another human being, rather than serving her own ego" (2003, 239). For Ward, "marriage is therefore a moral salvation" (ibid.). This reading, however, overemphasizes Ward's conservative strain and allows the pressure of other Ward novels (in which marriage does "save" the heroine in certain ways) to cover over the much more grim and radical strain in *David Grieve,* where marriage is not—for David, or Elise, or anybody—a salvation of any kind, but rather a giving up and giving in. Elise fails in her art because she marries, and marriage offers her no real solace. Elise has merely become a caretaker; she says to David, "I am no longer an artist . . . I spend my life making *tisane,* in lifting weights too heavy for me, in bargaining for things to eat" (*Grieve,* 563). David asks if she is happy, and she says that she is, "if he will only live. He depends on me for everything. It is like a child, but it consoles" (564). We do not believe her, nor are we meant to. Certainly the fact that the grammar of her final comment makes it seem as if she is referring to her invalid husband as "it" ("it is like a child . . .") does nothing to lighten the mood.[9]

The narrative may introduce Elise's final fate as an ironic punishment (she who refused to marry and give up her art like a good woman has been forced to do just that) but nevertheless comes to view it as tragedy. Elise's fate participates in the more general plot trajectory toward disappointment; true to the hero's last name, Grieve, the novel is almost unbearably depressing. However, when considered alongside the other women in the novel, Elise gets off easy. Other women in the novel are punished with even more ferocious violence: Louie, David's angry and unconventional sister, leads a life of explosive misery and eventually commits suicide after the death of her daughter. The "proper" women in the novel fare no better: David's wife, feminine and nurturing if a bit vain of her appearance, gets cancer on her face and dies horribly disfigured. Dora, the traditional good girl who has loved David throughout her life, ends the novel not with the prospect of marrying David at last but as a lonely churchwoman. There is, finally, no model for positive femininity in this text. But the early vision of Elise, proud and independent with her art, comes closest; as a painter, she enjoys a fleeting but radical independence from men, from narrative structures, and from social responsibilities. Ward's New Woman artist might not triumph in the end, but she remains the sole illuminating female figure in the novel.

Other Ward heroines practice art and participate in Ward's ambiguous representation of female independence. In her next novel, *Marcella*, published two years after *David Grieve*, the eponymous heroine discovers in herself a talent for music and painting and embarks on a very brief (two-page) stint as a student in the South Kensington art schools:

> So began an experience, as novel as it was strenuous. Marcella soon developed all the airs of independence and all the jargon of two professions.... Working with consuming energy and ambition, she pushed her gifts so far as to become at least a very intelligent, eager, and confident critic of the art of other people—which is much. But though art stirred and trained her, gave her new horizons and new standards, it was not in art that she found ultimately the chief excitement and motive-power of her new life—not in art, but in the birth of social and philanthropic ardour, the sense of a hitherto unsuspected social power. (*Marcella*, 15)

That Marcella so quickly leaves the world of art suggests that Ward has perhaps had enough of the woman artist after Elise. Yet this excerpt from *Marcella* still hints at one of the disruptions that the figure of woman painter (as exemplified by Elise) introduces into Ward's fiction, a disruption caused by the woman painter's solitude. When she is an active artist, Elise lives alone, works alone, and explicitly rejects David for a life with art as her only companion. In *Marcella*, Ward turns her attention to a woman's "social power," focusing on the social and political interactions that a woman can embrace.

Figure 7.3. Illustration from *The Mating of Lydia,* facing page 68. Photo by author.

In one of her last novels, *The Mating of Lydia,* Ward once again returns to the figure of the woman artist and tackles the central problem of her professional independence. The atrocious title seems fitting for a novel that rather ruthlessly marries off a heroine who doesn't want to get married and who clings to the freedom art gives her. The transformation of Lydia Penfold, Ward's heroine, can be quickly seen in two of the illustrations by Charles E. Brock accompanying the novel (figures 7.3 and 7.4).

Figure 7.4. Illustration from *The Mating of Lydia*, facing page 490. Photo by author.

The first illustration comes near the beginning of the novel; Lydia is heading home from a painting excursion in the hills and comes upon an old shepherd. The caption reads, "They stopped to talk while he rested a few minutes." Lydia, significantly, is not resting; she is standing tall, carrying a largish load of painting equipment easily and in no need of a boulder to lean on. She is self-contained; her independence and solitude are visible in the distance she keeps from the shepherd and in her posture. She is dressed in the "rational dress" of a New Woman, with tailored menswear-inspired clothing and comfortable boots. In the second illustration, which comes at the end of the novel, Lydia presents a very different picture as she sits close beside her fiancé. Her posture—leaning into the man—and her feminine clothing, as well as the dismally domestic interior behind her, suggest her final submission to traditional femininity. The couple look down, not meeting the viewer's eyes—this could have the effect of increasing their enclosure as a couple, yet they do not meet one another's eyes either, which adds a note of unease into the seemingly loving picture. The empty mirror in the background echoes this unease, as if suggesting the possible end to representation and mimesis (i.e., the end of her art) which follows Lydia's marriage.

Lydia begins the novel as a struggling painter, earning a living for herself, her mother, and her sister (whose playwriting fails to earn fame or fortune). When we first meet her, she has just refused a position as a drawing mistress in a Brighton school, sold four drawings in Liverpool for twenty pounds, and gotten rave reviews in the public press. The twenty pounds she has earned, we are told, will "pay half the year's rent" (*Lydia*, 75), which suggests that her earning powers are considerable. By refusing the teaching position, Lydia is refusing all ties that might draw her away from a life as an independent productive artist. She is also steadfastly refusing to marry the wealthy and charming young Lord Tatham—"sweetly normal," one critic calls him (Greenwell Smith 1980, 103). Marrying Tatham would bring her and her family comfort and prosperity, but Lydia wants friendship between men and women without desire. She links herself implicitly with the New Woman when she tells Lord Tatham after she refuses him, "Why shouldn't we just be friends? I know it sounds an old, stale thing to say. But it isn't. There's a new meaning in it now, because—because *women are being made new*. It used to be offering what we couldn't give. We could be lovers; we weren't strong enough to be friends. But now . . . just try me" (273; emphasis added).

The irony here is that Lord Tatham, Lydia's admirer, is secretly the purchaser of those sketches that have earned Lydia twenty pounds—a drop in the bucket for Lord Tatham. Her independence is therefore a sham, based on female erotic potential rather than artistic talent. Motivated by desire rather than aesthetic judgment, Lord Tatham cannot exhibit the sketches openly in his home for fear Lydia might see them, so he hangs them in his private dressing room. Buying a woman's painting without her knowledge is, given the intimate connection between a woman's art and a woman's body that the *Punch* article so well represents, an aesthetic form of illicit access to a woman's body that is otherwise denied. Because the painting and the body come to stand in for one another, the purchaser of the former has certain metaphoric contact with the latter: Lord Tatham has a surrogate Lydia hidden away for his private use. Women's paintings do more than simply call to mind the artist; they metonymically stand in for the woman's body. Paintings become reductions of a woman's entire self into a contained, moveable commodity—able to be bought and sold by lovers or strangers. Thus when a heroine's works are purchased by a suitor (which occurs in many of the novels that feature professional women artists), he is literally taking her "off the market," returning her to her proper place as an object of desire within the private home—for his eyes only, as it were. (We see this in Mary Brunton's *Self-Control,* for example, published in 1810; the heroine's paintings are purchased by an admirer who feels he owns a piece of her by virtue of possessing her artworks.) A purchaser who is a lover short-circuits the public, social process of aesthetic judgment—by taking the works of the beloved off the market, he makes certain that her works can never be judged publicly by an *objective* audience.[10]

Here, this tactic emphatically does not work: Lord Tatham fails to win Lydia. The man who does win her—the morally questionable Claude Faversham—significantly does not remove her from the public sphere. When Lydia and Faversham first meet, for example, he has jumped down from his bicycle to help her collect a series of press cuttings that have blown off in a breeze. The cuttings are reviews of a recent art exhibit where Lydia's paintings have received much praise, and she is desperate to save one particular review that spoke of her work as "agreeable and scholarly, showing, at times, more than a touch of high talent" (62). Faversham jumps into a pond to save not the damsel in distress but the cutting that marks her successful participation in the public art realm. After their marriage, Lydia will remain involved with this world; Ward thus allows Lydia to reject Tatham's kind of aesthetic domination and to retain some form of artistic independence.

Critics have been rather more ambivalent about this novel than Ward's others, calling the characters too good and the ending "a bit insipid" in its romantic pairings (Greenwell Smith 1980, 101). However, *The Mating of Lydia,* while obviously concerned with Lydia's love life, also serves as Ward's treatise about the proper use of art and the role of the artist—male or female—in the social order. Lydia exhibits the same blend of practical economics and spiritual aesthetics that characterize so many of the nineteenth century's artistic heroines. Ward describes Lydia as "a professional artist, to whom guineas were just as welcome as to other people, and she had very industrious and methodical views of her business. But she was, before everything, one of those persons who thrill under the appeal of beauty to a degree that often threatens or suspends practical energy" (*Lydia,* 72). She is elsewhere described as "a Della Robbia angel—who has been to college. And she is an artist" (263). Her professionalism upsets one of the novel's characters, who whispers to another, "You say she paints? The modern girl must *do* something. *My* girls have been brought up for *home*" (ibid.). Lydia, on the other hand, is fiercely proud of her professional independence, ranking art above marriage or other traditional feminine goals: "That's where this generation differs," Lydia thinks to herself. "We needn't drift [into marriage]—we see clear. Oh! Isn't beauty enough?" (95).

The only male artist in the novel (again we see this contrast figure) is Delorme the portraitist, described as a painter in Whistler's style. Delorme has little sympathy for women artists:

> "*Mon Dieu!* Why do women paint? It is an infernal thing, painting; what can a woman make of it? She can only unsex herself. And in the end—what she produces—what is it?"
>
> "It pays the rent!—isn't that enough?" [replies Lady Tatham].
>
> "But a young girl like that! What, in God's name, has she to do with paying the rent! Let her dance and sing—have a train of lovers—look beautiful!" (280)

Delorme's complaint—"she can only unsex herself"—tells us that Ward is very much referring to the debates over the New Woman, even if the most fervent of those debates occurred twenty years before the publication of *The Mating of Lydia*. The defeminization of women was a familiar fear articulated by those in opposition to the New Woman; whether the New Woman was seen as "oversexed, undersexed, or same sex identified" (Pykett 2001, xii), her failure to display traditional feminine qualities was seen as a threat to culture, the state, even the future of the British race.

Delorme's view of women is never entirely supported or rejected by the narrative, as Lydia's character displays the conflicts that make Ward such a problematic writer for modern readers. In the course of just one page, Ward permits Lydia to espouse her theories of radical gender equality ("we women are starved . . . because men will only marry us. . . . Why can't they . . . open the treasure house to us . . . and let us alone? To be treated as good fellows! That's all we ask . . .") and then follows with the narrative comment: "In her simple gray dress, which showed the rippling beauty of every line, she was like one of these innumerable angels or virtues, by artists illustrious or forgotten" (166). Ward seems to be telling her reader that no matter how committed to equality, no matter how independent or artistic or professional a woman is, narrative itself will come back around and objectify her. The irony here, as in all narratives featuring an artist heroine, is that the woman artist attempts to remove herself from the traditional role of art object by becoming an artist herself and controlling the means of artistic production. In *The Mating of Lydia,* the tactic is less of a painful failure than it was in *The History of David Grieve.*[11]

Lydia's artistic career is not the only locus for aesthetic debate in the novel; another plot runs parallel and serves to highlight the public/private debate that Ward is staging through her treatment of Lydia's life. The novel begins by introducing us to Mr. Melrose, a miserly art collector. He is bringing his young Italian bride and their baby from Italy to his home in Cumbria, the Lake District of northwest England where the story takes place. Melrose explains that he collects

> clocks, watches, ironwork, china, stuffs, pots, brasses—something of everything. A few pictures—no great shakes—as yet. But some day I may begin to buy them in earnest . . . but meanwhile, Tyson, *economy!* All my income is required—for what is my hobby—my passion—my mania, if you like—the collecting of works of art. I have gradually reduced my personal expenditure to a minimum, and it must be the same with this estate. No useless outlay of any kind. (27)

"Useless outlay" includes—unfortunately for his wife and daughter—food, heat, clothing, transportation, company, entertainment, and baby supplies. Mrs. Melrose is kept a virtual prisoner, and both she and the baby suffer physical and emotional trauma from the privations. At length she steals one of his bronze statues, sells it, and flees back to Italy with her baby. Melrose severs all ties with her, and Ward picks up the narrative twenty years later when Claude Faversham falls off his bicycle near Melrose's estate and is forced to convalesce there.

Melrose offers Faversham a position as his steward, and the two struggle for moral control over the estate: Melrose is adamant that only the collection matters and that the local community can rot—as, indeed, they have been. Faversham, with Lydia to egg him on, attempts halfheartedly to make some amends to Melrose's tenants, servants, and the local community who have all been ruined by Melrose's Scrooge-like outlook. Eager to win Faversham over to the dark side, so to speak, Melrose offers Faversham the chance to become the inheritor of his estate and collection, valued at over a million pounds—but Faversham must agree to continue Melrose's miserly treatment of his tenants and to make certain that neither Melrose's wife nor his legitimate daughter receives a penny of the property. (Mrs. Melrose and her daughter

Felicia have by now returned to England, penniless and desperate—Melrose refuses to see them or to give them financial assistance.) Faversham is, for a large portion of the narrative, seduced by the thought of Melrose's money into acquiescence with his evil employer's desires, telling himself that he will do some good when Mr. Melrose dies. Eventually Melrose's lack of proper attention to his tenants results in several deaths, one of a child. When a tenant murders Melrose, Faversham inherits the property and collections. He (under Lydia's influence) has a change of heart and legally signs over the lot to Felicia Melrose on the condition that she turn the house into a museum and art school and engage him as curator. Faversham and Lydia marry and devote their lives to the arts. The novel ends with a sentimental call to the moneyed people of England to use their wealth to "restore the waste places—build—people—teach! . . . Rural England turns to you, its natural leaders, to shape it afresh" (512).

The Melrose plot bluntly argues against the rights of the individual collector; Ward states simply that art should not be for private consumption but should rather be used as part of a national plan for social improvement. Melrose is made oddly analogous to Lord Tatham—both want to keep art for their private viewing. Certainly Lord Tatham's motivation is love and Mr. Melrose's greed—but Ward brings these two into surprisingly close proximity. Tatham is, on the surface, a proper hero—charming, honest, noble. The reader certainly expects Lydia to marry him. That she falls for Faversham, who has little but his aesthetic interests to recommend him, creates a reevaluation of narrative expectation and aesthetics. Structurally, women and art are made equivalent: Lydia cannot marry a wealthy lord who would keep her for his private consumption, as these things are "of the past." Likewise, art cannot be "hoarded" by one man as a status symbol; art must be shared, made available in a public space. Faversham says, "I could spend, if not my life, at any rate a term of years, in making the Tower a palace of art, a centre of design, of training, of suggestion—a House Beautiful, indeed, for the whole North of England. And my promised wife says she will help me" (278). Lydia's profession allows her to enter the public world, and the politics of Ward's novel permit her to remain there. Thus the woman artist gets, if not the prize in money or a title, at least the prize in activity and work: she gets to continue some form of a career in art, though perhaps in a different form (Ward does not mention whether Lydia will continue to draw and paint, only that she will be instrumental in the new museum and art school). Ward's *The Mating of Lydia* is one of the few Victorian or Edwardian novels where we see even a hint that a woman's marriage won't hinder her artistic work; it certainly argues that a woman cannot be kept like an artwork in a man's private collection.

Through her representation of women artists, Ward suggests that women must be allowed to circulate freely in the social realm; any time art tries to escape from the realm of the social (into the realm of the sensual) it is doomed. *The Mating of Lydia* can be read as Ward's belated plea for a return to the mid-century Victorian belief that art must have moral, social, and political use. In arguing for the everyday value of art, Ward stakes her allegiance to an older, mid-Victorian aesthetic and implicitly rejects fin-de-siècle artistic styles. Kathy Psomiades traces two main historical narratives that underpin turn-of-the-century British Aestheticism: the first is "a narrative about the separation of art from the praxis of everyday life" (1997, 9); aestheticism involves the fantasy of art as a retreat from the sordid realities of the social and political bourgeois world. The second narrative, in tension with the first, tells the story of "art's increasing involvement with commodity culture" (ibid.). Psomiades points out that critics, while they tend to read aestheticism as either disavowing mass culture (in the aesthetes' disdain for the bourgeois) or entirely co-opted by it (in their passion for decoration and material goods), still inevitably arrive at an argument that aestheticism does both simultaneously. Ward is writing—well after the main flowering of aestheticism, certainly, but with a wary eye still on it—specifically against such a creed. She positions women artists as the sole possible hope for a moral, socially uplifting art—one which rejects the personal, the erotic, or the private.

Unfortunately, the New Woman artist is, in Ward's novels, thwarted in her ability to become this kind of socially regenerative artist by the social pressures that insist on reinforcing her sexuality. Lydia's tepid success stems in part from her refusal to enter the traditional narrative of marriage to the noble lord; she chooses a man (one lacking the requirements for romantic hero) who keeps her in contact with the art world she loves. Elise's failure, similarly, stems from the pressures of sexuality: her sexual desire for David destroys her creative abilities—the abilities that support her financially as well as emotionally. And when she does marry, she finds that the social pressures of being a supportive wife make art equally impossible. Admittedly, in their final fates neither of Ward's New Women artists serves as an ideal model for female liberation, aesthetic or otherwise. Yet they both figure as mouthpieces for Ward's critique of an ideological structure that makes artistic achievement nearly impossible for women.

Coda

Contemporary Representations of the Woman Painter

> As far as being a woman painter nowadays, it seems a lot like being a housewife, only you paint more.
> —Lisa Petraitis-Harrington, contemporary artist.

IN THIS STUDY I have suggested that in the nineteenth century, particularly the middle decades, women painters achieved significant strides in education, income, and public prestige, even if these strides did not necessarily position women as the equals of male artists. Nor did rising prestige make women painters immune from the discourse of erotic scrutiny which, as we have seen, regularly plagued women painters. Novelists of the period recorded these strides and setbacks in their fictional representations of women painters. Although a site for feminist critique, the fictional female painter is nowhere a representation without turmoil; we have no wholly positive vision of an unembattled woman painter in the Victorian era.

This holds true, alas, for subsequent fictional representations of women painters. Lily Briscoe of Virginia Woolf's *To the Lighthouse,* perhaps the most famous woman painter in fiction, is far from untroubled in her artistic life. She might be allowed to end the novel with a vision, but the status of that vision is highly problematic (is it celebratory? or merely exhausted? or both?). Fictional women painters later in the twentieth century are similarly ambiguous, as we see in Mary Gordon's *Spending,* Iris Murdoch's *The Sandcastle,* and Margaret Atwood's *Cat's Eye,* among others.[1] A spate of fictionalized retellings of the troubled life of the Renaissance painter Artemisia Gentileschi (by Anna Banti, Susan Vreeland, and Alexandra Lapierre) make it clear that the persistent eroticization of women painters is not a thing of the past; taken together, these novels (and the various film adaptations of the painter's life[2]) suggest that the best way for a woman painter from the past to achieve fame in the present is to have been raped in the past.[3]

Contemporary real-life women painters face a similarly oppressive interest in their physical beings. My aim in this coda is quite simply to suggest that the Victorian discourse that insists on evaluating women artists as physical or sexual bodies rather than as artistic producers is still very much with us. A *New York Times* headline from 18 April 1999 says it all: "The Artist Is a Glamour Puss." The article, written by Elizabeth Hayt, appears *not* in the Arts and Leisure section but in "Sunday Styles," a section on *fashion,* and it bears the subheading: "Young women in fine arts present themselves as stylish and sexy, reflecting their work." Work is secondary; appearance is primary. The article contains but a whisper of information on the work of the women artists discussed; it is their bodies and their clothes (their "gorgeous frames," to recall the *Punch* review) that are considered newsworthy. A caption below a photograph of one woman sculptor reads: "Rachel Feinstein . . . now 27, wore leg warmers with garters and a see-through plastic miniskirt to an interview at Yale." Granted, one of Hayt's points is that these women are no longer bound by ideological codes that dictate female sexuality; that they are free to do and wear whatever they choose; and that because of this freedom, their art is more alive, more frankly sensual. Yet nevertheless, when Tracey Emin, an installation artist, is quoted as saying, "when I go out, I show an amazing amount of cleavage because I've got really nice breasts," it is not her *artwork* that is receiving acclaim. Her best-known work is described as "a tent inscribed with the names of all the people she has slept with." Taken together with the artist's own valorization of her breasts, the reader of the *Times* article has no choice but to read art and artist as part of the same package: a package that represents and offers sex. The *Times* review cannot consider Emin's work in any way other than directly linked to her "really nice breasts."

Another late-twentieth-century *New York Times* article (2 November 1997), by Steven Henry Madoff, titled "After the Roaring 80's in Art, A Decade of Quieter Voices," details the new "quietness and modesty" of the nineties' art scene. After the "giddy, go-go art market" of the previous decade, he claims that the 1990s is a quiet period, during which fears of stock market crashes make artists and dealers reticent on the subject of money and fame. Madoff heralds this new quietness in art by discussions of and with four contemporary artists: Kiki Smith, Matthew Barnew, Ann Hamilton, and Robert Gober. The text of the article, which is front-page news for the Arts and Leisure section, is embedded within a full-page color collage of four photographs of these artists. The collage is divided into two large sections: the top is a photograph of Matthew Barney dressed up in his installation piece as a strange Poseidon-like figure with plastic bubbles for hair; the bottom half is a shot of Robert Gober hard at work on the base of an installation sculpture, kneeling on a plaster-covered floor. Superimposed on these two large images sit two smaller images: on the top left nestles a small impromptu-looking photograph of Ann Hamilton, holding her 3-year-old son on her shoulders. On the lower right is a more formal portrait photo of artist Kiki Smith, beautifully made up, posing elegantly but barefoot in a forest.

What does this conglomeration of photographs tell us? Kiki Smith, for instance, appears to be her own artwork. Her posture is contrapuntal, her surroundings dryadic, her hair Pre-Raphaelite. Nothing exists in the photograph but Smith herself—no artwork, no work at all, just the lovely form of the artist. Ann Hamilton looks cheerful and maternal; she smiles hugely at the camera and hugs the legs of her son (Emmet, the caption tells us), who sits triumphantly astride Mom and has his mouth full of some sticky-looking treat. As with the shot of Kiki Smith, there is nothing visible that might be "art" in the photograph, no evidence of creative work (nonbiological creative work, that is). Both male artists, however, are actively creating art—one in the costume of his latest installation (he too *is* art, but not simply in his normal garb; to become art, he must wear a plastic bubbly wig, ear extensions, and face paint), the other male artist grubbing around on a studio floor littered with visible evidence of productivity.

If, as the article suggests, 1990s art has "replaced the frontal force of Neo-Expressionism with images and scenes full of obscure, unexpected juxtapositions and emotionally charged references to the body," the layout artist at the *Times* has successfully captured this in their collage. Certainly the modern Madonna-and-child photo and the thoughtful Pre-Raphaelite Dryad image contain "emotionally charged references to the body." Certainly the four portraits of the artists form a well-patterned juxtaposition. But how "unexpected" is this juxtaposition? Women artists are mothers or models; male artists work. What is so new about this?

The text of the article maintains these gender distinctions. Madoff interviews each artist listed above and discusses them in four separate sections; the sections are as carefully positioned—alternating female/male/female/male—with regard to gender as the collage. The interviews begin with a section on Kiki Smith, our modern dryad, which starts with a quote from the artist, saying: "I want to get quieter and quieter. I want to have an opulent interior life and a spare existence." As she describes the 1990s reaction against 1980s art, Smith traces a rather startling parallel with the Victorian reaction to certain elements of Romanticism: "The 80s were still playing out that idea of the artist as genius romantic, but it just got tired. All that drinking, drugs;

all that money and pressure. When you see it destroy people you know, you realize you're willing to give up a whole lot of that stuff to do your work." Smith articulates the same anti-"cult of personality" work ethic as the mid-Victorians espoused in response to what they perceived as the excesses of the Byronic style.

After Smith's musings, the article immediately provides a physical description and setting for Smith: "Relaxed, with bright blue eyes, long black hair and an easy laugh, the artist is sitting at the kitchen table in the old three-story building she bought as home and studio . . . the rooms are comfortable and unassuming." Only after we get this pleasant domestic scene are we offered any description of Smith's decidedly *uncomfortable* work: "a woman on all fours with her entrails pulled out like so much rope." This, however, is Smith's older work. Her newer pieces "live in a world that is far more dream-like."

Contrast this portrait of the woman artist with the next description, of Matthew Barney. We are not told whether his eyes are blue or brown or magenta, whether his domestic space is unassuming, or what his laugh sounds like. We are told that he is "nothing less than a prodigy" and that his work is "audacious . . . tackl[ing] everything from notions of biology and team sports to the vaudeville of Harry Houdini." When physical descriptions do enter in, they show Barney in the costume of his installation pieces: "Barney appears as a fantastic sheep-man, with slick red hair, a protruding snout and a formal suit." The woman artist appears as a physical, desirable bodily presence ("bright" eyes, an "easy" laugh); the male artist appears as a sheep—but all in the service of art.

The article now turns to Ann Hamilton, the artist pictured with her child on the front page. Again we are offered a brief physical description: "a warm woman with graying hair and an air of bright engagement." The article mentions the "social interaction and sensuousness" of her work; the artist says, "[My work], early on, became something very social, something larger than my own labor." This insistence on the social dimension in art mirrors, again, a Victorian-like turn away from solipsistic creation to a Ruskinian art-for-society's-sake. Hamilton's "labor," then, is twofold: childbirth and social art, both for the larger good of the community. That her art's "sensuousness" is mentioned, however, seems to bring us back to a bodily awareness (as does her photograph, with child)—a bodily awareness that is resolutely absent in the interview with Barney. Barney's corporeal identity remains hidden behind a façade.

The art of the 1990s, the article insists, is made by "artists who aren't selling shares in their identities": instead, the artists described seem private, a little jittery, wary of the "cult of personality" that dominated the 1980s art world. The last artist interviewed, Robert Gober, is so wary that he does not let the interviewer take notes and insists on having a hand in the construction of the article. As with the other male artist interviewed, the first description in the Gober section is of an artwork in his studio. However, after the writer describes Gober's almost preternatural shyness and concern over public representation, the writer goes on to describe Gober's appearance, briefly—almost, it seems, as a punishment for the mildly feminine trait of reticence. Gober's "pleasant face and watchful brown eyes" suit a man whose art is consistently described by the article in delicate terms: "lovingly miraculous," "dreaming," "uncannily provocative," and so on. Contrast this to the decidedly unfeminine terms used to describe Matthew Barney: audacious, prodigy, tackled, sleek execution. Add this to the fact that the author is careful to include the sexual preferences of both male artists: we are told, that Barney, "When he's not working . . . spends time with his wife, Mary Farley . . ." and Gober is quoted as saying, "I'm a gay man."

The article's central theme—that today's art world is a "kinder, gentler" scene, a decade of quieter voices—relies on women artists to represent the peace and security of motherhood or feminine natural beauty, and asks homosexual male artists to hover in the dream world and the unconscious. Meanwhile, the "audacious" heterosexual male artist tackles "internally lubricated self-threading flight blocks" and, like some rebellious artistic James Bond, plays opposite Ursula Andress in his video pieces.

Yet another late 1990s periodical article on women artists is provocatively entitled "Lady Painters? Smile When You Say That." Written by Peter Plagens and appearing in *Newsweek* in 1996, the article focuses on three "postfeminist" women artists—Nicola Tyson, Elizabeth Olbert, and Lisa Yuskavage. "Postfeminist" is Plagens's term; "Tyson," he writes, "prefers to call it a 'complex female subjectivity.'" To which he so wittily replies, "OK, she's earned the right." Plagens describes the third artist, Yuskavage, as an "overtly sexual artist." This rather ambiguous phrase might refer to Yuskavage's pictures of "ghostly, grotesque bimbos" or it might be aimed in a more personal direction. The article offers images of the women's works that—coincidentally?—are all representations of deformed female bodies. As with the work of Craik and Yonge, the reviewer here seems to tolerate the feminism of the painters only because the female body is defiled somewhere in the background.

This all sounds remarkably familiar to Victorian ideological constructions of women painters, which, as we have seen, ruthlessly focused on the female artist's body to the almost complete neglect of her artwork. As the late-Victorian critic George Moore wrote, "In her art woman is always in evening dress" (1898, 223). We might compare this with a *New York Times* article from 5 July 2000: in "Portrait of the Artist as a Young Woman," Roberta Smith writes, "The incidence of female artists in evening wear may be on the rise." Smith's is yet another article emphasizing the appearance of the body of women artists rather than their art. Smith does at least notice and object to this phenomenon; one of Smith's main points is her alarm at the prevalent fascination with photographing female artists in the nearly-nude. But the woman artist's *art* itself is still missing.

This is but a smattering of examples from a vibrant discourse still very much under debate; whether they are truly representative I can only speculate. But this random collection does seem to suggest that the gender politics of the art world have not changed as profoundly as we might like to think. In this book, I have attempted to trace the moment when this gender politics was first configured and to suggest that the woman painter has faced an arduous fight against a set of remarkably tenacious ideological discourses. As a potentially transgressive figure, the woman painter was, and remains, a cultural obsession. And no one has been more obsessed than her sister artist, the woman writer.

Notes

Introduction

1. For an excellent discussion of Eliot's knowledge of and literary use of painting, see Witemeyer 1979.

2. See Nunn 1987, 3.

3. Poovey (1988, 12) traces some of the "contested images" of gender that threatened the precarious (indeed, in her argument, untenable and fantastical) stability of Victorian gender norms. The "border cases" that she investigates "had the potential to expose the artificiality of the binary logic that governed the Victorian symbolic economy." These border cases—divorce, childbirth, the governess, etc.—could "challenge the social arrangement of separate spheres and everything that went with it: the sexual division of labor, the model of moral influence, the notion that there was some boundary to the alienation of market relations." While less markedly a "border case" in that she more overtly challenged the cultural gender hierarchies, the Victorian woman painter was nevertheless very much a contested image—and is arguably as frequent a fictional figure as the governess.

4. I draw frequently on recent developments in art history to explore what nineteenth-century women writers might have been observing in the art world during their lifetimes. My work here has been made easier—indeed has been made *possible*—by a recent body of impressive recovery work on women painters of the nineteenth century. Through the work of art historians including Whitney Chadwick, Deborah Cherry, Paula Gillett, Griselda Pollock, Jan Marsh, Christina Campbell Orr, and others, previously unknown Victorian women artists have been brought to light and given comprehensive histories; serious aesthetic critique has at last been brought to bear on works hitherto dismissed as domestic or feminine art. I am also, of course, indebted to feminist literary scholars, who have made it possible to take seriously the works of many noncanonical writers whom I discuss in this book.

5. The woman painter is overwhelmingly a denizen of the realm of realist fiction. All the texts I consider here fall under the heading of domestic fiction, focusing on the marriage plot to varying degrees. *Jane Eyre* is the only text that strays significantly from the realist path—and Jane's paintings, while fantastic in their subject matter, are very much a part of the material side of the novel. Nancy Armstrong's influential *Desire and Domestic Fiction* (1990) argues that the domestic realist novel comes into being as a discourse of gendered subjectivity that plays out political issues in the private sphere of domesticity; the early novel's main concern, she argues, is sexuality and marriage, but these mask socioeconomic and political threads running just below the surface. Helene Moglen similarly argues for the "centrality of sex and gender as the novel's defining concern" (2001, 1) rather than the more traditional class-based argument, derived from Ian Watt, which locates the novel within the history of capital and the rise of the middle class. In Moglen's alternate history, changes in the sex-gender system were inextricably tied to the economic and social changes traced by Watt and his followers; the novel both "imposed and resisted" such transformations in gender ideology (4).

Some writers on realism, such as George Levine 1981 and Leo Bersani, argue that realism struggles to repair social fragmentation, to present a (however doomed) picture of a unified subject—a kind of "consolations of fiction" argument. Along similar lines, but with stronger disapproval, D. A. Miller argues that novels (realist and otherwise) are a form of social policing, an effort at containment and ideological domination. Catherine Belsey in *Critical Practice* argues that this aspect of realism is politically dangerous; in this reading, realism is a part of the bourgeois and capitalist project to cover up the fissures in social order and individual identity caused by economic oppression. The novel becomes a way of collapsing social heterogeneity into homogeneity (marriage, stability, closure, etc.).

In response to such critiques, feminist critics of the 1980s and 1990s often turned away from realist texts to the gothic novel or sensational fiction to find evidence of women's voices. But Penny Boumelha in "Realism and the Ends of Feminism" set out to reclaim realism for feminist critics: Boumelha argues that women writers used the conventions and constraints of realism with purpose, to reveal and critique the social and ideological pressures that limited Victorian women's lives. If critics were attuned to its nuances, argued Boumelha, women's realist fiction had radical and transgressive statements to make. I argue similarly that these women writers are actively working through aesthetic and ideological issues, offering critiques of varying stridency.

6. The most obvious kind of direct influence is work-to-work influence, as when a writer (W. H. Auden, for example) writes a poem specifically about a work of art (Brueghel's *Landscape with the Fall of Icarus*). In the nineteenth century, we see numerous examples of this, from the Pre-Raphaelites to the poets Katherine Bradley and Edith Cooper ("Michael Field"), who wrote several poems "to" or "about" paintings. In the other direction, direct influence also appears in painting when an artist represents a scene from a literary source. Less obvious kinds of direct influence abound, however. One kind is when a *style* from one medium influences an artist working in another medium, as when Katherine Mansfield writes a story explicitly in the style of abstract expressionism. More broad direct influence studies include numerous single-author studies such as Witemeyer's *George Eliot and the Visual Arts* (1979), or (more broadly still) Alexander and Sellars's *The Art of the Brontës* (1995). Works such as these argue for the direct influence of certain paintings, painters, or schools of painting on the

writings of individual authors. Single-author investigations have been done on most of the "major" writers, particularly in Modernism; era-wide studies are also common. Mariana Torgovnick, for example, notes the way certain Modernist novels exhibit similarities to Modernist art (1985); similarly, Wendy Steiner 1982 traces the influence of cubism on literature.

    7. The Zeitgeist approach is historically based and again ranges widely in content. Zeitgeist approaches argue that writers and visual artists in particular historical periods share some particular characteristics because of their simultaneous position in history. This can be overly broad, vague, and ultimately untenable, as in the work of Wylie Sypher; it can appear in a more subtle form in the works of Roston or Praz; or it can become quite specific and focused, as in Heffernan's work on the Romantics or Abel's analogies between Baudelaire and Delacroix. In Murray Roston's *Victorian Contexts,* for example, the overarching assumption is that art and literature can be discussed *together* as reacting to similar social events; writers and artists of all kinds respond to the shifting matrix of social and cultural concerns of their time. There is no single Zeitgeist of the Victorian era; there are, however, a complex series of events and issues to which artists responded—what Greenblatt has called a "shared code" (Greenblatt, 86). Roston writes, "shifts in social mores and changes in commodity culture have a simultaneous effect upon all media" (1996, 1). Artist and writer react to a "central complex of inherited assumptions, of emergent ideas, of urgent contemporary concerns" (3) and each artist adopts or resists or questions them in different ways. Roston labels his methodology a "synchronic approach," defined as "the focus upon the simultaneous response of writer and artist to current problems" (ibid.). In this same vein, Mary Ann Caws argues that "The mutual interference of two objects, a visual and a verbal one, involves a dialogue, which the reader or observer enters into and sponsors, and which with other dialogues forms part of a more general conversation" (1989, 4). Zeitgeist approaches can compare anything from iconography to composition style to expressive aims to explicit reactions to discrete historical events.

    8. This latter kind of interart analysis also includes studies in literary pictorialism (Hagstrum 1958), histories of ekphrasis (Heffernan 1993, parts of W. Mitchell 1994, Meltzer 1987), studies in representation and narrative (parts of Byerly 1997), spatial form theories of literature (Mitchell 1980, Joseph Frank 1948), and other examples, all of which explore ways in which visual media impact the stylistic and structural universe of specific fictions. Jeffrey Meyers's *Painting and the Novel* (1975) is another example of this type of interart project that imports definitions from one art into another. Hence he talks of fiction as making use of elements of painting: perspective, composition, foreshortening, foreground, and background.

    9. Theories of Visual Culture in general, such as the work of Claude Gandelman (1991), again make use of both literature and art without privileging one or the other. Much excellent cultural studies work likewise uses literature and visual art in equal measure to make sociocultural arguments (see Flint 2000, or Barrell 1986 as examples). Other theories of Visual Culture, such as those by W. J. T. Mitchell (1986, 1994), Mieke Bal (1991) or James Elkins, might be said to have dispensed with both literature and traditional visual art in favor of a discussion of the nature of images. Yet another body of work focuses on questions of aesthetics and ranges across multiple art media, as in the collection edited by Kemal and Gaskell (2000), or in Suzanne Langer's work (1957). Such theories do not purport to be theories of painting or literature as such, but rather

(in varying ways) are debating the philosophical meaning, social effect, or political role of art.

10. See also Christ and Jordan 1995, introduction.

11. As I suggest in chapter 3, I disagree with Smith's reading of paintings in *Jane Eyre* as "conventional" and used purely to "delineate character." Jane's paintings, in fact, are much more complicated artifacts involved in a complex web of economic, aesthetic, and social interactions.

12. A partial list of British Victorian texts which feature male painters includes : Wilde, *The Picture of Dorian Gray;* Hardy, *The Well-Beloved* and *Golden Arrow;* Dickens, *Little Dorrit;* Thackeray, *The Newcomes;* Marie Corelli, *The Master Christian;* George Du Maurier, *Trilby;* and George Eliot, *Middlemarch.* There are numerous others in British fiction, and many more in American and Continental novels; see Jeffares and Smith for additional lists. See also Bowie 1950 and O'Donovan 1994 featuring male painters.

13. See L. Lewis 2003.

14. For example, Andres pairs the scene from Collins's *The Woman in White* in which Walter Hartright first sees Marian at the window at Limmeridge with Millais's *Mariana* (noting too that the similarity of names suggests "a deliberate allusion to that painting"); Collins's transformation of that painting, Andres argues, reveals his criticisms of traditional gender constructs (2002, 374).

15. At least not paintings that I have been able to recognize. Several writers—Charlotte Brontë and George Eliot in particular—do often create narrative moments that call to mind paintings by male painters (Andres 2005 discusses Eliot's narrative revisions of several Pre-Raphaelite paintings, for example; similarly, Alexander and Sellars 1995 record that Brontë was heavily influenced by Bewick's illustrations and John Martin's grand gothic canvases).

16. Caroline Levine has argued persuasively that Victorian realism was itself more concerned with *process* than product: "Victorian realism's own theorists focused less on the verisimilitude of the product than on the labor that went into its making" (2000, 75). Rather than valuing the mimetic exactitude of realism, Victorian realists and theorists (like Eliot and Lewes) stressed the power—moral and political—of the struggle to see the world clearly enough to *try* to represent it. As we shall see, women writers often use the scene of painting to unfold and negotiate complex theories of realism (literary and otherwise). See in particular chapters 1, 2, and 4.

17. The *paragone,* or contest, between art forms, is a Renaissance tradition. In Leonardo da Vinci's treatise, painting was the clear victor because of its concreteness and reliance on the noblest sense—sight. In later versions—most prominently Lessing's (1766; 1984)—painting took second place to poetry, which could represent change across time rather than be limited to the static moment.

18. More recently, in *The Alphabet Versus the Goddess,* Leonard Shlain argues that women are image-oriented and men word-oriented, that men are linear while women see things all at once, and that the overthrow in prehistoric times of matriarchal cultures was directly related to the institution of the very linear, very masculine alphabet (a somewhat dubious paradigm).

19. See Smick 1996.

20. See Vickers 1985.

21. Wells works with early modern and classical definitions that distinguish between ekphrasis and enargeia; in later periods, enargeia is less prominent and definitions of

ekphrasis tend to include the kind of vibrancy once associated with enargeia. See Kreiger 1992, chap. 1. Wells associates ekphrasis with epic (and enargeia with lyric) and argues that it functions explicitly *against* enargeia, as a way to repudiate the destructive absorption of enargeia. Enargeia can be a description of anything, not just of a work of art (as with ekphrasis); however, the terms are often used interchangeably in the post-Classical period: Wells's description of enargeia as potentially destructive is applicable to many instances of ekphrasis. Enargeia "may be understood as facilitating a dangerous absorption in the feminine; . . . carried away by the force of enargeia, the lyric subject first identifies with the beautiful 'signifier' before him, and then attempts to appropriate it as the signified of his own interiority. . . . This absorption leads (inevitably) to a destructive 'defacement' of both self and other" (2002, 110).

22. In Wells's discussion of enargeia and ekphrasis, she begins the process of retheorizing ekphrasis by asking what happens when the viewer/describer of the object is female (although the producer of the object is not). One result of a "female focalizer of the ekphrasis" (namely Lucrece) is an emphasis on "personal grief and loss rather than, say, the political and historical implications of Troy's fall for Rome's subsequent rise" (2002, 117).

23. We do have numerous descriptions of art in nonfiction prose by women, but this does not specifically count as ekphrasis, which is a rhetorical device specific to fictional genres.

24. For examples of Victorian women's ekphrastic poetry, see Martinez (2003). The twentieth century has more examples of ekphrastic poetry by women (Marianne Moore, Sylvia Plath, May Swenson, Ann Lauterbach, and Barbara Guest have numerous examples), but there are still surprisingly few women writers who write ekphrastically about *women's* paintings. The contemporary poetry journal *Ekphrasis* has occasional excellent examples.

25. In her study of the novel of female artistic development, Linda Lewis writes, "My purpose is to trace the female *Künstlerroman* as developing parallel to but separate from its male counterpart and to illustrate that literary matriarchy proved to be nurturing—not an anxiety of influence—to literary daughters creating their own fictions of female genius" (2003, 4). In Lewis's literary history, Madame De Staël's *Corinne* and George Sand's *Consuelo* functioned as a kind of founding myth for women artists (Western culture and religions offering them none) which subsequent women writers embraced to represent their own artistic desires. I argue similarly that women painters and their works offered women writers positive touchstones for artistic exploration.

26. Other critics have gone further in attempting to recuperate the aesthetic without neglecting social and political concerns. Linda Dowling argues that we have been disposed to consider "the very idea of the aesthetic as mystification, to see all talk of art or beauty as no more than one of the ruses or stratagems through which societies perpetuate themselves as orders of domination" (1996, x). Dowling sets out the terms of the debate: Is aesthetics an evil discourse of cultural domination? Is it inherently apolitical in its very totalizing nature? Or is the aesthetic a field of revolutionary possibility? In arguing for this latter stance, Dowling encourages us to take seriously the view of art held by writers like Ruskin and Morris: that art can and should be morally and socially redemptive. Dowling reads Ruskin, Pater, Morris, and Wilde as aestheticians committed to community formation and individual transformation through art; she also argues against the received notion that Victorian aestheticism—as exemplified by the Art for Art's Sake

battle cry—was not a withdrawal into art and away from politics or an elitist retreat from the masses. On the contrary, Wilde and Pater, like Morris and Ruskin, had "egalitarian impulses" (2); in Dowling's reading, all the major Victorian aestheticians shared a desire to instill in the masses a feeling for beauty. She does not suggest that they are all successful pleas for democracy, simply that the writers in question shared a belief that art could lead us there, if done right and received properly.

27. Armstrong turns to affective life—"playing and dreaming, thinking and feeling" (2000, 2)—to remake the category of the aesthetic and develop what she, similar to Dowling, calls a "democratic aesthetic" (3) which requires an "uncoupling of the aesthetic and privilege" (4). Armstrong carefully controls her reintroduction of affect into the discourse of the aesthetic; she insists that the return to a consideration of beauty and the emotional power of art be done rationally (as, she argues, Adorno did in his *Aesthetic Theory*), with a strong theoretical base and an acknowledgment of political problems such as class, gender, and race. One of the most useful of Armstrong's points is that relying on a Kantian notion of disinterest to argue that art can be a space for radical free play is just as "conservative" as an argument that relies on common universal judgments to define art. (In other words, arguing that art is whatever you want it to be because it is a space apart from the real world is just as limited as arguing that art is what certain educated people say that it is.) Both arguments rely on a notion of art as a "special space" (13)—a notion that Armstrong and the Victorian women writers I discuss in this book object to strongly.

28. Subject formation is but one side of the aesthetic coin. Another arena in which aesthetic judgment features prominently is that of community formation. The project of aesthetic democracy, Linda Dowling ably demonstrates, did not originate or terminate with the liberal social theories promulgated by the Ruskin of "On the Nature of Gothic" or the socialist/artisan work of Morris. Aesthetic democracy—the notion that all humans have an innate sense of taste which, if shepherded correctly by a gentle state, can provide the basis for a unified moral community—was forged in the eighteenth century by such thinkers as Shaftesbury, Burke, and Kant. Shaftesbury called this innate sense a *sensus communis;* Burke wrote that "the standard both of reason and Taste is the same in all human creatures" (1990, 11). Nineteenth-century social critics agreed; aesthetic judgment was innate in all men—but rigorous training was needed to bring them all up to speed, and writers like Ruskin worked to school the mass of mankind in art. I use the terms "all men" and "mankind" advisedly here. For though eighteenth-century aesthetics may have been built upon an admittedly fraught belief in the universality of taste amongst *males,* the nineteenth century was not so certain that women contained the same potentiality. This book traces the struggles of women writers and artists to assert their aesthetic subjecthood into a masculine tradition—to be acknowledged as producers, viewers, and admirers of art.

29. As Christopher Prendergast argues, following Raymond Williams, artistic representation and social/political representation are inevitably linked. Prendergast argues that any time a representation (of either kind) is posited, the immediate question (and the one asked most frequently by contemporary theory) is, on *whose authority* does A stand in for B? Prendergast writes, "If representation is the process whereby 'a' stands for 'b' (where 'a' and 'b' can be terms in a linguistic system, a literary system, or a political system), by what *authority* does it do so? . . . The principal set of claims concerns a relation between representation and *power* . . ." (1988, 8–9; emphasis in original). The

writers I examine here realize that aesthetic production, perception, and judgment are socially and historically conditioned events that are radically affected by the gender of persons involved therein. These writers suggest that when a woman is doing the painting there is never any possibility of disinterested aesthetic experience, no freedom from the problems of power.

30. In the late Victorian era, aesthetics again shifted; Regina Gagnier points out a "shift in emphasis" in the fin-de-siècle period from "an aesthetics of production to an aesthetics of consumption" (1999, 271). This aesthetic shift, she argues in a later work, was tied to shifts in theories of political economy. During the first half of the century, political economists focused on production: "Most people's subjective and objective identities are centrally related to whether they make automobiles, books, contracts, breakfasts, hotel beds, music, speeches, or babies. The fact that the division of labor also reflects major social divisions of race, gender, and ethnicity, and internationally reflects relations of domination and subordination between nations is also crucial in establishing individual and collective identities" (2000, 3). In the second half of the century, thinkers started focusing on consumption rather than production, and "theory of economics became more psychological than sociological" (4), that is, more concerned with choices (why do consumers buy things?) than with how one's place in the division of labor impacts one's identity. The women writers I consider here—even later ones such as Mary Ward—remain steadfastly embedded within the productivist side of aesthetic debate.

31. Consider in this context Walter Benjamin's classic account of the traumatic etiology of Baudelaire's poetry.

32. On the other hand, Adorno also locates in this pivotal period the flowering of a kind of art that is most closely integrated into the social order, namely bourgeois realism. Adorno explains this seeming paradox (art in the nineteenth century is, at the same time, both more autonomous from society and more closely tied to it) by insisting that art is "social primarily because it stands opposed to society" (321). In other words, only an art "emancipated" (as Adorno terms it) from society (that is, no longer forced to be useful to society, no longer purely functional) can function as a reflection or critique of society: "this opposition art can mount only when it has become autonomous" (321).

33. Linda Dowling argues against the dismissal of the aesthetic in works such as that of Martha Woodmansee, who blasts aesthetics as "great minds speaking with one another over and above the historical process" (1994, 7); instead, Dowling advocates a turn to material facts and social forces that shaped art worlds.

34. Women artists also entered the art scene just as British concern for the quality of their national art was on the rise. The British were well aware that they had Shakespeare and Milton, but they didn't have Leonardo da Vinci or Rembrandt. In his introduction to a lady's drawing manual, one artist writes, "So great is the barrenness of genius in painting among English artists, that I am sure there is every reason to hope that these times may produce some female artists, who will bear the palm from the other sex" (Brookshaw 1801, 4).

35. Siegel explores the emergence of the modern idea of the artist, paying particular attention to the role of institutions (museums foremost, but also art schools and art history as a discipline) in this formation. For Siegel, as for nearly all the writers on "the artist" as an evolving concept in the nineteenth century, the artist is male. While grappling with the shifting meaning of the term "artist" during the 1800s, Siegel writes of the prevailing idea of an artist as "someone who does something (craft) so well that *he* is

in fact doing something else (art)—and thereby becoming another kind of person (artist)" (2000, xvi; emphasis added). The pronoun here is telling, though I do not wish to overreact. On the one hand, one might argue that Siegel uses "he" to refer to the nineteenth century because he (Siegel) wishes to follow that lead; that is, in the nineteenth century the artist in general would be "he," so Siegel preserves this. However, this is not in keeping with the dictionary entries that Siegel actually quotes, most of which use the gender-neutral construction "one who" in their attempts to define "artist."

Chapter One

1. Such an arrangement was not without its dangers, however: in Wilkie Collins's *The Woman in White*, the drawing master Walter Hartright is hired to teach young Laura Fairlie, with whom he falls in love. The erotic potential inherent in the male teacher/female student scenario is frequently represented in fiction—in Eliot's *Daniel Deronda*, Miss Arrowpoint marries her music teacher Herr Klesmer; the eponymous heroine of Charlotte Brontë's *Shirley* eventually marries her tutor; examples are numerous.

2. See (Mrs. E. M.) Henrietta Ward 1925, 196–203.

3. See Prieto 2001 for an excellent history of the rise of American artists during the eighteenth, nineteenth, and twentieth centuries.

4. See Nunn 1995, 139–56, for an account of the debate over women painting and exhibiting nude female figures. For an excellent history of female art education, with discussion of nude models, see Dodd 1995. See also Cherry 1993, 53–64; Gillett 1990, 158–72.

5. See Nunn 1987, chap. 3, for the best discussion of the SFA's checkered history.

6. At its founding in 1768, the Royal Academy boasted two female members, Mary Moser and Angelica Kauffman (whose story so fascinated the nineteenth century that Anne Thackeray Ritchie published a fictionalized account of the artist's life, titled *Miss Angel* [1876]). The famous painting of the founding of the Royal Academy offers a symbolic scene indicative of the social status of these two founding women artists: neither woman is physically present in the painting, which shows R.A. members in various poses in one of the Academy painting rooms. Instead, Moser and Kauffman are present only as dim, formal, framed portraits on the back walls, because Moser and Kauffman, as women, could not be present in a room where "life class" was under way (indicated by a nude model in the painting's foreground). But it is ironic that, of course, all the other R.A. members depicted are themselves merely portraits of the "real" men in question—they are portraits, however, unbounded by frames, unfettered by the conventions that kept women artists from full membership in this prestigious academy until the twentieth century.

7. For painting prices, see Reitlinger 1961.

8. See Gillett 1990, chap. 2, for more information on the increasing social prestige of the painter in the Victorian era.

9. Ibid. 18ff.

10. As Harman suggests, the public/private sphere distinction is dismantled consistently and insistently by women's forays into the public world; hitherto seemingly stable gender categories are thereby forcibly redefined in novelistic scenes that dramatize female characters' "defining public moment" (1998, 9). Although not "feminine *politi-*

cal novels" in the sense that Harman defines them ("texts in which female characters participate in the public universe conventionally understood to be owned and occupied by men—the world of mills and city streets, of labor and strikes, of Parliament and parliamentary debates, of national celebrations and urban investigations, of outdoor public speaking and political activism" [8]), the texts I examine in this study do make the art world a public arena that engages with social and cultural debates.

11. And the woman writer could, famously, hide her endeavors, as the tale of Jane Austen covering her manuscripts when anyone entered the parlor suggests.

12. The standard chronology for Royal Academy shows was this: The R.A. Summer Exhibit—the big one, of contemporary art—opened to the public on the first Monday in June and ran until the first Monday in August. The Wednesday before public opening was reserved for the reporters; on the Saturday before opening was held The Banquet, a male-only gathering of R.A. members, literati, politicians, art patrons, and wealthy Society members. Also preceding the public opening was the Royal Private View, for the queen and her family. Immediately after the Royal Private View was the Private View, "the first major social event that was an official exhibition function" (Gillett 1990, 209). This was the high-society event that marked the official opening of the elite London season (of parties, etc); tickets to the Private View were hot commodities and essential to anyone who wanted an entrée into the fashionable world.

The R.A. Winter Exhibit featured works by old masters, or perhaps recently deceased English artists. In the first week of April, artists put the finishing touches on whatever works they intended to send to the R.A. for possible exhibition. R.A. Members (about sixty total in any given year) were guaranteed acceptance and their paintings were generally hung "on the line"—that is, at eye level or slightly above (the best position for viewing). Nonmembers submitted their paintings to the selection committee and hoped for the best. The bulk of each exhibition consisted of nonmember pieces: for example, the 1862 Summer Exhibit showed 1,142 pieces: 146 were the work of Academicians, 996 the work of outsiders (Nunn 1987, 91). Women exhibitors at the Royal Academy show were, of course, in the "nonmember" category, since women were not admitted to full membership in the R.A. until the twentieth century. Of the thousand-plus works that the average R.A. show exhibited, between forty and one hundred women artists were represented. For more information on the ins and outs of the R.A., see ibid. 192–241, and Nunn 1987, 88ff.

13. See Gillett 1990, chaps. 1 and 2.

14. For information on Osborn, see Casteras 1992, 219–25. For an excellent analysis of this painting, to which my reading is much indebted, see Cherry 1993, 78–81.

15. Ward was a member of the Central Committee of the National Society for Women's Suffrage; Jopling campaigned for women's rights within the Society of Portrait Painters.

16. The declaration was originally published in *Fortnightly Review* (July 1889, 123–42). See also Cherry 1993, 93.

17. For an excellent biography of Bodichon, see Hirsch 1998, 1995.

18. Eliza Fox was also a well-known artist—her portrait of Bodichon still hangs at Girton College, which Bodichon helped to found. Mary Howitt was a writer, friendly with the Pre-Raphaelite circle, who often wrote on various art subjects—her novella "Margaret von Ehrenberg, Artist-Wife" is discussed in chapter 2. Mary's daughter, Anna Mary Howitt, was a painter, and part of the "pre-Raphaelite sisterhood" of women who

worked with and around the better known Pre-Raphaelite Brotherhood. Anna Howitt also married a painter and was the author of *An Art Student in Munich,* an account of her art education in Germany. Anna Howitt's serialized story "Sisters in Art" is discussed in chapter 3. Another signer, Amelia Edwards, was a novelist, journalist, and Egyptologist, but her involvement with the artists involved in the MWPA (and in particular her friendship with Barbara Bodichon) influenced her fiction: the heroine of Edwards's *Barbara's History* is a practicing artist. The art critic Anna Jameson was another signer; others were actresses, writers, and other professional women.

19. In her lifetime Bodichon exhibited roughly 250 works of art, mainly watercolor landscapes. Her paintings are airy, subtle, full of shadows and light and mood, always with a feeling of vastness characteristic of Romantic landscape art. Her main influences were the Romantic English landscape artists, such as Cox, Prout, or Turner. She was impatient with formal history painting, and she followed the dictates of the contemporary Barbizon school, which popularized out-of-doors painting. As an independently wealthy woman, Bodichon (unlike the majority of the fictional artist-heroines we shall encounter) had unusual access to varied landscapes because of her extensive travels. Dante Gabriel Rossetti wrote that Bodichon's intrepid *en plein air* drive meant she thought "nothing of climbing up a mountain in breeches, or wading through a stream in none, in the sacred name of pigment" (quoted in Hirsch 1995, 176). Bodichon was a friend and supporter of the Pre-Raphaelites, as well as a colleague: she, Rossetti, and Anna Mary Howitt began the Folio Club, in which each member would contribute a painting or drawing before passing it along to the next member.

20. One possible reason for this backlash—or more appropriately backsliding—is that in the later parts of the century, the issues surrounding women's involvement in the art world became less interconnected with political feminist movements; aesthetic considerations (generated and sustained by the Aesthetic movements) largely overshadowed social concerns. Feminist agitation focused more on issues of suffrage than on education or professional interests; art was pressed into service (in the form of banners, posters, etc.) for feminism, rather than the more reciprocal relationship of the middle decades. See Nunn 1987, 211–23.

21. For an excellent discussion of the myth in the eighteenth century, and its relationship to (specifically French) women artists, see Wettlaufer 2004. See also Rosenblum 1957 and Bermingham 1992 for information on the eighteenth-century interest in Dibutade.

22. *Punch* briefly lists other artworks in the exhibition but goes into little or no detail, and the litany sounds very much like a collection of classically *amateur* achievements, rather than the offerings for sale at a public exhibition:

> There are, also, watercolors, and copies from the Old, and a Tennysonian picture by Mrs. Ward, and a *genre* subject by Miss Breadstreet, and wonderful portraits of lace collars and Crinoline dresses . . . and oil paintings, large and small, modest and ambitious, and such suctorious birds'-eggs and glorious odoriferous flowers by Mrs. Harrison, that you suspect she must have borrowed the palette and brushes of Hunt to have painted them. ("Let Us Join the Ladies")

Watercolors and copies, a scene from a poem, a genre subject, feminine lace and crinoline, birds' eggs and flower pictures—all are traditionally the realm of the amateur. Only the oil paintings—which Punch does not describe in any detail, merely offering dimensions—stand out as the usual medium for serious artists. But all the other works mentioned have for their subjects traditionally female objects.

23. Actual self-portraits by Victorian women painters were, as Casteras 1992 and Yeldham (1984, 1: 167–68) note, surprisingly rare.

24. Although the market does make its shamefaced appearance briefly at the very end of the *Punch* article. After the brief list of the exhibit's subject matter, the *Punch* reviewer remarks, "Besides these, there are . . . an infinity of agreeable pictures, the majority of which are ticketed in the corner, "Sold." And, for a picture, many consider the height of criticism is to be "Sold!," and, in truth, but few artists go beyond it, while hundreds of poor struggling fellows never get so far." The market concerns of the art world, and woman's place within the market, form a sort of narrative counterpoint to the art-as-incitement-to-desire theme discussed earlier. For middle-class women in the nineteenth century, art provided a valuable alternative to the scarce money-making ventures offered: working as a governess, acting as a paid companion, schoolteaching, or writing. In Anne Brontë's *The Tenant of Wildfell Hall*, Eliot's *Daniel Deronda*, Anna Mary Howitt's writings, Dinah Mulock's *Olive*, Mrs. Oliphant's *Miss Marjoribanks*, Charlotte Yonge's *Pillars of the House*, Mary Howitt's "Margaret von Ehrenberg, Artist-Wife," and Mrs. Humphrey Ward's *The History of David Grieve*, we are offered female figures who paint for money, whose various forays into the market economy are the subject of intense scrutiny.

25. Other negative portrayals of women painters in fiction, with heavy emphasis on erotic themes, can be found in George Moore's novel *A Modern Lover* (1883); Henry James, *Roderick Hudson;* and Hawthorne, *The Marble Faun*.

26. Another of Alcott's novels, *An Old-Fashioned Girl*, features a pair of women artists who live and work together. The sculptor Rebecca Jeffrey is depicted as a strong, feminist woman who is at work on an Amazonian-size sculpture; her friend Lizzie Small "is an engraver and designs the most delightful little pictures" and is described as meek, quiet, dainty—and engaged (Alcott 1870, 225).

27. Siddal was an accomplished painter; for information about her life and work, see Pollock 1988, 91–114; Marsh 1985, 16–78, 133–35, 210–15; Marsh and Nunn 1989, 65–73.

28. Ellet begins as far back as "the Fair Egyptians" and proceeds century by century, finishing with a discussion of her contemporary sister artists. Ellet focuses mainly on European artists (mostly French, Italian, and German) with a few forays into Scandinavia and several chapters on nineteenth-century American women. No native British women are discussed at any length (few are even mentioned); the closest would be Angelica Kauffman and Mary Moser, both of whom worked in England for much of their professional careers, but neither was English-born. Yet Ellet does admit to being greatly indebted to English women *writers:* in her preface she admits that some of her information on contemporary artists has been taken, "with a little condensing and shaping, from late numbers of that excellent periodical, 'The Englishwoman's Journal'" (1859, v).

29. Ellet also tells the story of the Corinthian Maid as another means of emphasizing the naturalness of woman's drive-to-art (Ellet 1859, 2).

30. A glaring exception to this tradition is the Russian artist Marie Bashkertseff, whose memoir (1919) is anything but quotidian and domestic. Bashkertseff follows the

Romantic tradition of the tortured, melancholy, melodramatic artist to the letter in her stunning memoir.

31. For information on Beale, see Cherry 1993, 93.

32. Butler's fame was so great that, even as a woman, in 1879 she was just two votes away from being elected to membership in the Royal Academy. However, she was beat out by Hubert von Herkomer, a little-known painter whom some of the voters didn't even know, but preferred to vote for in preference to a woman artist (Gillett 1990, 109).

Chapter Two

1. Portions of this article were previously published as "The Professionalization of the Woman Artist in Anne Brontë's *The Tenant of Wildfell Hall*" (*Nineteenth-Century Literature* 58 [2003]: 1–41). Many thanks to *Nineteenth-Century Literature* for permission to reprint selections from this article.

2. Leading the way in this rediscovery—or reevaluation—of Anne's works were Naomi Jacobs 1986, Margaret Mary Berg 1987, Juliet McMaster 1982, and Elizabeth Langland 1989.

3. See especially Nash and Suess 2001. Such an extraordinary collection notwithstanding, some Victorianists still persist in devaluing Anne's work; Terry Eagleton's chapter on the Brontës in his recent *The English Novel* (2005), for example, contains but two paragraphs on Anne (and three *pages* on Branwell).

4. *Tenant* was first published in three volumes in June 1848 by T. C. Newby and was reprinted in July in one volume, and again in August with a preface by Anne. Charlotte's publisher, George Smith, eventually secured the rights to Anne's and Emily's works from Newby, who had served the two sisters no good turn in his treatment of their works.

5. See Alexander and Sellars 1995, introduction, for an excellent account of the Brontë family's artistic activities and interests.

6. Helen's diary, recording her courtship and marriage with Huntingdon and her eventual escape from him, forms the central portion of *Tenant*. Its extensive frame narrative is told by Gilbert Markham, the young farmer who falls in love with Helen after she has fled from her husband and come to live as the elusive "tenant" of the derelict Wildfell Hall.

7. Compare this with the comment of Gilbert (Helen's second admirer) while watching Helen paint: "If I had but a pencil and a morsel of paper I could make a lovelier sketch than hers, admitting I had the power to delineate faithfully what is before me [namely, the artist rather than her subject matter]" (88).

8. Recent *Tenant* scholarship has considered the novel in light of the "social problem novels" of the period 1840–60. In these readings, the social problems in question are marital abuse and drunkenness. However, I would argue that the problem of female aesthetic production is another "social problem" that *Tenant* tackles, and the one most closely aligned to the novel's own aesthetic. Another, equally central, reading of this novel would center on the heroine's role as *mother*. See Gruner 1997. I see many connections between Helen's role as mother (producer of children) and artist (producer of paintings).

9. The fact that the editor and introducer of the novel feels compelled to criticize it in this manner speaks volumes for Anne Brontë's place in the literary canon.

10. See Jacobs 1986 for an excellent summary of the opinions of the few critics of *Tenant* as regards the relative importance or quality of the frame narrative and nested diary.

11. Carnell's broader argument, however, sees Brontë's novel as politically reactionary, harking back to an earlier model of humanism and rationalism: "Brontë ultimately sought wholeness and integration between the sexes through an eighteenth-century ideal of the public good in which most women might participate indirectly as instructors and nurturers of their husbands and sons" (1998, 20). While I agree with Carnell's critique of the separate spheres doctrine, I do not consider the novel's ending to be a suppression of Helen's voice or a retreat into "a nostalgic vision of domestic harmony within the Enlightenment public sphere" (23). Critics who consider that the "end" of the novel is somehow Brontë's last word fail to take into account several crucial factors: first, there is no actual textual evidence that Helen gives up painting. Second, Helen has left one husband already in the course of the novel, and she is *absent from home with the children* while Gilbert writes his extremely extended letter to his brother-in-law. A small point, but Brontë does seem to be telling us that Helen has taken the children somewhere and is gone long enough for Gilbert to write a 300-page letter. We have only Gilbert's word that the marriage is the "nostalgic vision of domestic harmony" that Carnell sees, and Gilbert has not proven himself to be an entirely trustworthy narrator. Finally, the convention that privileges the outer frame narrative (the "beginning" and the "end") as the final answer over the inner narrative of Helen's diary is precisely the convention Carnell has successfully dismantled in her essay. Brontë has already, within Helen's diary, critiqued the narrative tradition of ending a tale with a marriage by showing us the breakdown of Helen and Huntingdon's marriage—we should not fall victim to the fantasy that marriage to Gilbert is meant to be Helen's final destiny.

12. Remember too that Moore compained that "Anne broke down"midway through her novel. By referring to the novelist by her first name rather than by her last, Moore compounds his familiar treatment of Brontë. Furthermore, the phrase "broke down" suggests a physical, or even a neurotic, breakdown.

13. If anything, the novel is *two* love stories—which is part of the problem. Another reason for Moore's concern over the structural break in the novel is that he is jealous *for* Gilbert. The tale is one of repeated jealousy—Gilbert is consumed with it (that's the heat *he* feels) and that becomes a base from which readers can't escape. So when Helen's diary begins to detail her intense passion for the young Huntingdon, the reader (still in Gilbert's shoes) is angry and jealous on his behalf. The dual love story in which a prior love (Helen and Huntingdon) breaks in on a later but narratively immediate one (Helen and Gilbert) is intensely unsettling.

14. Moore, it must be remembered, is writing during the decade that experienced the emergence of and furor around the New Woman, whose ambivalent sexuality (some contemporary detractors saw her as oversexed, some as frigid) was a central issue for debate. Similarly, the New Woman raised the specter of female professional identity, of which Moore did not approve. His explicit link between gender, aesthetics, and erotics was rarely so explicit in writings on women in art from Brontë's era, but (I argue) serves to make visible one crucial component of the debate over female artists.

15. Though the pictures are not described as watercolors or sketches or paintings in oil, we know that Helen paints in oil because Gilbert notes "bottles of oil" and canvas (rather than paper for watercolors) in her studio, and later in the novel she attacks one of her husband's randy friends with her palette knife. Both suggest the use of oil paints that

need scraping and mixing with a knife, while watercolors were sold in cakes. That Helen paints in oil rather than watercolor or pen and ink further removes her from the "typical" feminine artists of her time, who were more likely to use the "feminine" medium of watercolor than smelly, messy, and expensive oil paint.

16. The house in fact belongs to her brother, Mr. Lawrence, who is the same "somebody" we will meet later who takes Helen's paintings to London to sell them.

17. Alexander and Sellars makes compelling connections between the Brontë sisters' artworks and Martin.

18. See Bicknell and Munro 1988 for an excellent discussion of drawing manuals for young women. Also see Ruskin 1857.

19. See Mrs. E. M. Ward 1925, Butler 1922, and Jopling 1925 for autobiographical accounts of female artists' negotiations between art and social life.

20. In contrast, popular photographs and paintings of male artists' studios show clearly that their painting space is for painting—socializing is secondary. See Gillett 1990, chap. 1.

21. Helen's artwork is but one of the hotly contested kinds of property that circulates in *Tenant*. Arthur Huntingdon marries Helen for her considerable property (in money and land); he later takes possession of Helen's moveable property (jewels, artworks, etc.) to prevent her from leaving him. Part of their marital strife surrounds another sort of property: their son. And much later in the novel, after Arthur's death, Gilbert struggles to propose to the now wealthier Helen in spite of her property; though he is loud in his protestations of his dislike for her wealth, their marriage under British law does make him sole possessor of Helen's considerable property.

22. For a more detailed account of the married life and political activities of Caroline Norton, see Holcombe 1983, chap. 4; see also Poovey 1988, chap. 3, for an excellent reading of the political and social significance of Norton's story; for a complete biography, see Perkins 1910.

23. Meredith's heroine in *Diana of the Crossways* is also loosely based on Norton.

24. See Nunn 1986, 19–25. For a fictional sketch of Mary Howitt, see L. E. Landon's *Romance and Reality* (1847).

25. The novella contains about a dozen illustrations, labeled as portraits by Margaret herself. That the novella reproduces her portraits but not her other works suggests that even in fiction, portraiture may be more valuable than other genres of art.

26. The chapter on the Brontës in Eagleton's recent compendium *The English Novel* (2005) displays similar disregard for *Tenant* and for issues of gender. In fact, Eagleton begins the Brontë chapter—in a book about the English *novel*, it should be remembered—with a long recuperative discussion of the merits of *Branwell* Brontë. He also spends considerable time lauding *Patrick* Brontë's nonfiction works. Anne Brontë merits *four sentences*.

27. Paintings, obviously, can be and were viewed in galleries with the artist someplace else entirely, but in the nineteenth century the presence of the producer was frequently expected—often, the sale or viewing of art was done in the artist's own studio. Similarly, exhibition in a public gallery required the artist to be present at "Varnishing Day" and other public events.

28. Because there is no omniscient narrator, the novel is effectively devoid of a stable point on which to place the scales that measure truth. Gilbert's letter, Helen's diary, Helen's letters—all are written with a personal bias that makes both their representation

of events and their subsequent judgment of them untrustworthy. It is a typical Brontë family tactic, the unreliable narrator; but in *Tenant* this unreliability radically unsettles a purportedly realist text. The frame-within-a-frame structure of the novel calls into question the ability of any one frame to contain or represent "truth"—each frame tells a different story.

29. Later in the preface, Brontë narrates another scene of uncovering and discovery—this time not a gendered discovery, as before, but a literal discovery *of* gender. She writes,

> I would have it to be distinctly understood that Acton Bell is neither Currer nor Ellis Bell, and therefore, let not his faults be attributed to them. As to whether the name be real or fictitious, it cannot greatly signify to those who know him only by his works. As little, I think, can it matter whether the writer so designated is a man, or a woman as one or two of my critics profess to have discovered. (31)

Just as housecleaning raises some dust, so too does the writing of fiction. The end product, the works, cannot simply be taken at face value; speculations as to authorial identity or difference (Acton is not Currer is not Ellis) and authorial gender must intervene. That womanhood is something one must discover—that it is not immediately obvious—becomes Brontë's basis for an androgynous theory of art, offered at the end of the preface. She argues for a complete irrelevance of the sex of an author—not, as Virginia Woolf was to state decades later, because genderless art could be objective, measured, reasoned, but because of a more radical belief in the similarities between the sexes:

> I am at a loss to conceive how a man should permit himself to write anything that would be really disgraceful to a woman, or why a woman should be censured for writing anything that would be proper and becoming for a man.

Coming from a century that spent an enormous part of its time dissecting the differences between the sexes, and prescribing guidelines for masculine and feminine behavior, this calm philosophy shocks. Yet as we leave the preface and enter the world of the novel, moments such as this will become more and more common. Brontë's modus operandi, when it comes to gender, is to quietly ignore ("I am at a loss to conceive") and simply refuse to refute traditional gender norms.

30. The connection between female artists and monstrosity or deformity will be important later on as well, when I discuss Yonge's *Pillars of the House* and Craik's *Olive,* both of which contain female artists who are in some way physically deformed.

Chapter Three

1. See, for example, Gilbert and Gubar 2000, chap. 5. See also Gezari 2000, 85–86, and Maynard 1984, 138–40.

2. Jane performs a similar maneuver earlier in the novel when, after the marriage of Miss Temple, Jane stands at her window at Lowood and looks out: "My eye passed

all other objects to rest on those most remote, the blue peaks: it was those I longed to surmount; all within their boundary seemed prison-ground . . . I traced the white road . . . vanishing in a gorge between two [mountains]: how I longed to follow it further" (74).

3. This way of reading is very much in keeping with the radically Jane-o-centric readings that the novel has generated since its publication. Everything in the novel is considered an emanation of Jane's psyche—and rightly so, on many levels. Even the dominant reading of the novel's structure—best represented by Gilbert and Gubar's discussion in *The Madwoman in the Attic*—takes Jane as the source of all actions and events in the novel. When Bertha comes down from her attic the night before Jane's (first, failed) wedding and rends the bridal veil, it is read as a displacement of Jane's anger against Rochester and her ambivalence toward sexual initiation. Even Bertha herself is often read as almost not "real"—that is, she is read allegorically as Jane's alter ego, her angry double.

4. Two little-known novels whose plots borrow heavily from *Jane Eyre*—an 1866 novel by Eliza Tabor called *Hester's Sacrifice*, and *Barbara's History* by Amelia Edwards (1864)—both take up the question of women's interior aesthetic vision where Brontë leaves off. In both novels, the heroine paints with more professional seriousness than in *Jane Eyre*, but both Tabor and Edwards embroil their heroines in similar romantic scenarios. Tabor's novel in particular follows *Jane Eyre* surprisingly closely—except in its ending, which kills off the English artist-heroine and the West Indian former mistress in a fire, and leaves the Rochester-type hero to mourn them both. These refractions of Brontë's plot gives additional insight into the narrative potential that the figure of the woman painter has to articulate the relationship between desire and aesthetic production. Both novels allow us to see how other female writers similarly transformed ekphrasis—in Edwards's case a particular and radical kind of kinetic ekphrasis—into a tool for female liberation and power.

5. Even in the opening scene with the Bewick illustrations—which Jane does not herself create—it can easily be argued that Brontë represents the illustrations as in some sense a product of Jane's own imagination. Jane might not have painted them herself, but her interpretation of them is so powerful as to become an appropriation of the images. This seems to be good training for the young Jane, who will later produce her own images frequently.

6. For a discussion of Renaissance 'blazoning' in *The Rape of Lucrece*, see Nancy Vickers's influential article (1985).

7. If we consider this description from an ekphrastic point of view, we see that word and image work in tandem: the image shows us the unsubmerged portion of an object while the word hints at the remainder.

8. In addition to the symbolic readings by Starzyk 1991, Smith 1995, Byerly 1997, Gilbert and Gubar 2000, and others, critics have also speculated frequently on the possible sources for the paintings. The Brontë family was familiar with the wild and sublime works of John Martin as well as the illustrations of Bewick; both are possible influences on the style and content of Jane's watercolors.

9. Since *Jane Eyre* and *Tenant* were written at the same time (1846–47) by sisters who regularly read one another's work-in-progress, one assumes that the comparable scenes in the two novels are in dialogue.

10. We think of furniture normally as chairs, tables, and the like, moveable objects

to sit on, eat off of, etc. For Brontë, furniture would have had a similar connotation but would have had an extended meaning, encompassing furnish*ings*, such as curtains and bed linens (which were sometimes called bed-furniture), wallpaper, even such things as door handles. It was also used to imply that something was fitted up properly, with all the elements; to comment on someone's "mental furniture" was one way of describing personality characteristics. Taken this way, Rochester's remark that internalizes Jane (her life is both inside her head and inside a room) should remind us of the early window-recess scene, and other enclosure scenes—Jane in the Red Room, in the alcove during the fancy evening revels, inside her curtained bed, in her little schoolroom later in the novel (the schoolroom that she furnishes and cleans just as she likes); and finally to her culminating, after her legacy, in cleaning and redecorating Moor House. This reference to a well-furnished interior space also might make us think of Virginia Woolf's *Room of One's Own*—which is precisely what Rochester suggests Jane possesses on a metaphoric level because, on a social level, she does not own a room of her own.

11. Review of Society for Female Artists exhibit, *Athenaeum*, no. 1588, April 3, 1858, 43. The same *Athenaeum* review that bemoaned the "unimaginative" nature of women's art significantly favored one particular drawing in the Society of Female Artists exhibition and in addition showed how Jane's unusual subject drawings made their way into the popular press. The *Athenaeum* reviewer uses Jane's drawings as a problematic touchstone for female aesthetic excellence: "For pungent caricature, sarcastic and yet playful, we have seldom seen anything better than Scenes from the Life of a Female Artist, by F. A. Claxton—the child drawing from the looking glass, the studio with the strong-minded woman, and the rejected picture, are such sketches as Jane Eyre would have made had she painted instead of written." This description of Florence Claxton's work represents it as decidedly different from the reviewer's earlier characterization of the bulk of women's artworks: Claxton's "Scenes" represent neither spaniels, nor roses, nor firstborns, nor anything else in the dismissive litany quoted above.

The *Athenaeum*'s reference to Jane Eyre carries with it ironic complications as well. The reviewer remarks that Claxton's drawings are "such sketches as Jane Eyre would have made had *she painted instead of written*" (emphasis added). The reviewer seems to have forgotten that Jane Eyre *does* paint (as well as "write" her memoirs); it's Charlotte Brontë who only "writes." Additionally, the *Athenaeum* reviewer fails to note that Jane Eyre's actual artwork bears no resemblance whatsoever to Claxton's realistic sketches. The radical subject matter of the three watercolors has been conveniently ignored. The reviewer seems to be taking "Jane Eyre" as a symbol for a certain kind of aesthetic style—"sarcastic, yet playful" with a tinge of feminism. But Brontë has carefully shown Jane to be a very different kind of artist.

12. We saw in chapter 2 that Helen Graham, in *The Tenant of Wildfell Hall*, runs up against similar problems of subject matter—but her way out is different. She takes trips, moves through the landscape, discovers new locales rather than sitting at home painting the same thing again and again. Her persistent uprooting—her inability or disinclination to be domestically static—is both reflected in her art productions and made possible by them.

13. In further contrast to Ellis's paeans on the benefits of painting, Jane does not keep her productions to herself (though commanded to exhibit them to Rochester, Jane *further* exhibits them to the reader, in detail).

14. That Lewes considered Bertha to be a jarring, unrealistic element in the narrative

is painfully ironic when one considers the public gossip surrounding "Currer Bell's" dedication of *Jane Eyre* to Thackeray, who unfortunately *did* have a mad wife—though not in his attic. When Brontë heard of this circumstance, she wrote apologetically, "Well may it be said that fact is often stranger than fiction!"

15. Charlotte Brontë to W. S. Williams, quoted in *Jane Eyre,* Norton Critical Edition, 438.

16. Latmos (or Latmus) is the mountain where Endymion kept his sheep and where Selene, goddess of the moon, fell in love with him and cast a spell over him so that he would sleep and have vivid dreams of, among other things, herself (Hamilton 1999, 118).

17. Brontë revisits this kind of symbolic painting when Jane makes four sketches when she returns to visit the dying Aunt Reed. To occupy herself, she makes four vignettes very much in the manner of Bewick, whose volumes she has just seen "occupying their old place on the third shelf" (*Jane Eyre,* 200) of her Aunt's bookcase: "A glimpse of sea between two rocks; the rising moon, and a ship crossing its disk; a group of reeds and water-flags, and a naiad's head crowned with lotus-flowers, rising out of them; an elf sitting in a hedge-sparrow's nest, under a wreath of hawthorn-bloom" (204–5). Again, we can sort out these images symbolically with relative ease (which is not to say that my interpretation is correct or the only one, only that the images are rich enough to suggest narrative connections quickly). Most of the figures in the vignettes can be read as images of Jane or her experiences; the third sketch is particularly readable as Jane, the naiad crowned with flowers "rising out of" or above a group of reeds (i.e., Reeds). The final sketch of the elf, too, can be taken as an image of Jane herself, whom Rochester likens to all manner of supernatural things (fairy, sprite, etc.). This elf appears to have found some manner of flowery domestic bliss, albeit borrowed, temporary, and possibly prickly—as Jane's will turn out to be, because of her volatile and bigamous bridegroom—from another species.

18. In Shakespeare's *Lucrece,* Lucrece herself reenacts Aeneas's absorption in the same images; as Wells argues, "The poem seems to invite an appreciation of the difference between male and female absorption" (1997, 111). She asks, "What difference does it make that Lucrece views these pictures of fallen Troy *as a woman?*" (112; emphasis in original).

19. In addition to offering a "private release for her own emotions," as one critic has suggested (Byerly 1997, 95), Rochester's portrait also functions as a very *public* statement of Jane's erotic life for the benefit of Eliza and Georgiana, the Reed sisters, who hover in the background as Jane recalls and reproduces Rochester's features. Jane draws in a public place, in the sitting room with both Reed sisters present. She makes a show of "hiding" her drawing only *after* the sisters have seen it and commented on it. With a similar desire to make visual artifacts public, Jane chooses not to detail her three strange pictures to us at the time of their inception—a holiday at Lowood—but instead waits to unveil them before a more populous audience (namely, Rochester, in his drawing room).

20. Jane's earliest attempts at ekphrasis show this same use of the rhetorical device to articulate her own opinions rather than to provide an objective description. Of the Bewick illustrations, Jane says: "The two ships becalmed on a torpid sea, I believed to be marine phantoms. The fiend pinning down the thief's pack behind him, I passed over quickly: it was an object of terror. So was the blacked horned thing seated aloof on a rock, surveying a distant crowd surrounding a gallows" (40).

21. In Gezari's *Charlotte Brontë and Defensive Conduct*, for example, each of Brontë's novels becomes linked to a body: hands for *The Professor;* the stomach for *Shirley;* the mouth or voice for *Villette*. In *Jane Eyre*, it is the "prominence of the eye" that draws Gezari's attention, "the powerful move according to which *Jane Eyre* conceives of the threat to the 'eye' as a threat to the 'I.'" When Charlotte Brontë began *Jane Eyre*, her second novel, her father was being treated for cataracts, and the manuscript of *The Professor* had just been rejected and returned. Gezari writes, "*Jane Eyre* registers these two events—the denial of Brontë's vision as a writer and the threat to her father's sight—not only in one of its central events, the blinding of Rochester, but also in its representation of seeing, being the object of sight, and looking as the essential forms of relatedness at every stage of Jane Eyre's experience" (49). These real-life attacks on vision (literal and metaphoric) stimulated Brontë to a relentless shoring up of vision, such that Jane's vision comes to contain or obliterate all others in the course of the novel.

Chapter Four

1. The well-documented and varied problems encountered by governesses in the period were caused, in part, by this social prejudice against women who were forced to work. See Poovey 1988, chap. 4, and other works on governesses in the period.

2. For more detailed information on Howitt's life, see Nunn 1986, 19–25.

3. See Nunn 1986, 20. Painting was prevalent in almost all of Howitt's fictional work. Howitt's third novel, *School of Life*, tells the intertwining stories of two young male artists, Leonard Mordant and Johnny Wetherley, in their struggles to overcome class boundaries and family disapproval to become artists. There are no female visual artists in the novel; there is a woman writer, Agnes, a hard and unsympathetic character who lacks the imaginative and ethical force Howitt always gives to her painter-characters.

4. See for example Burke 1990, 11–12, and Kant 1992, §§20–22.

5. See Nunn 1987, 44–48 and n. 66.

6. See Lambourne for a discussion of design and craft in England during the Victorian period.

7. Charles Eastlake (1836–1906) was the nephew of Sir Charles Eastlake, who was president of the Royal Academy from 1855 to 1865. It was Sir Charles, not his nephew, who was married to Lady Elizabeth (Rigby) Eastlake, who wrote the scathing review of *Jane Eyre*.

8. One "danger" of Judaism for Daniel, at least according to the Christian leisure classes in the novel or among its Victorian readership, is that his embrace of his parents' culture is coded in the language of occupation. He might not "convert" officially to Judaism, but it does become, in every sense of the word, Deronda's "calling." He *professes* it, and it becomes his profession. Late in the novel, after Daniel has discovered his Jewish heritage, he visits Kalonymos to discover more about his grandfather. When Kalonymos asks, "What is your vocation?" Deronda is embarrassed, as he "did not feel it quite honest to allege his law-reading as a vocation." He answers, "I cannot say that I have any," and Kalonymos tells him, "Get one, get one. The Jew must be diligent" (*Deronda*, 620). Before this, he belongs (and yet does not quite belong) to the leisure class—and his idleness is ridiculed with a bitterness strange for Eliot, who otherwise lavishes praise on her young hero. When Daniel is rowing on the Thames, just before he finds Mirah, the narrator

begins dreamily, "He was in another sort of contemplative mood perhaps more common in the young men of our day—that of questioning whether it were worth while to take part in the battle of the world." But suddenly the tenor shifts from dreamy to derisive: "I mean, of course, the young men in whom the unproductive labour of questioning is sustained by three or four per cent on capital which somebody else has battled for" (156). Furthermore, the name that Deronda conspicuously does *not* carry, Mallinger, bears a resemblance to the word for sailors or workers who invented ailments or problems to shirk their work: "malingerers." One who malingers gets out of work by devious routes, and the Mallinger family represents the idle rich—though some of them, like Sir Hugo, are amiable. But Grandcourt—or Henleigh Mallinger Grandcourt to give him his full title—incarnates lethargy and represents what Deronda might possibly become if he does not find himself an occupation.

9. See Byerly 1989 for a discussion of the significance of music in *Daniel Deronda* and other works by Eliot. See Marshall 1999 for a reading that considers references to actors and the theater in the novel.

10. For Eliot's art historical knowledge, and a list of the artworks she saw, see Witemeyer 1979, chap. 2.

11. Sophia Andres (2005, 98–101) argues that Eliot was also influenced by the Pre-Raphaelites, particularly Burne-Jones, so that in *Daniel Deronda* she relied heavily on mythological figures, casting Gwendolyn as a series of mythological women that the Pre-Raphaelites had immortalized in paint (Pandora, the Magdalene, Proserpine, Medusa, etc.).

12. This summary of the relationship between the Meyrick brother and his sisters sounds surprisingly similar to the situation the Brontës found themselves in. Branwell was given money—at the expense of the sisters, who were forced to work for their living—to follow his inclination toward art. Branwell, like Hans Meyrick, did not succeed as an artist—the true story of Branwell's ill-fated attempts to enter the Royal Academy of Arts in London is unknown, but, as Jane Sellars writes, "The general theory is that he lost his confidence when faced with the realities of the great metropolis . . . and, having squandered his money in public houses, came home" (Sellars 1995, 77). Branwell became, before his death from opium and alcohol, an unsuccessful provincial portraitist—a branch of art we see Hans "descend" to at the close of *Daniel Deronda*. But Hans, unlike Branwell, shows no sign of becoming in any way debauched or a trial to his loving sisters; in Hans Meyrick, Eliot has revised the Brontë legend so that nothing occurs to mar the happiness of the sisters in art, even though Hans, like Branwell, never succeeds in becoming a truly talented painter.

13. Likening Eliot's prose to cabinet pictures is oddly ironic, considering it is a cabinet picture that terrorizes Gwendolyn at Offendene and disrupts her dramatic tableau.

14. But by using the word "charter" at the last, the Alcharisi subtly opens out the other side of the argument, as the word heightens the *political* implications of her statement. Eliot's fiction is filled with scenes surrounding the Chartist movement of the early 1800s; the Alcharisi's statement that her nature gave her a "charter" hints at the existence of a nascent "working *women's* charter" to supplement the better-known Working Men's Charter.

15. Note that the sister paints a scene from the popular *Arabian Nights* while the brother tackles classical history. Yet Hans's series of paintings are considerably less successful than his sister's works.

16. But pictures are also people: the art on the Meyrick's walls—the "glorious company of engravings" (312)—participates actively in the life of the women living between the walls. Literally the pictures do become "company" in the sense of guests or companions rather than an assemblage or group of things. When Klesmer takes his leave after approving Mirah's singing, the narrator paints the following picture of the scene:

> Thereupon Klesmer bowed round to the three sisters more grandly than they had ever been bowed to before. Altogether it was an amusing picture—the little room with so much of its diagonal taken up in Klesmer's magnificent bend to the small feminine figures like images a little less than life-size, *the grave Holbein faces on the walls, as many as were not otherwise occupied, looking hard at this stranger who by his face seemed a dignified contemporary of their own.* (416; emphasis added)

The "small feminine figures" of the Meyricks are here again made to seem doll-like, dwarfed by the enormity of Klesmer's genius. But, lest he entirely overwhelm the tiny Meyrick family, the "grave Holbein faces" of the Meyrick's engravings look upon Klesmer and, by claiming kinship to him, draw this "real" individual into a canvas-life, much the way the narrator does when she prefaces this scene with, "altogether it was an amusing picture." The Holbein faces aren't the only faces enclosed within a frame: Klesmer shares this fate as well.

17. When her family loses their income, Gwendolyn forms the romantic plan of going on the stage. She summons Klesmer for advice and tells him, "We have lost all our fortune . . . I must get my own bread. . . . The only way I can think of is to be an actress—to go on the stage. But of course I should like to take a high position, and I thought . . . to study singing also. . . . Naturally, I should wish to take as high a rank as I can" (215). She has no concern for art, of course—her desires are for money and fame. Klesmer responds with the language of True Art, the exaltation of struggling without return for an "inward vocation." Gwendolyn, who cannot believe she doesn't possess all talents, insists, "I don't mind going up hill. It will be easier than the dead level of being a governess" (217).

18. For an introduction to Oliphant and the recent critical debates, see Losano 2002. Portions of this chapter are drawn from that article. Also see Elisabeth Jay's impressive critical biography, *Mrs. Oliphant: A Fiction to Herself* (1995).

19. The system of political economy that Lucilla purports to follow might not, in the novel's first volume, be recognized as political at all—though certainly "economy" is a good metaphor for Lucilla's management of Carlingford's social resources. Lucilla's political economy is derived roughly—very roughly, and very ironically in parts—from the well-known theories of Comte (as translated and popularized by Harriet Martineau). Comte sought to apply the methods of experimentation and observation used in the sciences to disciplines not traditionally considered scientific: religion, philosophy, social science. Social reform, he believed, could be achieved only through the scientific method. At first glance, Lucilla might seem the ultimate utilitarian, and hence influenced as well by the theories of John Stuart Mill or Bentham: she is always considering the greater social good, as when Mr. Cavendish switches his attentions to Barbara, and the women of Carlingford urge Lucilla to oust Barbara from the "evenings." Lucilla refuses and remarks placidly: "After all, there are thousands and thousands of gentlemen,

but it is not so easy to find a voice that goes with mine. All my masters always said it was a quite peculiar second I wanted; and suppose Barbara is foolish, that is not to say I should forget *my* duties" (110). But one would not attribute a laissez-faire position to Miss Marjoribanks; her theories are utilitarian only in the sense that she believes she, as monarch, can provide the greatest happiness for the greatest number. When a beggar woman approaches the Marjoribanks' house in Grange Lane, Lucilla refuses to dispense money, "for that was contrary to those principles of political economy which she had studied with such success [at school]" (54). Instead, Lucilla says to the beggar woman, "If you are honest and want to work, I will try to find you something to do" (54).

20. Lucilla's great plan for Carlingford, the narrator is careful to imply, involves little more than organizing "Thursday Evenings"—social gatherings of the town's more well-to-do members at which music, food, and talk are enjoyed. Lucilla thinks that she has made great strides in her mission, but the narrative gives the reader no real markers of any great success. In fact, Lucilla's endeavors are very often marked by failure of one kind or another—individual humans (like Mr. Cavendish, who cannot squelch his attraction for Barbara Lake) turn out to be just beyond her manipulation. She has succeeded, however, in impressing on the citizens of Carlingford the *belief* that she is their sovereign; she has succeeded in acquiring power itself, if not in transforming actual events or individuals (although she does, in essence, influence the outcome of a parliamentary election—an event that should have profound significance but is drawn rather irrelevantly by Oliphant's satirical pen). But no matter the actual tally of success or failure, Lucilla *feels* that she has accomplished great things; and when, at the end of her career, Lucilla prepares to marry and leave Carlingford, she disdains the town's fate: "They will go back to their old ridiculous parties, as if they had never seen anything better. . . . That will be the end of it all, after one has slaved like a—like a woman in a mill!" (317). Here Lucilla, daughter of a prosperous doctor, compares herself to a factory worker, and compares the "work" of organizing genteel parties with manual labor; and other wealthy women in the novel also bemoan their lot as laborers: Mrs. Centum asks: "I should like to know what they [men] would do if they had what we have to go through: to look after all the servants—and they are always out of their sense at Christmas—and to see that the children don't have too much pudding, and to support all the noise. The holidays are the hardest work a poor woman can have" (109). At the close of the novel, Lucilla plans to continue her career as a social innovator after her marriage. When Lucilla and her betrothed (her cousin Tom Marjoribanks—Lucilla will not change her name upon marriage, significantly) are discussing their future, she remarks, "The thing that we both want is something to do." And he replies quickly, "That is what *I* want. But as for you, Lucilla, you shall do nothing but enjoy yourself, and take care of yourself. The idea of *you* wanting something to do!" Whereupon "Miss Marjoribanks regarded her betrothed with mild and affectionate contempt" and tells him, "Do you know that I have always been doing something, and responsible for something, all my life?" (315). Lucilla and Tom pool their money and buy the derelict estate—Marchbanks—which has a village near it that needs Lucilla's managerial touch. She dreams of her new occupation as the novel ends: "It gave her the liveliest satisfaction to think of all the disorder and disarray of the Marchbank village. Her fingers itched to be at it—to set all the crooked things straight, and clean away the rubbish, and set everything, as she said, on a sound foundation" (321).

21. Lucilla is often accused of acting a part: "'She is such an actor, you know,' Barbara said; 'she will never give in to let you know how she is feeling'" (166). Barbara thinks

Lucilla must be heartbroken by the loss of Mr. Cavendish, when in fact, Lucilla is characterized by a sincerity so rigid as to be unintentionally humorous.

22. The young artist's name suggest her intimate connection to the art world. The name "Rose Lake" is the name of a paint color—similar to Rose madder—which would have been regularly used in Oliphant's time. See *The Dictionary of Art,* vol. 18, ed Jane Turner, entry under "Lake."

23. " À l'Académie," *Journal des femmes* 8 (July 1892): 1, quoted in Garb 1994, 43.

Chapter Five

1. See, for example, the fictional treatments of her life by Susan Vreeland (2002) and Alexandra Lapierre (1998), as well as the film versions (1998 dir. Merlet, and 1992 dir. Clarkson) of her life. Anna Banti is also discussed in Wendy Wasserstein's play *The Heidi Chronicles* (1988).

2. The *Companion* was recently revised to become *The Oxford Dictionary of Art.* The third edition, published in 2004, offers a new entry for Kauffman which includes much of the same information but adds a list of names of "other distinguished men who were charmed by her" (373). It also claims that her large paintings have "prettiness" and "great charm" but are "insipid," and that "she was much more successful with ladylike decorative vignettes" (373). No doubts about her gender here.

The 2000 *Yale Dictionary of Art and Artists* runs along similar lines. Kauffman's entry has no references to her appearance—but still mentions her two marriages. Likewise, the entry for Frida Kahlo includes the following information: "She had met Rivera when he was painting a mural at her school; in 1929 she married him and though their married life swung between passion and conflict and both had relationships outside it (in 1939 they divorced; in 1940 they remarried), they were emotionally dependent upon each other" (ed. Langmuir and Lynton 2000, 362). Rivera's entry, on the other hand, mentions Kahlo in this manner: "In 1928 he married the painter Frida Kahlo" (2000, 595). The love lives of women artists obviously remain a matter of abiding interest.

3. The staging of the choice itself nods toward the well-known (at the time) allegory of Hercules choosing between Vice and Virtue. The scene was painted frequently and was used by Shaftesbury as *the* allegorical representation of art itself, which in his aesthetic system had to choose between private aims (Vice) and the public good (Virtue) (See Barrell 1986 and Shaftesbury 1710). In her self-portrait, the real Kauffman places herself in the idealized position of Hercules; and while neither music nor painting is explicitly Vice, she still suggests by the classical allusion that her choice between media is a noble and (possibly) immortalizing one. See Burlin 1986 for an excellent discussion of how women writers and painters used this scene in their works.

4. For brief discussions of Ritchie's influence on Woolf, see Trodd 2000; Gerin 1981, 241–43, 279–84; and Mackay 2001, 82. Fuller exploration of the literary relationship between these two writers will hopefully be undertaken as Ritchie scholarship increases.

5. Ritchie may also have been attracted to Kauffman because of her (Ritchie's) close friendship with Julia Margaret Cameron, the photographer. Cameron's biography does not in the least resemble Kauffman's, but it is possible that Ritchie's interest in Kauffman as a female visual artist was strengthened by her interest in her friend's profession.

6. Historical fiction and so-called "romantic historiography" (Simmons 1990, 53) peaked in the 1830s and 1840s and was in serious decline by the 1860s, due in part to the previous deluge (which sated the reading public), in part to the rise of realism, and in part to a new kind of professional historiography which came into vogue in the second half of the nineteenth century (ibid., 58). Although writers were still writing historical novels in the 1870s, it was rare: outright history was more popular.

7. Trodd writes that *A Book of Sibyls* begins with a kind of "ghost story, and invokes the supernatural throughout as a means to describe the occult presence of women in literary history, the difficulty of evaluating its traces, and her worries about women's relation to the official literary tradition" (2000, 196). Ritchie's many memoirs and biographies made her "increasingly associated with the re-creation of the lives of dead writers" (ibid.). Ritchie's ghost story in *Sibyls,* Trodd argues, initiates a long tradition—from Ritchie and Oliphant to Virginia Woolf and Alice Walker—of figuring past women artists as occult presences, working in secret and hidden from history.

8. Anne Seymour Damer (1749–1828) was a well-known cultural figure. The caption of the cartoon, placed on the pedestal ("A Model to make a boy from"), suggests that Damer's well-placed chisel is causing the cartoonist considerable anxiety.

9. Ritchie was acquainted with Ruskin personally; they had several meetings and were correspondents. Ritchie also wrote an article on Ruskin, first published in *Cornhill* and *Harpers* and later in book form in *Records of Tennyson, Ruskin and Browning.* She had attempted to write something on Ruskin earlier but was incapable of it—certainly he was influential enough in her life and thinking to be a force to be reckoned with.

10. Jeremy Maas's excellent survey of the subject, *Victorian Painters* (1969), has a brief discussion of portraiture, as does John Walker's historical overview *Portraits: 5,000 Years* (1983, chap. 9).

11. For obvious reasons, Kauffman's life in England, for example, provides the bulk of Ritchie's book—when in fact it was just over a decade. Additionally, the character of "Lady W—," based on the real historical figure Lady Wentworth, becomes a fully realized, detailed figure whose machinations have serious plot repercussions in Ritchie's narrative, while in other sources she is either mentioned briefly or elided entirely.

12. For more on Dicksee, see Cherry 1993, 2000.

Chapter Six

1. Dinah Maria Mulock Craik (1826–1887) wrote fiction, periodical essays, and children's literature. She believed in equality in marriage and was a champion of many women's causes. Her book, *A Woman's Thoughts about Woman* (1858), argued for increased job opportunities for women. See Mitchell 1993.

2. Charlotte Mary Yonge (1823–1901) wrote over two hundred books. Influenced heavily by Keble and the Oxford Movement, Yonge's fiction emphasizes middle-class domesticity, the importance of spiritual discipline, and family affection. Though generally conservative, her novels often show intermittent veins of more radical views on the nature of the family and the role of women in society. See Mare and Percival 1948.

3. Perhaps because of their already monstrous state, women were thought to influence the physical appearance of their offspring when this appearance was unusual

in any way. (Thus we find the famous traditions of the pregnant woman who looked at a picture of John the Baptist in furs giving birth to an excessively hairy child or the folk tradition that a harelip on a child was caused by the mother seeing a rabbit during pregnancy.) Serious deformities were thought to be divine punishment for some parental crime—the most famous Greek cripple, Hephaistos (Vulcan), was the product of Hera's sole creation, in revenge against Zeus for giving birth to Athena all by himself. Hera's hubristic parthenogenesis, in an era when the male seed was though to be the primary creator of new life, results in a deformed offspring. But Hephaistos became an artisan, a skilled worker in valuable materials. His artistic talent was thought to be restitution for his physical imperfections—and the famous myth in which he traps Aphrodite in Ares' arms symbolizes the triumph of his arts over the lusts of the more perfect divinities (see Garland 1995, chap. 3).

4. Eighteenth-century aesthetics continued the idea of deformity as incompleteness. In Edmund Burke's *Philosophical Enquiry,* for example, the issue of deformity arises in relation to his struggles to define beauty. Proportion, says Burke, has nothing to do with beauty; the common belief that beauty lies in proportion stems

> from a wrong idea of the relation which deformity bears to beauty, to which it has been considered as the opposite; on this principle it was concluded, that where the causes of deformity were removed, beauty must naturally and necessarily be introduced. This I believe is a mistake. For *deformity* is opposed, not to beauty, but to the *compleat, common form.* If one of the legs of a man be found shorter than the other, the man is deformed; because there is something wanting to complete the whole idea we form of a man. So if the back be humped, the man is deformed; because his back has an unusual figure, and what carries with it the idea of some disease or misfortune. (93; emphasis in original)

Oddly, we see that the two disfigurements we are dealing with, the ones unified in Jenny Wren, seem to be the most common illustrations for deformity—"queer" legs and humped backs. These deformities are coded not as "ugly" (opposed to beautiful) but rather as "incomplete."

5. Many writers have explored this connection between women and deformity; Craik and Yonge inherit a rich tradition of representations of deformity, gender, and art from the eighteenth century and from early Romanticism. For example, in Sarah Scott's feminist utopia *Millenium* [sic] *Hall,* published in 1762, a colony of the deformed and disfigured people find refuge and occupation in the enclave Millenium Hall, a retreat from capitalist patriarchy run by six women who renounce marriage and motherhood in favor of "sisterhood" and the arts. The proximity of the deformed and the female correlates the two as similarly deviant from the perfections of the masculine; at Millenium Hall, however, the aesthetic model is transformed and deformity becomes an aesthetic virtue, while beauty is despised. As Felicity Nussbaum writes, "at Millenium Hall the culture's devaluation of deformity is reversed" (1997, 166). The unmarried, the disfigured, the independent woman—these become icons for perfection in this feminist utopia.

6. This accretion of deformity makes these characters almost monstrous. Jeffrey Jerome Cohen 1996 offers "Seven Theses" postulating the position of the monster—

anything or anyone deformed, disfigured, outside the boundaries of the normal—in culture. The seven theses are:

1. The Monster's Body Is a Cultural Body (that is, monstrosity is a cultural construct)
2. The Monster Always Escapes (cannot be pinned down, permanently captured)
3. The Monster Is the Harbinger of Category Crisis (monsters evade categorization)
4. The Monster Dwells at the Gates of Difference
5. The Monster Polices the Borders of the Possible (monsters serve as visible cultural borders, representatives of boundaries not to be crossed lest we become like them)
6. Fear of the Monster Is Really a Kind of Desire (the repulsive/seductive structure)
7. The Monster Stands at the Threshold of Becoming (by their difference, monsters incite change)

The disfigured artist-heroines in this chapter support all seven of these theses. They are "monsters" in their deformity, and in their marginal cultural status; they are also monsters because they fracture gender codes and attack the very foundation of aesthetics.

For other discussion of the monstrous, the deformed, or the grotesque in literature, see Harpman 1982 and Russo 1995.

7. As, significantly, does another *Jane Eyre* take-off, *Hester's Sacrifice,* which contains the same plain heroine-artist pitted against a cast-off West Indian wife. In this 1866 novel by Eliza Tabor, however, both women drown together in a shipwreck (caused by a fire started by the West Indian wife); the "hero" survives and no one lives happily ever after.

8. When we consider his progeny, we must call into question the "purity" of the father's blood. Indeed, Craik offers a powerful critique of paternal purity. Olive's mother may be represented as physically impure (and indeed she herself becomes disabled—blind—in her middle age), and Christal's mother may be "impure" because of her racial difference, but both mothers are finally represented as victims of Angus Rothesay's so-called pure blood. On the one hand, his racial purity is linked to the depredations of imperialism; on the other, his physical perfection is not balanced by human warmth or sympathy (which his "impure" child and wife possess).

9. Hemans is another woman writer—like Caroline Norton, Anna Jameson, or Margaret Oliphant—who was forced by circumstances to support herself and her children with the proceeds of her writing. When she was in her teens, her father left the family; several years later Hemans's own husband followed suit, leaving her with five children to support.

10. Kauffman (Swiss, 1741–1807) is discussed in chapter 5. Prosperia Rossi (sculptor, Italian Renaissance), was the only Italian woman artist to become famous for works in marble (she is the subject of a poem by F. Hemans). Elisabetta Sirani (Italian, 1638–1665) opened her own school for women painters; her early death caused her entire native city of Bologna to go into mourning.

11. For a well-documented and detailed(!) explication of the historical connection between women and the particular, see Schor 1987, esp. 11–22.

Chapter Seven

1. For more on women artists in the period 1880–1920, see Cherry 1993, 73–77, 86–95. See also Elliott and Wallace 1994.

2. Louisa, Marchioness of Waterford, was an amateur watercolorist and illustrator who exhibited frequently at the Grosvenor Gallery and other venues. For more information on Lady Waterford, see Nunn 1987, 174–86. Annie Robinson Swynnerton was one of the founders of the Manchester Society for Woman Painters in 1876 and exhibited briefly at the Royal Academy. Henrietta Ward, wife of E. M. Ward (a Royal Academy member), was a popular artist and art teacher who painted both domestic and historical subjects (see Cherry 1993, 93–130). Laura Alma-Tadema was the wife of Lawrence Alma-Tadema; she painted primarily domestic subjects (see Cherry 1993, 41–43).

3. For more on the Macdonald sisters, see Cherry 1993, 203–7; Helland 1996; Marsh and Nunn 1989; and Burkhauser 1990.

4. Other New Women painters of the period tackled the problem of feminine sexuality by controlling their own *self*-representation, crafting their images as resolutely professional. Margaret Foster Richardson's self-portrait, *A Motion Picture* (1912), suggests the unfettered possibility represented by the New Woman painter. She is ready for work, brushes in hand, moving toward the light. The painter has effaced all markers of feminine sexuality: her smock and severe collar are androgynous; she wears glasses and has drawn-back hair, in contrast to the Gibson Girl poufs of the period. She strides, showing purpose; her glance at the viewer doesn't break her motion. Similarly, Dorothy Carleton Smyth's *Self-Portrait* (1921) shows her working, smocked; she will have none of the ornate outfits we see in earlier self-portraits or portraits of women painters, in which the artist's sexuality was still present for appreciation (compare, for example, the painter's outrageous outfit in *Self-Portrait with Two Pupils* by Adelaide Labille-Guiard from 1785. Would an artist paint in blue satin?).

5. Ward was the granddaughter of Dr. Thomas Arnold (the headmaster of Rugby) and the niece of Matthew Arnold. Her husband, Thomas Humphry Ward, was a tutor at Oxford and later art critic for the *Times*; her husband's writing career seems to have contributed to her knowledge of and interest in the visual arts.

6. For more discussion of Ward's relationship to feminism and her anti-suffrage activities, see Sutherland's excellent biography of Ward (1990, 301–6) and Sutton-Ramspeck (1999).

7. Elsmere to Patricia Meyer Spacks's use of Ward's *Robert Elsmere* as a test case in a discussion of books which were once bestsellers but are now considered "boring." Spacks argues, among other things, that shifts of taste in literature "tell us what ideas we can no longer afford to admit to consciousness, as well as what forms of literary embodiment have come to seem meaningless" (1994, 289). Ward's particular treatment of the professional woman artist fits into precisely this category for twentieth- and twenty-first century feminist academic readers (who would be the main ones to recuperate and re-read Ward).

8. The character of Elise Delaunay was modeled on the Russian émigré Marie Bashkirtseff, a young artist whose extraordinary journal and letters were known to Ward. See Collister 1984.

9. Lewis's reading equally overplays Ward's sympathy for David; Lewis argues that Elise is punished "for the pain she has caused David" (2003, 239). However, Ward tells

us that David, after steeping himself in French and German Romantic literature, travels to France ready and willing to indulge himself in a grand, tortured passion—which is precisely what he gets. His adoration of Elise is founded not on what we might call "true love" or rational knowledge of his loved object, but rather on a desire for a fantasy-based, essentially fictional woman.

10. Buying a poor woman's artworks behind her back is also in part a structural counterpart to another common narrative device: buying a poor woman a piano. Frank Churchill does it for Jane Fairfax in *Emma;* Colonel Brandon does the same for Marianne Dashwood in *Sense and Sensibility;* and in *Little Women,* the wealthy Mr. Lawrence gives a piano to the shy Beth March. In all these instances, the gift is obviously based on economic superiority, but the action also implies masculine control over female creativity. Where visual artworks are concerned, the wealthy man cannot control the woman's production, so he limits, instead, her access to the market. In both cases—music and painting—the result of the male characters' action is to ensure that the artistic production of the women serves male pleasure. Churchill and Brandon do not offer pianos to their beloveds so that they can practice and become famous public musicians, but rather so that they can entertain within the home.

11. Ward's oeuvre offers other instances of women who dream of becoming professional artists of one kind or another. In *Robert Elsmere,* Robert's pious wife Catherine's sister Rose trains as a professional musician—which serves, as Spacks writes, "mainly to make her attractive to London society and to draw two men to her" (1994, 293). Rose marries in the end, but as with Lydia and Elise, the reader is not at all certain that the marriage will be a happy one. Rose "has clearly established her longing for more than ordinary social life has to offer" (ibid., 296); her artistic temperament and training would seem to make her marriage destined for difficulty if not failure. Curiously, the artistic pretensions of one of the few writers in Ward's work, Lydia's sister Susan in *The Mating of Lydia,* who is attempting to write a verse tragedy (possibly in Greek; Ward is unclear), are consistently dismissed. Susan has "gone overboard," so to speak; she has become a suffragette and hence (Ward suggests) can neither produce good art nor become a suitably romantic female character for fiction.

Coda

1. See White 2005 for excellent discussions of these novels and other twentieth-century fiction featuring women painters as characters.

2. *Artemisia* (film), directed by Agnes Merlet (Miramax, 1998); television production, directed by Adrienne Clarkson (Canadian Broadcasting Company, 1998).

3. For discussions of the fictionalized versions of Artemisia's life, see Benedetti and Elizabeth Cohen.

WORKS CITED

Abel, Elizabeth. 1980 "Redefining the Sister Arts: Baudelaire's Response to the Art of Delacroix." *Critical Inquiry* 6, no. 3 (Spring): 363–84.
Adorno, Theodor. 1984. *Aesthetic Theory.* Translated by C. Lenhardt. London: Routledge and Kegan Paul. German original, 1970.
Agamben, Georgio. 1999. *The Man without Content.* Translated by Georgia Albert. Stanford, Calif.: Stanford University Press. Italian original, 1994.
Alcott, Louisa May. 1868–69. *Little Women.* New York: W.W. Norton, 2003.
———. 1870. *An Old-Fashioned Girl.* New York: Grosset and Dunlap, 1974.
Alcott, May. 1879. *Studying Art Abroad. And How to Do It Cheaply.* Boston: Roberts Bros.
Alexander, Christine, and Jane Sellars. 1995. *The Art of the Brontës.* Cambridge: Cambridge University Press.
Altick, Richard. 1978. *The Shows of London.* Cambridge: Belknap Press.
Amigoni, David. 1993. *Victorian Biography.* New York: St. Martin's.
Andres, Sophia. 2002. "Wilkie Collins' Challenges to Pre-Raphaelite Gender Constructs." In *A Companion to the Victorian Novel.* Edited by William Baker and Ken Womack, 365–76. Westport, CN: Greenwood.
———. 2005. *The Pre-Raphaelite Art of the Victorian Novel: Narrative Challenges to Visual Gendered Boundaries.* Columbus: The Ohio State University Press.
Anonymous. 1879. "Contemporary Literature: Biography, Travel and Sport." *Blackwood's Edinburgh Magazine* 125 (April): 482–506.
Anonymous. 1810. "Observations on Fancy Work, as Affording an Agreeable Occupation for Ladies." *Ackermann's Repository of the Arts, Literature and Commerce* 3, no. 17, June.
Anonymous reviewer. 1894. "Glasgow School of Art." *Glasgow Evening News*, August 18.

Armstrong, Isobel. 2000. *The Radical Aesthetic*. Oxford: Blackwell.
Armstrong, Nancy. 1990. *Desire and Domestic Fiction*. New York: Oxford University Press.
———. 1999. *Fiction in the Age of Photography: The Legacy of British Realism*. Cambridge: Harvard University Press.
Apter, Emily, and William Pietz, eds. 1993. *Fetishism as Cultural Discourse*. Ithaca: Cornell University Press.
Aristotle. *Generation of Animals*. Translated by A. L. Peck. Cambridge, MA: Harvard University Press, 1963.
Atwood, Margaret. 1998. *Cat's Eye*. New York: Anchor Books.
Austen, Jane. 1816. *Emma*. Reprint, edited by James Kinsley. Oxford: Oxford University Press, 1971.
———. *Sense and Sensibility*. 1811. Reprint, edited by Ros Ballister. New York: Penguin Books, 2003.
Bal, Mieke, 1991. *Reading Rembrandt: Beyond the Word/Image Opposition*. Cambridge: Cambridge University Press.
Banti, Anna. 1947. *Artemisia*. Translated by Shirly D'Ardia Caracciolo. Lincoln, NE: Bison Books, 2003.
Barker, Deborah. 2000. *Aesthetics and Gender in American Literature: Portraits of the Woman Artist*. Lewisburg, PA: Bucknell University Press.
Barrell, John. 1986. *The Political Theory of Painting from Reynolds to Hazlitt*. New Haven: Yale University Press.
Barrett, Dorothea. 1989. *Vocation and Desire: George Eliot's Heroines*. London: Routledge.
Barrett, Michele. 1992. "Max Raphael and the Question of Aesthetics." In *The Politics of Pleasure: Aesthetics and Cultural Theory*. Edited by Stephen Regan, 33–58. Buckingham, England: Open University Press.
Bashkertshiff, Marie. 1919. *The Diary of a Young Artist*. Translated by Mary J. Serrano. New York: Dutton.
Battersby, Christine. 1989. *Gender and Genius: Towards a Feminist Aesthetics*. Bloomington: Indiana University Press.
Baudelaire, Charles. 1995. *The Painter of Modern Life and other Essays*. Translated by Jonathan Mayne. London: Phaidon Press. French original, 1863.
Baumgarten, Alexander Gottlieb. 1735. *Reflections on Poetry*. Translated by Karl Aschenbrenner and William Holther. Berkeley: University of California Press, 1954.
Beale, Sophia. 1908. *Recollections of a Spinster Aunt*. London: Heinemann.
Beaumont, Averil (Margaret Raine Hunt). 1874. *Thornicroft's Model*. 2 vols. Leipzig: Tauchnitz.
Belsey, Catherine. 2002. *Critical Practice*. New York: Routledge.
Benedetti, Laura. 1999. "Reconstructing Artemisia: Twentieth-Century Images of a Woman Artist." *Comparative Literature* 51, no. 1 (Winter): 42–61.
Benjamin, Walter. 2006. *The Writer of Modern Life: Essays on Charles Baudelaire*. Translated by Howard Eiland, Edmund Jephcot, Rodney Livingstone, and Harry Zohn. London: Belknap Press. First published, 1938.
Bennett, Tony. 1987. "Really Useless Knowledge: A Political Critique of Aesthetics." *Literature and History* 12: 38–57.
Berg, Margaret Mary. 1987. "*The Tenant of Wildfell Hall:* Anne Brontë's *Jane Eyre*." *Victorian Newsletter* 71: 10–15.

Bermingham, Ann. 1992. "The Origin of Painting and the Ends of Art: Wright of Derby's *Corinthian Maid*." In *Painting and the Politics of Culture*. Edited by John Barrell, 62–83. Oxford: Oxford University Press.

———. 2000. *Learning to Draw: Studies in the Cultural History of a Polite and Useful Art*. New Haven: Yale University Press for the Paul Mellon Centre for Studies in British Art.

Bersani, Leo. 1969. *A Future for Astyanax: Character and Desire in Literature*. New York: Columbia University Press.

Bicknell, Peter, and Jane Munro. 1988. *Gilpin to Ruskin: Drawing Masters and Their Manuals*. Cambridge: Fitzwilliam Museum; Grasmere: Wordsworth Museum.

Blake, Kathleen. 1995. "*Armgart*—George Eliot on the Woman Artist." In *Victorian Women Poets: A Critical Reader*. Edited by Angela Leighton, 82–87. Oxford: Blackwell.

Bodichon, Barbara Leigh Smith. 1857. *Women and Work*. London: Bosworth and Harrison.

Bohls, Elizabeth. 1995. *Women Travel Writers and the Language of Aesthetics, 1716–1818*. Cambridge: Cambridge University Press.

Booth, Alison. 1991. "Incomplete Stories: Womanhood and Artistic Ambition in *Daniel Deronda* and *Between the Acts*." In *Writing the Woman Artist: Essays on Poetics, Politics and Portraiture*. Edited by Suzanne Jones, 107–32. Philadelphia: University of Pennsylvania Press.

Boucherett, Jessie. 1881. "Gallery of Lady Artists." *Englishwoman's Review* 15:151.

Boumelha, Penny. 1998. "Realism and the Ends of Feminism." In *Grafts: Feminist Cultural Criticism*. Edited by Susan Sheridan. London: Verso Press.

Bowie, Theodore Robert. 1950. *The Painter in French Fiction*. University of North Carolina Studies in the Romance Languages and Literatures. Chapel Hill: University of North Carolina Press.

Brantlinger, Patrick. 1998. *The Reading Lesson: The Threat of Mass Literacy in Nineteenth-Century British Fiction*. Bloomington: Indiana University Press.

Brontë, Anne. 1847. *Agnes Grey*. Reprint. Edited by Angeline Goreau. Penguin Classics. New York: Penguin Books, 1988.

———. 1848. *The Tenant of Wildfell Hall*. Reprint. Edited by Winifred Gerin. Penguin Classics. New York: Penguin Books, 1979.

———. *The Tenant of Wildfell Hall*. VHS. Directed by Mike Barker. British Broadcasting Corporation, 1997.

Brontë, Charlotte. 1848. *Jane Eyre*. Reprint. Edited by Richard Dunn. Norton Critical Edition. New York: Norton, 1987

———. 1849. *Shirley*. Edited by Margaret Smith. Oxford: Oxford University Press, 1979.

———. 1853. *Villette*. Edited by Helen Cooper. New York: Penguin Classics, 2004.

———. 1857. *The Professor*. Edited by Margaret Smith and Herbert Rosegarten. Oxford: Oxford University Press, 1987.

———. 1995. *The Letters of Charlotte Brontë*. Vol. 1. Edited by Margaret Smith. Oxford: Clarendon Press.

Brontë, Emily. 1847. *Wuthering Heights*. Reprint. Edited by Richard Dunn. New York: Norton, 2002.

Brooks, Peter. 1993. *Body Work: Objects of Desire in Modern Narrative*. Cambridge: Harvard University Press.

Brookshaw, George, (pseud.). 1801. *A New Treatise on Flower Painting; or, Every Lady Her Own Drawing Master*. London: Riley.
Brunton, Mary. 1810. *Self-Control*. Reprint, London: Pandora Press, 1986.
Burke, Edmund. 1757. *A Philosophical Enquiry into the Origin of Our Ideas of the Sublime and Beautiful*. Reprint. Oxford: Oxford University Press, 1990.
Burkhauster, Jude. 1990. *Glasgow Girls: Women in Art and Design, 1880–1920*. Edinburgh: Canongate.
Burlin, Katrin R. 1986. "'At the Crossroads': Sister Authors and the Sister Arts." In *Fetter'd or Free: British Women Novelists, 1670–1815*. Edited by Mary Anne Schofield and Cecilia Macheski, 60–84. Athens: University of Ohio Press.
Butler, Elizabeth Thompson. 1922. *An Autobiography*. London: Constable.
Byerly, Alison. 1989. "The Language of the Soul: George Eliot and Music." *Nineteenth-Century Literature* 44, no. 1 (June 1989): 1–17.
———. 1997. *Realism, Representation, and the Arts in Nineteenth-Century Literature*. Cambridge: Cambridge University Press.
Caird, Mona. 1894. *The Daughters of Danaus*. Reprint, with an afterword by Margaret Morganroth Gullette. New York: The Feminist Press, 1989.
Carlyle, Thomas. 1832. "Biography." *Fraser's Magazine* 27, no. 5: 253–60.
Carnell, Rachel. 1998. "Feminism and the Public Sphere in Anne Brontë's *The Tenant of Wildfell Hall*." *Nineteenth-Century Literature* 53: 1–24.
Casteras, Susan P. 1992. "'The Necessity of a Name': Portrayals and Betrayals of Victorian Women Artists." In *Gender and Discourse in Victorian Literature and Art*. Edited by Antony H. Harrison and Beverly Taylor, 207–32. Dekalb: Northern Illinois University Press.
Caws, Mary Ann. 1989. *The Art of Interference: Stressed Readings in Verbal and Visual Texts*. Princeton, NJ: Princeton University Press.
Chadwick, Whitney. 1996. *Women, Art, and Society*. London: Thames and Hudson.
Cherry, Deborah. 1993. *Painting Women: Victorian Women Artists*. London: Routledge.
———. 1995. "Women Artists and the Politics of Feminism 1850–1900." In *Women in the Victorian Art World*. Edited by Clarissa Campbell Orr, 49–69. Manchester: Manchester University Press.
———. 2000. *Beyond the Frame: Feminism and Visual Culture, Britain 1850–1900*. London: Routledge.
Chitham, Edward. 1979. *The Poems of Anne Brontë: A New Text and Commentary*. New York: Palgrave Macmillan.
Cholmondeley, Mary. 1899. *Red Pottage*. New York: Harper and Brothers.
Chopin, Kate. 1899. *The Awakening*. New York: Avon Books, 1982.
Christ, Carol, and John Jordan, eds. 1995. *Victorian Literature and the Victorian Visual Imagination*. Berkeley: University of California Press.
Claxton, Florence. 1871. *The Adventures of a Woman in Search of Her Rights*. London: The Graphotyping Co.
Clayton, Ellen. 1876. *English Female Artists*. 2 vols. London: Tinsley Brothers.
Codell, Julie. 2003. *The Victorian Artist: Artists' Lifewritings in Britain, 1870–1910*. Cambridge: Cambridge University Press.
Cohen, Elisabeth. 2000. "The Trials of Artemisia Gentileschi: A Rape as History." *Sixteenth Century Journal* 31, no. 1 (Spring): 47–75.
Cohen, Jeffrey Jerome. 1996. *Monster Theory: Reading Culture*. Minneapolis: University of Minnesota Press.

Collins, Wilkie. 2003. *The Woman in White*. New York: Penguin Books.
Collister, Peter. 1984. "Marie Bashkirtseff in Fiction: Edmond de Goncourt and Mrs. Humphry Ward." *Modern Philology* 82: 53–69.
———. 1985. "After 'Half a Century': Mrs. Humphry Ward on Charlotte and Emily Brontë." *English Studies* 5: 410–431.
Conrad, Joseph. *Arrows of Gold*. Philadelphia: University of Pennsylvania Press, 2004.
Corelli, Marie. 1900. *The Master Christian*. New York: Grosset, Dunlap.
Cotes, Mrs. Everard. 1894. *A Daughter of Today*. Toronto: The Toronto News Company.
Craik, Dinah Mulock. *Olive*. 1850. Reprint. Edited by Cora Kaplan. Oxford: Oxford University Press, 1996.
———. 1860. *A Woman's Thoughts about Woman*. Leipzig: Tauchnitz.
Culler, Jonathan. 1982. *On Deconstruction*. Ithaca: Cornell University Press.
Denisoff, Denis. 1999. "Lady in Green with Novel: The Gendered Economics of the Visual Arts and Mid-Victorian Women's Writing." In *Victorian Women Writers and the Woman Question*. Edited by Nicola Diane Thompson, 151–69. Cambridge: Cambridge University Press.
de Staël, Mme. 1807. *Corinne*. Translated by Sylvia Raphael. Oxford: Oxford University Press, 1998.
Dickens, Charles. 1850. *David Copperfield*. Edited by Jeremy Tambling. New York: Penguin Classics, 1997.
———. 1857. *Little Dorrit*. Reprint. Edited by John Holloway. London: Penguin Books, 1985.
———. 1865. *Our Mutual Friend*. Reprint. New York: Bantam, 1990.
di Rossi, Giovanni. 1810. Vita di Giovanni di Rossi. Florence: n. pub.
Dixon, Ella Hepworth. 1894. *The Story of a Modern Woman*. Reprint. Edited by Valerie Behlbaum. Longon: Ashgate Publishing, 2005.
Dodd, Sara M. 1995. "Art Education for Women in the 1860's: A Decade of Debate." In *Women in the Victorian Art World*. Edited by Clarissa Campbell Orr, 187–98. Manchester: Manchester University Press.
Dowling, Linda. 1996. *The Vulgarization of Art: The Victorians and Aesthetic Democracy*. Charlottesville: The University Press of Virginia.
Du Maurier, George. 1894. *Trilby*. Edited by Dennis Denisoff. Oxford: Oxford University Press, 1998.
Eagleton, Terry. 1975. *Myths of Power*. London: Macmillan.
———. 1990. *The Ideology of the Aesthetic*. Oxford: Blackwell.
———. 2005. *The English Novel: An Introduction*. Oxford: Blackwell.
Eastlake, Charles. 1868. *Hints on Household Taste*. Reprint, New York: Dover, 1969.
Edwards, Amelia B. 1864. *Barbara's History*. 2 vols. Leipzig: Tauchnitz.
Eliot, George. 1859. *Adam Bede*. Reprint. Edited byMargaret Reynolds. New York: Penguin Books, 2007.
———. 1871–72. *Middlemarch*. Reprint. Edited by W. J. Harvey. Harmondsworth: Penguin Books, 1986.
———. 1876. *Daniel Deronda*. Reprint. Edited by Graham Handley. Oxford: Oxford University Press, 1988.
———. 1954–78. *The George Eliot Letters*. Edited by Gordon Haight. 9 vols. New Haven; Yale University Press.
Elkins, James. 1988. *On Pictures and the Words That Fail Them*. Cambridge: Cambridge University Press.

———. 1994. *The Poetics of Perspective*. Ithaca: Cornell University Press.
———. 1997. *The Object Stares Back: Or the Nature of Being*. New York: Harcourt Brace.
———. 1999. *The Domain of Images*. Ithaca: Cornell University Press.
Ellet, Elizabeth. 1859. *Women Artists in All Ages and Countries*. New York: Harper.
Elliott, Bridget, and Jo-Ann Wallace. 1994. *Women Artists and Writers: Modernist (Im)positionings*. London: Routledge.
Ellis, Mrs. 1848a. "The Daughters of England." *The Family Monitor*. New York: Edward Walker.
———. 1848b. "The Women of England." *The Family Monitor*. New York: Edward Walker.
Fairer, David. 2004. Preface to *The Victorians and the Eighteenth Century*. Edited by Francis O. Gorman and Katherine Turner, xii–xvi. Aldershot, England: Ashgate.
Ferry, Luc. 1987. *Homo Aestheticus*. Translated by Robert de Loaiza. Chicago: University of Chicago Press, 1993.
Flint, Kate. 2000. *The Victorians and the Visual Imagination*. Cambridge: Cambridge University Press.
Foucault, Michel. 1990. *History of Sexuality*. Vol. 1: *An Introduction*. Translated by Robert Hurley. New York: Vintage Books.
Frank, Joseph. "Spatial Form in Modern Literature." 1948. In *Criticism: The Foundation of Modern Literary Judgments*. Edited by Mark Schorer, Josephine Miles, and Gordon McKenzie. New York: Harcourt Brace.
Frawley, Maria. 1996. *Anne Brontë*. New York: Twayne.
Gagnier, Regina. 1999. "Productive Bodies, Pleasured Bodies: On Victorian Aesthetics." In *Women and British Aestheticism*. Edited by Talia Schaffer and Kathy Alexis Psomiades, 270–90. Charlottesville: University Press of Virginia.
———. 2000. *The Insatiability of Human Wants: Economics and Aesthetics in Market Society*. Chicago: University of Chicago Press.
"Gallery of Lady Artists." 1868. *Englishwoman's Review*, April, 467.
Gandelman, Claude. 1991. *Reading Pictures, Viewing Texts*. Bloomington: Indiana University Press.
Garb, Tamar. 1994. *Sisters of the Brush: Women's Artistic Culture in Late 19th Century Paris*. New Haven: Yale University Press.
Garland, Robert. 1995. *The Eye of the Beholder: Deformity and Disability in the Graeco-Roman World*. Ithaca: Cornell University Press.
Garland-Thomson, Rosemarie. 1996. *Extraordinary Bodies: Figuring Physical Disability in American Culture and Literature*. New York: Columbia University Press.
———. 2000. "The Beauty and the Freak." In *Points of Contact: Disability and Culture*. Edited by Susan Crutchfield and Marcy Epstein, 181–96. Ann Arbor: University of Michigan Press.
Gaskell, Elizabeth. 1996. *The Life of Charlotte Brontë*. Oxford: Oxford University Press.
Gerin, Winifred. 1981. *Anne Thackeray Ritchie: A Biography*. Oxford: Oxford University Press.
Gezari, Janet. 1992. *Charlotte Brontë and Defensive Conduct: The Author and the Body at Risk*. Philadelphia: University of Pennsylvania Press.
Gilbert, Sandra, and Susan Gubar. 2000. *The Madwoman in the Attic*. 2nd ed. New Haven: Yale University Press.

Gillett, Paula. 1990. *Worlds of Art: Painters in Victorian Society.* New Brunswick, NJ: Rutgers University Press.
Golden, Catherine. J. 2003. *Images of the Woman Reader in Victorian British and American Fiction.* Gainesville: University of Florida Press.
Goodbrand, Robert. 1870. "A Suggestion for a New Kind of Biography." *The Contemporary Review* 14 (April–July): 20–28.
Gordon, Jan B. 1984. "Gossip, Diary, Letter, Text: Anne Brontë's Narrative Tenant and the Problematic of the Gothic Sequel." *ELH* 51: 719–45
Gordon, Mary. 1999. *Spending.* New York: Scribner's.
Goreau, Angeline. "Introduction." *Agnes Grey* by Charlotte Brontë. London: Penguin Books, 1988.
Greenblatt, Stephen. 1989. *Shakespearean Negotiations.* Berkeley: University of California Press.
Greenwell Smith, Esther. 1980. *Mrs. Humphry Ward.* Boston: Twayne.
Gruner, Elizabeth Rose. 1997. "Plotting the Mother: Caroline Norton, Helen Huntington, and Isabel Vane." *Tulsa Studies in Women's Literature* 16: 303–25.
Hagstrum, Jean. 1958. *The Sister Arts: The Tradition of Literary Pictorialism and English Poetry from Dryden to Gray.* Chicago: University of Chicago Press.
Haight, Gordon, ed. 1954–78. *The George Eliot Letters.* 9 vols. New Haven: Yale University Press.
Halliwell, Stephen. 2002. *The Aesthetics of Mimesis.* Princeton, NJ: Princeton University Press.
Hamilton, Edith. 1999. *Mythology.* New York: Grand Central Publishing.
Hardy, Thomas. 1998. *The Pursuit of the Well-Beloved and The Well-Beloved.* New York: Penguin Books.
———. *Jude the Obscure.* 1999. New York: W.W. Norton Publishers.
Harman, Barbara Leah. 1998. *The Feminine Political Novel in Victorian England.* Charlottesville: University Press of Virginia.
Harpman, Geoffrey Galt. 1982. *On The Grotesque: Strategies of Contradiction in Art and Literature.* Princeton, NJ: Princeton University Press.
Hawthorne, Nathaniel. 1860. *The Marble Faun.* Reprint. New York: Dover Publications, 2004.
Hazlitt, William. 1934. *The Complete Works of William Hazlitt.* Vol. 20. Edited by P. P. Howe. London: Dent.
Heffernan, James A. W. 1985. *The Re-Creation of Landscape: A Study of Wordsworth, Coleridge, Constable and Turner.* Hanover, NH: University Press of New England.
———. 1993. *Museum of Words: The Poetics of Ekphrasis from Homer to Ashberry.* Chicago: University of Chicago Press.
Helland, Janice. 1996. *The Studios of Frances and Margaret Macdonald.* Manchester: Manchester University Press.
Hemans, Felicia. 1830. "Corinne of the Capitol." In *Felicia Hamans: Selected Poems.* Edited by Susan Wolfson. Princeton: Princeton University Press.
Hennelly, Mark. 1984. "Jane Eyre's Reading Lesson." *ELH* 51, no. 4 (Winter): 639–717.
Hills, Patricia, ed. 1986. *John Singer Sargent.* New York: N. Abrams and the Whitney Museum of American Art.
Hirsch, Pam. 1995. "Barbara Leigh Smith Bodichon: Artist and Activist." In *Women*

in the Victorian Art World. Edited by Clarissa Campbell Orr, 167–86. Manchester: Manchester University Press.

———. 1998. *Barbara Leigh Smith Bodichon: Feminist, Artist, and Rebel.* London: Chatto & Windus.

Holcombe, Lee. 1983. *Wives and Property: Reform of the Married Women's Property Law in Nineteenth-Century England.* Toronto: University of Toronto Press.

Hollander, John. 1995. *The Gazer's Spirit: Poems Speaking to Silent Works of Art.* Chicago: University of Chicago Press.

Howard-Zophy, Angela, and Sasha Rana Adams Tarrant, eds. 1997. *Redefining the New Woman: 1920–1963.* New York: Routledge.

Howitt, Anna Mary. 1852. "Sisters in Art." *The Illustrated Exhibitor and Magazine of Art* 2 (March–July): 214–26, 238–40, 262–63, 286–88, 317–19, 334–36, 347–49, 362–64.

———. 1854. *An Art Student in Munich.* Boston: Ticknor, Reed, and Fields.

———. *School of Life.* Boston: Tickner and Fields.

Howitt, William, and Mary Howitt. 1853. "Margaret von Ehrenberg, The Artist-Wife." In *Stories of English and Foreign Life*, 1–148. London: Bohn.

Huet, Marie-Helene. 1993. *Monstrous Imagination.* Cambridge: Harvard University Press.

Jacobs, Naomi. 1986. "Gender and Layered Narrative in *Wuthering Heights* and *The Tenant of Wildfell Hall.*" *Journal of Narrative Technique* 16: 204–19.

Jacobus, Mary. 1997. *Psychoanalysis and the Scene of Reading.* Oxford: Oxford University Press.

James, Henry. 1875. *Roderick Hudson.* Edited by Leon Edel. New York: Harper, 1960.

———. 1884. *The Art of Fiction.* In *Literary Criticism, Volume One.* Edited by Leon Edel and Mark Wilson. Library of America, 1984.

Jameson, Anna. 1834. *Visits and Sketches at Home and Abroad with Tales and Miscellanies Now First Collected and a New Edition of the Diary of an Ennuyee.* 2 vols. New York: Harper.

Jay, Elisabeth. 1995. *Mrs. Oliphant: A Fiction to Herself.* New York: Oxford University Press.

———. 2004. "The Cultural Politics of Eighteenth-century Representation in Victorian Literary Histories." In *The Victorians and the Eighteenth Century.* Edited by Francis O. Gorman and Katherine Turner, 98–118. Aldershot, England: Ashgate.

Jeffares, Bo. 1979. *The Artist in Nineteenth-Century Fiction.* Atlantic Highlands, NJ: Humanities Press.

Jopling, Louise. 1925. *Twenty Years of My Life.* London: John Lane, The Bodley Head.

Kant, Immanuel. 1992. *Critique of Judgement.* Translated by James Creed Meredith. Oxford: Clarendon. German original, 1978.

Keen, Suzanne. 1998. *Victorian Renovations of the Novel.* Cambridge: Cambridge University Press.

Kemal, Salim, and Ivan Gaskell. 2000. "Contesting the Arts: Politics and Aesthetics." In *Politics and Aesthetics in the Arts.* Edited by Salim Kemal and Ivan Gaskell, 1–10. Cambridge: Cambridge University Press.

Klages, Mary. 1999. *Woeful Afflictions: Disability and Sentimentality in Victorian America.* Philadelphia: University of Pennsylvania Press.

Kochanck, Lisa. 1987. "Reframing the Freak: From Sideshow to Science." *Victorian Periodicals Review* 30: 227–43.

Krieger, Murray. 1992. *Ekphrasis*. Baltimore: Johns Hopkins University Press.
Kromm, Jane. 1998. "Visual Culture and Scopic Custom in *Jane Eyre* and *Villette*." *Victorian Literature and Culture* 26: 369–94.
Lambourne, Lionel. *Utopian Craftsman*. London: Astragal Books, 1980.
Landon, Letitia Elizabeth. 1831. *Romance and Reality*. 3 vols. London: H. Colburn and Richard Bentley.
Langer, Suzanne. 1957. *Problems of Art: Ten Philosophical Lectures*. New York: Scribner's.
Langland, Elizabeth. 1989. *Anne Bronte: The Other One*. London: Macmillan.
———. 1992. "The Voicing of Feminine Desire in Anne Brontë's *The Tenant of Wildfell Hall*." In *Gender and Discourse in Victorian Literature and Art*. Edited by Antony Harrison and Beverly Taylor, 111–23. Dekalb: Northern Illinois University Press.
Lapierre, Alexandra. 1998. *Artemisia: A Novel*. Translated by Liz Heron. New York: Grove Press, 2001.
Laqueur, Thomas. 1990. *Making Sex: Body and Gender from the Greeks to Freud*. Cambridge, MA: Harvard University Press.
Ledger, Sally. 1997. *The New Woman: Fiction and Feminism at the Fin de Siècle*. Manchester: Manchester University Press.
Leighton, Angela, and Margaret Reynolds, eds. 1995. *Victorian Women Poets: An Anthology*. Oxford: Blackwell.
Leonardo da Vinci. *Paragone*. Edited and translated by Irma Richter. Oxford: Oxford University Press, 1949.
———. 1998. *The Notebooks of Leonardo da Vinci*. New York: Oxford University Press.
Lessing, Gotthold Ephraim. 1984. *Laocoön: An Essay on the Limits of Painting and Poetry*. Translated by Edward Allen McCormick. Baltimore: Johns Hopkins University Press. German original, 1766.
"Let Us Join the Ladies." 1857. *Punch, or the London Charivari*, July 18, 27.
Levine, Caroline. 2000. "Visual Labor: Ruskin's Radical Realism." *Victorian Literature and Culture* 20: 73–86.
———. 2003. *The Serious Pleasure of Suspense: Victorian Realism and Narrative Doubt*. Charlottesville: University Press of Virginia.
Levine, George. 1981. *The Realistic Imagination: English Fiction from Frankenstein to Lady Chatterley*. Chicago: University of Chicago Press.
———, ed. 1994. *Aesthetics and Ideology*. New Brunswick, NJ: Rutgers University Press.
Lewes, G. H. 1847. Review of *Jane Eyre*. *Fraser's Magazine*, December. Reprinted in C. Brontë, *Jane Eyre*. Norton Critical Edition, 436–37.
Lewis, Linda. 2003. *Germaine de Staël, George Sand, and the Victorian Woman Artist*. Columbia: University of Missouri Press.
Linton, Eliza Lynn. 1891. "The Wild Women as Social Insurgents." *The Nineteenth Century* 30: 596–605.
Losano, Antonia. 2002. "Margaret Oliphant." In *British Writers: Retrospective Supplement 9*. Edited by Jay Parini, 209–26. New York: Scribners.
Maas, Jeremy. 1969. *Victorian Painters*. New York: Harrison House.
Mackay, Carol Hanbery. 1988. "Hate and Humor as Empathetic Whimsy in Anne Thackeray Ritchie." *Women's Studies* 15: 117–33.
———. 2001. *Creative Negativity: Four Victorian Exemplars of the Female Quest*. Stanford, CA: Stanford University Press.

Mare, Margaret, and Alicia Percival. 1948. *Victorian Best-Seller: The World of Charlotte M. Yonge*. London: Harrap.
Marsh, Jan. 1985. *The Pre-Raphaelite Sisterhood*. New York: St. Martin's.
———. 1995. "Art, Ambition and Sisterhood in the 1850s." In *Women in the Victorian Art World*. Edited by Clarissa Campbell Orr, 33–48. Manchester: Manchester University Press.
Marsh, Jan, and Pamela Gerrish Nunn. 1989. *Women Artists and the Pre-Raphaelite Movement*. London: Virago.
Marshall, Gail. 1994. "Actresses, Statues and Speculation in *Daniel Deronda*." *Essays in Criticism* 44:117–39.
Martineau, Harriet. 1859. "Female Industry." Reprinted in *Criminals, Idiots, Women and Minors: Nineteenth-Century Writing by Women on Women*. Edited by Susan Hamilton, 29–70. Peterborough, Ontario: Broadviews Press, 1995.
Martinez, Michele. 2003. "Women Poets and the Sister Arts in Nineteenth-Century England." *Victorian Poetry* 41, no. 4 (Winter): 621–28.
de Mattos, Katharine. 1884. "The Artist in Fiction." *The Magazine of Art* 7: 157–59.
Matus, Jill. 1993. "Looking at Cleopatra: The Expression and Exhibition of Female Desire in *Villette*." *Victorian Literature and Culture* 21: 345–67.
Maynard, John. 1984. *Charlotte Brontë and Sexuality*. Cambridge: Cambridge University Press.
McCormack, Kathleen. 1996. "George Eliot, Julia Cameron, and William Henry Fox Talbot: Photography and *Daniel Deronda*." *Word and Image* 12: 175–79.
McMaster, Juliet. 1982. "Imbecile Laughter and Desperate Earnest in *The Tenant of Wildfell Hall*." *Modern Language Quarterly* 43: 352–68.
Meltzer, Françoise. 1987. *Salome and the Dance of Writing*. Chicago: University of Chicago Press.
Meredith, George. 1888. *Diana of the Crossways*. London: Roberts Brothers.
Meyers, Jeffrey. 1975. *Painting and the Novel*. Manchester: Manchester University Press.
Michie, Helena. 1989. "'Who is this in Pain?': Scarring, Disfigurement and Female Identity in *Bleak House* and *Our Mutual Friend*." *Novel* 22: 199–212.
Miller, D. A. 1988. *The Novel and the Police*. Berkeley: University of California Press.
Mitchell, David, and Sharon L. Snyder. 2001. *Narrative Prosthesis: Disability and the Dependencies of Discourse*. Ann Arbor: University of Michigan Press.
Millett, Kate. 1970. *Sexual Politics*. Garden City, NY: Doubleday.
Mitchell, Sally. 1993. *Dinah Mulock Craik*. Boston: Twayne.
Mitchell, W. T. J. 1980. *The Language of Images*. Chicago: University of Chicago Press.
———. 1986. *Iconology: Image, Text, Ideology*. Chicago: University of Chicago Press.
———. 1994. *Picture Theory: Essays on Verbal and Visual Representation*. Chicago: University of Chicago Press.
Moglen, Helene. 2001. *The Trauma of Gender: A Feminist Theory of the English Novel*. Berkeley: University of California Press.
Moore, George. 1898. *Modern Painting*. London: Scott.
———. 1924. *Conversations on Ebury Street*. New York: Boni and Liveright.
Mortensen, Phoebe. 1997. *Art in the Social Order*. Albany: State University of New York Press.
Mourao, Manuela. 1997. "Delicate Balances: Gender and Power in Anne Thackeray Ritchie's Non-fiction." *Women's Writing* 4: 73–91.

———. 2000. "Interrogating the Female *Bildungsroman*: Anne Thackeray Ritchie's Marriage Fictions." *Nineteenth-Century Feminisms* 2: 73–87.
Murdoch, Iris. 1957. *The Sandcastle*. New York: Viking Books.
Nash, Julie, and Barbara A. Suess, eds. 2001. *New Approaches to the Literary Art of Anne Brontë*. Aldershot, England: Ashgate.
Nochlin, Linda. 1989. "Why Have There Been No Great Women Artists?" In *Women, Art and the Power and Other Essays*. London: Thames and Hudson.
Norton, Caroline. 1837. *Observations on the Natural Claim of the Mother to the Custody of Her Infant Children, as Affected by the Common Law Right of the Father*. London: John Murray.
———. 1854. *English Laws for Women in the Nineteenth Century*. Printed for private circulation. On line at VictorianWomenWritersproject: www.indiana.edu/~letrs/vwwp/norton/englaw.html
Nunn, Pamela Gerrish. 1986. *Canvassing: Recollections by Six Victorian Women Artists*. London: Camden.
———. 1987. *Victorian Women Artists*. London: Woman's Press.
———. 1995. *Problem Pictures: Men and Women in Victorian Painting*. Aldershot, England: Scolar Press.
Nussbaum, Felicity A. 1997. "Feminotopias: The Pleasures of 'Deformity' in Mid-Eighteenth-Century England." In *The Body and Physical Difference*. Edited by David Mitchell and Sharon Snyder, 161–73. Ann Arbor: University of Michigan Press.
O'Donovan, Patrick. 1994. "Avatars of the Artist: Narrative Approaches to the Work of the Painter." In *Artistic Relations: Literature and the Visual Arts in Nineteenth-Century France*. Edited by Peter Collier and Robert Lethbridge, 222–36. New Haven: Yale University Press.
Oldcastle, John. 1883. "The Love Affairs of Angelica Kauffman." *The Magazine of Art* 5: 32–35.
O'Mealy, Joseph. 1966. "Mrs. Oliphant, Miss Marjoribanks, and the Victorian Canon." In *the New Nineteenth Century: Feminist Readings of Underread Victorian Fiction*. Edited by Barbara Leah Harman and Susan Meyer, 63–76. New York: Garland Publishing, Inc.
Oliphant, Margaret. 1866. *Miss Marjoribanks*. Reprint, Leipzig: Tauchnitz, 1870.
———. 1869. *Historical Sketches of the Reign of George II*. Edinburgh and London: William Blackwood and Sons.
———. 1883. "The Ethics of Biography." *Contemporary Review* 44 (July): 76–93.
———. 1899. *Autobiography and Letters of Mrs. Oliphant*. Edited by Mrs. Harry Coghill. New York: Dodd, Mead.
Orr, Clarissa Campbell. 1995. Introduction to *Women in the Victorian Art World*. Edited by Clarissa Campbell Orr, 1–32. Manchester: Manchester University Press.
Osborne, Harold, ed. 1970. *The Oxford Companion to Art*. First ed. Oxford: Oxford University Press.
Oxford Dictionary of Art. 2004. 3rd ed. Edited by Ian Chivers. Oxford: Oxford University Press.
Panofsky, Erwin. 1972. *Studies in Iconology: Humanistic Themes in the Art of the Renaissance*. New York: Westview Press.
Pater, Walter. 1888. "Robert Elsmere." In *Essays from* The Guardian, 53–70. London: Macmillan, 1906.

———. 1897. *Greek Studies*. New York: The Macmillan Company.
Perkins, Jane Gray. 1910. *The Life of Mrs. Norton*. London: Murray.
Phelps, Elizabeth Stuart. 1877. *The Story of Avis*. Reprint. Edited by Carol Farley Kessler New Brunswick, NJ: Rutgers University Press, 1985.
Plagens, Peter. 1996. "Lady Painters? Smile When You Say That." *Newsweek,* September 30, 82–83.
Pliny the Elder. *Natural History: A Selection*. Translated by John F. Healey. New York: Penguin Classics, 1991.
Pollock, Griselda. 1988. *Vision and Difference*. London: Routledge.
Poynter, Edward. 1885. *Lectures on Art*. London: Chapman and Hall.
Poovey, Mary. 1988. *Uneven Developments: The Ideological Work of Gender in Mid-Victorian England*. Chicago: University of Chicago Press.
Praz, Mario. *Mnemosyne: The Parallel between Literature and the Visual Arts*. Princeton: Princeton University Press.
Prendergrast, Christopher. 2000. *The Triangle of Representation*. New York: Columbia University Press.
Prieto, Laura R. 2001. *At Home in the Studio: The Professionalization of Women Artists in America*. Cambridge: Harvard University Press.
Psomiades, Kathy Alexis. 1997. *Beauty's Body: Femininity and Representation in British Aestheticism*. Stanford, CA: Stanford University Press.
Purnell, Thomas. 1861. "Women and Art." *Art Journal* 23: 107–9.
Pykett, Lyn. 1999. "Portraits of the Artist as a Young Woman: Representations of the Female Artist in the New Woman Fiction of the 1890s." In *Victorian Women Writers and the Woman Question*. Edited by Nicola Diane Thompson, 135–50. Cambridge: Cambridge University Press.
———. 2001. Foreword to *The New Woman in Fiction and in Fact: Fin de Siècle Feminisms*. Edited by Angelique Richardson and Chris Willis, xi–xii. Hampshire, England: Palgrave Macmillan.
Regan, Stephen, ed. 1992. *The Politics of Pleasure: Aesthetics and Cultural Theory*. Buckingham, England: Open University Press.
Reitlinger, G. 1961. *The Economics of Taste: The Rise and Fall of Picture Prices, 1760–1960*. London: Barrie.
Review of Society for Female Artists exhibit. 1858. *Athenaeum*, no. 1588 (3 April): 43.
Reynolds, Sir Joshua. 1769–91. *Discourses*. Reprint. Edited by Pat Rogers. London: Penguin Books, 1992.
Rigby, Elizabeth (Lady Eastlake). 1848. "*Vanity Fair*—and *Jane Eyre*." *Quarterly Review* 84, no. 167 (December): 153–85.
Ritchie, Anne Thackeray. 1863 and 1873. *The Story of Elizabeth; and Old Kensington*. Reprint. Edited by Esther Schwartz-McKinzie. Bristol: Themmes Press, 1995.
———. 1866. "Sleeping Beauty in the Wood." *Cornhill Magazine* 13 (May): 556–66. Reprinted in *Forbidden Journeys: Fairy Tales and Fantasies by Victorian Women Writers*. Edited by Nina Auerbach and U. C. Knoepflmacher, 21–34. Chicago: University of Chicago Press, 1992.
———. 1876. *Miss Angel and Fulham Lawn*. London: Smith Elder.
———, 1883. *The Book of Sybils*. London: Blackwood and Sons.
———. 1885. *Mrs. Dymond*. Reprint. Edited by Esther Schwartz-McKinzie. Stroud, Gloucester: Sutton Publishers, 1997.

———. 1892. *Records of Tennyson, Ruskin and Browning*. London: Macmillan and Co.
Roston, Murray. 1996. *Victorian Contexts: Literature and the Visual Arts*. New York: New York University Press.
Ruskin, John. 1857. *The Elements of Drawing*. Reprint. Edited by Bernard Dunstan. London: Herbert Press, 1991.
———. 1866–84. *Modern Painters*. 5 vols. Boston: Dana Estes.
———. 1903–12. *The Works of John Ruskin*. 39 vols. Edited by E. T. Cook and Alexander Wedderburn. London: Allen.
———. 1972. *Sublime and Instructive: Letters from John Ruskin to Louisa, Marchioness of Waterford, Anna Blunden and Ellen Heaton*. Edited by Virginia Surtees. London: Michael Joseph.
Russo, Mary. 1995. *The Female Grotesque: Risk, Excess and Modernity*. New York: Routledge.
Saintsbury, George. 1876. Review of *Daniel Deronda*. *Academy* 10 (9 September): 253–54.
Sand, George. 1843. *Consuelo*. Translated by Fayette Robinson. New York: Lupton Books, 1882.
Schor, Naomi. 1987. *Reading in Detail: Aesthetics and the Feminine*. New York: Methuen.
Scott, Leader. 1884. "Women at Work: Their Functions in Art." *The Magazine of Art* 7 (June): 98–99.
Scott, Sarah. 1762. *Millenium Hall*. Reprint New York: Virago Press, 1986.
Sedgwick, Eve. 1985. *Between Men: English Literature and Male Homosocial Desire*. New York: Columbia University Press.
Shaftesbury, Earl of (Anthony Ashley Cooper). 1710. "Sensus Communis: An essay on the Freedom of Wit and Humour." Reprinted in *Characteristics of Men, Manners, Opinions, Times*. Edited by Lawrence E. Klein. Cambridge: Cambridge University Press, 2000.
Shakespeare, William. *The Tragedy of King Richard the Third*. Edited by Alfred Harbage. Pelican Shakespeare. Baltimore: Penguin Books, 1969.
———. *The Rape of Lucrece*. In *The Norton Shakespeare*. Edited by Stephen Greenblatt, 635–82. New York: W.W. Norton, 1997.
Shaw, Harry. 1983. *Forms of Historical Fiction: Sir Walter Scott and His Successors*. Ithaca: Cornell University Press.
Shlain, Leonard. 1998. *The Alphabet versus the Goddess: The Conflict between Word and Image*. New York: Viking.
Sicherman, Barbara. 1989. "Sense and Sensibility: A Case Study of Women's Reading in Late-Victorian America." In *Reading in America: Literature and Social History*. Edited by Cathy Davidson, 201–25. Baltimore: Johns Hopkins University Press.
Siegel, Jonah. 2000. *Desire and Excess: The Nineteenth-Century Culture of Art*. Princeton, NJ: Princeton University Press.
Signorotti, Elizabeth. 1995. "'A Frame Perfect and Glorious': Narrative Structure in Anne Brontë's *The Tenant of Wildfell Hall*." *Victorian Newsletter* 87 (Spring): 20–25.
Simmons, Claire. *Reversing the Conquest: History and Myth in Nineteenth-Century British Literature*. New Brunswick, NJ: Rutgers University Press, 1996.
Smick, Rebekah. 1996. "Evoking Michelangelo's Vatican *Pieta*: Transformations in the

Topos of Living Stone." In *The Eye of the Poet*. Edited by Amy Golahny, 23–52. Lewisburg: Bucknell University Press.

Smith, Alison. 1997. *The Victorian Nude*. New York: Watson-Guptill Publications.

———. 2002. *Exposed: The Victorian Nude*. New York: Watson-Guptill Publications.

Smith, Barbara Leigh. 1854. *A Brief Summary, in Plain Language, of the Most Important Laws concerning Women*. London: J. Chapman.

Smith, Mack. 1995. *Literary Realism and the Ekphrastic Tradition*. University Park: Pennsylvania State University Press.

"The Society of Female Artists." 1858. *Englishwoman's Journal* 1, no. 3 (May): 205–9.

Spacks, Patricia Meyer. 1994. "A Dull Book is Easily Renounced." *Victorian Literature and Culture* 22: 287–302.

Spivak, Gayatri. 1985. "Three Women's Texts and a Critique of Imperialism." *Critical Inquiry* 12: 243–61.

Starzyk, Lawrence J. 1991. "'The Gallery of Memory': The Pictorial in *Jane Eyre*." *Papers in Language and Literature* 75: 288–309.

———. 1999. *"If Mine Had Been the Painter's Hand": The Indeterminate in Nineteenth-Century Poetry and Painting*. New York: Peter Lang.

———. 2002. "*Ut Pictura Poesis*: The Nineteenth-Century Perspective." *Victorian Newsletter* 102 (Fall): 1–9.

Steiner, Wendy. 1982. *The Colors of Rhetoric: Problems in the Relationship between Modern Literature and Painting*. Chicago: University of Chicago Press.

———. 1988. *Pictures of Romance: Form against Context in Painting and Literature*. Chicago: University of Chicago Press.

Stoddard Holmes, Martha. 2004. *Fictions of Affliction: Physical Disability in Victorian Culture*. Ann Arbor: University of Michigan Press.

Sutherland, John. 1990. *Mrs. Humphry Ward: Eminent Victorian, Pre-eminent Edwardian*. Oxford: Clarendon.

Sutton-Ramspeck, Beth. 1999. "Shot out of the Canon: Mary Ward and the Claims of Conflicting Feminisms." In *Victorian Women Writers and the Woman Question*. Edited by Nicola Diane Thompson, 204–22. Cambridge: Cambridge University Press.

Sypher, Wylie. 1960. *Rococco to Cubism in Art and Literature*. New York: Random House.

———. 1978. *Four Stages of Renaissance Style*. New York: Peter Smith Publisher.

Tabor, Eliza. 1866. *Hester's Sacrifice*. London: Hurst and Blackett.

The Tenant of Wildfell Hall. 1997. DVD. Directed by Mike Bowker. BBC.

Thackeray, William. 1855. *The Newcomes*. Reprint. Edited by D. J. Taylor. The Everyman Library. London: Dent, 1994.

Torgovnick, Marianna. 1985. *The Visual Arts, Pictorialism, and the Novel*. Princeton, NJ: Princeton University Press.

Tolstoy, Leo. 1865–1869. *War and Peace*. Translated by Anthony Briggs. New York: Penguin Classics.

Trodd, Anthea. 2000. "'The Mothers of Our Mothers': Ghostly Strategies in Women's Writing." In *Rethinking Victorian Culture*. Edited by Juliet John and Alice Jenkins, 196–208. New York: St. Martin's.

Turner, Jane, ed. 1996. *The Dictionary of Art*. 34 vols. London: Macmillan.

Vickers, Nancy. 1985. "The Blazon of Sweet Beauty's Best: Shakespeare's Lucrece." In

Shakespeare and the Question of Theory. Edited by Patricia Parker and Geoffrey Hartman, 95–115. New York: Methuen.
Vreeland, Susan. 2002. *The Passion of Artemisia.* New York: Penguin Books, 2002.
Walker, John. 1983. *Portraits: 5,000 Years.* New York: Harry N. Abrams, Inc.
Ward, Mrs. Humphry. 1884. *Miss Bretherton.* Available on line at www.gutenberg.org/dirs/1/3/4/3/13432/13432.txt.
———. 1888. *Robert Elsmere.*
———. 1892. *The History of David Grieve.* New York: Macmillan.
———. 1894. *Marcella.* London: Virago Press, 1985.
———. 1906. *Fenwick's Career.* New York: Harper, 1906.
———. 1913. *The Mating of Lydia.* 2 vols. Leipzig: Tauchnitz.
Ward, E. M., Mrs. 1925. *Memories of Ninety Years.* Edited by Isabel G. McAllister. New York: Holt.
Wasserstein, Wendy. 1990. *The Heidi Chronicles.* New York: Dramatists Play Service.
Watt, Ian. 2001. *The Rise of the Novel.* Berkeley: University of California Press.
Wells, Marion. 2002. "To find a face where all distress is stell'd: Enargeia, Ekphrasis and Mourning in *The Rape of Lucrece* and *The Aeneid.*" *Comparative Literature* 54, no. 2: 97–126.
Wendorf, Richard. 1996. *Sir Joshua Reynolds: The Painter in Society.* London: National Portrait Gallery.
Wettlaufer, Alexandra K. 2004. "Dibutades and Her Daughters: The Female Artist in Postrevolutionary France." *Nineteeth Century Studies* 18: 9–38.
Whistler, James Abbott McNeil. 1890. *The Gentle Art of Making Enemies.* Reprint New York: Dover, 1967.
White, Roberta. *A Studio of One's Own: Fictional Women Painters and the Art of Fiction.* Madison: Fairleigh Dickinson University Press, 2005.
Wilde, Oscar. 1890. *The Picture of Dorian Gray.* Reprint. Edited by Michael Gillespie. New York: W.W. Norton.
Williams, Raymond. 1985. *Keywords: A Vocabulary of Culture and Society.* New York: Oxford University Press.
Wilt, Judith. 1996. "Transition Time: The Political Romances of Mrs. Humphry Ward's *Marcella* and *Sir George Tressady.*" In *The New Nineteenth Century: Feminist Readings of Underread Victorian Fiction.* Edited by Barbara Leah Harman and Susan Meyer, 225–46. New York: Garland.
Wise, T. J., and J. A. Symington. 1932. *The Brontës: Their Lives, Friendships and Correspondence.* 4 vols. Oxford: Oxford University Press.
Witemeyer, Hugh. 1979. *George Eliot and the Visual Arts.* New Haven: Yale University Press.
Wolfson, Susan. 1998. Introduction to "Ideology and Romantic Aesthetics: A Forum," special issue. *Studies in Romanticism* 37: 3–5.
Woodmansee, Martha. 1994. *The Author, Art, and the Market: Rereading the History of Aesthetics.* New York: Columbia University Press.
Woolf, Virginia. 1919. Obituary of Anne Thackeray Ritchie. *Times Literary Supplement,* March 6.
———. 1929. *To the Lighthouse.* Reprint San Diego: Harcourt Brace, 1989.
———. 1929. *A Room of One's Own.* Reprint New York: Harvest Books, 1989.
———. 1938. *Three Guineas.* New York: Harvest Books, 1966.

———. 1950. *The Captain's Deathbed and Other Essays*. Reprint New York: Harcourt Brace, 1973.

———. 1966–67. *Collected Essays*. 4 vols. London: Hogarth Press.

Yale Dictionary of Art and Artists. 2000. Edited by Erika Langmuir and Norbert Lynton. New Haven: Yale University Press.

Yeldham, Charlotte. 1984. *Women Artists in Nineteenth-Century France and England*. 2 vols. New York: Garland.

Yonge, Charlotte. 1856. *The Daisy Chain*. Reprint edition. New York: Virago Press, 1988.

———. 1857. *The Dynevor Terrace: or, The Clue of Life*. 2 vols. London: John W. Parker and Son, 1857.

———. 1865. *The Clever Woman of the Family*. Reprint edition. In *Novels and Tales by Charlotte M. Yonge*. Vol. 10. London: Macmillan, 1882.

———. 1873. *Pillars of the House*. 5 vols. Leipzig: Tauchnitz.

Index

(Page numbers in italics indicated illustrated matter.)

ability, critique of, 181
academic art, 215
act of painting, 8
Adam Bede (Eliot), 131
Adorno, Theodor, 15, 17
adultery in literature, 197
Adventures of a Woman in Search of Her Rights, The (Claxton), 49–50, *50*, 150
Aeneas (mythical character), 115
aesthetic democracy, 18, 244n28
aesthetic ideology: 18th-century, 167; 19th-century, 169–71
aesthetic interactions, paintings as artifacts in, 242n11
aestheticism, 44, 209, 231
aesthetic movements, 248n20
aesthetics: debate over, 13–20; detail, level of acceptable, 204–5; history of, 115; literary commentaries on, 99, 145, 165, 166–67, 195–96, 240n5; political nature of, 16; and women artists, 62, 165–66
Aesthetic Theory (Adorno), 15

Agamben, Georgio, 17
Agnes Grey (Brontë), 64, 71, 75
Alcharisi, the (fictional character), 129, 130, 133–34, 135, 136
alcoholism in literature, 64, 72, 250n8
Alcott, Louisa May, 49, 266n10
Alcott, May, 27
Alda Underwood (fictional character), 198
Alexander, Christine, 98, 240n6
Alice Law (fictional character), 122, 123, 124, 128
allegory in art, 152–55, 171
Allegory of Imitation (Kauffman), 152, 154
Allingham, Helen (née Paterson), 130–31, 178–79, *179*
Alma-Tadema, Laura, 38, *41,* 42, 212, 257n2
Alma-Tadema, Lawrence, 257n2
Alphabet Versus the Goddess, The (Shlain), 242n18
alter-ego, woman painter as, 8
Altick, Richard, 182

ambition, plot of, 135–36
Amy March (fictional character), 49
Amy Meyrick (fictional character), 130
Andres, Sophia, 5–6
androgynous theory of art, 253n29
Angelika Kauffmann in the Studio of Joshua Reynolds (Allingham), 178–79, *179*
Angus Rothesay (fictional character), 186
animals as art subjects, 108
Arabian Nights, 135
Aristotle, 94, 183
Armgart (Eliot), 133
Armstrong, Isobel, 15
Armstrong, Nancy, 6, 240n5
Arnold, Matthew, 265n5
Arnold, Thomas, 265n5
Arrangement in Grey and Black ("Whistler's Mother") (Whistler), 221
art: as accomplishment, 23, 24–25, 26; as bride (metaphor), 187, 190; commercialization of, 122, 123, 128; defined, 3, 244n27; education and training, 25, 26–27, 30, 41, 78, 106–7, 109, 122, 124–26, 128, 146, 210, 216, 232; and life, disjunction between, 7; literary references to, 12–13; marketing of, 35–38, 210, 211, 249n24; social and aesthetic debates about, 4; and society, 14; theory of, 167–68 (*see also* aesthetics); viewing of, 34
art history, recent developments in, 239n4
Arthur (artist's son) (fictional character), 77, 83, 93–94, 186
artisan class, 140–41
artistic freedom: versus economics, 84; in literature, 78
artistic sensitivity versus creativity, 2
artistic taste, improving, 126–28
Artist in Her Painting Room, An (Best), 79, 80
artist/model relationship, 28, 28–29, 29
artists: economic conditions of, 60; focus on, 17–18; public contact of, 252n27; public perception of, 18–19, 21, 60; public visibility of, 36, 252n27; qualities required in, 3, 19; social status of, 18–19, 32–33
art media, similarities across, 5
art nouveau, 215
art objects, 8
art objects, women as, 9, 10, 44, 54, 74, 88–89, 100, 101, 102, 229, 250n7. *See also* women artists: as objects of art
Art of Fiction, The (James), 5
Art of the Brontës, The (Alexander and Sellar), 240n6
Art Student in Munich, An (Howitt), 27, 122, 248n18
art traditions, women artists role in, 3
artwork, entering into, 162–63
asexuality, literary portrayals in disabled people, 181, 182, 190–91
Atwood, Margaret, 232
"Aurora Leigh" (Browning), 133–34
Austen, Jane, 101, 105, 137–38, 157, 158, 183, 247n11, 266n10
autobiography, drawings as, 113
Autobiography (Oliphant), 146, 147, 148
Awakening, The (Chopin), 209, 210
Awakening Conscience, The (Hunt), 51

Banti, Anna, 232
Barbara Lake (fictional character), 139, 140, 142–43, 144, 146
Barbara's History (Edwards), 254n4
Barbauld, A. L. (Anna), 157, 160
Barker, Deborah Ellen, 8
Barnew, Matthew, 233, 235, 236
Barrell, John, 168, 169
Barrett, Michele, 14
Bashkertseff, Marie, 190, 249n30, 265n8
Battersby, Christine, 20
Baudelaire, Charles, 204, 205
Beale, Sophia, 59–61, 62
beauty (defined), 3
Belsey, Catherine, 240n5

Benjamin, Walter, 245n31
Bennett, Tony, 14
Bentham, 260n20
Berenice (Jewish woman), 135
Berg, Margaret Mary, 70–71
Bermingham, Ann, 105
Bersani, Leo, 240n5
Bertha Mason (fictional character), 105, 183, 185, 192, 254n3, 255n14
Bertram, Anthony, 211, 213, 216
Best, Mary Ellen, 79, *80*
Beth March (fictional character), 266n10
Bewick illustrations, 118, 242n15, 254n5, 254n8, 256n17, 256n20
biographical interpretation of artwork, 68–69
biography writing, 172–73
blindness in literature, 97, 186, 257n21
Blunden, Anna, 39, 45, 107, 108, 171
Bodichon, Barbara, 31, 38–39, *40*, 40–41, 83, 84, 119, 121, 122, 129–30
body: discourse on, 3, 19 (*see also* female body); novels linked to, 257n21
Bohls, Elizabeth, 15
Bonheur, Rosa, 56, 58, 190, 212
Book of Sibyls, The (Ritchie), 157–58, 160, 174
Boumelha, Penny, 240n5
bourgeois realism, 245n32
Bouvier, Agnes, 45
boy and his drawing, fictional scene of, 174
Braddon, Mary Elizabeth, 157
Brandon, Colonel (fictional character), 266n10
Brantlinger, Patrick, 97
Brontë, Anne: art education of, 26, 78; artistic status of, 4; artwork of, 65–68, *66*; on gender, 253n29; low-public profile of, 34; works of, 21, 30, 63–65, 73, 172, 185–86, 219, 249n24 (*see also specific title, e.g.: Tenant of Wildfell Hall, The* [Brontë]); writings on, 157

Brontë, Branwell, 26, 64, 65, 201, 252n26, 258n13
Brontë, Charlotte: art education of, 26, 106–7; artistic interests and ambitions of, 65, 98, 99; artistic status of, 4; low public profile of, 34; paintings, real cited by, 242n15; works of, 2, 21, 73, 185 (*see also specific title, e.g.: Jane Eyre* [Brontë]); writings on, 157
Brontë, Patrick, 252n26
Brooks, Peter, 6
Broughton, Rhoda, 157
Browning, Elizabeth Barrett, 133–34
Browning, Robert, 12
Brownlow, Emma, 46, 49
Brutus, 188
Brynhild (mythical character), 201–2, 203
Burke, Edmund, 244n28, 263n4
Burne-Jones, Edward, 32
Butler, Elizabeth Thompson, 33, 61–62, 79, 131, 212
Bylerly, Alison, 7, 13
Byron, 193, 199
Byronic hero, tradition of, 21

cabinet pictures, 132
Caird, Mona, 209
Cameron, Julia Margaret, 261n5
Carlyle, Thomas, 17–18
Carnell, Rachel, 73
Cassell's children's book series, 131
Casteras, Susan, 52, 178
Cat's Eye (Atwood), 232
Cavendish, Mr., 140, 142
Caws, Mary Ann, 241n7
Celia Manners (fictional character), 183, 185, 186, 196–97
Charlotte, Queen, 159
Charlotte Brontë and Defensive Conduct (Gezari), 257n21
Charles Tansley (fictional character), 75
charter, nature as origin for, 134
Cherry, Deborah, 38, 40, 178
child custody laws, 82–83

children: of artists in fiction, 77, 83, 93–94; as art subjects, 108, 193
Chitham, Edward, 65, 67
Cholmondeley, Mary, 157, 209
Chopin, Kate, 209, 210
Christal Manners (fictional character), 186, 197
Chronicles of Carlingford series, 136
Churchill, Frank, 266n10
class: boundaries and art, 141, 257n4; gender and, 87; literary commentaries on, 99; middle class, 240n5, 262n2; triadic structure, 86–87; working class, 220
Claude Faversham (fictional character), 227, 229, 230
Claxton, Florence, 39, 45, 49–50, 50, 150, 255n11
Clayton, Ellen, 23, 56–57, 58, 62, 175–76
Clever Woman of the Family, The (Yonge), 200, 207
Codell, Julie, 18, 58–59
Cohen, Jeffrey Jerome, 263–64n6
Cohen, Mrs. (fictional character), 123, 124
collaborative art ventures, 124–25
Collins, Wilkie, 242n14, 246n1
Colonel Brandon (fictional character), 266n10
community formation, 244n28
companion, paid, serving as, 249n24
composite characters, women artists as, 8
Comte, 259n20
Consuelo (Sand), 189, 209, 243n25
consumption, aesthetics of, 245n30
contemporary issues, literary commentary on, 159
"contested image," woman painter as, 2
Cooper, Anthony Ashley. *See* Shaftesbury, Earl of (Anthony Ashley Cooper)
Corelli, Marie, 242n12
Corinne (de Staël), 133, 188–89, 209, 243n25

"Corinne of the Capitol" (Hemans), 189
Corinthian Maid (Dibutade), 43, 44, 58
Cotes, Mrs. Everard (Sara Jeannette Duncan), 209, 217
courtly love poem, 10
courtship, art as, 47, 102–3, 104–6, 113
Craik, Dinah Mulock, 4, 22, 30, 180, 182–83, 184, 185–88, 190–98, 200, 208
creation process, description of, 117
creative producer, woman's role as, 161
crippled people in literature, 199
Critical Practice (Belsey), 240n5
cubism, 241n6
cult of personality, 235, 236
cultural change, art as medium for, 3

Daisy Chain, The (Yonge), 207
Damer, Mrs. Anne Seymour, 165, 166, 167, 171, 172
"Damerian Apollo" (engraving), *166*
Dance, Nathaniel, 176
Daniel Deronda (fictional character), 130, 131, 133, 134–35
Daniel Deronda (Eliot), 21, 121, 129–30, 131–33, 134–36, 140–41, 246n1, 249n24
Daughter of Today, A (Cotes), 209, 217
Daughters of Danaus, The (Caird), 209
David Copperfield (Dickens), 222
death, painting as harbinger of, 6
debauched artist (stereotype), 21
Declaration in Favour of Women's Suffrage 1889, 38
deformity or disability: in Greek culture, 183; as incompleteness, 263n4; moral defect connection to, 186; mothers blamed for, 262–63n3; in Victorian culture, 181, 182; women artist connection to, 22, 180, 182, 183–85, *184*, 205, 253n30 (monstrosity)
de Horn, Count, 157, 161–62, 165, 176

Delorme (portraitist) (fictional character), 228
democracy and art, 15, 244n26
DeMorgan, Evelyn, 216
Denisoff, Denis, 192
Derby Day (Frith), 4
de Rossi, Giovanni, 176
design (art): in literature, 120, 123, 124, 125, 128; taste in, 126
Desire and Domestic Fiction (Armstrong), 240n5
de Staël, Madame Germaine, 133, 188–89, 209, 243n25
Diana of the Crossways (Meredith), 252n23
diary as literary device, 72–73, 90, 91
Dibutade (Corinthian Maid), 43, 44, 58
Dickens, Charles, 6, 159, 181, 201, 242n12
Dicksee, Margaret Isabel, *177*, 177–78
Dido (mythical character), 115
disabled people, representation of, 180–81
Discourses (Reynolds), 168
disinterest, Kantian notion of, 244n27
diver as seeker after truth (metaphor), 91
division of labor, 245n30
divorce reform bills, 83
Dixon, Ella Hepworth, 209, 217
domestic fiction, 164, 198
domestic mess, figurative cleaning up of, 91–92
domestic subjects of art, 29–30, 42, 108, 203, 257n2
Dora (fictional character), 222, 223
Dorothea Brooks (fictional character), 134
double-drawing, 92–93
Dowling, Linda, 18, 243–44nn26–28
drama, history as, 159
drawing as required accomplishment, 23
Du Maurier, George, 242n12
Duncan, Sara Jeannette. *See* Cotes, Mrs. Everard (Sara Jeannette Duncan)

Dutch painting, 130, 131
Dynevor Terrace (Yonge), 207

Eagleton, Terry, 3, 13–14, 15, 86–87
Eastlake, Charles, 108–9, 126–28
Eastlake, Charles, Sir, 108–9, 113, 257n8
Eastlake, Lady (Elizabeth Rigby), 38, 113, 257n8
economic interactions, paintings as artifacts in, 242n11
economics, theory of, 245n30
Edgar Underwood (fictional character), 201–3, 205, 206
Edgeworth, Maria, 157
Edna Pontellier (fictional character), 209, 210
education and training, women's access to, 8
Edwards, Amelia, 248n18, 254n4
ekphrasis, 8–11, 12–13, 21, 69, 71, 99–100, 102, 114–15, 116, 117–18, 160, 194, 201, 241n8
Elements of Drawing (Ruskin), 107, 169, 170–71
Elfride (fictional character), 209
Eliot, George: art and social power, commentary on, 1; categorization of, 4; M. Oliphant compared to, 147, 148; paintings, real, cited by, 242n15; A. Ritchie's writings on, 157; teacher-student romances in fiction of, 246n1; women artists, perception of, 56; works of, 21, 120, 121, 129–30, 131–36, 193, 242n12, 249n24 (see also *Daniel Deronda* [Eliot])
Elise Delaunay (fictional character), 219, 220, 221–23, 231
Ellet, Elizabeth, 57–58, 62, 175, 176
Ellis, Sarah Stickney, 24–26, 109–10
Elton, Mr. (fictional character), 101
emasculation fear, 165, 166
Emin, Tracey, 233
Emma (Austen), 101, 105, 137–38, 266n10

emotional abuse in literature, 64
emotionality, attitudes toward, 20
enargeia (rhetorical device), 10
English Female Artists (Clayton), 56–57, 175–76
English Laws for Women in the Nineteenth Century (Norton), 83
English Novel, The (Eagleton), 252n26
engraving in literature, 120, 132
entertainment, vocation of, 30
Ermine Williams (fictional character), 200, 207
eroticism and art: as barrier to female aesthetic production, 76, 89–90, 212–13; link between, 3, 17, 21, 28–29, 43, 44–52, 214, 214–16, *215,* 218, 232–33, 256n19
erotic plot, 135–36. *See also* marriage: in literature
espieglerie (prankishness), 157
Esther (fictional character), 123, 124, 128
esthetic critiques, paintings as medium for, 3
Ethel May (fictional character), 207
ethical qualities of artists, 19
Eve, role of, 161
Extraordinary Bodies: Figuring Physical Disability in American Culture and Literature (Garland-Thomson), 181
eye, prominence of, 257n21
Eyre, Jane (fictional character). See *Jane Eyre* (Brontë)

Falkland, Dr. (fictional character), 123, 124
fame, women and, 189, 195
family and career: compatability between, 207; conflict between, 133–34, 146, 189
Far From the Madding Crowd (Hardy), 131
Feinstein, Rachel, 233
Felix Underwood (fictional character), 198
female artistic tradition, 157

female body: artist's, 45, 47, 95, 153, 162, 233, 234, 236–37; perceptions of, 183; problematic aspects of, 22, 43, 150, 161, 176, 183
female creativity, male control of, 52, 266n10
female deformity in literature, 181–83
female identity: art role in revealing, 101–2; representations of, 37–38
female independence, 223, 225, 226
female nude portraits, 216–17
female professionalism: in literature, 197, 219, 228–29; problems of, 79, 81–82
female publicity, debate over, 33
Female School of Art, 34
Female School of Design, 125–26
female stereotypes, 163–64
female writing tradition, 157
feminism: aesthetics and, 74–75; in *Jane Eyre,* 97; realism and, 240n5; turn-of-century, 218–19
feminist literary scholarship, 2
feminist movement: women artist involvement in, 38–41, 49, 130, 178; women writer involvement in, 84, 261n1
feminist utopia in literature, 263n5
feminity, social codes of, 96, 114, 134
Fenwick's Career (Ward), 218
fiction, appreciation enhanced by biographic appetite, 18
fictionalized biography, 159, 172
Fictions of Affliction (Stoddard Holmes), 181
figure painting, 30
Finishing Touches (Hayllar), 79, *81*
Firth, William Powell, 32
Flint, Kate, 5, 34, 96
flowers as art subjects, 29, 30
Folio Club, 121, 248n19
Forbes (painter) (fictional character), 218
foreigner, woman artist as, 87–88
formalism and materialism, balance between, 15
Fountain, The (Sargent), 52–54, *53*

Fox, Eliza, 31, 38, 39
frame, as metaphor, 160, 163
freak shows, 182
Frith, William Powell, 4
fruit as art subject, 30
Fuseli, Henry, 176

Gagnier, Regina, 245n30
Galloway, Mr., 61, 62
Garland-Thomson, Rosemarie, 181, 182
Gaskell, Elizabeth, 98, 157
gay artists, 236
gender: and aesthetics, 19–20, 155; and class, 87; and disability, 185, 186, 187, 190, 199, 206, 207, 263–64n6; distinctions of, 234–36; and ekphrasis, 8, 9, 10; equality, 219; ideology of, 16; literary commentaries on, 99, 145; politics of, 62, 114; power struggles and, 87; relations in literature, 251n11; resistance in art, 11; similarities between, 253n29
Gender and Genius (Battersby), 20
gender equality, 228
gender norms: challenging, 118, 129, 141, 239n3; women artists and, 7, 121, 141, 175, 185, 221, 237
Generation of Animals (Aristotle), 183
genius: concept of, 17, 20; women and, 187–88, 189, 199
Gentileschi, Artemisia, 151, 232
Gentle Art of Making Enemies, The (Whistler), 221
George Eliot and the Visual Arts (Witemeyer), 240n6
Geraldine Underwood (fictional character), 180, 182, 183, 194, 198, 199, 200–204, 205–6, 207–8
Gerin, Winifred, 72, 156
Gezari, Janet, 257n21
"ghost story," 160
Gilbert, Sandra, 92–93
Gilbert Markham (fictional character), 71–72, 76, 77, 79, 87, 88–89, 90, 94, 95, 250nn6–7, 252n21

Gillett, Paula, 20
Gillies, Margaret, 39
Glasgow School of Art, 213
Gober, Robert, 233, 236
Goethe, 18
Golden Arrow (Hardy), 242n12
Goodbrand, Robert, 173
Gordon, Mary, 232
governesses: employment for, 249n24; in fiction, 140, 239n3; public perceptions of, 2, 55, 56, 257n1
Grandcourt (fictional character), 129
Grand Style, 170
Grant, Francis, 32–33
Greek statues, 169
Greek Studies (Pater), 43
Greenaway, Kate, 42, *42,* 131
Grote, Harriet, 31
Gubar, Susan, 92–93
Guest, Barbara, 243n24
Guiseppe (sculptor) (fictional character), 122–23, 124, 128
Gwendolyn Harleth (fictional character), 129, 130, 132, 133, 134

Halliwell, Stephen, 167
Hamerton, Philip Gilbert, 32–33
Hamilton, Ann, 233, 234, 235
Handbook to the Louvre, A (Beale), 59–60
Hans Meyrick (fictional character), 130, 134, 135, 192
Hardy, Thomas, 131, 209, 217, 242n12
Harold Gwynne (fictional character), 192, 195
Harriet Smith (fictional character), 101
Hawthorne, Nathaniel, 249n25
Hay, Jane Bentham, 122
Hayllar, Jessica, 79, *81*
Hayt, Elizabeth, 233
Hazlitt, William, 169, 173
Heffernan, James, 9–10, 11, 12, 115
Helen Graham (fictional character), 21, 30, 65, 68–71, 72, 73, 74–75, 76–78, 79, 83, 85, 87, 88–90,

92–93, 94–95, 98–99, 104–5, 172, 186, 255n12
Hemans, Felicia, 189–90
Henry Gowan (fictional character), 201
Hephaistos (Vulcan) (mythical character), 199, 263n3
Hercules (mythical character), 261n3
Hereford, Laura, 39
Hermans, Felicia, 157
heroines, women artists as, 7, 8, 16, 22
heroine's story, possible plot lines for, 135–36
Hester (fictional character), 209
Hester's Sacrifice (Tabor), 254n4, 264n7
High Art, 4, 20–21, 24, 45, 120, 127, 128, 133, 146, 190, 193, 194, 196, 201, 207–8, 217
Hints on Household Taste (Eastlake), 108–9, 126–28
historical fiction, 158–60, 161
Historical Sketches of the Reign of George II (Oliphant), 159
historiography, 262n6
History of David Grieve, The (Ward), 218, 219–23, 229, 231, 249n24
history painting, 4, 30, 108, 120, 128, 150, 168–69, 178, 193
Hollander, John, 12
Homer (fictional character), 13
"Horse-market, The" (Bonheur), 58
housekeeper, as seeker after truth (metaphor), 91–92
Howitt, Anna Mary, 4, 21, 27, 38, 84, 120, 121–25, 128–29, 193, 248n19, 249n24
Howitt, Mary, 38, 83–85, 87–88, 121, 247n18, 249n24
Howitt, William, 83–85, 87–88
Huet, Marie-Hélène, 94
Huntingdon, Arthur (fictional character), 64, 68–69, 70, 72, 73, 78, 85–86, 87, 89, 92, 93–94, 95, 104–5, 252n21

Iconology (Mitchell), 9
ideal beauty in art, 169
idealism in art, 204
identities, production as basis for, 245n30
ideological barriers of women artists, 3
ideological domination through literature, 240n5
ideological issues in literature, 240n5
ideological screen, history as, 159–60
ideology and aesthetics, 14–15
Ideology of the Aesthetic, The (Eagleton), 13–14
idle rich in literature, 142, 258n9
"Idylls of the King" (Tennyson), 159
illustration and illustrators in literature, 5, 120
imaginary works of art: in Brontë's *Jane Eyre*, 106, 111–12 (see also *Jane Eyre* [Brontë]: paintings described in); in Brontë's *Tenant of Wildfell Hall*, 68–71, 76, 77–78; in Craik's *Olive*, 193–94, 196; overview of, 12; in Yonge's *Pillars of the House*, 201–4, 205, 206
imagination-based art, 107–8, 171–72, 174
imitation in art, 167–68, 169–70, 174
imperialism in women's fiction, 97
Impressionism, 221
individualism, reading as act of, 96–97
interart blending, barriers to, 11–12
interart criticism, 4–5, 7–8, 12. *See also* ekphrasis
interart theory, 21
interior design, 126–27
interior design in literature, 138
internal experience revealed through art, 111–12
international influence on English art, 126
interpretation versus imitation, 166–68, 169–71
Isabel (actress) (fictional character), 218
Isabel Conway (fictional character), 207

Jacobs, N.M., 73
Jacobus, Mary, 96

James, Henry, 5, 249n25
Jameson, Anna, 18, 31, 38, 83, 264n9
Jane Eyre (Brontë): art, giving up, 219; art as courtship in, 47, 102–3, 104, 105–6; feminism in, 97; fiction influenced by, 254n4; *Olive* (Craik) compared to, 183, 185, 186, 192, 194, 195, 197–98; paintings described in, 6, 21, 65, 98–99, 100, 101, 102, 103–4, 108, 109, 113–14, 115–17; real artists compared to, 255n11; realism versus, 240n5; reviews of, 113, 257n8; self-expression in, 95; *Tenant of Wildfell Hall* compared to, 63, 87; visual imagery in, 97–98, 100
Jane Fairfax (fictional character), 266n10
Japanese prints, 215
Jenny Wren (fictional character), 180, 181, 263n4
job interview, courtship linked with, 105–6
Jo March (fictional character), 49
Jopling, Louise, 27, 29, 38, 59, 62, 79, 190
journal as literary device, 90
journals, 15
Judaism in literature, 129
Jude the Obscure (Hardy), 209, 217

Kahlo, Frida, 151, 261n2
Kant, Immanuel, 16–17, 244n27, 244n28
Kaplan, Cora, 185
Kate Meyrick (fictional character), 130, 134
Kauffman, Angelica: aesthetic views of, 166–67, 171–72; as art subject, 152–55, *153,* 176–79, *177, 179;* artwork of, 150, 161, 165, 175, 176; background of, 150, 249n28; biographical treatment of, 58, 149–50, 151, 155, 175–76; evaluation of, 212; femininity, capitalizing on, 190; fictional character based on (See *Miss Angel and Fulham Lawn* [Ritchie]); literary references to, 192; marriage of, 164–65; as Royal Academy founder, 161, 165, 246n6; self-portraits of, 152–55, *153*
Kauffman, Joseph, 176
Keats, John, 9, 10, 12
Keen, Suzanne, 133
Keywords (Williams), 14
Klages, Mary, 181
Klesmer (fictional character), 129, 134, 136, 140–41
Kochanek, Lisa, 182

Labille-Guiard, Adelaide, 265n4
Lady Macbeth (fictional character), 138
"Lady Students at the National Gallery" (cartoon), *184*
Lady W. (Wentworth), 157, 163, *177, 178*
landscapes, 29, 128, 168, 172
Langer, Suzanne, 11
Langland, Elizabeth, 73
Lapierre, Alexandra, 232
Laqueur, Thomas, 183
Latmos (mythical mountain), 112, 256n16
Laurencin, Marie, 211, 213, 216
Lauterbach, Ann, 243n24
Lawrence, Mr. (fictional character), 266n10
Lawrence, Thomas, 192
Lectures on Art (Ruskin), 19
Ledger, Sally, 210
Leighton, Frederic, 33
Leighton, Lord, 32–33, 61
leisure class in literature, 142, 258n9
Leonard Mordant (fictional character), 257n4
Leonardo da Vinci, 242n17, 245n34
lesbian desire: in art, 29, 216; in literature, 191–92
letters as literary device, 90
"Let Us Join the Ladies" (caricature of women artists), *48*
Levine, Caroline, 242n16

Levine, George, 15, 240n5
Lewes, George Henry, 97–98, 110–11, 129, 130
Lewis, Linda, 189, 209, 217–18, 222, 243n25
Lily Briscoe (fictional character), 1, 43, 219, 232
Linton, Eliza Lynn, 210–11
literary critiques, paintings as medium for, 3
literary pictorialism, 241n8
Literary Realism and the Ephrastic Tradition (Smith), 6
literature: and painting, interplay between, 1, 3, 4–11, 12; power of, 174; taste, shifts in, 265n7
Little Dorrit (Dickens), 6, 201, 242n12
Little Loves (Greenaway), 42
Little Women (Alcott), 49, 266n10
Lizzy (fictional character), 123, 125, 128
Lord Tatham (fictional character), 226–27, 230
Louie (fictional character), 220, 221, 223
Louisa, Marchioness of Waterford (Lady Waterford), 212, 257n2
love and art, conflict between, 133–34, 221–22, 231
love story versus feminist aesthetic, 74–75
low arts, 120, 121
Lucilla Marjoribanks (fictional character), 137–38, 141, 142, 143, 144, 145
Lucrece (fictional character), 10, 256n18
Lucy Snowe (fictional character), 110, 118
Lydia Penfold (fictional character), 218, 224–28, 229, 230

Mab Meyrick (fictional character), 130, 134, 135
MacDonald, Frances, 213, 214, 214–16, 215, 217

MacDonald, Margaret, 213
madness in literature, 110–11, 183
Madoff, Steven Henry, 233
Maggie Tulliver (fictional character), 134
Making Sex (Laqueur), 183
Manchester Society for Women Painters, 257n2
Marble Fawn, The (Hawthorne), 249n25
Marcella (Ward), 217, 223
"Margaret von Ehrenberg, Artist-Wife" (Howitt), 83, 84–85, 87–88, 121, 247n18, 249n24
Marianne Dashwood (fictional character), 266n10
marital abuse in literature, 64, 69, 72, 73, 92, 250n8
marriage: art as alternative to, 182, 186, 187, 188, 189; and career, 230; equality in, 262n1; in literature, 134–35, 136, 161–62, 164–65, 192, 195, 219, 222, 230, 231, 240n5; as metaphor, 187, 190
Married Woman's Property Act (MWPA), 39–40, 83
married women, property laws affecting, 81–82, 83, 84, 85–86, 195
Martin, John, 78, 254n8
Martineau, Harriet, 39
Martinez, Michele, 243n24
Marxist methodology of aesthetic investigation, 15
Master Christian, The (Corelli), 242n12
masters, study of old, 168, 170
materialism, artistic beauty versus, 128, 193, 201
materialist aesthetics, 16, 21
materialist thinking, 14, 15
Mating of Lydia, The (Ward), 218, *224*, 224–30, *225*, 231
matriarchal cultures, prehistoric overthrow of, 242n18
McMaster, Juliet, 72
medieval art and architecture, 126
Meliora, Miss (fictional character), 192

Melrose, Mr. (fictional character), 229–30
Melrose, Mrs. (fictional character), 229–30
Meltzer, Françoise, 6–7
memoirs, 15
men: demasculinization as art models, 28–29; dominion of, 188
mental furniture, artwork as, 106
Merritt, Anna Lea, 27–28, 216
Meyer, Jeffrey, 241n8
Meyrick family (fictional family), 129, 130, 131–33, 134–35
Michael (art teacher) (fictional character), 186–87, 188, 190–91, 192, 193, 194, 195, 201
Michelangelo, 188
middle class, rise of, 240n5
middle-class domesticity, 262n2
Middlemarch (Eliot), 129, 134, 242n12
Mill, John Stuart, 260n20
Millenium [sic] Hall (Scott), 263n5
Miller, D.A., 240n5
Mill on the Floss (Eliot), 134
Milton, John, 245n34
Mirah (fictional character), 129, 131, 133, 134, 135, 136
miscegenation, 186, 197
misogyny, cultural, 20
Miss Angel and Fulham Lawn (Ritchie), 22, 58, 131, 140, 149, 155, 156–57, 158–63, 164, 165–67, 170, 171–72, 173–75, 176, 246n6
'*Miss Angel'—Angelica Kauffmann, introduced by Lady Wentworth, visits Mr. Reynolds' studio* (Dicksee), *177*, 177–78
Miss Bretherton (Ward), 218
Miss Marjoribanks (Oliphant), 21, 26, 121, 125, 136–46, 249n24
Mitchell, David, 181
Mitchell, Sally, 185
Mitchell, W. J. T., 9, 10
models: finding, 29; men as, 43, 52–54, 53, 134–35, 220; women as, 2. *See also* art objects
Modernism, 209

modernist art and literature, 241n6
Modern Lover, A (Moore), 249n25
Modern Painters (Ruskin), 19, 130, 169–70, 174
Modern Painting (Moore), 75, 212
Moglen, Helene, 240n5
monster, position of, 264n6
monstrosity (defined), 94
Moore, George, 71, 72, 74, 75–76, 212–13, 236–37, 249n25
Moore, Marianne, 243n24
moral community, forming through art, 244n28
morality, art role in, 21, 203, 231
Mordecai (fictional character), 130, 135
Morisot, Berthe, 29
Morris, William, 32–33
Moser, Mary, 151, 152, 246n6, 249n28
motherhood in literature, 250n8
Motion Picture, A (Richardson), 265n4
Mrs. Dymond (Ritchie), 156
Mulock, Dinah, 249n24
Mulvey, Laura, 13
Murdoch, Iris, 232
muses, women as, 2
music as courtship, 92, 104–5
"Music" (figure) as allegory, 154
music in literature, 129
Mutrie sisters, 39
"My Last Duchess" (Browning), 12
mythological women in art, 201–2, 203, 258n12

Nameless and Friendless (Osborn), 36–38, *37*
narrative fiction, commentary on, 206
narrative moments, symbolic potential of, 173–74
Narrative Prosthesis (Mitchell and Snyder), 181
narrative signals, paintings as, 6
nationality and art, 87–88
natural history, study of, 25
Natural History (Pliny), 43
nature as art subject: drawing from, 107; fidelity to, 172, 175, 203;

imitation of, 166–67, 168, 169, 170–71
nature of woman versus artist, 134
Neoclassicism, 168
Neo-Expressionism, 234
nested narrative structure, 72–73, 74
Newcomes, The (Thackeray), 242n12
New Woman: artists, 42, 213, 217, 223, 231; discourse on, 212, 228; in fiction, 217–18, 219, 226, 231; public backlash against, 42, 210–11, 213, 251n14; scholarship on, 210
Nietzsche, Friedrich, 16, 17
Nochlin, Linda, 149
nonfiction: aesthetic treatises within, 15; women's art described in, 243n23
nonworking married woman as ideal, 119
normalcy, critique of, 181, 264n8
Norton, Caroline, 39, 81–82, 83, 86, 264n9
notional ekphrasis, 12
novel, characteristics of, 160
novel structure, critique of, 71–74
nude figures, painting of, 27–28, 29, 30, 108, 123, 215, 216–17, 220, 221, 246n6
Nunn, Pamela Gerrish, 122

objectivity in art, 172
Observations on the Natural Claim of the Mother to the Custody of her Infant Children (Norton), 82
occupation, importance of, 258n9
occupation, language of, 257n9
"Ode on a Grecian Urn" (Keats), 9, 12
Oedipus (mythical character), 199
oil paintings in literature, 251n15
Olbert, Elizabeth, 236
Oldcastle, John, 175
Old-Fashioned Girl, An (Alcott), 249n26
Old Kensington (Ritchie), 156
Oliphant, Margaret, 4, 21, 26, 120, 121, 125, 136–48, 157, 159, 164, 173, 193, 206, 249n24, 262n7, 264n9
Olive (Craik), 22, 30, 180, 182–83, 185–88, 190–98, 200, 201, 207–8
Olive (Mulock), 249n24
Opie, Amelia, 157
Orr, Clarissa Campbell, 20
Osborn, Emily Mary, 33, 36–38, 37, 39, 40, *40*
Our Mutual Friend (Dickens), 181
outsiders, women artists as, 7
Oxford Companion to Art, 151, 152
Oxford Dictionary of Art, 176
Oxford Movement, 262n2

painter-hero in fiction, 7
painters as outsiders, 7
painting: entering into, 162–63; mythical origin of, 43
Painting and the Novel (Meyer), 241n8
"Painting" (figure) as allegory, 152–53, *153*, 154, *154*
paintings, real, fictional references to, 118, 128, 130, 165, 242n15, 254n5, 256n17, 256n20
Parable of Love (Love's Mirror), A (Rossetti), 50–52, *51*
paragone (contest between art forms), 12–13, 242n17
Parkes, Bessie Rayner, 121
pastoral, history as, 159
Pater, Walter, 43
paternal purity, critique of, 264n8
Paterson, Helen. *See* Allingham, Helen (née Paterson)
patriarchal culture, 147
personal versus political focus in art, 243n22
Phelps, Elizabeth Stuart, 58, 219
Philoktetes (mythical character), 199
Philosophical Enquiry (Burke), 263n4
photography, advent of, 5
physical being of artist, 19
physical difference, art as compensation for, 186–87
pictorialism, 9

Picture of Dorian Gray, The (Wilde), 242n12
pictures, characters as, 135, 197
Picture Sunday, 35–36, 194
Picture Theory (Mitchell), 10
Pillars of the House (Yonge), 22, 180, 182, 193, 198–99, 200–204, 205–6, 249n24
Plagens, Peter, 236
Plath, Sylvia, 243n24
Plato, 17, 101, 167
Pliny, 43
poetry: paintings in, 240n6; women's paintings in, 243n24
"Poetry" (figure) as allegory, 152, 153, 154, *154*
points of view, shifting, 90
political economy, education in, 137, 146
political fiction, 198
political reform: art role in, 3, 231; in literature, 138
politics and art, 16, 244n26
Politics of Pleasure, The (Regan), 14
Pond, A (MacDonald), *214*, 214–16
Poovey, Mary, 2
portraiture: biography writing compared to, 173; breaking into, 30; of children and animals, 108; in literature, 6–7, 84, 92, 93–94, 100–101, 102, 115–16, 120, 160–61, 165, 201
postfeminist artists, 236
power relations, Foucaldian "dense transfer point" of, 2
Poynter, Edward, 169
Prendergast, Christopher, 244n29
Prince Camaralzaman (fictional character), 135
private focus in art, 169
production, aesthetics of, 245n30
professionalization, women's access to, 8
Professor, The (Brontë), 257n21
"Properzia Rossi" (Hemans), 189
prostitution, 119
Psomiades, Kathy, 44, 231
psyche: literary emanations of, 254n3; painting role in revealing, 65, 98, 104, 114
psychological events, artwork representing, 65
public virtue, art role in, 169
Purnell, Thomas, 119
Pygmalion (mythical sculptor), 17
Pykett, Lyn, 210

"Quatre Bras" (Butler), 62
Queen of the Air (Ruskin), 19

race issues in literature, 197
Rachel (fictional character), 207
racial purity, critique of, 264n8
Rae, Henrietta, 27–28, 216
rape: as art theme, 11; figurative form of, 86
Reading in Detail: Aesthetics and the Feminine (Schor), 204
reading scenes in literature, 96–97
real characters, fictional artists based on, 22
real historical paintings, literary references to, 8
realism: in art, 108–9, 127–28, 131, 172, 174, 204, 242n16; in literature, 4, 6, 7, 13, 64, 69, 90–92, 110–11, 133, 206, 262n6; movement, 6
real versus imaginary, blurred division between, 173–74
Recollections of a Spinster Aunt (Beale), 59–61
Red Pottage (Cholmondeley), 209
Regan, Stephen, 14
religious art subjects, 203–4
Rembrandt, 130, 245n34
representational art, 215
representation and narrative, studies in, 241n8
representation and power, relation between, 244n29
Reynolds, Joshua: as art subject, 175, *177*, 178, 179; art theory of,

167–68, 171, 172; critics of, 170; fictional portrayal of, 159, 161, 163, 165, 166, 171, 172; A. Kauffman relationship with, 150, 151, 161, 163, 165, 212; literary references to, 130, 192; wealth and status of, 32

Richardson, Margarget Foster, 265n4

Ritchie, Anne Thackeray, 4, 22, 58, 131, 140, 149, 155–63, 164–65, 166–67, 170, 171–72, 173–75, 176, 246n6

Rivera, Diego, 151, 261n2

Robert Elsmere (Ward), 218, 219

Rochester (fictional character), 47, 97, 98, 102–3, 104, 105, 106, 107, 109, 111–12, 113, 115–16, 117, 118

Roderick Hudson (James), 249n25

"Roll Call, The" ("Calling the Roll after an Engagement, Crimea") (Butler), 61, 79

romance narratives: alternatives to, 193, 207; dismantling of, 222; traditional, 133

romance tragedy, 165

romantic biography, 160

romantic historiography, 262n6

Romantic period: aesthetics during, 15; genius, concept in, 20; ideal of, 7; painting origin story, decline following, 43; Victorian reaction to, 234; word and image relationship during, 9

Room of One's Own, A (Woolf), 60, 155, 255n10

Rosamond Oliver (fictional character), 100–101, 102

rose blooming in snow (metaphor), 95

Rose Lake (fictional character), 121, 137, 139–40, 141–43, 144–46, 147, 148

Rose (musician) (fictional character), 218

Rossetti, Dante Gabriel, 50–52, *51*

Rossi, Properzia (Prosperia), 189, 192

Roston, Murray, 241n7

Rothesay family (fictional family), 185, 186

Royal Academy: art exhibited and sold through, 31, 33, 34–35, 35, 38, 61; founding of, 161, 165, 246n6; in literature, 194; presidents of, 169, 257n8; rise of, 32; schools of, 216; women admitted to schools of, 39, 41; women elected to, 150, 216–17, 250n32; women's art displayed through, 59, 107, 122

Royal Female School of Art, 126

Rubens paintings, 128

Ruskin, John, 19, 107, 108, 112, 130, 168, 169–71, 174, 203, 244n28, 262n9

safety in art, 172

Salome and the Dance of Writing (Meltzer), 6–7

Sand, George, 157, 189, 209, 243n25

Sandcastle, The (Murdoch), 232

Sara Derwent (fictional character), 191, 192

Sargent, John Singer, 52–54, *53*

scene of painting (term), 3, 242n16

School of Life (Howitt), 257n4

Schools of Design, 125–26

Schor, Naomi, 204

Schwartz-McKinzie, Esther, 156

science education for women, 25

science in literature, 129

Scott, Sarah, 263n5

sculptors in fiction, 165

sculpture, mythical origin of, 43

Sedgwick, Eve, 192

seduction through art, 101, 102

self, submersion of, 175

self-expression, attitudes toward, 20

self-expression in literature, 93, 95, 108, 110

Self-Portrait (Kauffman), 152, *153*, 154

self-portraits, 87–88, 98, 152–55, 249n23, 265n4

Self-Portrait (Smyth), 265n4

Self-Portrait with Two Pupils (Labille-Guiard), 265n4

self-repression in literature, 93

Sellars, Jane, 67, 240n6
Sense and Sensibility (Austen), 266n10
sensitivity, attitudes toward, 20
sensus communis, 124, 244n28
sentimental art, criticism of, 107–8
sentimental fiction, 160
sentimental narrative mode, 161
separate spheres doctrine, 218, 251n11
"Seven Theses" (Cohen), 264n6
sexes. *See* gender
sexual equality, 219
sexuality in fiction, 219, 240n5
Shaftesbury, Earl of (Anthony Ashley Cooper), 244n28
Shakespeare, William, 10, 245n34, 256n18
Shaw, Harry, 159
Sheridan, Caroline. *See* Norton, Caroline
Shirley (Brontë), 257n21
Shlain, Leonard, 242n18
Shows of London, The (Altick), 182
Show Sunday, 35–36, 194
Sickert, Walter, 5
Siddal, Elizabeth, 50, 84
Siegel, Jonah, 19
Signorotti, Elizabeth, 73
Silver, Mr. (fictional character), 122, 123–24, 128
single women in literature, 163, 164
Sinnett, Sophia, 46
Sirani, Elisabetta (Elizabeth), 58, 192
Sisters, The (Alma-Tadema), *41*
"Sisters in Art" (Howitt), 21, 84, 121, 122–25, 128–29, 248n18
Sleeping Beauty (fairly tale), modernized revision of, 164
Smith, Barbara Leigh. *See* Bodichon, Barbara
Smith, Kiki, 233, 234–35
Smith, Mack, 6
Smith, Roberta, 237
Smyth, Dorothy Carleton, 265n4
Snyder, Sharon L., 181
social barriers of women artists, 3
social change, art as medium for, 3
social conventions, challenging, 21
social critique, art as medium for, 3, 95
social events, artwork representing, 65
social fragmentation, repairing through realism, 240n5
social hierarchy, 140
social interactions, paintings as artifacts in, 242n11
social issues in literature, 8, 73, 195, 207
social mores, shift in, impact on media, 241n7
social policing, novels as form of, 240n5
social/political versus artistic representation, 244n29
social position, art as means of revealing, 102
social power and potential, painting as medium for, 1
social problem novels, 250n8
social process, art as, 8
social reform, art role in, 230, 231
social reform in literature, 138
social unfairness, anger at, 156–57
Society of Female Artists, 31, 45, 49, 59, 84, 108, 122, 206
Solomon, Rebecca, 39
Spacks, Patricia Meyer, 219
spatial form theories of literature, 241n8
spectator and art object, 16–17, 115
Spending (Gordon), 232
spinsters, stereotypes of, 164
Spivak, Gayatri, 97
St. John Rivers (fictional character), 101, 102, 195
Starzyk, Lawrence, 51, 98, 242n17
Stella Underwood (fictional character), 203, 206
still lives, 108
Stoddard Holmes, Martha, 181, 182, 200
Stoddart, Frances, 45
Stories of English and Foreign Life (Howitt), 83
Story of a Modern Woman, The (Dixon), 209, 217
Story of Avis, The (Phelps), 58, 219

Story of Elizabeth, The (Ritchie), 156, 164
"Studies from Nature: A Model to Make a Boy" (engraving), *166*
studio: access to, 78–79; artistic depiction of, 80–81; as literary setting, 76, 78, 79
Studying Art Abroad (Alcott), 27
subconscious mind, paintings as agent for revealing, 104
subject, history as, 159
subject formation, 244n28
subjects of art: access to, 29–30; in literature, 107, 193, 203–4; restrictions on, 108; unconventional, 107, 211
Sue Bridehead (fictional character), 209, 217
Sunrise at Sea (Brontë), *66, 67*
Sutton-Ramspeck, Beth, 219
Swenson, May, 243n24
Swift, Kate, 45
Swynnerton, Anne Robinson, 216–17, 257n2
Sybilla Rothesay (fictional character), 185, 186
Sypher, Wylie, 241n7

Tabor, Eliza, 254n4, 264n7
Tale of Two Cities, A (Dickens), 159
Tatham, Lord (fictional character), 226–27, 230
teacher-student romances, 246n1
teaching, 30, 120, 249n24
Tenant of Wildfell Hall, The (Brontë), 21, 30, 63–65, 67, 68–75, 76–78, 79, 83, 84–87, 88–95, 98–99, 104–5, 118, 172, 185–86, 219, 249n24, 255n12
textile work, 120, 125
Thackeray, William Makepeace, 155, 156, 242n12
Thorneycroft, Mary, 39
Tiny Tim (fictional character), 181
'Tis a Long Path That Wanders to Desire (Macdonald), *215*, 216

Titian, 130
Titus (Roman emperor), 135
Torgovnick, Mariana, 241n6
To the Lighthouse (Woolf), 1, 43, 75, 219, 232
travel narratives, 15
triadic class structure, 86–87
Trilby (Du Maurier), 242n12
Troy, destruction in art, 115
truth, literary revealing of, 90–92, 94
Twenty Years of My Life (Jopling), 59
Tyson, Nicola, 236

unconventional subject matter in literature, 73
unrepresantable, representation of, 104, 111–12
utopias, female artistic, 121, 122, 124, 134, 136, 148, 263n5

Valkyries as art subjects, 201–2
"Vanishing Day at the Royal Academy," 34, *35*, 252n27
Vice and Virtue, choosing between (allegory), 261n3
Victoria, Queen, 61
Victorian Contexts (Roston), 241n7
Victorians and the Visual Imagination, The (Flint), 5
Vigée-Lebrun, Elizabeth, 212
Villette (Brontë), 2, 110, 118, 257n21
visual and literary representation, joint evolution of, 6
visual arts, literary emphasis on, 5–7
Visual Culture, Theories of, 241n9
Vita di A. Kauffman (de Rossi), 176
von Glehn, Jane Emmet, 52–54, *53*
von Glehn, Wilfred, 52–53, *53*
von Herkomer, Hubert, 250n32
Vreeland, Susan, 232

Walker, Alice, 262n7
Ward, Henrietta (Mrs. E. M.), 27, 31, 36, 38, 212, 257n2

Ward, Mary (Mrs. Humphrey), 4, 22, 157, 163–64, 193, 210, 217–31, *224, 225,* 245n30, 249n24
Ward, Thomas Humphrey, 265n5
watercolors in literature, 103–4, 113–14, 116
Waterford, Lady (Louisa, Marchioness of Waterford), 212, 257n2
Watts, Alaric, 122
Watts, George Frederic, 32
weaving by women, 11
Well-Beloved, The (Hardy), 242n12
Wendorf, Richard, 173
Wentworth, Lady, 157, 163, *177,* 178
West, Benjamin, 150
West Indian women in fiction, 183, 185, 186, 196–97
Wetherley, Johnny (fictional character), 257n4
"Whistler's Mother" (Whistler), 221
Whistler v. Ruskin libel trial, 1877, 221
Wilde, Oscar, 18, 242n12
Williams, Raymond, 14, 244n29
Williams, W. S., 111
Wilmet Underwood (fictional character), 198, 199–200
Wilmot, Miss (fictional character), 104–5
wind, painting, 112
Witemeyer, Hugh, 240n6
Woeful Afflictions (Klages), 181
Wolfson, Susan, 15
"Woman and Fame" (Hemans), 189
Woman Gazing (Brontë), *66,* 67–68
Woman in White, The (Collins), 242n14, 246n1
"Woman Question," 1–2 (women painter emblematic of), 157
Woman's Thoughts about Woman, A (Craik), 30, 261n1
women: aesthetic backlash against, 209; defeminiization, fear of, 228; and deformity, 262–63n3, 263n5; economic freedom of, 8; education for, 137, 146, 218; and fame, 189, 195; job opportunities for, 158; occupations for, 30, 54, 64, 119, 120, 137, 138–39, 141–42; status of, 8, 211; unequal opportunities of, 158
Women and Work (Bodichon), 119
women artists: as art subjects, 46, 47, *48,* 49–54, 79; barriers of, 3, 13, 19, 20, 33, 41–43, 62, 146, 147–48, 149, 156–57, 209, 231, 232–33; biographical treatment of, 58, 150–52; as deviants, 113; economic conditions of, 3, 21, 59–61, 77, 192–93, 194–95, 227; employment for, 30–32, 58, 119, 120–21, 125; eroticization of, 44–52, 62; legacy of, 161; memoirs of, 59–62; modern pressures on, 22; negative portrayal of, 49, 163–64; nonfictional works on, 56–58, 165–66; as objects of art, 46, 48–49, 88–89, 162–63, 180, 206, 220, 233, 234; as occult presences, 262n7; property laws affecting, 79, 81, 84, 85–86, 195; public perception of, 1, 2, 20, 42–43, 44–52, 58–59, 75–76, 143–44, 145, 164, 165, 167, 175, 179, 187–88, 234–35, 236–37; public visibility of, 33–34, 36–38, 54–57, 55, 156, 205–6; qualities required in, 19; rise of, 2, 20, 23–25, 26, 30, 43, 209, 232, 245n34; separation from art produced, 74–75; social conditions for, 21, 121, 143–44, 145, 148, 231, 232; study abroad by, 27; successful examples of, 149 (discovering), 210; writings on, 210
Women Artists in All Ages and Countries (Ellet), 57–58, 175, 176
women doctors, 54
Women Householder's Declaration of 1889, 59
women in entertainment, public perception of, 54–56, *55*
Women in the Victorian Art World (Orr), 20
women lawyers, 54
women musicians: writings on, 210
women readers, cultural discourse on, 96–97

women's art: amateur, 23, 24, 25, 92; attitudes toward, 44–45, 46–49; commercialization of, 24; evaluation of, 3, 16, 20–21, 204, 205, 211–13; ignoring and downplaying of, 165–66, 234, 235, 236; interpretation of, 68–69, 70–71, 100, 114; literary references to, 10–11, 12, 13 (*see also* imaginary works of art; paintings, real, fictional references to); popular appeal of, 193–94, 205, 207–8; purpose of, 102, 109–10

women's music, 92, 104

women's suffrage, 38, 54, 59, 218

women writers: anonymity of, 33, 34; and artists, connection between, 2–3, 8, 57, 62; attitudes toward, 1; economic conditions of, 264n9; employment for, 30, 249n24; in fiction, 49, 200, 207; ideological barriers for, 209; property law impact on, 39, 81–82; writings on, 157, 210

Woodmansee, Martha, 14, 245n33

Woolf, Virginia: A. Brontë's views compared to, 253n29; female artistic tradition recovery project of, 157; M. Oliphant, commentary on, 147; past women artists, views on, 262n7; as A. Ritchie's niece, 156; *Room of One's Own, A,* 60, 155, 255n10; Victorian writer influence on, 1; works of, 75, 219, 232; writing-painting connection recognized by, 1, 43

word and image relationship, 9, 117, 118, 196

working-class heroes in literature, 220

working women: art education for, 125; deformity in, 187, 194; in literature, 129, 140, 141–44, 146, 187, 194; prejudices against, 119, 183; scholarly interest in, 64; separate spheres doctrine and, 218–19

work-to-work influence, 240n6

writing and painting, relationship between, 1, 3, 4–11, 12

Wuthering Heights (Brontë), 63, 64, 73, 87

Yale Dictionary of Art and Artists, 261n2

Yonge, Charlotte, 4, 22, 157, 180, 182, 183, 184–85, 193, 198–204, 205–8, 249n24

Yuskavage, Lisa, 236

Zeitgeist approach to art and literature, 241n7

Zucchi, Antonio, 151–52, 157, 162, 163, 164

www.ingramcontent.com/pod-product-compliance
Lightning Source LLC
Chambersburg PA
CBHW020942230426
43666CB00005B/134